Adventures in Pragmatic Psychotherapy

Adventures in Pragmatic Psychotherapy

Douglas A. Quirk

Rev. date: 03/11/2019

To order additional copies of this book, contact:
Xlibris
1-888-795-4274
www.Xlibris.com
Orders@Xlibris.com
788819

CONTENTS

ADVENTURES IN PRAGMATIC PSYCHOTHERAPY[1]

Felicity Alice Constance True

My good friend, Douglas Quirk (1931 to 1997) was a gentle genius. Born in India, the son of Baptist missionaries, he attended English boarding school(s) where, he informed me, the teachers were not allowed to whip their students with a cane that was any thicker than the teacher's thumb. He was educated in the classics as well as in the classical English music hall ballads – and I enjoyed hearing him reciting them, particularly the story of young Mr. Reese, *An Overworked Elocutionist*, which he could be persuaded to do when he had enough to drink.

Doug received his B.A. and M.A. from the University of Toronto, and completed all of the requirements for his Ph.D. except for his dissertation – and he subsequently taught Psychology for Psychiatrists and Nurses in the U. of T. Department of Psychiatry for many years. He was a Clinical Fellow of the Ontario Society for Clinical Hypnosis, the Behavior Therapy and Research Society, the American and Ontario Associations of Marriage and Family Counsellors, and a Fellow of the Royal Society of Health. He had a very quirky sense of humour, as witness his decision to tell these psychotherapy stories under the pseudonym of Felicity Alice Constance True (FACT), perhaps not wanting to be identified with them.

He was a devout Christian – I remember his prayer that Jesus would save a place for him in heaven. Nevertheless, I expect that, like the rest of us, he probably had more to repent of than his writing, although that was bad enough in itself.

One eminent psychologist has said that everything Doug did would eventually be judged psychotic. I would contend, however,

---

[1] This manuscript is an amalgam of three separate papers written by Douglas A. Quirk, MA, CPsych – *Psychotherapy Off The Wall (or Proclivities Of A Psychotherapist Made Indefensible), Psychotherapy Out Of Bounds (or Presumptuousness Of A Psychotherapist Made Preposterous)*, and *Psychotherapy Beyond The Fringe*.

that it would probably be no more deserving of that epithet than any of our religious mythologies. If Doug was crazy, he was "crazy like a fox" – he always knew what he was doing (and most of the time it was slowly killing himself through chain-smoking, but that is another story entirely!). The stories in this manuscript are illustrative of Doug's simple-minded but very effective approach to psychotherapy.

Reg Reynolds, Editor

PREFACE

I know that you know that psychotherapy is a terribly serious and expensive enterprise, that it delves painfully into the deep unconscious horrors that drive people crazy, and that the person who needs it most is "the other guy" – although you may sometimes wonder about yourself. I know that you know that one of the problems encountered with psychotherapists is that they use their own language which nobody else understands. Have you ever wondered if it's just to hide the fact that they don't know what they're talking about? If they did, you'd think they'd realize that what they do is meaningless, since it's obvious that you can't have a scientific enterprise whose subject matter is ephemeral and governed by an individual's free will.

Actually, psychotherapy can be terrific fun for all concerned. It can be quite inexpensive. It can ignore the unconscious – if that exists in the form in which most people think it does. It's just a way to provide relevant assistance to solve resistant problems that don't yield to help from friends, clergy, or physicians. It does address pains, but mostly to get rid of them. Almost everybody can benefit from psychotherapy. Almost nobody has to be crazy, crooked, or addicted.

It is true that, as in any enterprise, there are some practitioners who don't know which side is up But the use of specialized languages is intended to create greater precision than could be achieved using the often ambiguous and non-referential words of everyday language. And it sometimes happens that adopting the language helps the treatment. Finally, you can make a science of psychology and its stepchild psychotherapy, even acknowledging free will. Some of the basis for these statements should become clearer as you make your way through this text.

But why bother saying all this? Partly it's to pique your interest. Partly it's to question some common stereotypical misconceptions about psychotherapy, some of which may be due to exposure to inadequately trained therapists. Partly it's intended to explain why "psychologise" is used at times in this volume in addition to English. Partly it's to create confusion, since uncertainty is necessary if new learning is to take place. And finally it's because a book is supposed to have a preface, whose purpose is to mislead you into thinking you know what the volume is about. So let's mislead you in the usual way. This volume seeks to offer some solid information about psychotherapy, disguised as light-hearted science fiction, carried out by an odd psychotherapist trying to solve psychological mysteries as if he were a detective on the police force.

INTRODUCTION

As editor of this nonsense, I have taken the liberty of moving Doug's INTRODUCTION to Appendix B (and you will see why should you care to peruse it).

Reg Reynolds, Editor

CHAPTER 1

SEX

NOW THAT YOU'RE PAYING ATTENTION... If you are going to talk about psychology, there is a rule (maybe an unwritten one) that you have to start right off talking about sex. Partly, this is because many people think that that's all psychotherapists think about. And maybe some do. Partly, this common misconception comes about because many people don't know that psychology has advanced a long way past Freud's (a dirty old man who fathered psychotherapy) pre-scientific grasp of what people are about. Partly, the notions about sex in life come from other dirty old and young men and women who haven't discovered that life holds out any other kinds of fun. Partly, the idea about the importance of sex comes from everybody's vicarious pleasure from talking and thinking about it. In any case, one just has to start off by talking about sex, if only to get people's attention.

But what is there to say about sex which is not just the same old stuff that people have been talking about for centuries, and which psychotherapists have been getting other people to talk about for decades? You might think that everything interesting about it has already been said. So we might have to get our vicarious oral gratifications from chewing over stuff that other people have talked about at some length. Let's see.

Hypo-sexuality – Affectionateness – How Not to Get It Up

This chapter is about hypo-sexuality and not hypno-sexuality. 'Hypo' refers to 'beneath' (an interesting position), as in hypo-dermic (beneath the skin) or 'less than' (a less interesting position) as in hypo-chondriasis or less than sick. It is the opposite of 'hyper' or 'hyped', which refers to 'above' or 'more than (usual)' as in hyper-active or overly active, or hyper-tension or high blood pressure. So this chapter is intended to address less than usual levels of sex drive.

Some people like digressions and some don't. If you don't like digressions, perhaps you should skip the rest of this section. Did the idea of hypno-sexuality pique your curiosity? Picture having a relaxed body and a sharply focused mind. Let the mind increase the intensity of the sensations from your body. Have you ever tried it? It could be fun. But perhaps you think you can't …be hypnotized. If so, hypno-sexuality wouldn't interest you.

Actually, hypnosis is easy and you ought to …try it some time. If you think you can't …be hypnotized, you could …try it for yourself. If …you wish, you could …try it right now. Of course, when you are done with …testing your ability to …be hypnotized, reading the next section heading can …be used by you to …wake yourself up again so that …you can be fully alert.

Meanwhile, if …you want to …test your ability to …be hypnotized, …do it. It's easy, and only …you need to …know …that it worked for you. Read the following statement carefully until …you understand it, and then …try not to …think about it and …remember it. Then when you …wake up in the morning, and …you find that …the following phrase just pops into your head and you will …know that you can't …be hypnotized: Always learn something new. Now, aren't you …happy that …you can …know that you can't …be hypnotised.

Of course, if …it is something you can do, it could be quite useful to you. It could …help you …feel comfortable the next time you visit your dentist. It could …help you …relax and …feel comfortable throughout the day. It could even …add too …your pleasure in all sorts of experiences. So isn't it …wonderful that …you can …be hypnotized?

Living Loving

Frank was a brilliant man of about forty. He found Felicity on his own. See, he was brilliant. He came in to see Felicity for a personal problem about which he was concerned. When he appeared, the man Felicity met was short, soft-spoken, and very gentle. His main concern seemed to be that he was worried about hurting his wife's feelings when she found out about his current 'affair'. He had been seeing this other lady for a couple of years, and now he wanted to spend more time with her, including staying overnight. He was worried that his wife might not understand his wishes in this and that she might divorce him or, worse, feel hurt.

Now to the untutored ear, including Felicity's, this problem might seem a trifle strange. Of course his wife would feel hurt, probably angry, and she might very well leave him. After all, the marriage agreement or promise usually includes some commitment such as '… forsaking all others, cling only to her/him as long as you both live'. Did he really think that he could induce his wife to be willing to share him, half and half, with another woman? Thankfully, Frank was a patient man so he took the time to explain the matter to Felicity.

You see, he was not interested in the other woman sexually. For that matter, he was not interested in his wife sexually. Indeed, as his wife knew, it had been such a long time, years in fact, since he had experienced an erection or an ejaculation that his penis had shrunk, atrophied perhaps, to a mere fraction of its former flaccid size. All he wanted to do was to love and to look after both his wife and his other lady.

Felicity would never be able to do justice to the warmth and tenderness of Frank's words and manner. Affection permeated his whole being as he rhapsodized about his gentle, loving feelings for these two women. His words were sheer poetry, spoken softly and with caressing sibilants throughout. Felicity could feel himself being transported to a world of feeling far removed from the crass and sensory experiences of sex. Felicity could almost grasp that sexual arousal would feel far too impassioned and worldly in the heady mystical elevation, beyond the flesh, that Frank's spirit had achieved.

Felicity could almost grasp it, but not quite. Felicity's earthy mind strained to understand what his body could not. He remembered occasions with other patients who were wrestling with changes in their sexual lives and feelings during which, as sexual drive increased the expression of affection decreased. And as they became more affectionate their sexual drives seemed to decrease. Certainly, those people with the strongest sexual drives or preoccupations, namely the homosexuals he had seen in his practice, usually had a hard time expressing affectionate feelings, and tended to have 'contract sex' – that is, they would agree to have sexual contact instead of courting one another. But Frank seemed to be the extreme case of non-sexualized affectionateness. Felicity could see no way to understand or help Frank with his dilemma.

Felicity told Frank he did not know what to say or how to help, although he thought he could almost empathize with Frank's situation. Frank thanked Felicity for his help, saying that all he had wanted was a listening ear so he could think the whole problem out for himself. There was nothing more he wanted. This surprised Felicity. But he expressed his gratitude to Frank for his acceptance of his inability to help him.

Was there something Felicity should have done about Frank's feelings or his life circumstances? Was there some psychopathology present that Felicity should have tried to treat? The court of last judgement in this is the client. He did not want to change.

A Foregone Orgone

But Frank was not the only person to consult Felicity about a lack of sexual desire. A couple of years later, an absolutely beautiful woman with a statuesque figure consulted Felicity about a problem similar to Frank's. Frances was a very effective and efficient professional woman in her mid-thirties. She was married, and she professed an exquisite love for her husband. However, she was 'frigid'. She felt a great sense of remorse that she was unable to respond with any kind or degree of arousal to any stimulation or contact with her husband, other than the warmth of love that she felt for him. She wanted desperately to find a way to increase her responsiveness in order to add to his pleasure, joy and happiness. But nothing worked to evoke in her any erotic sensations. She thought of herself as a chiselled statue. The task she seemed to be giving Felicity was to breathe life into her alabaster body. He didn't know how to perform such a task by means of any known form of psychotherapy.

The first guidance he could find as he thought about how to accomplish this task came from Reich. Strange images of laminated coffin-like devices ran through his mind, coupled with vague ideas that Reich may have died in an 'insane asylum'. Since he was sure that he would not try to use any of Reich's ideas about how to enhance Frances' 'orgone' (Reich's notion of the energy of libido), Felicity tried to push that kaleidoscope of pictures out of his head. Psychoanalysis, aimed at releasing any 'repression' of libidinous impulses, had already received more than a fair trial with Frances. The use of electrical stimulation to reinstate sensation in small patches of insensitive skin (skin anaesthesia) had been reported in the literature. This method seemed utterly inappropriate in this case. He considered hypnosis, but recalled that its use might increase the risk of suicide in an appetitive problem such as this one.

Of course, he forgot about at least one option that might have worked. He might have tried a procedure he called CARRA, described in in some detail later, when talking about Susan and Shirley. However, he still doubts that he would have taken the chance of using it with Frances without access to the control of round-the-clock monitoring in a hospital.

Having recently been called upon to assess another bright professional woman complaining of anorgasmia (inability to have a sexual climax) but without any real pathology, Felicity was cautious and detailed in his inquiry with Frances. The other lady had said that she was unable to achieve any discharge during sexual contacts. The psychological tests had revealed no sexual conflicts at all. So Felicity had undertaken a thorough inquiry. He was informed that this woman regularly became aroused during sexual contact, experienced a peak of arousal and then achieved a sense of relief – but there was no discharge. It turned out that she had expected to have an ejaculation equivalent to that of the male. When she was offered simple information about the respective sexual events in the two genders, she was satisfied with the information and required no further psychotherapy.

But this was not Frances' problem. She understood the sexual functions of the two genders. But she experienced no sensation at all from stimulation of her erogenous zones in any way different from that of rubbing any other area of her body. In those days, the idea of sexual abuse of children by adults was rarely considered as an issue, let alone a fad used to account for every psychological problem. Felicity did not even think of that possible explanation for Frances' lack of erotic arousal. In those days, the Freudian view of infantile sexual fantasies was the main window through which psychotherapists looked at early sexual arousal or conflicts. And Frances had already been psychoanalysed for a great many years, without benefit or understanding. By this point in her life, all she wanted was results – she wanted to be able to become aroused by her husband's sexual advances.

If Frances had been a man, Felicity would have known right away what to do. He was already using the phallometer to condition erotic responses in order to retrain sexual object preferences in male homosexuals, as described later in Englebert's story. But there was no equivalent device available for measuring a female's erotic responses. Felicity considered how it might be possible to construct a clitorometer to perform the equivalent conditioning procedure. His thoughts rambled around what he knew about the female sexual response, and the speed of reaction of each part – response speed is important if a response is to be conditioned or trained. A clitorometer wouldn't help anyway because the erectile response of the clitoris, if he remembered rightly, was really quite slow – slower, he recited to himself, than the erectile response of the vulva, which, in turn, was slower than the erectile response of the nipples of the breast.

With a start, he caught himself staring at the voluptuous curves of Frances' breasts under her tight sweater. Felicity began to blush at the thought that he may have been responding in an inappropriate way to the lady in front of him. Then the blush vanished as he realized there was a real treatment possibility associated with the fairly rapid erectile response of the breast.

Erectile tissue becomes erect as a result of dilation of the blood vessels infusing the area. The resulting increased volume of blood suffuses into the porous erectile tissue causing it to become firm and thus erect in preparation for its function – in the case of the breast to make it easy for the baby to feed. Given the relative size of the penis, it is easy to use a device to measure changes in penile volume (in an enclosed glass tube displacing air) or circumference (with a mercury strain gauge around the penis) or stiffening (with a clasp as a strain gauge). The problem with the female erectile tissues is that they are too small to accommodate any known type of device. However, erectile tissues do not only become erect, the volume of their blood contents also increases.

Felicity reasoned that even if the erectile response could not easily be measured in order to permit it to be conditioned, the blood volume might be capable of being used. As blood volume in any part of the body increases, so does the temperature of the skin in the area. If Frances taped a skin temperature thermistor in contact with the nipple of her breast, it might be possible, using simple rewards, to train any, however minor, existing erotic responses to increase in response to fantasies about sexual involvement with her husband.

Frances agreed to try the experiment on the clear understanding that there was no existing evidence that such a procedure might work. She seated herself in a room by herself, and scotch taped a thermistor (a temperature sensor attached to a biofeedback temperature unit) in contact with the nipple of her breast. She then installed a dentist's curved suction tube in her mouth (over her teeth). The tube led to an i/v drip bottle containing a favourite juice, with another tube leading from the bottle to a rubber hand pump operated by Felicity, with which he could administer small sips of juice as a reward for each increase in nipple temperature. [**WARNING** : Beware not to drown the client!] Meanwhile, he monitored the skin temperature device from the adjoining room. Frances was asked to relax herself and to picture scenes in which she could see her husband caressing her, could hear his affectionate or sexualized remarks, and could feel his caresses. For every, even momentary, increase in the recorded skin temperature, she was given a small sip of her selected fruit juice as a reward. [**WARNING** : Beware not to drown the client!]

During the approximately fifteen sessions involved in this training, the skin temperature from the nipple rose fairly consistently – although during each session there was a good deal of variation occurring, as would be expected of erectile tissue. Frances reported that she was able to get the pictures she was trying to create more and more clearly in her mind. She was able to see and feel her husband's arousal in her mind, and that gave her what almost seemed like an internal sense of excitement.

But she was unable to notice any increase in the erotic response of her erogenous zones when she was touched by her husband at home. She became discouraged and thought she would quit. But another thought occurred to her. She had persisted without benefit for many years in psychoanalysis. There seemed to be some slight feeling developing in this short period of treatment. Privately, Felicity considered the possibilities that she was reacting to a sense of being demeaned by the rather direct nature of the procedure, or that fear of sexual arousal was driving her from treatment as the risk of such arousal 'breaking through' seemed imminent. These may well have been part of her response because she decided to terminate treatment for the present and to see what developed from the first murmurings of internal excitement she had felt. Frances said she would report back in six months to a year. However, Felicity moved his practice during that time and he never heard from Frances again.

The idea seemed sound enough to warrant some research attention. But Felicity did not receive any more clients exhibiting an equivalent presenting problem to make it possible to undertake a research study using the method. Nor has he since been asked to treat any females for whom skin temperature training might have served as an appropriate replacement for the phallometric training element in the treatment of males.

CHAPTER 2
SEXUAL OFFENCES

Rape! The Delight of the Media

Of course, the most sensational subject to talk about is rape. Most people seem to have the idea that rape is a sexual act that just happens to involve violence in order to achieve the sexual purpose. In fact, it looks more as though rape is a violent act that just happens to involve the genitals to achieve its angry or aggressive purpose. But even this is not always true. Oh dear, now we are going to get confused if we aren't careful. Actually, of course, nothing is quite as simple as we often try to make it out to be. And remember, one of the purposes of this discourse on psychotherapy is to try to make some sense out of the things that happen in people and the things which make life go badly for some people – in this case, particularly the victims.

So what is rape about? Well, that depends on who is doing the rape, and to whom. For example, date rape is usually motivated partly by sex, but it is also (and possibly more so) motivated by anger over frustrated wishes and/or a self-righteous sense of 'rights' or 'possession' over the other. Rape of a stranger is likely motivated by sexual wishes and fantasies, but it seems commonly to be more a product of such issues as anger, sadistic fantasies of the other's helplessness, the wish to punish another as perceived retribution for a sense of personal injury, the felt need to control another, or just plain violent rage due to other events in the rapist's life. Rape by a convict on a fellow prisoner is likely partly a sexual act, though it is likely also to be motivated by a desire to dominate another. There are several possible factors involved in rape. It is for this reason that several stories are concocted in this chapter to address some of the imagined reasons why rape occurs.

Before telling these stories, however, a couple of things need to be said and understood. First, there is risk that talking about rape and rapists will lead one to imagine that rape is as common an event as the media seem to suggest. That can increase people's fears about being raped. Rape is still a relatively very rare event, and the media have done us a real disservice by barraging us with accounts of it and other sensational events, and thus making it seem that such events are commonplace. Second, some people will be offended by the consideration that may seem to be afforded in these stories to the perpetrator and his feelings. It needs to be understood that Felicity never met these perpetrator's victims, so he has been protected from direct exposure to the pains that they suffered. Also, he had to treat the perpetrators in order to try to prevent victimization of other people in the future. In order to be able to do that he has had to prevent himself from critical or hostile attitudes toward these people and, in fact, to foster in himself positive feelings toward them. It takes quite a while to be able to adjust to this fact in listening to stories about this kind of criminal offence. Third, Felicity has to present the perpetrators as fairly ordinary people (which, if fact, they are) since, when he succeeded in the work he did with them, they returned to the community as ordinary people with an ordinary and decent concern with the well-being of others – and not in any sense more dangerous than anybody else. So, while understanding that we too feel horror about their crimes, please try to bear with the way in which we may talk about these offenders.

A Victimized Victimizer

There is a growing lore to the effect that most, or at least many, sex offenders have been the victims of sexual abuse when they were children. Certainly, lots of sex offenders report such abuse in their early lives. However, there is growing evidence that many of the alleged instances of child sexual abuse never happened. These instances are created either intentionally to justify the perpetrator's own actions, or unintentionally as a result of the effort to understand the roots of personal distress or absent early memories. Before talking about Allen, it might be well to take a few moments to explain the false memories some people possess.

Sex offenders, as a group, are among those who failed to achieve adequate socialization as young people. They often don't know things like how to talk to people, how to court, or how to express their feelings. After they have performed a sex offence, they are often terribly ashamed of themselves. Like most of us, when they feel ashamed they are likely to try to find some way to explain what they did.

Some of their explanations can be quite imaginative, and others can be just plain silly. One of the explanations that seems satisfactory to some of them is that they themselves were sexually abused as children. Quite often the reports of this childhood sex abuse amount to little more than elaborations about the normal consensual exploration of one another's bodies that occurs during preschool and early school years. Sometimes the reports appear to be attempts to make sense out of memories of childhood phantasms – early dreams remembered partly because they seemed real and because they made no sense at the time. And some of the reports are of real events of childhood sexual misadventures or sexual abuse by older people. The latter lend credence to some of the other stories in the eyes of people working with offenders.

The more insidious false memories, however, stem from two other sources. When we become upset or troubled, most of us try to find ways in which to understand or explain why. Since most of us look for causes in the past (i.e., 'initial causes'), like Freud, we feel forced to poke back farther and farther into our histories to find the causes in forgotten or buried painful events. Absent memories seem to confirm that there must be something buried. This can happen, but the chances are that the memories were never stored for retrieval in the first place. There are at least two ways in which this can happen.

Most people don't have 'real' memories – in this case, meaning other than feelings – before three or four years of age. The reason for this is that these memories are stored as images that are cued by words. Prior to three of four years of age the child just doesn't have enough verbal language to store memories effectively for retrieval at a later date. So most of the really early memories some people report are pseudo-memories most likely recreated at a later age by stories told by other older family members or incautious questioning or acceptances by other confidants, or even psychotherapists – who may listen for the things they consider 'important', or to which they are sensitive, or which they think accounts for other people's experiences or distresses.

Many people complain that they can't remember anything of their childhoods, and they may conclude that this means they have buried something terrible. Most of these people date their first memories from between nine and eleven years of age. When this happens the reason is nearly always the same. Either due to felt conflict with parents, or due to fairly intense introversion, the child has refrained from much verbal interaction with older family members. During the early 'self-conscious' years of life (about three to nine) the child has very little history with which to contend or to create backward-looking thoughts. The present and the anticipated future (when he/she will be able to do this or that) is about all the child is concerned with.

By about 10, two things happen: the child has enough history to make it appropriate, even necessary, to date the past in an historical sequence, and he/she develops a greater involvement with peers than with parents, and feels the need for a sense of his/her identity (differences and similarities) with respect to his/her peers. In the 'normal' course of development, the dating of past events ('how old was I when ...'), and its resultant sense of continuity of identity, is provided in conversations with parents and older siblings. In those young people who do not participate actively in communication with older family members (due to conflict or introversion), the memories of the past fail to be dated so that it often seems to them that their childhood memories date only back to the point of intense social consciousness or peer involvements – at about ten. The memories are there, they just have not become organized in memory in an age-related time sequence.

Allen was sentenced to prison on a conviction for rape. He was extremely embarrassed about his action, and he was terrified about what the other inmates might do to harm him. He had heard how sex offenders could be treated in prison, both by the staff and the other inmates who mutually tended to view sex offenders as the lowest form of vermin, and who frequently abused or injured them. Although he was a solidly built young man in his late twenties, he tended to stand in corners or walk near walls, watching the other inmates furtively and trembling visibly.

His offence began with a break and enter committed when he was drunk and doing drugs. He was looking for money or anything he could sell to allow him to buy more drugs. In the apartment he entered, he found a young woman asleep in her bed. He tripped over something and the woman was awakened by the noise. She was clearly scared, but she was also angry and she began to scream. He ran to the bed, grabbed her around the shoulders with one arm, covered her mouth with his other hand and whispered a warning that she had better not make any noise. In holding her, he pulled her up from the bed and the covers fell away showing her naked body. She grabbed the covers and tried to cover herself with them.

Allen liked the sight of her body, and he was half aware that the woman seemed more concerned that her nudity be covered than that he was holding her or that he had threatened her. When he had obtained her nodded assent that she would make no noise, he took his hand away from her mouth and pulled the covers down to look at her body again. Although she had not struggled with his hand on her mouth, she fought to keep herself covered. Partly due to the effects of the alcohol and drugs which disinhibited some of the anger he had harboured toward his parents, partly due to feeling frustrated at being unable to wrestle the covers from the woman's grip, and partly due to his awareness of her sense of vulnerability about her nudity, Allen began to feel a towering rage building in himself. It built very quickly.

He was wearing a scarf. He pulled it off and tied it around the woman's head to act as a gag. She released the sheets and tried to remove the gag. He grabbed her arms, pushed them behind her back and used a blouse on her night table to tied them behind her. He pulled the bedding off her. She tried to struggle. He took hold of her breasts and pressed her into the bed. The woman winced. For a moment he hesitated reacting to her discomfort. But his anger took over and he began brutally to maul her genitals. He might still have stopped with the manhandling, but she looked as though she was terrified. A dark image crept into his mind which involved some intense excitement. He felt tense all over, and his excitement got the better of him. He hit her hard a couple of times to warn her to be still. Then he clambered out of his trousers and raped her viciously.

While telling Felicity this story, Allen wept often. He said he knew he had hurt her, scared her, and injured her. He said he felt awful remorse about what he did. But, like many offenders, he seemed almost more preoccupied about 'why' he did such a thing than about his victim's suffering. He moved easily to that question.

Allen complained that he had no clear memories at all before the age of eleven, but that he was sure he had been sexually abused as a child – why else would he have no childhood memories? Almost as a plea, he asked whether any early sexual abuse he may have suffered would account for 'why' he abused this woman. He was not really interested in Felicity's opinion on the matter. He was sure that must be why he did this terrible thing. But Felicity was quick enough to notice that there was no other explanation offered, even one to tie such possible abuse of himself to his abuse of his victim.

This story is told in considerable detail because it illustrates quite well several of the common features found in sex offenses. Commonly, there has been use of disinhibiting substances, there is a sudden opportunity which was at least not entirely expected (if it had been expected, controls might have been in place before the opportunity presented itself), the victim is alone and vulnerable, the surroundings are dark (making anonymity possible), parts of the person's body can be seen unclothed, the victim seems helpless or terrified, the victim seems submissive or acquiesces to demands, the perpetrator has felt angry at abuse or mistreatment he/she believes to have been given to him/her, the perpetrator has justifications or excuses available in his/her mind to serve as an additional disinhibitor, and there is usually a progression of changing plans or purposes which unfold as the act proceeds, often changing from one set of intentions and actions to others. These are some of the elements that may lead to dangerous behaviours. Fortunately, Allen believed that it was dark enough in the room that the woman would be unable to recognize and identify him. If he had realized that his features could be seen quite clearly, the situation might have shifted from a dangerous one to a lethal one.

An Importuned Opportunist[2]

A Repugnant Pugilist

A Vicious Vileness

Incest, Creating New Scars

An Absolute Absolution

---

[2] I am sure that these next five stories would have been fascinating, but I have not been able to locate them. RR

CHAPTER 3

A-SEXUALITY

Exhibitionism, Sadism, and Pyromania

Felicity is strange. Surely exhibitionism and sadism are sexual phenomena, if anything associated with intensified sexual drive. Maybe, and maybe not. Perhaps Felicity is living up to his 'odd' psychologist nature in believing that they are probably more like rape, which is an aggressive act rather than not a primarily sexual one. That does not mean that sexual arousal is not involved in exhibitionism, rape, or sadism. It often is. But the sexual motives are infantile and essentially pre-sexual. And the excitement generated by them probably only includes sexual arousal as part of a complex pattern of arousal involving all sorts of other needs or drives – anger, power, dependency, and the like.

How do we know these facts? We don't. Felicity just made them up. Of course, a lot of other people think the evidence points that way too. But just let's see if we can glean anything from the cases presented, such as they are – admittedly, not a representative bunch if, indeed, there is such a thing.

A Flagging Flasher

Felicity heard about George years before he met him. A pair of colleagues treated George for his exhibitionism using Wolpe's systematic desensitization method almost ten years before Felicity and he met. Apparently, there had been a slight reduction in the frequency of his exhibitionistic acts following the systematic desensitization, a reduction that lasted for about three months. But the frequency of 'flashing' had quickly returned to its former rate – a rate that varied between one and four or more times per day when he was not incarcerated. A psychiatrist characterized George as the most malignant and intractable case of exhibitionism ever recorded in the literature.

From the time when he was treated with the desensitization, George had been carried by the psychiatrist of the team, who had tried 'every known form of therapy' with George, ranging from intensive psychotherapy to aversive conditioning. Since the psychiatrist was moving his practice, he transferred the case to another psychiatrist who, upon reviewing the treatment provided this man, determined that the only thing that hadn't been tried yet was something out of Felicity's bag of tricks. Consequently, George was referred to Felicity for treatment.

Felicity listened to George's story. The man was clearly desperate. He disliked his compulsion to exhibit himself, and not just because it regularly landed him in jail. He had accepted every kind of indignity in order to free himself of his actions. He had even accepted his wife playing the role of custodial officer. To prevent his misdeeds, she accompanied him everywhere, including to and from work. He still managed to elude her daily in all sorts of clever ways in order to perform his act.

Unlike most exhibitionists Felicity had known, George did not give himself the justification that he only wanted to give pleasure to the ladies to whom he exposed himself. His psychotherapy and his frequent experiences in court had disabused him of that idea. Besides, the treatments he had received also included covert sensitization – a modern way of treating exhibitionists. In this method, he had been induced to image the guilt and shame he felt in court when his unacceptable acts were being described in detail in public. As soon as he was feeling the guilt and shame strongly enough, he was then required to exhibit himself to a female staff member. This 'cold' exhibitionistic act, repeated many times, had not reduced his exhibitionistic frequency a bit. It was not that he wanted to do the act, nor did he report much pleasure or arousal in it. He felt compelled to do the act.

Believing, on the basis of the tests administered to George, that there was a negative, anxiety-mediated arousal at the root of his compulsive actions, Felicity started George on Quirk's stimulus conditioned autonomic response suppression (SCARS) method (described in greater detail later). Galvanic skin resistance (GSR) electrodes were attached to George's right hand to record moment-to-moment changes in his palmar sweat response – as one way of measuring activity of the autonomic (emergency/stress/anxiety) nervous system. Meanwhile, George was shown pictorial slides, mostly representing people in various stages of undress, usually in public or looking as though they were embarrassed by being thus unclothed. The purpose of the pictures was to evoke in George ideas related to mild embarrassment associated with being seen by others in various ways 'exposed' to public scrutiny – the feelings usually associated with shame. Strange and contradictory as this may seem, the idea was to desensitize or decondition (get rid of) his uncomfortable arousal or shame. Every time, as soon as the GSR recorded a 1,000 ohms increase – less sweat and, therefore, less anxiety – beyond its former levels, the slide George was looking at was changed. In this method, slide *change* (not slide content) was used as if it were a 'reward' for the *increase* in skin resistance (less sweat, more 'comfort') as measured by the GSR. The idea was to train George's physiological anxiety responses toward comfort *in* the situations represented by the slides, hopefully to reduce the associated uncomfortable feelings he might experience in such situations.

His wife continued to accompany George everywhere, as she had for the past many years. The treatment seemed interminable to George. It actually lasted three months, at the (maximum) frequency of three sessions a week. There were thirty-five sessions in all. There was no discussion of his exhibitionistic acts. As the treatment was reaching its planned end, Felicity was surprised when, upon inquiry, George said that his exhibitionistic acts had stopped about a month previously. Of course Felicity was a little sceptical, but he thought he would not press the issue too much as George would eventually be in court and in jail again if he was not telling the truth.

Treatment was concluded according to plan, and follow-up visits were arranged monthly. At the first follow-up visit, George reported that there had been no 'flashing' now for a bit more than two months. As if to confirm this, George had attended the session not wearing manacles and without an escorting correctional officer waiting for him. Felicity congratulated him, another appointment was made for a month away, and they parted.

Just before the next planned session, George phoned Felicity in a panic. He said, "It's happened again." There was genuine despair in his voice. Felicity suggested that they could talk about it at their planned session in a few days time. When George appeared for that appointment, he carried on his face a mixture of self-depreciation and wonderment. He said he had indeed exposed himself on the one occasion a few days earlier, but he had not felt compelled to repeat the action since. Felicity decided to respond in a matter-of-fact and supportive way, and he encouraged George to 'forget about it'. George thought Felicity was out of his mind and told him so. Felicity shrugged and said, "Probably."

Of course, George could not know what was behind Felicity's lack of concern. Felicity had observed two interesting things about people who were undergoing the SCARS procedure that he had used with George. First, if the frequency of sessions was such that there was less than 48 hours between sessions (i.e., sessions held daily), it tended to take almost a half again as many sessions to complete the basic anti-anxiety treatment task as it did if there was at least 48 hours between sessions. He had concluded that what is called *short-term* consolidation of learning requires about 48 hours. So, with those people seen daily, short-term consolidation of the learning from one session was not yet complete before the learning from the next session was introduced. This may have been why treatment was 'slowed down' in these cases.

Second, he had noticed something else which was more relevant to George's situation. Following completion of this kind of treatment, at about six week intervals, many people reported a temporary recurrence of their symptoms. The recurrence was often accompanied by an increased intensity of reported anxiety or distress. Felicity had concluded from this observation that *long-term* consolidation of learning must take about 6 weeks. He thought that new learning must be stored in temporary memory for a while. At some point in time (perhaps after 6 weeks), the brain's executive function decides that the new learning is appropriate, and that it should become part of the long-term habit storage system. At this point, the new learning is probably 'dumped' into the more or less permanent organization of behaviour, which is called personality. But the existing structure of habits in the personality would be somewhat inconsistent with the new learning, for example, from treatment. Consequently, the personality would have to re-adjust itself and its motivational force fields to accommodate the new learning. This action should involve a general disruption of the organization of the personality system. This disruption might well be experienced as distress, and might well allow old habits to re-appear temporarily, particularly if they were anxiety-related.

Given this way of looking at the process of consolidation of new therapeutic learning, Felicity was not surprised to observe a periodic re-emergence of symptoms. And, in fact, it was even reassuring to him when it occurred. But it had been about two months – that is, more than six weeks – since George and Felicity had terminated their treatment work together. Didn't that bother Felicity? Not really. Felicity had no idea at all about when to start counting off the 6-week intervals. With the benefit of 20/20 hindsight, Felicity was ready to argue to himself that the treatment had really been completed when

George, unbeknown to Felicity, had stopped exposing himself. And that had now been about three months ago, or an interval equal to two six-week long-term consolidation periods.

Although troubled by Felicity's capricious nonchalance about his criminal behaviour, George accepted the reassurance that Felicity was not worried and went home. They completed their follow-up interviews together a little short of the planned two years. There were no further incidents reported during that time, and George remained out of court and out of jail.

As if to tell Felicity that the termination of the follow-up was premature, just after it was completed and almost exactly two years following the last incident, George phoned Felicity again in a panic. "It's all over me again," he moaned. Felicity invited him in for another interview.

George looked scared and despondent when he appeared for the session a couple of days later. Felicity asked him what had happened. He said his wife had stopped accompanying him everywhere about a year previously, since he had not exposed himself for a long time. He was driving home from work on Friday. He saw a woman walking on the sidewalk. He parked in a lane way ahead of her and, when she passed the lane, he stepped out and exposed himself. But he was not sure that she had seen him as she did not react in any way. He drove on until he reached a shopping mall. He parked and got out of his car, found a couple of women and exposed himself again. He was sure they saw him this time. Then he felt overwhelmed by panic. He leaped into his car, drove home as fast as he could, ran in and hid under the bed.

Felicity wanted to laugh at the image this account painted in his mind, but the fact that he was still unsure about why this incident had occurred sobered him. He asked George whether he was suffering from any infectious illness – he was not. He could see that George had not aged appreciably. He asked if he had been imbibing alcoholic beverages in any unusual quantities – he had not. He asked if George was under any other acute source of stress – he was not. He asked if George had been particularly tired. That would have exhausted

Felicity's intelligence about the conditions under which old habits are inclined temporarily to re-emerge. George acknowledged that he had been particularly tired. The incident in question had occurred while he was driving home on the Friday evening having just completed a week of double overtime shifts at work. Fatigue, and the above other factors, can reduce usual conscious controls, and can reinstate old habits temporarily.

Felicity breathed a sigh of relief and told George to go home and get some rest. George shook his head and stared at Felicity in disbelief. There was no doubt Felicity was mad. However, mad or sane, he felt he could trust Felicity, and he did as he was told. Over the next few years, Felicity had periodic contact with George about matters concerning his family – George and his wife had appointed Felicity as their family psychologist. During this time there were no further incidents of exhibitionism reported.

Eight years passed, and Felicity received yet another frantic phone call from George. "It's all over me again." He rushed over to see Felicity that day and reported that he had just exposed himself again on his way home from work. Felicity inquired into the above issues once more. There was nothing noteworthy in George's responses to the questions. There had been some family stressors during the past year, but nothing that Felicity considered to be relevant to the re-emergence of the old habit after so long a time.

The better to think about the problem, Felicity went to light up a cigarette and he offered one to George. George declined the offer politely. Felicity was taken aback by this refusal. He remembered George to have been almost as heavy a smoker as he was. He thought George shared with Felicity one of the latter's lifelong objectives, namely, to burn up the products of those awful tobacco companies, usually one at a time in order to extend the period of the tobacco companies' suffering. He asked George when he had quit. George reported, with some pride, that he had quit three days earlier. Felicity gave a snort of disgust. "Get out of here!" he laughed. George was confused. What had he just said? Did Felicity want him to start smoking again? Was smoking a part of whatever had 'cured' his exhibitionism? Seeing George's sense of bewilderment, Felicity explained. The third day after quitting smoking is the point of maximum physiological stress and emotional disruption. The nicotine is just about out of the system, but there remains enough to create an increased craving for the poison. George was simply suffering a particularly strong physiological stress reaction, which would be gone by the next day.

George left. Although there have been further contacts about family matters, there has been no report of any exhibitionistic act. The last incident is now about 12 years old. In his own peculiar way, Felicity imagines there might be another recurrence in maybe four more years – to represent the steady strengthening of the new habit and the decline of the old.

A Much Maligned Marquis

Sexuality has had little to do with the compulsive 'flashing' acts of nearly all the exhibitionists that Felicity has seen. Their sexual activities have usually been quite within normal limits with one or many women, or as limited as that of many other men. This has been as true of males as of females – although the latter may react sexually to the appreciative reactions of males, or in the anticipation of such reactions. To a slightly lesser extent, the same has been true of the transvestites (cross-dressers) Felicity has seen. The latter often do obtain some tactile sensations of an erotic nature from the softness of female clothing – especially those who specialize in silks and satins. But this is largely from auto-sexual impulses, or the desire to enhance masturbatory sensations and fantasies. The major part of the transvestite image, whether in males or in females, seems to be one of social role adoption, largely associated with an exaggerated valuation of the sex role qualities of the other gender – delicacy and refinement of taste, or aggressiveness and efficiency of movement. Sadism is also quite distinct from sexuality, and really quite similar in its function to transvestism. Sadism's function appears to be that of the over-valuation of something akin to punishment. Everybody is capable of at least some sadism – a sense of excitement (often misconstrued as satisfaction) in the helplessness of the other, best represented by the other's acceptance of pain. Most people, exposed to this view that sadism is widespread, reject the idea out of hand. Damn it, some people are just plain vicious and sadistic!

In fact, everybody has some sadistic impulses whether or not they ever get acted out. Sadistic acts usually express sadistic fantasies. And these may range all the way from inflicting pain or death on another, to revenge or 'getting back' at someone perceived to have injured the avenger or hurt his feelings. Everyday sadism rarely gets reported. It may involve fantasies of another's helplessness and suffering inflicted as if in retaliation (for example, the "Just you wait" song in "My Fair Lady"), vengeful reactions to perceived injury (next in degree of offence to a slight), and abuse (for example, earlier generations' practices, methods of discipline or habits of ignoring children, reviewed, revised, and up-dated).

Some people may feel offended about the apparently rather cavalier attitude adopted here toward, for example, abuse. By way of clarification, it should be stated that in most cultures acts such as murder, inflicting injury, non-consensual sexual acts, and sexual acts with children are considered to be crimes. There is *no* intention to imply here that crimes are acceptable in any terms. The point being made is that the specific acts involved notwithstanding, the sadistic impulse which may serve to motivate some criminal and many non-criminal acts (or which may never be acted out) is the same impulse, and is quite commonplace.

Following the second World War there was a good deal of concern about how quite nice people, such as large numbers of Germans, could apparently accept inflicting pain and degradation on other human beings – as in the concentration camps. It was discovered that two factors were important: first, that the internees passively accepted the brutality inflicted upon them and, second, that the existing political attitudes permitted violence against them. It was this lethal combination that served to stimulate and release any sadistic feelings in those charged with confining the internees. It was partly because of this discovery that the Israelis decided never again to 'sit back and take it' – which may have led to at least some of the 'stiff necked' response of Israel to any sense of being victimized by others.

The way sadism works is well illustrated in the famous Zimbardo prison experiment. Zimbardo, a researcher at Stanford University, decided to find out what would happen if people became prisoners or guards. He advertised for students to serve as paid subjects in a research study. A bunch of nice college students volunteered. Zimbardo divided them at random into two groups, and assigned one group to serve as 'the prisoners' and the other group to serve as 'the guards'. A set of wooden cells was constructed in a research space, and the 'prisoners' were installed in the cells, with the 'guards' to look after them – all in good, clean fun, right?

Well, the good clean fun turned out not to be fun at all. The prisoners, without prompting, started to act like prisoners. They became passive, submissive and accommodating. As if in response to these roles the prisoners were playing, the guards started to become exacting, demanding, demeaning and, yes, modestly sadistic. So profound were the changes which took place in the two groups of individuals that Zimbardo had to cancel the whole experiment within days. In fact, one of the students playing the role of a prisoner became quite seriously disturbed in the experience. And similar kinds of observations have been made in a series of other studies trying to examine the same kind of thing.

There is no 'sexuality' involved in the development of the sadistic impulses on the part of those possessed of power, unless the gender of the passive person coincides with that of the other's sexual object preference. However, it appears that it is not the sexualizing of the female that provokes sadism, any more than it is the sexualizing of the female that stimulates rape. Rape is usually an act of aggression, just as sadism is viewed by the perpetrator as an act of punishment (which is most likely to be acted out when the perpetrator is in a position of power over another and typically harboured as angry ruminations when he or she is not).

In the case where pain is to be inflicted on a member of the perpetrator's own gender, the action is most likely to be aimed at creating social disgrace, as by leaving visible marks by punching or scratching the other's face. In the case where the object of the aggression or of punishment is of the opposite gender, the reason why the genitals may sometimes be selected as a target of action is likely merely because they may seem to the perpetrator to be the part of the person most vulnerable to attack or to the evocation of pain or humiliation. The point being made is that sadistic behaviour is involved in any intent to inflict pain or humiliation. The effects or the circumstances of the behaviour are, from the point of view of its sadistic intent, irrelevant to the nature of its motivation, even although we typically judge the behaviour in just those terms.

From the point of view of the actual behaviour or the circumstances or effects of the act, one may refer to it as 'an attack', or as an 'unprovoked act', or as having 'harmful' or 'dangerous' effects. The sadistic act nearly always involves an 'attack' (whether real or imagined); it commonly (but not always) has 'dangerous' or 'harmful' consequences (at least in its intent); but it is rarely considered to be 'unprovoked' in the eyes of the perpetrator – even although nobody else may be able to understand the 'provocation'.

In the eyes of the perpetrator, any attack is deemed to be 'retaliatory' in nature, even if the act against which the retaliation is directed may not be detectable by others. Either internationally or individually, an attack is 'justified' by the attacker as if it were a response to having been provoked in the form of actual or imagined attack, intimidation, humiliation, or misdeed. And the attacker's response is perceived by him or her (or it, if a nation) as the appropriate, and possibly even necessary, response in the face of the provocation – if only to use the pain or humiliation as a means to draw the other's attention to his or her or its misdeed.

Most victims of sadistic attack would find the notion that the attack was perceived as retaliation by the perpetrator, hard or impossible to understand or to accept. And, indeed, the provocation involved is often very nearly invisible. The attack may be conceived as a reaction to the other's aggressive stance, moral turpitude, former misdeeds, unfair advantages, invasiveness, faults, errors of judgement, or even attempts to achieve social empowerment (as through make-up, attire, or manner). And, in order to act out sadistic impulses, the perpetrator usually views him/her self as morally or rightfully (e.g., as a parent or an official) in the position of judging the other's apparent or real conduct.

And the sadistic response is not restricted to males. The response of the rape perpetrator or the sadist is really little different from that of a woman if she is going to fight with a man. She is likely to choose the most vulnerable point for attack. And, the intense excitement and sense of gratification which many women feel during training in rape-proofing, or in successful counter-attack when they are attacked, although it is called a sense of 'empowerment', is probably completely equivalent to the experience of sadism – even although sadism has usually in the past been attributed almost exclusively to the male.

This point of view is certainly not a popular one. The most usual counter-arguments are that there is an important difference between attack and retaliation, that no attack is ever justifiable, and that the sense of 'empowerment' is a product of relief from fear of the anticipated danger in the situation. Unfortunately for these counter-arguments, the difference between attack and retaliation is largely that of the point of view of victim and perpetrator (which, of course, does not in any way justify any attack); although surely wrong, the perpetrator obviously does think of the attack as justified; and the experience of empowerment, far from being one of reduced distress (i.e., relief), is usually experienced as an increase in positive feelings approaching exhilaration. The whole point of this argument, of course, is not in any way to diminish the experience of any victim, but rather to remark that sadism, and particularly sadistic impulses, are common to almost everyone – they are not qualitatively different events occurring in a number of particular and anomalous people. That is, we all share in the experience of sadism in some degree, if only when we judge another's conduct and/or criticize or rebuke another.

Returning to a lighter vein, the Marquis de Sade never truly understood 'real' sadism. A real sadist is one who, without the social grace to make an excuse, refuses point blank to be mean to a masochist. Now, that is sadistic!

But the aggressive (rape) or punitive (sadism) 'retaliation' is not always directed at people. Its target is sometimes an object, to which the attacker attributes his or her sense of being demeaned, and on which he feels justified or permitted to inflict pain or damage. So it was no surprise to Felicity when, while reviewing his fantasies, he discovered that his patients Harry, Hector and Hugh, who most markedly evidenced sadism, were not involved at all in the expression of their sadism sexually, or toward people. Harry expressed his sadism toward animals, and Hector and Hugh expressed their sadism toward things.

A Surreptitious Sadist

Harry, a man in his early thirties, was admitted to the correctional centre having been convicted of several counts of sadistically killing cattle. He had been employed as a farm labourer and thus had access to some cattle. The details of what he did are better left to your imagination, if you care to imagine such things. He had no sense that there was anything wrong with what he did. The dumb beasts were about as passive and yielding as anybody might wish.

On the Differential Diagnostic Technique (DDT), which is described in the story about Chester, Harry performed in the same way as Chester had done. This suggested that he had an irritative brain focus, equivalent to non-convulsive epilepsy, in the general region of the 'drive centre' of the old brain. Based on Chester's reaction, one might assume that it was the sex drive centre that was being accidentally and artificially stimulated in Harry's brain to evoke his sadistic behaviour. But there was no sexual involvement with the cattle he had killed, and Harry's sexual history was in no significant way different from that of any other 'normal' man. Instead, based on a history of sudden and unprovoked violent acts toward other children during his developmental years, it would seem more likely that it was Harry's 'rage' centre which was being stimulated by the short-circuiting activity involved in his 'complex seizures'.

And his fantasy life was replete with images or impulses of sadistic acts of various kinds, always with the victim being vulnerable, rendered incapable of self-protection, and helpless. His fantasies had many of the staff genuinely fearful of what he would do after he was released from his current incarceration.

He was treated, for a total of forty half-hour sessions, with a biofeedback procedure based on the concurrent use of Sterman's EEG-SMR training method that had been used with Chester, and with Quirk's GSR-SCARS procedure that had been used with George. EEG electrodes were attached to his scalp near the C3-C4 site, and the EEG apparatus set to provide him with a whistling sound whenever and while there was evidence of sensorimotor rhythm (SMR) activity from the site. The whistling sound was interpreted to him as being equivalent to Felicity saying 'fantastic' to him – as a reward for producing some of the desired behaviour.

Galvanic skin resistance (GSR) electrodes were attached to his right hand to measure changes in his palmar sweat production while he was seated looking at pictorial slides. The slides were used to facilitate the transfer of the training from the lab to the world in which he lived, and they dealt with animals, people, and things of various types and under various conditions – that is, they were pretty neutral pictures from life. The role of the slides in the SCARS treatment, in addition to fostering transfer of training, was merely to allow something to occur at the 'right times' which could be used as discrete and contingent rewards – the slide changes. Every time the GSR value increased by 1,000 ohms (i.e., less sweat, more 'calmness'), the slide was changed to a new one. And Harry was told that slide change was Felicity's way of saying 'good' to him.

Shortly after the forty treatment sessions were completed, Harry was released, having satisfied his sentence. He returned to the community. Felicity has been 'pulling' Harry's cumulative correctional file from time to time over the six years since Harry was released to see whether he had received further charges or convictions. He has not. Assuming that he is still alive and resides, as he always had since birth, in the jurisdiction covered by these records, the record indicates that, to date, he has remained free from further offenses. This may represent something of an accomplishment for Harry, considering that he had not spent more than six months at a time on the street (i.e., not incarcerated) since he had become an adult. Does this mean that Felicity's hypothesis was validated? It does not. Felicity regularly experiences some trepidation when he obtains Harry's file. There is, of course, no way to know if or when he will offend again.

A Wired Pyro

Hugh was an arsonist. He had set fires all over the city in which he lived. In setting each fire, he felt 'in control' of the social world which he felt ostracized him, and he obtained a kind of exhilarating excitement in the sense of 'getting back' that he felt over the things he burned. However, he did not experience any sexual excitement, nor was he sexually excited by the ensuing activity when the fire trucks and fire fighters arrived – such as that noted in the reports of (rare) pyro-erotic cases. In fact, he rarely waited around to see that part of the sequence of events.

Hugh's psychological test performances were quite different from Harry's and Hector's. The DDT scores were within 'normal' limits. But the tests did reveal a high level of anxious tension which, in his case, seemed to be projected and experienced mainly internally in his viscera (his 'guts'). It was as though internal tension accumulated within him in a manner similar to that of most pyro-maniacs. When tension reached an intolerable peak intensity, he seemed to feel the need to create a colourful and intense experience (a fire) to relieve the tension.

Because Felicity concluded that the anxious tension targeted the internal parts (viscera), he thought it might be appropriate to use a desensitization method targeting the bodily autonomic response most directly. So, viewing Hugh's behaviour as though it was a compulsive act similar to George's, Felicity started Hugh on Quirk's method of stimulus conditioned autonomic response suppression (SCARS).

There were thirty-five half-hour treatment sessions using the SCARS procedure. By half-way through this treatment, Hugh seemed calmed down and he reported that the fire-setting behaviour had stopped. His calmness and comfort grew through the rest of the treatment. He claims to have set no more fires in the intervening twenty years, and he has not been arrested or charged in that time.

But how could Felicity possibly think of Hector's and Hugh's criminal actions as 'sadistic'? Surely sadism is evidenced only in relation to living things, if not only toward people. Maybe so, and maybe not. Certainly, the way in which Harry, Hector, and Hugh described their actions and the ways they were feeling while performing their offenses had all the qualities which characterize most descriptions of 'sadistic' acts. They experienced intense excitement, the sense of exercising power, control, and revenge over other things, and apparent pleasure in inflicting damage and harm. It's true that their acts were not directed at people, and that they involved no sexual excitement. The reasons why sadism has become associated with sexuality in the minds of most people probably lie in three directions.

First, there may be a secondary arousal of sex drive when sadism is activated. The accompanying tense excitement may be interpreted as sexual arousal by the person, and that may serve to lead some people to focus their sadism in sex-related activities. The resulting acts could well create in the minds of the perpetrator, the victim, and the police the idea of an association between sex and sadism, even if the sexual arousal was only secondary.

Second, the media love to find and exploit the sensational to their own commercial advantage. And what could be more sensational than acts involving both sex and violence. The media have taught us to become excited by these, their two exploitable favourites. And the media have been aided in their training of us because part of the process of anybody's sexual excitement involves arousal of the sympathetic (stress/anxiety/fear) branch of the Autonomic Nervous System. That is, fear, aroused in us by media accounts, may feel equivalent to sexual excitement, so that we may even feel 'excited' by media stories of sexual and violent acts. Our minds have been drawn by the public media, including literature, to associate violence and sex with sadism, as if that is the commonly occurring connection.

Third, the first voice to try to make sense out of sadism was that of Fraud ... er ... Freud.[3] Now Freud thought that everything about people was motivated by one thing – sex. He even thought that defecating was a sexual act, referring to it at times as anal erotic. My goodness, he must have had a restricted sex life! On a topic more relevant to this section, he spoke of the infant, who has not yet achieved bowel control, and thus lays waste in its environment, as 'anal sadistic'. What rot! Hopefully, we have learned a great deal more about people since Freud was spinning his fancies about humankind – which was years before we had a productive science of psychology. Certainly, we know of at least two human inhabitants of this planet who are not exclusively motivated by sex – you and me. And if there are two, there may even be three.

---

[3]   The main problem with Freud's theories was overgeneralization. His formed his conclusions on the basis of his observations of his patients, and then he applied those conclusions to people in general. The same problem occurs whenever anyone applies to the population from which a sample was drawn conclusions based on observation of that sample alone, and Doug was as guilty of that as was Freud. R R

A Total Totalitarian

Now Hector was followed more closely by Felicity. Felicity met him when he too was admitted to the correctional centre. He was in his late teens, and he was considered to be a genuinely dangerous person at that age. Indeed, his remote community considered him sufficiently dangerous that they dispatched a police officer to the correctional centre when Hector was admitted. The officer brought with him a large, two-and-a-half inch thick file describing and picturing Hector's misdeeds, to supplement the information received through normal channels by the correctional centre's staff. Hardly in boyish exuberance, he had vandalized, trashed, and torched a number of buildings including the school he was attending, several businesses and several houses of people he did not even know. On more than one occasion he had left in his wake a trail of destruction that might have mimicked a maelstrom. But he seemed indifferent to the fact and the extent of the damage he had done – well, perhaps not indifferent, more like proud of his accomplishments.

Again, the DDT revealed the pattern of scores that Felicity had found repeatedly in deep, old brain, 'complex seizures' probably affecting the 'drive centre'. Again, it appeared from his recent, as well as his juvenile, history that the 'drive centre' site implicated in the short-circuiting electrical stimulation, would be the 'rage' centre – certainly, he had given many, many evidences of towering rages. Again it seemed appropriate to treat him in the biofeedback lab, using SMR conditioning of the EEG and the SCARS conditioning of the GSR, concurrently.

But there was something quite different about Hector. On the Eysenck test, his Extroversion score was at the first percentile point. That is, he would be thought of as very introverted, as only one percent of the population would score lower than he did on extraversion. This, in turn, would mean that he ought to learn new emotional habits very slowly – that is, his conditionability would be very slow. Based on his experience with other patients undergoing the SCARS procedure, Felicity estimated that it would require as many as 125 half-hour treatment sessions to complete treatment with Hector. Without allowing for vacations and other sources of missed appointments, at the maximum frequency of twice per week that Felicity could afford, that would mean he would need sixty-three weeks, or sixteen months, to complete the treatment.

But Hector had only twelve months of sentence time left to serve when Felicity was able to start treating him. Considering Hector's rather cavalier attitude toward his offenses, Felicity did not expect him to give up any of his 'earned remission' ('good time') off the end of his sentence in order to complete the treatment programme. But, in fact, Hector did give up enough of his earned remission to complete the treatment. By about half way through the treatment, Hector's attitude changed and he expressed what sounded like real remorse for the things he had done. And it seemed to Felicity that giving up earned remission confirmed the seriousness with which he finally viewed his offenses.

Eleven years have elapsed since Hector was released from this sentence. He enrolled in school, took courses, and became involved in a variety of interesting or frankly weird projects in the ensuing years. With each new project, Hector sent Felicity some memento of what he was doing – a copy of his certificate or a photograph – or he wrote or phoned to tell Felicity what he was up to. Also, by chance, Felicity had several face-to-face encounters with Hector on the street. Hector used these opportunities to talk about what he had been doing. Felicity used them as follow-up contacts. And Felicity's repeated 'pulls' of Hector's correctional file has continued to show a clean record, right up to date.

CHAPTER 4

SEXUAL ANOMALIES

Unjustifiable Justification

Some Tales About Trying to Understand Homosexuality. You may well ask why homosexuality is a topic of interest to a psychotherapist – is he a homosexual? Actually, although he was confused about his gender identity for some time, Felicity is not gay. Surely, you may want to point out, homosexuality is a genetic and given state of some people and not a psychological disorder. Let's be clear about this matter. First, the subject interests Felicity because, when he first became a psychologist, homosexuality *was* considered to be a psychological disorder, and trying to understand it formed part of the process by which he learned how to apply to the task of psychotherapy the psychology he had studied. Second, there is no satisfactory evidence to support the notion that homosexuality is always a genetic given, except for the fact that early attempts to treat it (and many other human conditions) using early forms of psychotherapy typically failed. Third, there are perfectly understandable causes that determine the preferences and turn-ons that we have and, in the case of homosexuality, some of the 'causes' have to do with fears and irritants that would ordinarily be thought of as 'neurotic' types of distress. Of course, that does *not* mean that a person should not adopt whatever preferences turn him or her on. Fourth, of course, the positions just offered are not popular ones at present, and they seem to be contradicted by the fact that the American Psychiatric Association has dropped the 'diagnosis' of homosexuality from among the diagnostic categories listed in its *Diagnostic and Statistical Manual (DSM III-R)*. It may be worth noting in passing that this was done under political pressure from the gay membership within psychiatry.

The foregoing having been said, Felicity would want to make three confessions. First, he has never been greatly impressed with knowledge derived from either political action or authoritative edict. Second, he has no quarrel with anybody being any way, or doing anything he or she likes as long as it does not harm other people. Consequently, as a psychotherapist, his only interests in whether or not a person is homosexual are concerned with those people who afflict others with their homosexual (or, for that matter, heterosexual) actions, or those people who ask him to alter their sexual preference. Third, Felicity's mother notwithstanding, just because anybody or everybody believes something does not necessarily mean it is true – whether the belief is that the person is Napoleon, or a homosexual, or a transsexual. Indeed, it seems entirely possible that if a million people believe anything, it's almost bound to be wrong.

Transsexuality illustrates the last point in perhaps the most telling way. There are people who believe they were 'supposed' or 'intended' to be one gender even although the genitals with which they came equipped are those of the other gender. Of course, it has never been clear just who, other than themselves, 'supposed' them to be of the other gender. If someone wants to be surgically altered, that has got to be his or her own business. However, to believe that someone or something external to themselves made a mistake in creating them, having 'intended' them to be of the other gender, has to mark that supposition both as wrong, and as a grandiose delusion – implying that the person is privy to the intentions of the Creator. To go the next step to affirm that their wrongly assigned gender ought to be changed surgically should suggest to someone that the person is self-destructively depressed or masochistic or created to provide surgeons with income. Such a non-adapting and maladaptive delusion is in no clear way different from the alternative delusion that the person is an alien displaced from some other planet such as Mars. What seems bewildering about this particular delusion is that, in contrast to how they react to other delusions, some psychiatrists enter this delusion and arrange for the person to be surgically mutilated to mimic the appearance of the other gender. Of course, the resulting man-made apparatus does not perform any function other than making the person over into a freak and *maybe* pleasing the sexual partner.

Whether the above helps in any way to reveal either why I am going to spin fairy-tales about homosexuality, or that I am an arrogant and wrong-thinking old fogey, I can't discern. I'm afraid you'll have to decide that for yourself – and, as you are helping in making sense of this treatise, we both share in your judgement. Regardless of our respective opinions on this subject, you may find the fantasies I am planning to talk about interesting, if not entertaining. With that pseudo-explanation, let's proceed.

A Rectified Rectum

Deryk was referred by a psychiatrist for treatment of his homosexuality. Felicity was, even for him, in a remarkably and devoutly lazy period of his life, and so he nearly turned the referral down. However, he was about to start a psychotherapy research study for which Deryk was seen to be a suitable subject. So Felicity agreed to see him to find out if he would be willing to participate as an experimental subject without any assurance that the procedure to which he might be assigned would be relevant to his presenting problem. Felicity was obviously out of his skull. Who would agree to such a silly, even improper, proposal? But then, Felicity may have been hoping that Deryk would turn him down.

Deryk came to Felicity's office at the appointed time. He was a grossly obese man in his late twenties. He had very little to say about himself other than that he was a homosexual. He had no specific expectations about treatment except that he really did not expect it to work. However, since he had no interests in activities, and thus had little to occupy his time, and since there was to be no charge for the treatment, he accepted the risk that he might be assigned to a program without any treatment benefits for him. Some people are wonderfully accommodating to other's needs.

The treatment work was done by a psychological assistant, and so Felicity had no further contact with Deryk until the treatment research program was completed. By prior agreement, Felicity then met with Deryk to determine the outcome of the treatment. There was none. Deryk presented at the end of the program as he had at the beginning, with no noticeable change in his appearance, manner, or presenting symptoms. Felicity was surprised and somewhat disappointed. Deryk had been assigned by chance to an appropriate treatment method which Felicity's experience and expectations suggested should have modified Deryk's homosexuality.

He undertook a detailed inquiry into Deryk's life and condition. Nothing seemed unusual. Almost by chance, Felicity asked Deryk how many bowel movements he had each day. Deryk wasn't sure, but he knew there were 'several'. Felicity woke up with a start and asked Deryk to come back in a week, after having recorded the time of day each time that he had a bowel movement. Deryk agreed to this unexpected request.

When Deryk returned the following week he handed Felicity a sheet of paper on which he had recorded each day's bowel movements. Using a calculator, Felicity computed that Deryk had averaged 17 bowel movements per day. He asked Deryk if he thought the week had been different in any way from other weeks, and then whether he thought he had more or fewer bowel movements that week than on any other. Deryk assured Felicity that there was nothing different about the week or about the number of his bowel movements. The penny dropped in Felicity's head.

Felicity arranged to see Deryk weekly, and asked him to undertake some homework faithfully. He calculated the average times of each day when Deryk would be having a bowel movement, and constructed a bowel movement timetable for Deryk to follow in which he was to average 16, rather than 17, bowel movements per day. The idea was that Deryk would wait until the mid-point in the interval between each pair of bowel movements before relieving himself. This would result in one less bowel movement per day during the next week. When he came for his next session, Deryk claimed to have followed his timetable and to have averaged 16 bowel movements a day during the week. A new timetable was prepared for the following week such that Deryk would average 15 bowel movements a day. He was given the new timetable and asked to follow it until the next session. Each week, one more bowel movement per day was dispensed with. Deryk reported each week that he had some difficulty sticking to the timetable at the beginning of the week, but that it became easier as the week wore on. The weeks passed.

Deryk started to take off weight. Then, at the end of the week during which he had only three bowel movements a day, he reported that he was no longer feeling attracted to or interested in males as sexual objects. In fact, he had been surprised to notice that he saw several quite attractive women during that week. Perhaps his improving appearance as he took off weight made him feel better about himself, and thus in a better position to entertain the possibility that he might have a mutual relationship with a woman. Or perhaps there was another explanation.

He kept his appointments with Felicity for the next two weeks. He was still in contact when his bowel movements reached one per day. However, at that point, reporting he no longer experienced any sexual interest in men, and indicating that he had met a woman with whom he had started courting activity, he decided to terminate the contact. He phoned a few months later to tell Felicity that he had married the lady he had been courting. He phoned again about a year later to say that a daughter had just been born to them. There was no further contact for about four years.

Felicity usually doesn't open his mail until it has been sitting around for a respectable period of time – to allow it to age properly. In this way, it has the opportunity to ferment or to become obsolete. While lawyers (in Deryk's dialect, pronounced 'liars') might object to this practice, any reasonable person would acknowledge that it reduces the amount of reading and letter-writing Felicity had to do, especially since this behaviour results in an ever-diminishing supply of mail. On this occasion, however, he made a mistake and performed a 'break and enter' on his mail box without awaiting 'due process'. It turned out, it turned out all right because there was only one letter, and it was from Deryk.

The letter informed Felicity that Deryk had moved with his wife and daughter to the mid-west. Quite suddenly, he had noticed that his sexual interest in his wife had declined and that he was once more a homosexual. He wondered what he could do about it as it was disrupting his marriage.

Felicity wrote back asking Deryk to record and return the time of his bowel movements each day for a week. The reply showed an average of 15 to 16 bowel movements per day. Felicity's response included a bowel movement timetable splitting the toilet times to provide for 14 bowel movements per day. He asked Deryk to write each week indicating how well he was sticking to the timetable and reporting his sexual feelings toward his wife and also toward men. He promised to send Deryk a new timetable each week. The mail-mediated psychotherapy continued regularly. At three bowel movements a day, Deryk reported no further homosexual interests and an improved sexual relationship with his wife. The mail contact dried up.

Three more years passed. Felicity received a frantic phone call from Deryk complaining that his homosexuality was back again. In the meantime, Deryk, his wife and daughter had returned to their original home base, so Deryk could attend appointments in person. Felicity gave Deryk an appointment for a week away, and asked Deryk to come with a record of his bowel movements in the intervening time. He recorded an average of 15 bowel movements a day.

Felicity had never explained to Deryk about the relationship between his homosexuality and his bowel movement frequency. While giving him the new set of timetables, on this occasion he explained what had happened and why – hopefully in a way that Deryk could understand well enough to use the information in the future.

The autonomic nervous system (ANS) has two branches – the sympathetic (arousal/stress/emergency or anxiety) branch and the parasympathetic (calmness, pleasure) branch. Messages are sent *out* by the brain to most organs along these two branches depending on what the brain 'wants' the body parts to do – to get aroused, activated or uptight, or to get calmed down and relaxed. And, by means of its internal (proprioceptive) sensory tracts, the brain *receives back* information about what the body organs are doing – information which may be experienced by the brain as discomfort, anxiousness or uptightness, or as calmness, comfort or pleasure, respectively.

When the rectal sphincter is closed tightly, that is done by the sympathetic branch of the autonomic nervous system; and when the rectum is relaxed or opened, that is done by the parasympathetic (calm/relaxed) branch of the autonomic nervous system. Felicity thought that Deryk needed this much basic neurophysiology. But of what importance was this information?

When the bowel is evacuated too frequently, say more than once or twice a day, it does not have time to do its job of retrieving fluid from the bowel contents. This has two effects. First, it over-taxes the body's fluid retention system so it has to over-work to retrieve enough fluid. This can result in failure to retrieve enough, and thus in too little fluid retention and loss of weight. Or the over-work can result in excess retrieval, and thus in too much fluid retention and weight gain. Deryk might remember the latter as a difficulty he had experienced each time he had felt he was a homosexual.

Second, it results in relatively fluid bowel contents. This requires the person to keep his rectal sphincter tightly closed – to prevent the social embarrassment of leakage. Maintaining strong tightening of the rectal sphincter creates and maintains a strong sympathetic nervous system response in the body – in order to achieve and hold the closing of the sphincter. This results in the person feeling a growing sense of anxiety, discomfort, and uptightness. Moreover, this tense uptightness is mainly located in the general region of the genitals. Tension around the genitals can increase sexual excitement. If the arousal becomes associated in the person's mind with the genitals, and thus with sexuality, the anxiety and its local tension may increase the person's sexual drive and thus the probability of homosexuality (see next section).

Felicity explained that this was why he had asked Deryk to reduce the frequency of his bowel movements each time he had complained about homosexuality. That is, the purpose of reducing the bowel movement frequency was to reduce the fluidity of the bowel contents, so that he would not have to maintain a strong and continuous sympathetic (anxiety-like) response to hold the sphincter tightly closed.

Deryk said he understood what he had to do. He kept in touch with Felicity until his bowel movement frequency was down to one per day, and he reported the loss of homosexual interests with an increased sexual interest in his wife. There has been no further contact during the fourteen years since this last episode.

Discussion (Explanatory Recapitulation)

Why is it that you find sections like this one being titled Discussion? The discussion is really a mono-scussion because the reader doesn't get to put his or her two or more cents worth in. Be that as it may, this is the kind of section that is usually called a 'discussion', so that's what it is called. Anyway, what is there to discuss? Surely the peculiar phenomena that have been presented so far have nothing whatever to do with the advertised topic of homosexuality. These four unusual phenomena are admittedly rare. How can they possibly help to unravel the causes underlying homosexuality in general – or do they? At least there may be some point in trying to find out what, if anything, is common to these four quite different types of factors fabricated to account for some few cases of homosexuality.

Alton and Alvin were simply not homosexuals. It is likely that they both considered homosexuality to be distasteful and, more importantly, leading to 'dirty' activities such as rectal intercourse. It is also probable that, like most people during the so-called 'physiological' period of homosexuality, they wondered about whether they might be homosexual. After all, since they were not yet psychosocially ready for heterosexual experience, just after the activation of sexual drives with the onset of puberty (between the ages of 11 and 14), most people tend to establish fairly intense friendships with same-sex peers. And these relationships sometimes involve some exploratory sexual intimacies. The intensity of such friendships, coupled with the post-pubertal increased interest in sexual matters, leads many people to wonder whether they are homosexual. Indeed, many of those who get hung up with words and identities (mostly introverted people), may give themselves the 'identity' of homosexuality as a result of their intense relationships with members of their own gender. This can then provide the 'meaning' filter through which they process future evidences from their experiences, noticing confirming and failing to notice contradictory evidence concerning their identities.

This is likely what happened to Alvin. But Alvin remained what he said he considered himself to be – a closet homosexual. Meanwhile, both he and Alton had characteristically been children with scrupulously clean habits – they both avoided dirt as much as they could; and they could both avoid dirt most of the time in their middle-class, spotlessly clean homes. But when a person successfully avoids something with which he is uncomfortable, he feels a tinge of relief – he feels better. Feeling better is the best kind of reward for the body – it loves it – and so it rewards anything which occurred just before the feeling better. The habit that is thus rewarded is both the anxiety response in the situation (this time, dirt), and the avoidance act in that situation in the future. This is how most phobias develop.

Thus, both Alton and Alvin quite accidentally, by their avoidance of dirt throughout their developing years, were teaching themselves to become both more and more anxious about dirt and more and more likely to avoid dirt if they could.

As they spent less and less time in their homes in their late teens and early twenties, both men were less protected from contact with a dirty world. Dirt was everywhere, and they could do little to clean it up. But by reducing eye focus in vision, and later extending this to becoming 'fogged out', they both apparently learned to drift toward sleep as a way of being less aware of the dirt around them. Felicity could understand that. He has a phobia about work, and he reacts to it either by going home sick (sick of work) or else by going to sleep too.

At this point, they might have adopted means for staying awake similar to those adopted by others. The hyperactivity of some young children is sometimes (but by no means always) a means for keeping themselves alert. This is only one of the reasons why Ritalin has its apparently paradoxical effects on hyperactivity – it settles down hyperactivity, even although Ritalin is a 'psycho-activating' or alerting or anti-sleep chemical. Alton and Alvin did not come equipped with activity-provoking motors, so that hyperactivity was not a solution available to them. Aggressiveness or hostility are means by which some people drive themselves to keep awake, or these may function as stimuli for others so that the others' reactions keep them awake. Anger or hostility would not have felt right or acceptable to either Alton or Alvin.

The reason why homosexuality worked for them as a moment-to-moment solution to their sleepy response to dirt is a bit convoluted. These two men viewed homosexual behaviour as the ultimate in filth. Consequently, thinking about homosexuality or anything related to it allowed them almost instantly to 'fog out' by drifting toward sleep in order to avoid paying attention to anything else which upset them, including other dirt stimuli such as dust or grime. That, however, made homosexuality a common last thought in their minds when they fogged out, and thus kept them focused on homosexual ideas.

Their problem then was to prevent themselves from crumpling to the sidewalk and going to sleep.

Alton found that making gross 'homosexual' comments shocked others, and that awakened him – which was gratifying because it relieved his fear that he was dying as his consciousness declined. However, his comments committed him to homosexual activities, which perpetuated the cycle of more 'fogginess' and more homosexual behaviour. Alvin felt strong anxiety arousal when he found himself pursuing his last (homosexual) thought before fogging out. He experienced this foggy anxiety as excitement. The (anxious) excitement (about the homosexual thought) both awakened him (protectively) and led him to believe that homosexuality excited him. Any resulting homosexual behaviour fogged him out again, so that he wouldn't know he didn't enjoy it – that is, until he stopped fogging out once he was started on the Ritalin. For both these men, the reduced level of alertness that followed thinking about homosexuality and their homosexual actions also reduced their ability to control their behaviour. This led to a rather foggy involvement in the last thing they were thinking about – the very crux of their *phobias*, homosexuality. In these two men, what appeared to be homosexuality was simply a complex neurosis.

The same was not true of the other men described. Bart and Benny had both learned symptom-producing anxiety habits following traumatization in traffic accidents. The test of this fact was that they both experienced reduction in their homosexual (and paedophiliac) interests following anti-anxiety conditioning treatment concerned solely with traffic situations. Chester and Chuck were both subject to accidental electrical stimulation of their brains due to 'short-circuiting' or epilepsy. The short-circuiting seemed to occur in an area of their brains containing both a sex drive centre and the anterior (front-end) roots of the autonomic nervous system – stimulation of the sympathetic branch of which results in quite intense anxiety. The test of this was the fact that they both experienced reduction in their bisexual (and paedophiliac) interests following treatment in which they were trained to increase the available neural inhibition in their brains. This presumably diminished the chance of 'short-circuiting' activity – to prevent any accidental triggering of arousal in these centres. Finally, Deryk created high levels of autonomic (anxiety) arousal in himself accidentally by having to maintain tight constriction of his rectal sphincter – a response which is only accomplished by maintaining arousal in the sympathetic (anxiety) branch of the autonomic nervous system.

The thing that is common to all of these people was the heightened level of anxiety they were experiencing. Anxiety is a learned drive and, like all drives, it adds drive intensity to any other drive or response with which it becomes conditionally associated or habitually connected. So it increases sex drive if anxiety becomes connected to it. But what would connect these different forms and sources of anxiety to the sexual drive?

In Deryk's case, it was probably the physical proximity of the evoked anxious tension to the genitals. Tension in the genital region can increase sexual excitement and thus establish the association in the brain between the tense arousal and sexuality. In the cases of Chester and Chuck, it is possible that the electrical stimulation from the epileptiform 'short-circuiting' affected not only the centres for the perception of visual angle (resulting in the DDT performances) and the autonomic nervous system roots (to create anxiety), but perhaps also the sex drive centre (and perhaps also the reinforcement centre). The concurrent activation of some of these centres might establish a connection between autonomic arousal (the 'fight or flight response') and the sexual drive, or the short-circuiting may merely have activated strong sexual drive.

The sequence of events in Bart's situation was complicated. It probably involved two pairs of associations, with his neighbour as the common element in the pairs. On the one hand, there was an obvious association between the 'helpful' neighbour and his son (the first victim). On the other hand, there would have been a traumatically-conditioned association formed in his mind between arousal of traumatic anxiety from the traffic accident and its most immediately associated stimuli when Bart was looking at the helpful neighbour 'sensuously' rolling the retrieved cigarette between his fingers. The sensuousness in the immediate stimulus may have transformed the *traumatic* anxiety to sex drive. But Felicity was never able to figure out the connections involved in Benny's life between the traumatically-conditioned anxiety and the sexual drive.

Perhaps all these possible habit-related connections did in fact take place. And perhaps sexual drive was increased by anxiety having become associated with it. But what is the relevance of all this to homosexuality? The information bearing on this question comes from a different source – research by two of the leading sexologists in the field of variant sexual object choices, Freund (not Freud) and Barlow. Although the conclusions they drew from their data led them in almost diametrically opposite directions, these two researchers adduced the same kind of information. It is likely that they might have been led in the same direction by their data if either one had also considered some other known facts. The other known facts need to be mentioned first.

First, all drives oscillate in a wave-like fashion. At times we are hungry or sleepy or need air, and at times we are not or do not. Drives go up and down over time.

Second, drives cumulate with each other, so that if we are tired and hungry we are apt to feel both the fatigue and the hunger as stronger or more poignant than the amount that each alone would warrant. That is, drives add together if more than one are high at the same time.

Third, if we were to plot on a graph the relationship between *drive* strength or intensity (on the horizontal axis) and 'turn-on' or felt excitement (on the vertical axis), we might be surprised by what we would find. Of course, with low drive there is a low level of subjective 'turn-on', interest or excitement. As drive increases, turn-on or excitement increases – at first. However, after a certain intensity of drive, if drive increases still farther, turn-on or arousal flattens off. And then, if drive is increased farther still, turn-on actually declines (turns off). For example, if you had a high level of sex drive, but you were also very sleepy and very hungry, the cumulation of these three drives together would result in such a high level of drive that you would feel neither sexy nor sleepy nor hungry – you would be more likely to feel just 'blah'. The graph between drive and felt turn-on is called the 'inverted U' relationship between drive and excitation. This much is basic Introductory Psychology and it has been known for many, many years.

Fourth, we come to a bit more speculation. It is Felicity's belief, with emphasis on belief, that each one of the 'partial sexual impulses' (kissing, being kissed, hugging, being hugged, looking, being looked at, touching, being touched, etc.) is more easily or more fully gratified heterosexually than homosexually for both genders. Felicity believes that's a given for all people. Now, <u>if</u> that were true, and if, throughout the course of growing up, everybody had free and uncomplicated sexual experience (the idyllic notion of 'free love on the beaches'), then, due to the slight advantage afforded by each of the 'partial sexual impulses' in heterosexual experience, in the long run everybody would end up being heterosexual – quite apart from relationship complications. That is, for example for males, over time the female would become the high drive preferred sex object. The male would also be a sex object, but associated with low sex drive and low turn-on.

To the extent that this picture is correct, on the 'inverted U' graph for males, the female as a sex object would be at the high point on the curve (i.e., moderately high drive, high turn-on), and the male as a sex object would be down near the beginning of the curve (i.e., low drive, low turn-on). If you find the above hard to follow, why not draw a picture of an upside down U graph for yourself, put marks to show the male and female as sex objects on the graph as suggested, and look at it.

Given that the above picture is based on an assumption, why not go over-board with it. Let's do a little imaginary magic with it. If, by some magic, an amount 'x' (unknown) of another kind of drive is added to the sex drive along the base of the 'inverted U' graph, something strange ought to happen. The drive would be added to the female object preference *and* to the less preferred male object, pushing the position of each farther along the curve to the right. That is, the female object would start to move down the upper end of the curve, and the male object would start to move up the lower end of the curve. If 'x' is only a fairly small amount, both female and male would shift only a bit, perhaps bringing the female down and the male up until both come to be at about an equally high level of excitement or turn-on (height up the curve) – and the person might say that he feels bisexual. If 'x' is a larger amount, the female would be pushed way over and down the upper end of the 'inverted U', and the male would be pushed up to the top of the curve – and the person might say that he feels only homosexual feelings or turn-on. Conversely (or, if you prefer, perversely), if you were to remove that added 'x' amount of drive, the male and female objects should slide back along the curve to their 'original' places, and the person should revert to heterosexuality. If this were so, and if that's what could happen if 'x' were added and if it were removed, where might this 'x' possibly come from?

Remember, the addition of the amount 'x' to the sex drive, to achieve this miracle of change in preferences, was done on a 'let's see what happens' basis. Obviously, there was some reason for trying to see what happens if 'x' is added or is taken away. Let's turn to that now. Here's where Freund and Barlow's work comes in.

What both of these researchers did was to plot on another graph the relationship between sexual excitement on the vertical axis, and the various steps toward sexual experience along the horizontal axis. For most people, at the point of seeing an attractive person at a distance there might be a slight sexual excitement. At the point of meeting this other person there might be a bit more sexual excitement. During social contact, when they are getting acquainted, there might be a little more sexual excitement. During courting and the expression of loving feelings there might be still more sexual excitement. During necking and foreplay, sexual excitement would likely increase a whole lot more. During the sex act, sexual excitement would be expected to increase even more. Then, following climax, sexual excitement should decline back to a low level. This much seems obvious, and it is what most people report. That is, sexual excitement increases in progression through the steps leading up to the sexual act.

In people who call themselves homosexuals, however, the picture of sexual excitement is a bit different. There is a rapid increase in sexual excitement on the approach of an attractive potential partner, and this reaches quite a high peak just the moment before meeting the other person. Then there is a steady decline in sexual excitement after meeting and during social interchange. This decline reaches a very low point during courting activity when expressions of affection might be expected to occur. It then rises quickly again during foreplay, on through the sexual act and, as expected, declines sharply after climax.

The low point at the point of courting is easier to understand. People who call themselves homosexuals tend to be quite anxious about expressing their feelings to another, and tend to avoid doing so if they can. That is why homosexual activity is very often 'contract' sexual activity – 'let's have it on together', rather than 'I love you'. Their anxiety about courting activity serves to get in the way of or to lower their sexual excitement, creating the trough at that point in the sequence of events. The other feature of the picture, the peak just before social contact, seems to be due to anxiety felt by people who call themselves homosexuals concerning whether or not they, themselves, are attractive and can excite the sexual interest of the other. This anxiety is experienced as tense excitement (more often than as anxiety or avoidance), and it reaches its peak at the point just before meeting the other person. The (anxious) excitement increases (instead of reducing) the sexual excitement at that point in the sequence of events.

But what has all this to do with 'x'? We are now ready to guess at the possible nature of the drive 'x' we have added to the sex drive in the upside down U graph. 'X' may be the sum of the learned anxiety drive that gets attached to the sex drive and to sexual excitement in those people who call themselves homosexuals. Is it possible that x = Anxiety about (Courting + Attractiveness)? But that doesn't make sense, right? Many people, especially women, get hung up about how attractive they are; and many people, especially men, get anxious about expressing their feelings and emotions. And that may be true, although this view of things may only express a set of faulty gender-related stereotypes. However, it may be that what keeps heterosexuality going and children being produced is the fact that most of those who get hung up about how attractive they are tend to be fairly comfortable about expressing their emotions; and most of those afraid to express their emotions tend to be less concerned about how attractive they are. It seems that to create homosexuals, both kinds of anxiety have to be present to load the sex drive (and not just other derived needs – see below) enough to change the relative positions of the male and female on the upside down U curve of sexual drive.

Besides, homosexuality is not the only possible consequence of high anxiety in either or both of these areas of living. People who are said to be 'paranoid' also exhibit these kinds of fears, and so do some people who used to be called 'hysterics'. Quite apart from the fact that some shrinks claim that these conditions are often or always associated with 'latent homosexuality' (a point of view which only justifies the definition of psychiatry as the study of the id by the odd), there is a good reason why a different way of reacting is found in these people as compared to those who call themselves homosexuals. The difference lies in the fact that these kinds of anxieties do not become attached to the sexual drive in these other people. Instead, these fears get attached to their social needs. The one group (paranoid) attaches these fears to its emotional need to be loved, so that it too easily feels rejected and mistreated by others. The other group (hysteric) attaches these fears to its sense of personal identity, so that these people avoid 'being themselves', and can feel and act like anybody else (except themselves). So 'paranoids' go around feeling angry at the rejection they expect from others, and 'hysterics' play roles in life, often becoming actors or actresses.

But how would you test the hypothesis that homosexuality is a result of little more (it is a bit more) than an increase in sex drive – brought about by attaching to it high anxiety about the expression of loving or closeness feelings and about whether or not the person is attractive enough? One way to check this hypothesis out would be to desensitize these two kinds of anxieties in people who call themselves homosexuals. Does that work to change homosexuality 'back' to heterosexuality? With some additional work done on the 'obsessional' qualities that are also usually present in such people, the answer seems to be a cautious 'yes'. At least it seems to be yes in most cases with which it has been tried.

Now, aren't you glad you waded through all that? Be brave! There are only a couple more sections in which the reading gets to be nearly that heavy, and they're shorter than this one. You had to expect to have something laid on you about how the 'id' works. Of course, you might have preferred that this part of the id remain as unconscious as the rest of it. If so, it ought to be pointed out that the unconscious, being by its nature unknowable (in becoming known, it becomes conscious), cannot properly be affirmed to exist. Moreover, if you harboured such a preference, you might overcome it by reminding yourself of the Taoist saying: 'The Great Way is not difficult for those who have no preferences'.

An Inscrutable Scrotum

Englebert exhibited most of the features which have been seen in most of the homosexuals Felicity has been called upon to treat. Englebert, was a garden variety homosexual. He was living with a man, and they frequented gay bars together from time to time both for entertainment and to have little adventures. He had been involved in a fair amount of sexual exploration and tickling as a young child, and had been used by a couple of adult males as a source of sexual gratification during his pre-adolescence. He enjoyed the tickling of and by other males, and had even felt some excitement, as well as discomfort and fear, in anal intercourse during his youthful experiences. Indeed, as with many children who are introduced to sexual experiences by adults, Englebert was not entirely sure that he had not been responsible for encouraging or even instigating these activities – perhaps due to some unexpressed or now-forgotten guilt from the experiences. But it remained for him to reach puberty, when he had a special boy friend towards whom he felt strong affection and intimacy, before he became convinced he was a homosexual. When he broke up with his special friend in his mid-teens, he hid his homosexuality 'in the closet' for a couple of years, yearning to find someone who would want to share sexual joy with him, and masturbating frequently while imagining this contact – thereby further conditioning a link between the pleasure of orgasm and homosexuality. He came out of the closet under the tutelage of a slightly older man when he reached his late teens.

He had always had lots of female friends and, in his mid-twenties, one of these began to pursue him with the clear wish that they establish a permanent relationship. He divulged to her, as he had to several others, that he was a homosexual. At first she felt rejected by this declaration. However, they had been friends for quite a long time and she felt that his 'condition' must be due to some personality problem for which he ought to consult a shrink. She told him her thoughts and refused to argue with his assurances about himself, saying only that she was not qualified to comment on the subject and that he should talk it over with somebody who was.

Mainly to placate his female friend, he saw a psychiatrist, who referred him on to Felicity. Englebert thought Felicity must be a transsexual who had changed his-her name prematurely, and he did not expect to get much of a straight answer from this contact. However, just to say that he had accommodated himself to his female friend's wishes, he kept the appointment that had been made for him with Felicity.

Felicity listened thoughtfully during Englebert's story about his background and the reasons for the present contact. As always, Felicity got the communicated message all wrong. So, he didn't do the usual 'shrink thing' of taking what Englebert told him at face value and reassuring Englebert that he was indeed a homosexual and that he might as well accept it since nothing could be done about it anyway. Instead, Felicity told Englebert that they ought to check into the question. He said that, if Englebert or his friend had any doubts about the matter, he could undertake some psychological tests to determine just what, if any, were the causes underlying his homosexuality. This was not what Englebert had expected based on the experiences of many of his homosexual friends who had, for various reasons, seen shrinks. Taken off guard, Englebert agreed to the suggestion about a psychological investigation.

The testing was ridiculous. He met Felicity's psychometrists on three occasions. One of them, a pretty female, showed him a bunch of inkblots on cards and asked him to tell her what he saw on them, asked him to copy a number of geometric forms from a booklet, and asked him all sorts of questions from an intelligence test. She then gave him a bunch of questionnaires to take home, to complete, and to return at his next visit. At the next session, another one of them, an ugly male, took him into a small room, asked him to put a little metal crescent thing around his penis, and then showed him all sorts of pictures of nude and semi-nude boys, girls, men and women. As if this were not enough of an indignity, Englebert was then asked to answer a lot of personal questions about his sexual experiences since he was a child. At the third session, he met the pretty girl again, having no idea what sort of collusion may have gone on between these two people. She sat with him while he answered another bunch of long, boring questionnaires about all sorts of issues most of which he had never thought about. He was relieved when he was told at the end of this meeting that the testing was done. He was given his appointment with Felicity who was to unravel the mysteries of this invasive set of procedures.

Since he had gone through all these unceremonious rituals, he decided he should at least find out what it all meant by attending his appointment with Felicity. After the usual greetings, he let Felicity know that, if he had known what was involved, he would not have agreed to do all that junk. Perhaps for the first time in his life Felicity was in a benign frame of mind, and so he smiled inanely at Englebert as though totally unaware of why he was so annoyed. He said that the purpose of this interview was to answer Englebert's original question concerning his homosexuality. He then began to leaf through the thick file he had in front of him. Felicity grunted and wheezed as he examined each page.

Finally, Felicity looked up and asked the astonished Englebert, "Do you want to be a homosexual?" Almost spluttering indignation, Englebert stammered, "I _am_ a homosexual!" "Yes, I know," Felicity replied, "but do you want to be a homosexual?" "What sort of a question is that?" Englebert was close to being furious. "You are what you are and I'm a homosexual. It's not a question of whether or not I want to be. That's like asking me whether or not I want hair on my body." "Exactly," Felicity replied. "If you want hair, you can probably grow it or have it grafted or otherwise attached. And if you don't want hair, you could probably have it shaved off or you could use some of the available methods for hair removal. The question here, though, is whether you want to be homosexual."

This had gone far enough. "Of course I do," Englebert affirmed. "Fine then," Felicity said, "you're welcome to be one." Englebert looked suspiciously at Felicity. "What would you have said if I said I didn't want to be a homosexual? I suppose you would say: 'Well, too bad, you are one', huh?" "No," Felicity said simply. "Do you really want to know what I would have said, or is that just a rhetorical question?" After a few moments pause, Englebert said, "No, I really would like to know. Certainly after all those tests you did you must have something more to tell me than what you've just said." "If you like," Felicity shrugged.

Felicity then told Englebert that the tests showed that he did respond on the phallometric testing with greater erections in response to males than to females, and that he had responded as strongly to adults as to youthful males. This certainly confirmed that his present sexual or erotic preference was in the homosexual direction, at least in his fantasies. In addition to this, there were some other test indicators that scored quite differently from those of most other people. These scores indicated that he experienced more guilt feelings, more sensitivity to what others thought about him, more anxiety about close emotionalized relationships and expressing his feelings to others, and more anxiety about his appearance and other people's reactions to him. Also, he did experience some confusion about himself, who he was and what his sexual 'identity' was like. His tests showed that he was prone to use some psychological 'distancing' defenses, such as hostility toward others and finding it hard to trust others, as means by which to prevent himself from getting too emotionally involved with others. In this way, his anxiety about close relationships would not be aroused. "These are not 'serious' or 'terrible' psychological 'problems'," Felicity concluded. "They are merely mildly uncomfortable feelings which are somewhat stronger in you than in most other people, and they are feelings which you have in common with most people who call themselves homosexuals".

Englebert was annoyed at Felicity's manner, and particularly at the way he kept on referring to homosexuals as 'people who call themselves homosexuals'. He demanded to know why Felicity kept using that phrase. He justified his annoyance by pointing out that homosexuals were homosexuals because they were only aroused by same sex partners, just as the, what had he called it, 'phallometric testing' had shown to be true of him. Felicity looked exactly like the inscrutable Sphinx as he asked Englebert if he really wanted an answer to his question, or whether he was just letting Felicity know how things were. "Of course I want to know!" Englebert exploded. "I've got to get some value for the time and money I've expended here."

Felicity seemed like a duck in a rainstorm with water pouring off its water-proofed back. He told Englebert that what he was about to tell him was *not* the intelligence about homosexuality that was currently accepted among sexologists. So, if Englebert liked, he could simply choose to ignore as fiction what he was about to hear. Felicity then gave the explanation of homosexuality given in the last section, drawing the associated curves and graphs on his blackboard for Englebert to see. While the explanation was going on, Englebert repeatedly gazed off into space referencing his own experience to confirm the statements Felicity was making.

At the end of the explanation, Felicity slumped back in his chair as if exhausted by the exercise of standing and talking at the same time. Englebert lapsed into a quiet reverie. Then he pulled himself together and asked, "So, if that's true, what can be done to change it? I am what I am, right?" Felicity was delighted at the rare opportunity to deliver one of his favourite replies. "Wrong!" he boomed. "If what I have just said happens to be true, and we are both sure it is not, then all we would have to do would be to unlearn or desensitize the anxieties which go to make up 'x' – after all they were learned in the first place, so it ought to be possible to unlearn them. If that was accomplished, in this fiction, the total sex drive should be diminished, moving the female object back up the high-drive tail of the upside down 'U', and the male object back down the other side of the upside down 'U'. If that happened, the person would feel "oh dear, I'm turned on by females and not by males – so maybe I am a heterosexual."

Felicity added that the problem was not really quite as simple as that. There were at least four other complications. First, the unusually high sex drive, brought about by the addition of the 'x' drive to the sex drive, would be reduced, so the person would tend to feel less chronically sexy. The main effects of that would be that he might think about masturbating a bit less often. And also, because the sex drive would be lower, the sexual experience would probably be a little less 'exciting' in a tense way, and a little more 'enjoyable' in an intense way. At least that was what some people reported after treatment.

Second, the person might feel heterosexual, but his penis might not respond, at least at first, as though he were a heterosexual person. This is because he has had a great deal of learning experience (with others and in masturbation with associated fantasies) of rewarding his penis for becoming and staying erect in response to male sex objects. After all, ejaculation is a mighty strong and pleasant reward, and it had occurred many, many times following becoming excited and erect with males and fantasies of males. If it turned out he wanted to be completely heterosexual, it might be necessary to do some things to help his penis to learn to become erect in response to females.

This could be accomplished on his own by ensuring that, during masturbation, he was always fantasizing about women for some time before he ejaculated. Alternatively, it could be accomplished in the phallometric lab by training erectile responses to female images, using a reward administered for each progressive increase in erectile response while he was looking at pictures of females.

Third, he was used to talking to men and to making sexy and provocative comments to men as part of their preparations for sexual activity. He knew that was easy to do. Either the man would react with anger or shock and turn him down, or the man would go along with the preparations for an agreement to fool around. But women would pose quite a different problem. They are strange people who not only don't understand that sex is sex and that you ask directly for it, but who even seem to become offended if the matter is broached too directly. It's almost as though they don't want sex. At least that's how some men perceive women. If he decided he wanted to be heterosexual, he would have to learn a whole new set of courting skills, including a new kind of assertiveness, a set of ways in which to give expression to his feelings, and even a greater sense of freedom in experiencing and expressing the softer, perhaps 'unmanly', emotions.

Fourth, and perhaps most importantly, he would have to learn how to be much less 'in his own head' or introverted. Felicity felt that he had to go into a lot more detail here. He pointed out that Englebert had always been somewhat more introverted and in his own head than extroverted and action-oriented. Introversion is a result of little more than the mediation of experience with words. Of course, Englebert wanted to know what that meant. Felicity gave an example. A mother, seeing a child walking toward a hot stove has three choices of response. She can say nothing and let the child get burned. If she does that, the child's flesh will soon heal, and the child will have learned a valuable lesson by direct contact with part of his world. She can 'flip out' and start screaming out warnings. The child will think something is wrong with his mother and, if anything, he may end up a bit paranoid. Or the mother can tell the child: "Don't touch the stove; it's hot and you'll get burned." If the child then does not touch the stove he will have learned to be a bit more introverted. He will have learned to mediate his experience with words: that box thing over there that he hasn't touched yet is a 'stove' and it will burn you. And he will have learned to reason by association between ideas: "It's hot. Does she mean like the hot water tap is hot? I'll get burned. Does she mean like a sun burn?" Words and ideas mediate his experience.

But words have no existence except as sounds made or as ideas or thoughts in the head. Unlike the world around us, they have to be kept alive by being repeated. This is done in thought, or by talking to ourselves. But to think or to talk to yourself, you have to pay attention to the thoughts going on within. This turns the attention inward, and that is called 'introversion'.

In addition to being events going on within ourselves, words or thoughts have another characteristic. They don't change. The world around us is constantly changing, but the words do not. This means that once anything has been assigned an 'identity' with a word allotted to it, the verbal identity does not change even if the thing it refers to changes quite a bit. One of the most important things to a person is the 'identity' he assigns himself. Even although he keeps on changing, the stream of his memories of his past keep him thinking of himself as the same person. Both the stream of memories and any verbal identity he gives himself remain almost fixed qualities. Felicity pointed out that Englebert had himself said that he *is* whatever it is he *is*, and that wouldn't change. If a person gives himself the verbal identity of 'being a homosexual', that would feel to him like his 'identity' – the word would stick with him.

But even that was not the end of the issue involved. We all have so much rich experience every day that our brains cannot handle it all, so we use verbal 'filters' through which to screen our daily experiences. These 'filters' tell us whether to notice or ignore our different experiences. Our brains pick and choose, by means of these filters, what we are going to notice or pay attention to and what we will simply ignore. These filters are conceptual or ideational filters formed through our beliefs from our values (the things we consider to be 'important' to us). If I come to believe that I am a homosexual as part of my identity, my attentional filters will allow me to notice confirming evidence – "See, I did get turned-on by that man" and they will prevent me from noticing dis-confirming evidence – as if I happened also to turn-on to a woman. In fact, having a homosexual identity, if I did notice an attraction to a woman, I would be inclined to attribute the turn-on to something else such as "Yes, she's a nice friendly person," or "she's dressed well," or "her make up looks good'" or "Women try to 'look' sexy, and that's what she's doing."

The problem all this creates for a person who wants to become heterosexual is that it will be hard for the person to change the beliefs and the 'filters' he uses, so that he could actually notice the evidences of the changes in himself. Indeed, it is because of using these kinds of filters and beliefs and identities that all of us manage to hang on to our clear ideas of ourselves as either homosexual or heterosexual. Felicity ended by adding that, as he had pointed out from the test results, Englebert was still a bit confused about his sexual identity – that his beliefs and filters were not entirely excluding him from alternative bits of evidence. And this was probably why he had come to ask Felicity about his homosexuality in the first place and, incidentally, why Felicity had offered him a thorough psychological assessment.

Englebert had listened intently throughout this explanation. It was evident that his introspective and obsessional nature had created many more thoughts, and much more complex thinking, in response to the already fairly complicated ideas Felicity had been talking about. He shook his head when Felicity was finished and offered the opinion: "You know, Felicity, you really aren't nearly as dumb as you look. On second thought, though, if you think I was able to put all that together, understand it and remember it, perhaps you are even dumber than you look." He sat for a few moments in thought. "Do you want to know what the mush inside my head is like right now?" he asked. "If you'd like to tell me," Felicity replied. "Right now, my thoughts remind me of a poem I learned when I was a child. Do you remember the one about Robert Reese?" Felicity said he didn't think he had ever heard it. So Englebert recited it.[4]

So Englebert recited it.

"There once was a little boy whose name was Robert Reese,
And every Friday afternoon he had to say a piece.
So many pieces had he learned that soon he had a store
Of recitations in his head, and still kept learning more."

Englebert went on misquoting Carolyn Wells' little masterpiece and ending with its marvellous punchline:

"His elocution was superb, his voice and gesture fine.
His school-mates all applauded as he finished the last line.
'I see', said Robert to himself, 'it doesn't matter what you say
As long as you declaim with oratorical display."

Englebert and Felicity shared a good laugh. There was perhaps a touch of nervous self-consciousness on Felicity's part as he considered the possibility that he was more than a little pompous in his delivery of his earlier recitation. However, Englebert's good humour suggested that he was disposed to forgive him for any possible responsibility he may have had for the tumult in Englebert's head. And Englebert's next remark verified Felicity's observations and set him quite at ease again. "Well, I suppose I'll just have to go home and think through what you have said. I'm sure what I need to know will sort itself out in my head in time. I'll call if I need to be reminded about anything." Felicity agreed with these suggestions. Englebert left in deep thought, shaking his head as if to confirm that his brain was still there by hearing it rattle.

It was almost six months before Felicity heard from Englebert again. There was a message to call him. Felicity returned the call with some concern. Englebert sounded quite buoyant. He said:

---

[4]   Parts of *An Overworked Elocutionist* by Carolyn Bailey Wells

"Well, I've thought about what you said, and I've talked the whole thing over with several of my friends, both gay and straight. It looks to me as though I've been elected by my gay friends to serve as the sacrificial goat to see just what happens if you're right about homosexuality." Felicity was not too pleased with this basis for undertaking psychotherapy, but he was swift enough to grasp that this might just be Englebert's way of expressing embarrassment or anticipatory anxiety about asking for or entering psychotherapy. So he suggested that they should at least get together to talk over what Englebert might want to do.

Englebert was much less flamboyant when he appeared for his appointment. With a serious voice and a steady gaze he told Felicity that he wanted to find out whether he could be straight. He had several reasons for concluding that the straight life would be better for him than the gay life, if indeed the straight life were possible for him. He also wanted to make it clear to Felicity that he was not concerned about how long the treatment might take, and that he wanted Felicity to do the whole task to make a fair and complete test of his unlikely sounding ideas about homosexuality.

Treatment was started at once. Englebert came twice a week. The early sessions involved anxiety desensitization using deep muscle relaxation, as described in previous stories. The scenes used involved interpersonal contacts in which others found or did not find him attractive, liked or did not like him, and where he progressively expressed himself as having caring feelings about things, other people and, finally, about the person with whom he was talking.

After a while in this sort of program, he was asked to come for longer sessions. During the first part of these sessions he went into the phallometric lab, put the metal crescent around his penis and watched slides. The slides usually started off as pictures of males, and then slowly faded and changed into pictures of females. He had a dentist's fluid-suction tube in his mouth hooked over his lower teeth and attached to a tube leading into another room. Every now and then he would receive a small squirt of grapefruit juice (his favourite kind of juice) into his mouth from this tube. **[WARNING** : Beware not to drown the client!] He was told this was being used as a reward for each heterosexually-appropriate erectile response being recorded on the phallometric equipment being monitored by the psychometrist in the next room.

After a few of these sessions, and after he had become used to the treatment routine, some of the treatment time was devoted to conversations with Felicity, in addition to the continuing anxiety desensitization and phallometric conditioning. During these conversations, a good deal of time was spent at first on the language Englebert used in talking both to Felicity and (while thinking) to himself. He learned to use verbs where possible in place of nouns. In place of saying "I am gay", he was encouraged to say, "I am homosexualizing". And instead of talking as though he was an effect at the mercy of events outside himself, he was encouraged to talk as though he was himself the cause of how he felt. For example, he was encouraged to say, "I arouse myself," in place of "I get aroused." At first that felt uncomfortable and somehow wrong. But, as he practised these skills and as he learned to seek and find specific examples of what he was talking about (referential statements in place of abstract ideas), he found, to his shock, quite noticeable changes in how he felt, the way he looked at things and the things he noticed about the world around him. What's more, for reasons he could not grasp, he felt happier than he had ever before felt, to the point of almost being able to feel a real sense of joy. Although delighted when Englebert reported some of these changes, Felicity seemed not to share Englebert's surprise and, indeed, seemed to accept the news as though it was expected.

Once this 'psychotherapy' had become a matter of course to Englebert, he was introduced into a group run by the pretty psychometrist. The group was concerned with assertive training. He was taught how to reduce his anxiety about dealing directly with situations in which he had previously felt 'put upon' by others. He learned to use a number of assertive skills such as the 'I' sentence in place of 'You' statements, and the 'three-part statement' in which he (1) confirmed his understanding of what the other had just said,

(2) indicated how he felt about the matter, and (3) affirmed what he would do about the issue. And he was shown quite clearly some of the mistakes of thinking he had always made and by which he made himself upset and angry. He was impressed.

But he was more impressed by something else about this group. By the second session he found himself quite distracted by the psychometrist's shapely legs that seemed to have been hung with malice of afore-thought right in front of his eyes. By the fourth session he could not take his eyes off her plunging neckline, which he was sure she had arranged just to tempt him. He found several excuses to get up and move about the room, passing near her and trying to peak down her blouse at her cleavage. After a few more of these group sessions, he found himself having consciously to fight the urge to walk up to her and take her breasts in his hands.

Finally, after one group in which the tingling in his hands and in his penis were such that he could hardly stand it, he asked her for a date. He had expected to be told in no uncertain terms to leave her alone and to get his mind out of the gutter. Instead, she smiled beautifully, thanked him for the compliment and said that it sounded as though his treatment was progressing very well. Although she did not accept his offer directly, she suggested that they should talk over what he was feeling and whatever it was he had in mind to do with her, either in the group or in her office. The cold water splash of in her reaction, almost thankfully, brought Englebert back to the issues he was trying to address within himself. He noted that he was not in the least bit offended or upset and that, if anything, he felt relieved by her reaction.

Although he continued to revel in the attractiveness of the psychometrist, he chose to talk the matter over with Felicity. He almost expected Felicity to punch him out him for being so fresh with one of his staff. Instead, Felicity congratulated him and asked how things were going in his love life at home and with his friends. Englebert frowned. He observed that he had not had any sexual contact at all with his partner for some time, although, as he was quick to add, he still loved him. He paused and sighed. "I suppose you know that I've never said that I loved him before to him or to anyone else." He frowned again. "My great-aunt's tusche," he exclaimed, "I believe I've got the hots for Phoebe – you know, the girl who suggested I come to see you in the first place." He lapsed into quiet shock.

The treatment took about a year to complete. At the end of that time, Englebert told Felicity that, although he still harboured many doubts about how he would cause himself to feel in the future, he felt fully heterosexual now. He said that his boy friend and he had split up, that Phoebe and he were living together, and that they were talking about getting married. Felicity congratulated him. But Englebert was not finished. He wanted Felicity to know that he was not sure how he would feel once he got away from the treatment program, that he was not confident that his inclinations would not still be toward men as sexual partners, and that he had real misgivings about the day to day business of living as a married man. "Welcome to the human race, my friend, and to the uncertainties everybody has," was Felicity's only reply.

The years have brought to Felicity's door many Ernestines and Ernests, whose experiences were quite similar to Englebert's. Many of them sought help by the briefest or least costly routes, and the results they achieved tended to be about in proportion to the investment they were willing or able to make in the task. It seems clear that if only part of a task is done, only part of the effect will be achieved.

As for Englebert, Felicity bumped into him from time to time in shops or on the street. He and Phoebe did marry. They did have two children. They did separate and then divorce. And both Englebert and Phoebe did re-marry. Did Englebert have any further homosexual contacts? He did. He told Felicity about two such contacts between his divorce and his re-marriage and, of course, there may have been more. He did report, however, that during the two contacts to which he admitted, although he had expected to enjoy them, he had actually been disgusted by them. Such may be the price we pay for changing how we go about experiencing life.

Felicity was not surprised by the change in how Englebert felt. He had also treated a couple of entertainers for their anxiety about how other people might react to them and how they appeared 'on stage' (anxiety about personal appearance). After the anxiety desensitization was completed, both these people lost their interest in being entertainers and found other careers for themselves. Apparently, in these cases, the excitement, bred of anxiety about being attractive and the centre of attention, had provided the motivation to wish to be 'the centre of attention'. It had apparently motivated their careers as entertainers and, once that anxiety was taken away, reduced that motivation.

Discussion? Recapitulation to Confusion

So, do you think you understand homosexuality yet? If you do, perhaps you'd be good enough to explain it to Felicity. He claims not to understand it at all. Each of the stories he made up served as a piece of a puzzle. One piece showed a face looking shocked. Another displayed a face looking sleepy. Two pieces had crumpled fenders on them. Two looked like bare wires with electricity sprouting from them. One showed a toilet bowl. And one might be part of a person getting sexually excited. We know where these scattered pictures came from – Felicity's normally unconscious mind. But, where do the pieces fit? And what's the whole picture about? Partly based on other pieces he has seen or others have described, Felicity tried to fit the pieces in places in which they made sense – at least to him. Has he succeeded in making sense of the puzzle? Who knows? Although he clearly fails, he thinks it's best to keep an open mind on any subject. But perhaps you think he abuses the privilege and drifts along with his mind ... vacant?

Or perhaps you think it would be important to add other pieces to the puzzle. There are lots of other features that are fairly common among homosexuals. Many are flamboyant and showy, perhaps consistent with their anxiety about 'being attractive' or the centre of attention. Many seem angry, some in a restrained way (see restraint-rage) and some in a resentful way (see closeness-hostility). Many exhibit misogyny (see sadism), etc. While such observations may be valid (or just stereotypes), Felicity would argue that there is a danger in creating too much complexity if you want to understand something. Later in this volume a few comments are made about the effects on understanding of varying the amounts of information included. At least Felicity says he needs to keep things simple if he is going to be able to comprehend anything.

But you must be asking yourself what there is to comprehend, since all this stuff is make-believe anyway. But that's the very point Felicity would make. The goal of science is to construct or make up theories that are as general as possible. A theory is simply a made up story to account for the greatest number of the facts which it seeks to explain. Theories are fictions offered to account for facts. Since Felicity always does things backwards, his objective was to find a set of truthful statements (in place of a theory) to account for fictional events. If you think that's nuts, just think about how any goal planning is done. You start with where you want to get to, and you argue back to make up a way to get there. If you make up workable steps along the way, the goal may eventually, in fact, be achieved.

CHAPTER 5

FEAR!

Scare Scars: Protectiveness: The Learned Core Of Dis-Ease ...

Anxiety or fear or stress has long been recognized as the common core of the 'neuroses'. Selye and others have argued cogently that stress is also the common core of a great many of the physical illnesses which afflict humankind – certainly nearly all of the 'chronic' diseases, or those which are most likely to threaten life. He also showed that stress is a basic attribute associated with even acute or infectious diseases, and that it affects the person's ability to recover from acute illnesses.

Stress, of course, is the effect on the body of the repeated and/ or intense activation of the sympathetic branch of the autonomic nervous system. It is this system that both initiates and orchestrates the body's immune system, and eventuates in the proprioceptive sensory feedback to the brain which is experienced as anxiety or fear. That is, from a psychological perspective, fear is at once the core of the most commonly occurring psychological difficulties (the neuroses), the main basis of nearly all chronic diseases, and an important aspect of recovery from acute diseases. And, according to

                    Douglas A. Quirk

Felicity's observations, it is also the common core of the psychoses (or the major mental 'diseases') as well as the underlying root of anger and most violence. So if Felicity respectfully recognizes and treats anxiety in the majority of cases, at least from his perspective that would be the appropriate thing to do.

But anxiety is not just implicated in the 'causation' of all kinds of human ills and suffering, it is a source of distress in its own right. Perhaps spending a bit of time addressing anxiety for its own sake might help to cast some light upon the different kinds of anxiety, how each is learned and develops, what effects each has on daily living as a learned motive for avoidant actions, and how each may most effectively be treated. This issue is addressed below.

The *sensation* of anxiety is not really that different from one situation to the next. It is largely a result of sensations received by the brain from the proprioceptive (internal) sensory tracts, including kinaesthetic muscle sensations, temperature and pressure sensations, and chemical sensations (chemo-receptors). If these sensory tracts indicate that activation of these body parts has occurred as a result of arousal of the sympathetic branch of the autonomic nervous system, the experience the brain feels is anxiety or fear. It is a standard experience generated by a standard bodily response. Then what creates the differences in the ways anxiety can be experienced? The answer seems to be that they arise from the different ways in which anxiety is learned.

Anxiety can be learned through the necessity of depending on others, as in infancy and childhood. The judgements and feelings of the other on whom the infant and growing child depends are likely to achieve great importance in its mind. This kind of experience typically results in learning feelings of guilt or shame and sensitivity to others' attitudes and feelings. Occurring early in life, it also tends to have important effects in the development of personality characteristics such as guilt- or shame-proneness. Almost everyone experiences some of this early-learned or 'dynamic' anxiety.

Anxiety can also be learned through the accidental consequence of 'feeling better' when one avoids an uncomfortable situation.

Successful avoidance results in a relief experience. Relief from discomfort is inherently rewarding or reinforcing. The learning which is reinforced is the habit of feeling uncomfortable (or anxious) in that situation in the future <u>and</u> of avoiding that situation in the future as far as possible. This kind of learning tends to result in phobic or situational anxiety.

Anxiety can be learned from a dangerous or traumatic situation in which the person feels helpless or vulnerable, particularly when the event is sudden and unexpected. The autonomic nervous system is nervous tissue, which therefore learns. In fact, it is hard-wired into the body to detect, and rapidly to learn, what is to be construed as dangerous or survival-threatening. Traumatic learning is most commonly encountered these days following traffic accidents, frequently minor ones, and most often rear-enders – where the person does not anticipate the sudden impact.

Anxiety can be learned by assigning dangerous 'meanings' to events. Dangerous meanings are imputed by catastrophizing ordinary events in thought. This sort of 'cognitive' anxiety most often results in bodily disorders or psychosomatic ills. It is commonly associated with ideas of body weakness or susceptibility to sudden catastrophes, usually imagined to affect health.

And anxiety can be learned through errors of regulation of bodily functions. Accidentally learned errors regarding bowel regulation or in the way in which the person breathes may result in habits resulting in anxiousness. Interestingly, in Felicity's experience, this physiologically-derived form of anxiety is usually experienced as a kind of psychological anxiety, specifically panic.

Of course, there are many other ways in which anxiety may be experienced. A 'built in' automatic-anxiety response occurs with loss of support as in falling, some detected motions, and loud noise – the auditory world is spherical, receiving distant sensations from all directions, thus providing the primary alerting system, or 'orienting reflex'. The built-in response to these stimuli may be one reason why fear is learned so efficiently in traffic accidents – in one practice trial.

'Built-in' autonomic-anxiety responses are also evoked from inside the person. The autonomic-stress response is automatically aroused when the body detects infection, poison, or injury affecting its integrity – in order to activate the immune system. And a 'short-circuit' in the area of the 'drive centre' in the brain, can trigger off an autonomic storm since the front-end roots of the autonomic nervous system are located in that region.

Although all these types of anxiety responses are 'automatic', they can be triggered or intensified in various circumstances as a result of learning, and they can serve as means to evoke arousal so that other responses can be learned – derived from these primary bodily responses. The possibilities of how the body can get itself upset are almost endless.

Developmental Anxiety – Guilt Proneness

Guilt is a terrible judgement of oneself. But some people are not all that clearly aware of things like guilt within themselves. This is often because the guilty feelings have become 'worked into' their personalities such that they have assumed abstract forms, particularly values. Many of those who have achieved fame due to their good deeds may not feel particularly guilty even although the primary driving motive is often guilt. Instead, such people, thought of as exhibiting a highly developed morality or an advanced stage of moral reasoning development, probably are motivated by strong values concerned with service or caring for others.

How does this transformation of guilt to values come about? Felicity doesn't know. But let's pretend he does, so we can have some fun with it. Actually, we've borrowed most of our ideas about this subject from a couple of young up-starts, James and Woodsmall [Time Line Therapy and the Basis of Personality, 1988. R R], so we can blame them if it all sounds too confusing.

The body grows by cell division (which increases the number of body cells) and by specialization of function within the various organ systems. The mind grows in a similar way. Habits and memories are formed from the experiences we have, and they cluster themselves into various 'habit family hierarchies' from their different amounts of habit strengths. The hierarchies determine which habits or memories are most likely to be evoked first in any given situation. Habit and memory groupings then develop so as to be called up under different kinds of circumstances – a kind of specialization of function.

These groupings are formed at different levels of abstraction or generality, partly so that we are not always led to respond in exactly the same ways from situation to situation. That is, we develop clusters of habits into different personality traits at different levels of abstraction such as being a good listener or interested in others, or being creative or analytical, or a literate speaker. And we assemble them into personality types such as introversion (thinking things through before acting) or extraversion (acting at once with some emotional impact). The formation of personality structures allow us, for example, to be creative in an introverted (highly elaborated and thought through) or in an extroverted (highly emotional and reproductive or 'copying' reality) way. That is, an artist who paints what he sees (his paintings may look like photographs) is likely extroverted, and one who paints what he thinks of (for example, the aesthete who wrote seven thick volumes on the experience of eating a piece of cake) is likely introverted.

Now, what's all that about? Experience in which a person feels guilty is likely to form a set of increasingly strong habits to feel guilty in all sorts of situations. But the person's reactions to various types of situations become increasingly differentiated to allow different reactions to be evoked in different kinds of situations. If guilt is experienced regularly in certain kinds of situations, the person's discomfort may well drive him to try to avoid responding in the guilt-provoking way and to react increasingly strongly in the way which avoids guilt, with the reward of 'feeling good'. A 'part' is formed in him, as it were, that drives him away from doing things which evoke guilt, and drives him to seek to 'be good'.

That much is obvious. But then the person may start to make the 'feeling good' way of reacting into an abstract principle for living. For example, Gurdjieff quoted the 'universal principle for all living' from that master among men, Mullah Nassir Edin, as: "When you're on a spree, go the whole hog, including the postage." Well, perhaps that isn't quite the most laudable of values but, like many others, it comes from a response to living (i.e., selfishness) which may have been guilt-motivated originally, but it affirms the normally guilt-motivated pole and glories in it. In the more usual case, the position that is affirmed involves glorifying the non-guilt-motivated pole of response – such as unselfishness or service to others.

We're getting there. The guilt versus the non-guilt polarity involved in the two response extremes creates an importance for the idea involved which, as it is made more and more abstract or general in thought, becomes a value – a conceptual part of the person that pushes him to react in particular ways as opposed to other ways. These abstract values are formed by and comprised of a number of 'beliefs', each of which subsumes a number of 'attitudes' on the part of the person; and each of which, in turn, is comprised of a number of habits of both thought and action. But the values are the most abstract parts, each including and activating its own beliefs, attitudes, and habits of memory, thought and action. Their generality, affecting wide areas of living, make values terribly important aspects of the person.

'Values' (1) are the most basic 'guides' which select for us what is most important to us and influence our approaches to things, (2) are the most abstract and 'general' things about us, which therefore determine what we think of ourselves – our self-definitions, (3) provide the up-front 'motivation' which decides what we will do, how we will spend our time and how strongly we will be driven to do things, and (4) provide the after-the-fact means by which we 'evaluate' how well we have done in doing anything – that is, they also determine how pleased we are with ourselves or how guilty we will feel. Not only that, we all have values and those values do govern our lives. If we think that someone or some group does not have values, we are wrong – it's just that their values don't correspond with our own.

So, what has all this got to do with treatment? That's easy. If we want to help a person most generally to improve the quality of his or her life, the quickest way to do it might be to work at the level of values – the most abstract guides for the person's life that most widely affect everything about the person. However, the person may not make the distress in his or her life into abstract ideas. The distress may also be experienced in a quite concrete but generalized way, as a picture or image of that which either hurts most or is most idealized.

A Sympathetic Antipathy

Martha was about as depressed a person as one might wish to meet. A single mother in her early thirties, she spent most of her evenings staring down the barrel of her loaded handgun, trying to pull the trigger and end her misery. The only thing she clung to as a reason for living was her daughter. She feared what might happen to her daughter if she was not around to care for her. Martha's mother would gain custody and, from long personal experience, Martha knew how horrible that fate would be.

But her own life felt unbearable to her. She constantly judged herself and found herself to be guilty and unworthy. Her unworthiness seemed verified by a sudden and unexplained separation from the man with whom she had been making long-term plans. And although she was in a position of great responsibility in her work, she felt her boss disapproved of her, and she felt certain she would make a major mistake at any moment. So each evening she sat in a big, beautiful house, surrounded by expensive and tasteful things, well-fed and watching her lovely daughter play, and she held her gun in her hand trying to find a way to kill herself.

Martha knew that the way she felt was 'crazy', but that knowledge changed nothing. All she had to do was to get up and look in the mirror and she winced with disgust at what she saw. Anybody else looking at Martha would respond with warm appreciation to this very attractive and pleasant person – certainly that was how Felicity reacted when she consulted him about her 'crazy', but firmly held, beliefs about herself.

The tests that Felicity administered verified an extremely heavy burden of guilt as the active process underlying her introverted and obsessional personality and her severe depression. And there was really little more of interest in the tests. Certainly, the guilt feelings were well integrated throughout the personality system, indicating that they had been with her for a very long time.

Felicity decided that he might have to get her to rework large parts of her personality make-up, although his primary attack had to be on her felt guilt. While he was laying out his multi-facetted therapeutic plan for her, Martha told him that the main thing she needed to accomplish was to find a way to like 'the way she looked' – a seemingly rather specific and concrete issue. Although often unable to solve their problems, people's focus of attention is commonly the best indicator of what needs to be done. Felicity knew this and so he offered a series of alternative methods by which Martha might get to like the way she looked. Since they would have taken almost an eternity of time, it was fortunate they were unnecessary.

To get at the roots of her guilt feelings, Felicity got Martha to picture a series of scenes from her past and from her imagined future, and to locate where in space she saw these pictures in her mind. This allowed Felicity, following some work by James and Woodsmall, to determine the manner in which Martha had structured the memories stored in her mind, and thus represented for herself the process of time through her life. It turned out that her memories tended to be organized in front of her, with her past approaching her along a line at about a 45 degree angle to her right, and her future receding from her along a line at about 45 degrees to her left. Any image of time stretching from her remote past through the present to her distant future would have been fine. This one seemed to work for her.

Next, Felicity asked her to close her eyes, and in her mind to imagine herself floating way up above her time-line, leaving it as a line below her that she could see way off in the distance. Then he asked her to float slowly down over her time-line and back in time until, looking down on her time-line, she reached a point at which she felt good about herself. With some doubt, she selected a time at about 4 years of age. Felicity asked her to drift down into the memory at that point in her time-line, to face the present and to tell him how she felt. She was troubled. On the one hand, she felt comfortable about herself. On the other hand, she felt very sad. Felicity wanted to find out what caused her discomfort, so he asked her to walk forward toward the present along her time-line until she started to feel uncomfortable. At between 5 and 6 years of age she reported feeling very bad.

Felicity asked her to drift up again way above her time-line, to float over that place, and then to tell him what she had seen there. Her memory was hazy, but she described a normal and quite benign childhood experience in which (1) she became fearful and (2) which engendered guilt feelings in her. The guilt seemed to be based in her strict Catholic up-bringing – mostly because she could not really remember what, if anything, took place. Regardless of what had happened, the strength of her reaction told Felicity that this point in time and this experience were probably fairly critical in forming her strong guilty self-judgements.

But she had been sad even before that point. He wanted to know why. So he asked her drift back again over her time-line until she found a time in which she was no longer sad. She said she had found such a place. He asked her to tell him, if she knew, whether that time was before, during, or after birth. She said it was before birth. He asked her where she was before birth. She said she was in her mother's womb. He asked her to drift down into that time, face the present, and tell him how she felt. She said she felt awful. He asked her to back up along her time line until she no longer felt awful. She said there was never any such time. Felicity asked her to drift up again over her time line and to tell him what she meant by her last statement.

She said that she had always known that her mother didn't want her, didn't like her, and wanted to be rid of her. She felt that she was her father's favourite, and that her mother had always been jealous of her. He asked whether it was possible for her mother not to like or want her before her mother knew she was pregnant. Martha agreed that was not possible. So Martha was able to agree that for a while following conception and the associated enjoyable relations with her father, her mother could not 'not-want' her – at least until that time when she discovered she was pregnant. Martha drifted down into her time-line during that time – granting that, although she might have no awareness of that time, it was still part of the time of her existence. She reported no feelings during that time. That was all Felicity wanted to know. He asked her to drift up again and to float forward along her time-line and down into the present.

As she had organized it in her mind, the problem was clearly two-fold. In spite of the fact that she spent a great deal of time with her mother, she thought of herself as having always been rejected by her mother, unwanted and made to feel bad or guilty for existing. And she also thought of herself as one who had earned her guilt for some unknown act she might have done in her early childhood.

At first, Felicity asked Martha to tell him about the picture that popped into her mind when she thought about her mother as a rejecting and jealous person. The image she reported of her mother as a scowling witch seemed to be workable, if a bit too concrete. He asked her for her image of acceptance and being wanted. A gentle picture of her father smiling attentively at her was reported. Felicity was sure that both of these images were too concrete and that the procedure he was going to try would therefore probably not work too well. But she was unable or unwilling to find another pair of images to represent rejection and acceptance. So he tried the visual squash (see below) with these two images. Although the procedure went smoothly, the result was only mildly gratifying, and the new image produced seemed weak to both Martha and Felicity.

On the one hand, it was probably a good idea to undertake the procedure (see squash below) with a 'lesser' issue first, if only because it gave her some practice with the procedure – making the next application easier. On the other hand, in principle, the more general and more powerful intervention should involve a personal (herself) abstract image rather than a 'projected' (of someone else) image. So, if only one procedure were to be run, it ought to have been one in which the image was non-specific or perhaps relating to herself.

He asked Martha what picture popped into her mind when she thought about herself as ugly or bad. She saw herself looking in the mirror and wincing with disgust at what she saw. That image was much too concrete to suit Felicity. He asked her again and again to let pictures pop into her mind about feeling bad or ugly. Finally, in sheer impatience and disgust, while looking downwards in embarrassment, she said, "I suppose you mean I'm looking at the green devil." Felicity was surprised and delighted. He wanted her to tell him what she meant. She said she could see herself in the mirror, and what she saw was the green devil. What green devil was she talking about? "The green devil that is just under my skin". From where to where? "From the top of my head to the end of my toes". Felicity knew he had found the level of abstraction that he was looking for.

He asked Martha to put the green devil up on a shelf, and then to tell him what popped into her mind when she thought of innocence and loveliness. Without hesitation, she reported seeing a nice little country church with a steeple. It was cleanly kept up and pretty. That was a nice abstract image and Felicity was pleased. He asked her to put that up on the shelf too.

Felicity then explained to Martha that both images were just parts of herself. The past is gone and no longer exists. The future is yet to come. The only connections we have with the past or the future are in our memories and images – which exist only in our own heads, and which are parts of ourselves. Of course, we can always talk to ourselves. But when we do so, we often don't know which parts of ourselves we're talking to. So, just to be sure we are talking with the parts of ourselves we want to talk to, it might be wise to 'objectify' those parts as images, and to bring them out of ourselves and look at them objectively. So, if she was going to bring out the green devil part of herself and put it on one of her hands, which hand would she put it on? She indicated her right hand. Felicity said, "Fine, then please do so." He then asked her to hold out her left hand too and place the little country church part of her on her left hand. She sat with her palms up-turned as if holding the two images and waited.

Felicity asked her please to talk to the green devil part of her and ask it what its highest intentions for her were. She said, "That I kill myself so I will be dead." Felicity asked, "But why would that part of you want you to be dead?" She said, "So I could not do anything else bad or wrong." "But why would that part of you want you not to do anything else bad or wrong?" "So I can be good." "But why would that part of you want you to be good?" "So I can be perfect." "But why would that part of you want you to be perfect?" "So I can be happy ...?" Her voice trailed off in a question and with doubt. "You mean that the green devil part of you wants you to be happy!? How can that be?" Martha opened her eyes and stared at Felicity in disbelief. "I said that, didn't I?" "I think you did," Felicity replied. "Now," he continued, "close your eyes again. Now look at your right hand and describe to me what you see." She looked absolutely flabbergasted. She opened her eyes, looked around as if to find something she had lost, then closed her eyes again. Sheer amazement was written all over her face, and tears started rolling down her cheeks. Felicity asked what was wrong. "It's not there any more," she said, "It's just a little green rubber ball."

Without breaking rhythm, Felicity asked her to turn to her left hand and to ask the part of her that is the little country church what its best intentions for her were. For a few moments her face continued to look toward her right hand. Then it turned toward her left hand and she said, "For me to be perfect." "And why does that part of you want you to be perfect?" "So I can be happy," she replied. Her head turned back and forth as if to look at each of her hands in turn. There was a sense of both shock and conviction in her look.

Felicity pointed out that it seemed that both parts of herself, both that part which represented badness and ugliness, and that part which represented goodness and attractiveness, wanted the same things for her, namely that she should be happy. If they wanted the same thing for her, perhaps they could talk to each other and figure out how they could get along together to help her achieve their common purpose without hurting her any more. And, he added, perhaps they could find a way to show to each other that they wanted to get together as one part of her. While saying this, Felicity slowly brought his two hands (which had been held as Martha was holding her hands) together palm to palm to illustrate the idea of squashing the two parts into one. Although Martha's eyes were closed and her attention apparently rivetted on her hands, her hands began slowly to move together as if in a sign of union between them. But they stopped side by side. She looked up in bewilderment. How could two such unrelated things become related to each other? After much encouragement without success in finding a way, Felicity finally suggested a solution that he confirmed with her at each step.

The little green ball has something to do with childhood play. It probably is not particularly important to her adult life. But the church continues to play a part in her life. Childhood memories are usually put away in a safe place where they can be enjoyed without interfering with adult life. Perhaps she would like to put the little green ball away somewhere in the church, since they both had the same purpose. She might want to bury the green ball under the little church as she might bury other memories of the past. Martha seemed satisfied with that idea, and she closed her eyes and slowly allowed her hands to move together in a palm to palm union.

Now Felicity asked Martha what she saw as she looked at the new part of her contained between her hands. What she saw was the little country church surrounded by thick green foliage of grass, bushes, and trees. The whole thing looked beautiful to her eyes. Finally, Felicity asked her to imagine an infinite source of love and power and happiness flowing down through her head and out through her heart to this new wonderful part of her. Then he asked her to allow that infinite source of love and power and happiness to flow down through her head and out through her heart to all the other many parts of her as she drew the new part into herself and integrated it with all the other parts of herself. After a while, Martha opened her eyes, flowing with tears of happiness, and she smiled a wistful thank you at Felicity, still holding her joined hands gently against her chest.

Felicity maintained periodic contact with Martha during the next six months. There were no more events of staring at her gun. She put it away as if she had no further use for it. She reported that she was feeling content and reasonably happy in her life, and that these feelings were consistently there. She met another man, and although still in some conflict about 'giving up' her feelings for her former friend, she was beginning to establish strong feelings for her new friend.

Guilt is a terrible judgement of one's self that evokes strong arousal of negative feelings. It underlies much of what passes as depression, and it evokes its own sense of anxiousness. It is learned from early, perfectly normal and necessary, parental rebukes and criticism which, however, tend to be magnified in the child's mind partly because of its helpless and dependent state in its relationship to its parents. The function or job of guilt tends to be to prevent the expression of self-gratifying feelings, most commonly anger. It is the primitive way in which the child gains control over its anger and other personal feelings in the service of maintaining the relationships which are so necessary to its survival – since the child believes such feelings may drive a wedge between itself and its parenting ones.

Martha's case is interesting particularly because of the way in which she was able to image her 'green devil'. For everyone, guilt is a kind of devil that demeans the person and makes him or her feel ugly and unworthy of love or caring. It really only varies in size and colour. For some, guilt is 'puke green' and it represents an evil that can only escape as bilious vomit. For others, it is 'piss yellow' or 'shit brown' and it represents evil that can only be dispelled as body waste. For still others, it is red and it can only be released as anger and violence. But for nearly everybody, it cannot be released or removed by actions or by surgery. It can only be healed by some process in which the person can come to terms with the images of his childhood, leaving them behind as innocuous dreams.

A Precision Incision

Mary was a troubled and unhappy young woman in her early thirties. In terms of formal diagnosis, she suffered from a severe obsessive condition, complicated by post-traumatic anxiety from a traffic accident in which she had been involved. The post-traumatic anxiety was eliminated using Wolpe's systematic anxiety desensitization (RIT) method, which has been described in several stories already. That procedure should have taken a great deal of time to complete – probably well over a year since obsessive personalities are notoriously hard to treat because they learn new emotional habits so slowly (slow 'conditionability').

One main root of the obsessive personality lies in strong guilt feelings which, in this case, were magnified by the traumatically-conditioned increase of arousal from the traffic accident. If the guilt feelings could be relieved first, it should relieve the obsessive resistance to conditionability and thus remove an impediment to progress in desensitization of the post-traumatic anxiety. Yes, it's true, this sounds like putting the cart before the horse in a circular kind of reasoning. But a brief procedure to relieve some of her guilt allowed the longer procedure for removing the traumatically-conditioned anxiety to take a minimum amount of time. So, Felicity tackled her values at the outset – to reduce the pressure of her guilt feelings.

So, how did they approach her values? Felicity began by asking Mary to list all of the things that were important to her in the 'areas' of (i) work, (ii) daily living, (iii) relationships and (iv) feelings. He used a couple of brief procedures to help her to find any values she had forgotten. When she had done that, he asked her to rank order the list of values for each area from the most important to the least important. He used a couple of brief methods to help her check to make sure they were ranked in the right order. Eventually, she had a carefully ordered list of all the values that were important to her in each of four areas of living. Then, Mary and Felicity settled down to examine her lists of values to find out if there were any 'problems' or conflicts among or within them.

It turned out that Mary didn't like her values very much. When Felicity asked her to imagine that she had a job, or a life, or a relationship, or feelings which contained all of the values she had listed for that area of living, instead of 'lighting up like a beacon' with pleasure, she looked half bored and half unhappy. Felicity wasn't surprised by how she reacted because nearly all of her values in all areas of living were values expressed in 'negative' terms, as if she wanted to 'avoid' or move away from something that was unpleasant for her. He had two choices. He could help her to change the order of her values to get some happier ones at the top of her lists. Or he could help to heal the pain that she was obviously trying to avoid. That avoiding pain was important to her was clear since nearly everything she considered important involved avoiding pain. If the pain could be removed from her values, their quality might change. Once freed from their negative feelings, he could get her to relist them and see how she liked them. That seemed the way to go.

The visual 'squash', described by James and Woodsmall, and already illustrated in Martha's story, was used to address each of the main conflicted (negative, to be avoided) values listed by Mary in the various areas of living. The images she chose for each one, and the image resulting after the 'squash', were all fascinating. However, one of the 'squashes' will probably suffice to illustrate the process employed.

Mary had listed 'innocence' as a value in the areas of living, relationships, feelings, as well as in family life and values. Its generality across areas of living suggested it was an important value to her. But the only way she was able to 'notice' innocence in life was by the 'absence of' badness or guilt. That is, rather than ever being able to feel good because she thought of herself as innocent, she was constantly on edge, vigilantly on guard to avoid badness. The only innocence she said she ever felt was a kind of 'forced' or 'assumed' innocence when she had avoided guilt or badness. This is what is meant by a 'conflicted value'.

The way in which she represented for herself the pole of 'badness' was a picture of a cemetery with a fresh mound of earth, leaves falling all around and a grave marker which kept changing between a cross and a regular tombstone. A real psychologist would have had a field day with all this lovely imagery. Felicity accepted it as a good image for the purpose, and asked her to put it up on a shelf. The way in which Mary represented the pole of 'innocence' was described as a grey and white cloud through which a bright white light shone down. She never felt innocent – hence perhaps the dismal image. But Felicity liked it. He asked her to put that up on the shelf too.

Mary elected to hold the image of 'badness' on her left hand, and so Felicity asked her to put it there and to put the image of 'innocence' on her right hand. He asked her to talk to the part of herself that was the image of the cemetery, and to ask it what its highest intentions for her were. She replied: "It wants me dead."

Felicity tried again: "But why does it want you dead?" The reply was: "So I can pay for my sins." "But why does it want you to pay for your sins?" "So I can be cleansed and clean." "But why does it want you to be cleansed and clean?" "So I can be a good person." "But why does it want you to be a good person?" "So I will not be unhappy." "But why does it want you not to be unhappy?" "So I can get along better with others." "But why does it want you to get along better with others?" "So I'll have a good life and be happy." "So it wants you to have a good life and be happy?" This last question seemed necessary because what Mary had just said did not seem to register on her. She frowned deeply, pulled her left hand closer to her face and said: "You're kidding me!" The remark was apparently addressed to the hand and not to Felicity. So Felicity asked: "What did the part say? Is it kidding you?" "No!" she gasped in utter shock.

"What about the light streaming through the clouds on your right hand?" Felicity asked, "Could you ask it what its best intentions for you are?" "So that I will be innocent." "But why does it want you to be innocent?" "So I will do the right things." "But why does it want you to do the right things?" "So people will like me." "But why does it want people to like you?" "You're right, that's what it says, so I can have a good life and be happy." "You mean, it wants you to have a good life and be happy, too? That's nuts, isn't it? Surely those two different parts can't want the same thing for you?" Mary turned her closed eyes toward one hand and then the other. "I guess they do," she said.

Felicity asked Mary to get the two poles on her two hands to talk to each other. After all, if they wanted the same thing for her, they ought to be able to get along together as a single part to help her to 'have a good life and be happy' without hurting her or making her feel bad. And perhaps, if they could agree to get along in that way, they could find some way to express to each other their wish and agreement to come together into one part. As he was saying this, Felicity brought his two hands together to clasp one another gently. So did Mary.

Once her hands were clasped together, Felicity asked her to look carefully at this 'new part of herself' and to tell him what it looked like. Mary looked surprised. She shook her head in disbelief. The picture she described as being the image that she now saw between her hands was one of a field in which there was a tree with a thick, straight trunk and no leaves on the tree's massive branching system. The grass in the field was green. The trunk and branches of the tree were not assigned a colour, but they were seen as very 'bright'. Felicity said he thought that was a beautiful scene and he thought he might adopt it too.

He asked her to imagine an infinite source of love and peace and power and healing flowing down through her head and out through her heart to the wonderful new part of herself. Then he asked her to imagine that same infinite source of love and peace and power and healing flowing down through her head and out through her heart to all the other parts of herself, too, while she integrated this new part of herself with the other parts of herself. As if to help the process, she drew her clasped hands in toward her chest and she smiled warmly and beautifully.

Once all of her major 'negative' or 'avoidant' values were 'healed' in this way, Felicity asked Mary to list her values all over again. This time, he did not give her any help other than a page of blank lines for each area of living (that is, work, living, relationships, and feelings).

None of the values she now listed seemed to be in the 'negative', 'avoiding' or 'away from' form, and none seemed to contain hidden conflicts.

To check on this, Felicity asked Mary to imagine herself possessed, each in turn, of a job, a life, a relationship, and feelings in which the first six of her values for the area were present. With each area, her faced flushed, a grin of self-satisfaction and pleasure spread across her face, she nodded emphatically, her chin lifted a bit and her posture seemed to straighten. Felicity thought that the traces of lines in her face also smoothed out. While thinking of having her first half dozen values in a couple of areas she even giggled a little. Felicity was pleased. But he wasn't quite satisfied.

When Mary was thinking about having a job in which she had the first six values that she had listed, in addition to these reactions there was also a slight frown of puzzlement. He asked her why. She said it was just that she couldn't quite figure out how she could have a job in which she could feel busy and useful, and in which she could also feel relaxed and peaceful. She had placed these two values at positions three and four, respectively. Felicity said he understood the problem and she could probably fix it if she wanted to. She said she did.

Before doing that, however, Felicity asked her to look over her lists of values again carefully. Were these the values she 'wanted to have' as her values, or were there others she would prefer to have in addition to or in place of any of them – using any principles she wanted to use to make that determination. She examined the lists thoughtfully. She thought her life would be 'better' and happier for her if she was a little more 'thoughtful' or 'considerate' of others. This value was in ninth place in her list in the area of 'living'. She was asked whether she felt it was properly placed at the ninth rank. She affirmed that it was, at least the way she felt now, but she still felt it 'ought' to be higher. Felicity asked her at what rank position she thought it 'ought' to be placed. She thought it ought to come fourth. Felicity pointed out that would mean that her fourth value, 'assertiveness and courage' would come fifth, that 'sharing activities with others' would then come sixth, and that 'enjoying teasing others' would slide to seventh place. Is that how she felt the list 'ought' to be. She cocked her head thoughtfully, nodded firmly and gave a definite 'yes'.

Felicity asked Mary what picture popped into her mind when she thought of 'assertiveness and courage' (her fourth ranked value under 'living'). The picture was of a woman's fist raised in triumph. She saw the picture straight in front of her, about four feet away and just above her line of vision. Felicity asked about sensory qualities. It was a small, pink hand with long, bright red nails. The image was a clear one, but it had no surrounding. There was neither sound nor movement associated with it. Felicity asked her to put it up on a shelf.

For 'relating warmly to others' (her third ranked value under living), the picture was one of waves rolling in over one another and combining to make larger waves. Felicity asked about the location. The scene, which faded off at the edges, was slightly below her line of vision, directly in front of her and about ten feet away. Upon inquiry, she was able to report that the water was a mixture of blue and green, with white caps and little scintillating sparkles of light all over it. There was movement as the waves rolled in and grew, and waxing and waning swishing sounds as they moved. Felicity asked her how she felt when she moved the scene closer to her – she didn't like it as much. What if she put it farther away – she didn't like it as much. What if she took away the sparkles of light – she didn't like it as much. What if she added some sparkles to it – it was about the same. What if she made the water only blue without green – she didn't like it as much. What if she made the water only green without the blue – she didn't like it as much. What if she stopped the movement and made it a still picture – she didn't like it as much. What if she took away the sound – she didn't like it as much. What if she made the sound continuous instead of waxing and waning – she didn't like it as much. What if she added the sound of gulls flying overhead – it didn't add, and it may distract. What if she heard kids and other people playing and laughing in the background. She liked that better. She was asked to put that image up on the shelf as well.

Now she was asked to bring down the picture of the woman's fist and look at it. What happened if she moved it farther away – she didn't like it as much. What if she brought it closer – she didn't like it as much. What if she put it a little lower, beneath her line of vision – she liked it better as it seemed more like a petite woman. What if she took away the colour and made it black-and-white – she didn't like it as much. What if she changed it to other colours – she didn't like it as much. What if the picture was less clear and more misty – she didn't like it as much. What if she added movement, so the arm and fist waved – she liked it a little more, she thought. What if there was sound, like people talking – she didn't like it as much as it distracted her. What if she added sound, like fanfare – she liked that much better. What if she added sound, like people cheering – she liked that even more. She was asked to put it back on the shelf.

She was asked what picture popped into her mind when she thought about being 'thoughtful or considerate of others' – the value, currently ninth, which she wanted to move to fourth place. She described a waterfall that cascaded repeatedly over rocks so that each level broke the fall of the water and made each fall gentler. She was asked where she saw it. Again, it was straight in front of her, way up above her line of vision, and perhaps fifty feet away. On inquiry, she described the water as mostly white with blue lines in it. The rocks were 'sort of brown'. There was slow movement down each cascade. There was a steady swish of sound. Felicity asked her to change the scene in various ways and to tell him how it made her feel. Bringing it closer seemed much nicer. Bringing it down toward her line of vision made it seem nicer. Making it black-and-white (without colour), taking away the sound or increasing the sound all made it less pleasant. Adding sparkles made it more pleasant. Adding the sounds of birds made it more pleasant, but adding the sounds of people made it less pleasant.

Felicity asked her to keep looking at the waterfall scene. He said he would like her to enjoy this scene. He would like her to move the waterfall down to about even with her line of vision, to bring it quite a bit closer, say to about ten feet away, and to add a distant background sound of birds. She brightened noticeably as he talked. He asked her whether she enjoyed that. She affirmed warmly that she did. He asked her to take a picture of that scene as it now was in her mind and to put the T.V. screen on which it was displayed at ten feet directly in front of her. He asked her to make the T.V. set a heavy one so it stayed put. When she had done that, he asked her to bring down the picture of the woman's fist raised in the air, to put it up a little higher – above the T.V. screen. He asked Mary to push the image of the arm and fist up a little to have it just above the T.V. screen. He asked her if that was all right. She said it was, that she liked the waterfall front and centre, and that having the triumphant arm and fist above it made her feel that she had found the waterfall all by herself.

Felicity asked her to come back and to make out her list of values in the area of living again. She smiled at Felicity as though she thought he was rather sneaky. She started to write the remembered list of values. She stopped half way down the list and stared with surprise at what she had done. She broke into gales of laughter. "You know what I've done," she said, "I've put consideration as number four and assertiveness as number five." Felicity asked her to 'go inside herself' and see whether that new ordering 'seemed right to her'. She affirmed it did. She was asked to compare each pair of values in turn again to see which one of each pair was stronger in order to confirm that the order assigned was the correct one. She took her time. Finally, she looked up and emphatically stated that the list was now both the way she felt and the way she thought it ought to be.

They used the same procedure to reduce the possible conflict in work between 'being busy and useful' and 'being relaxed and peaceful'. 'Relaxed and peaceful' were already in the relationship and feelings areas, and she thought she could properly give it a lower ranking in the area of work to reduce any possible conflict. She decided on seventh rather than fourth. The work-associated images for 'relaxed and peaceful' and for the seventh and eighth values were elicited. The positions and sensory qualities of the three images were established. The effects on the way she felt of altering the positions and the sensory qualities of each were determined. Then, the position and qualities of the 'relaxed and peaceful' image were modified to create a slightly less demanding feeling for her than those of the seventh image, and a little more demanding than those of the eighth image. Again, the effects of thus changing (and fixating) the image of 'relaxed and peaceful' were checked by having her relist her values for the work area and confirm that the now adjusted new list 'felt' right and good to her. Finally, Felicity had her check the order by comparing her values in the work area with each other in pairs. A satisfactory modification of the order of values in this list was reported.

The approach to values used with Mary is fun and quick. She enjoyed it, and Felicity enjoyed seeing the apparently genuine increase in Mary's happiness with herself. Moreover, she did report a major reduction in her guilt feelings, and that was followed by a sharp reduction in her reported and observed obsessive behaviour. And the systematic desensitization of the traumatic anxiety from the traffic accident progressed at an unusually quick speed. It was accomplished in sixteen sessions.

Avoidant Anxiety – Phobia – Phobic Fibs

Much of what is experienced as anxiety is evoked by given situations – phobic situations. Some people are afraid of heights, some of flying in aeroplanes, some of being attacked, some of getting angry, some of authorities, some of emotional closeness. The list is almost endless. What these phobic responses have in common is the way in which they were learned.

Anxiety in given situations is learned as an accidental result of avoiding the (arousal occasioned by) situations. Suppose you get on an elevator. You have no fear at all of elevators. As you get into the elevator, you experience gas pains. They feel uncomfortable and you are afraid you might pass gas and embarrass yourself in front of the people on the elevator. So, just to be safe, you get off the elevator at the next floor. Suddenly, the gas pains subside. You feel a sense of relief – reduction of the pain and of the worry about a social embarrassment. Although this sequence of events is unrelated to the elevator, you could easily be started on your way to the development of an elevator phobia. The next time you get on an elevator, you are apt to feel a wee bit of unnamed discomfort and, if you notice you feel a bit better as you leave the elevator, an elevator phobia has just received its second practice trial.

Phobias tend to start with uncomfortable feelings – often unrelated to the situation in which you find yourself – which are relieved (for whatever reason) as you leave or avoid the situation (again for whatever reason). They may grow because the one occasion leaves a kind of 'shadow' of non-conscious memory which may re-evoke a mild discomfort the next time the situation is encountered. If that mild discomfort (which may not even really register on consciousness) is relieved in avoiding or leaving the situation, the 'relief' serves as a reward to add a quantity of habit-strength to what preceded it – in this case, the habits of avoiding or leaving the situation *and* feeling anxious in that situation the next time it is encountered.

Everybody has some, however mild, phobias – that is, really quite harmless situations in which they feel uncomfortable. It would be almost impossible to get any distance into life without having had some 'relief' experiences associated· with leaving some situations. The only way to avoid developing a phobia would be to 'cope' in some way, and to remain in the situation until all discomfort is gone, in absolutely every situation you encountered. But to bother to be that careful to avoid phobia development would mean that you were afraid of developing a phobia – called 'phobophobia'. This last statement may sound like a typical 'shrink' statement, giving you no way to win for losing. In truth, phobias are neither uncommon nor important enough to worry about. The importance of a phobia depends upon the effects it has on the person's life. Felicity has a genuine fear of heights (acrophobia). But it doesn't interfere with his life because it is almost never important for him to go up and to look down from a high place. But if a person was afraid of crowds, and the only job available to him was as a courier working downtown in a big city, his work life would likely be severely hampered. Similarly, if a person is afraid of leaving home (agoraphobia), it is likely to interfere pretty thoroughly with going to work, going shopping, or even having much of a social life. So the importance of a phobia tends to depend pretty much on the kind of situation that is feared and its significance in the person's life.

Of course, a phobia may have another kind of importance. Each phobia adds a certain amount of anxiety to the person's 'anxiety load'. If the 'anxiety load' is already a heavy one, it does increase the stress level in the body and it serves to deplete the body's coping-with-stress resources, as well as impairing the quality of life.

Fortunately, phobia is one of the problems (or dis-eases, if you wish) for which it is easy to get effective and permanent treatment. Wolpe's method for systematic desensitization (**RIT**), which has been described in many of the stories fabricated here, is the standard treatment of choice for phobias, and it tends to be quite widely available – being used by many psychologists and some psychiatrists.

An Employment Ploy

Nicole presented an easy phobia to treat. She was referred for agoraphobia. The 'diagnosis' sounds impressive to the patient, as it is supposed to. It really means that the person is afraid of wide open spaces. But the term is used to cover a great variety of people's reactions to going anywhere. Nicole arrived for her first interview in a tasteful and neat business suit, wonderfully groomed and looking very attractive. She told Felicity that, by her late twenties, she had completed university and had spent a few years at home nursing her ailing parents. They had both died recently, and she was now ready to enter the work force. Felicity asked her to tell him about the problem for which she was seeking help. She said she was suffering from 'agoraphobia'. Felicity asked her again what the problem was. She said that she wanted to get out and get herself a job but she was unable to do so because of her agoraphobia. Felicity asked her if she would please show him her agoraphobia. She laughed nervously at this crazy request, perhaps thinking he was being a bit sexually provocative. She told him it wasn't anything she could show him. So he asked how she knew she had this 'condition' if she couldn't see it or show it to him.

Nicole told Felicity that she knew she had the condition because her doctor had told her she had it. Felicity may have sounded a bit sarcastic. "Oh," he said, "then it is your doctor I should be treating if he's the one experiencing the condition." She looked at Felicity as if he was bent out of shape, decided he must be kidding and broke into a burst of charming laughter. Felicity joined the mirth, but then affirmed that he was serious. He said he had never seen anything called 'agoraphobia' before, even although he was a specialist in the area of phobias. So he wondered how she knew she had the condition.

Nicole was really very bright. She grasped the question and said that she knew she had it because she was afraid to go out and look for a job. Felicity looked as though he now understood and said, "I see, what you mean is that you are afraid to go to work. But what is this 'condition' agoraphobia?" "That's it," she said. Felicity countered: "OK, so how would you know if you no longer had the 'condition' called agoraphobia?" "I guess you or my doctor would have to tell me it was cured," she said. "And how would you know if you were no longer afraid to go to work?", Felicity asked. "If I was going to work and not being afraid," she replied. "So you have to pay a doctor to tell you if you lose the agoraphobia, but you can figure out for yourself when you lose the fear of going to work, right?" She agreed. "Let's not do it that way," Felicity suggested. "Instead, why don't you take back control over your own life from us doctors. If the agoraphobia and the fear of going to work are one and the same thing, as you said, then why not put yourself in the position of being able to decide for yourself when you are cured by only calling it 'fear of going to work'." Nicole giggled with delight and said that she saw what Felicity meant.

Next Felicity asked her how she had arranged it so that she was afraid to work. He laughed as he suggested that he would like to learn how to do that so he wouldn't have to go to work. Nicole examined his face cautiously, wondering whether Felicity was insulting her, laughing at her, or suggesting that she was putting on an act. His man-in-the-moon face was at rest and looked incapable of anything but innocence. Still, she decided to ask him: "Are you suggesting I'm pretending so I don't have to go to work? I want very much to be able to go to work." "I absolutely believe that," Felicity affirmed, "or else you would not be here paying me for treatment. The problem is that the words we use in thinking and talking about things may very well get in the way of doing anything about them and in knowing when we have succeeded in doing that." Nicole nodded in surprised understanding. "Can I really feel comfortable about going to work?" she asked. "Good for you," Felicity boomed, "that is exactly the right way to ask the question both of me and of yourself."

Felicity continued, "Yes, emphatically, you can learn to be perfectly comfortable. And, yes, this *is* going to work. Please note the right words you used: You can feel comfortable about going to work. All are the right words. Now let's look at how we will achieve that goal." Felicity explained that fear is the brain's sensory experience of arousal in the body parts when the brain has activated the sympathetic branch of the autonomic nervous system. As an uncomfortable experience, fear motivates one to avoid the thing that is feared. The sympathetic system, and the fear it evokes, respond to perceived real or imagined dangers. In this case, they would both agree the danger was an imagined one. It had probably started as a child in her valuation of the importance of work, as the hard thing her daddy did every day. Now she was an adult. She knew that everybody does it at times and that it is not dangerous or threatening. All they would have to do would be to teach her body not to fear it and thus not to want to avoid it.

Felicity went on to describe the procedure for systematic anxiety desensitization (Wolpe's RIT method). He said she would first be learning how to relax. Then, while she was relaxed, he would repeatedly ask her to picture various situations related to going to work and being at work. The situations would be imaginary so she would not feel the need to avoid confronting them. Once they had repeated these images in her mind often enough, her body would have learned not to fear those kinds of situations and she would no longer be afraid of work. Nicole thought the method sounded interesting, but she was sceptical. She asked if it would work with her. Felicity assured her it would. At this point the first contact hour was up, so they made another appointment for two weeks away and Nicole left.

At her second appointment, Felicity asked Nicole how she was feeling. She said she was fine. She giggled nervously as if she was being too cheeky and said, "I'm here for my doctor to withdraw my diagnosis of 'agoraphobia'." Felicity asked her what she meant. She sat proudly in her chair and said: "You told me the treatment was going to work. So I figured there was no point being afraid. So I went out, got myself a job, and I've been working for a week now." "That's wonderful," Felicity laughed, "and how have you felt going to work and working?" "I'll admit I was scared at first, but now I love it and I'm not the least bit afraid." "So, what's your 'diagnosis' now?" Felicity asked with an impish look. "Fear of going to work, cured!" she affirmed confidently, "And what's my diagnosis now, doctor?" "Agoraphobia, cured!" Felicity echoed.

A few months later, Nicole phoned just to let Felicity know he had been right. She was still working, and she was still enjoying it immensely. Felicity was delighted. "Now," he said, "how are we going to cure me? I've been gravely ill." Nicole's voice took on a tone of genuine concern. "What's the matter?" she gasped. Felicity chuckled. "I am possessed of a dreadful affliction of the spirit," he said, "characterized by an indisposition to go to work." Nicole laughed heartily. "The diagnosis is obvious," she said, "You are clearly suffering from agoraphobia. Maybe you ought to take a vacation or change jobs." "Nicole," he laughed, "I think those are lovely ideas. Please send me your bill." "I will," she replied with another burst of mirth.

A Fountain Mountain

Noel was a married professional man in his early forties. He was referred to Felicity for an aquaphobia. Now let's be clear. This was not hydrophobia – a symptom of rabies. This was aquaphobia. He was afraid of water. The real presenting problem was concerned with the two major effects his phobia had on his life. He could not drink water, and his physician had told him he had to drink water for his health. And he could not take a bath, and his wife had told him that she could no longer stand being near him – given his growing aromatic body odour.

It would have been deleterious to his health, his marriage and his work with other people to spend time trying to unravel the dark and mysterious causes, buried deep in his unconscious, which might underlie this strange condition. Instead, without further ado, Felicity began training Noel in the art of deep muscle relaxation. In two hours of training, Noel had achieved a deep enough level of relaxation to begin the systematic desensitization of his anxiety – using Wolpe's reciprocal inhibition therapy (RIT) method.

The imaginal presentations began with him looking at a drinking fountain at the end of a long hall, and very slowly approaching closer and closer to it. The pictures then began at a distance again, watching somebody turn on the drinking fountain and take a drink. Again, in imagination he was moved closer and closer, watching while the person took drink after drink. Privately, Felicity was worried Noel might suddenly become panicky for fear the man drinking at the fountain would drown himself. However, apparently the man did not drown, nor did the idea or the terror occur to Noel. Then he was asked to picture himself walking into a washroom and seeing a basin and tap, and slowly moving closer and closer to it. That sequence was repeated while he watched someone else turn on the tap and wash his hands in the water, and then his face. Then the pictures involved standing at a drinking fountain, and then at a tap, and merely turning on the water and looking at it. Then he was asked to picture himself washing his hands under the tap, then filling a cup from the tap, then drinking some water from the cup, and then drinking some water from the drinking fountain. Then he was asked to picture himself wetting his hands and rubbing the moist hands over his face, then washing his face in water splashed by his hands from the tap. Then he was asked to picture himself running an inch of water into the bathtub and standing in it barefoot. Then more and more water was added to the tub as he stood in it naked. Then he sat in the water in the tub. Finally he bathed himself in the water in the tub.

The pictures never progressed to the shower or to getting near, let alone in, a swimming pool. He terminated contact before these images could be introduced since he had met his goals – he was drinking water and bathing his body at the sink (not yet in the tub). The sequence of presentations was a long one, and progress through it was laboured and slow – RIT does tend to be both effective and boring. He was obviously opposed to the idea of dealing with water, and was not going to yield as easily as Nicole had done. But the result was as expected, and he was finally able to do the steps up to, but not including, the last situations 'desensitized'. It would seem that the 'real life' situation is essentially only 'one hierarchy step' above the scene as it is represented by the imagined picture.

A Toasted Tootsie

Natalie was a beautiful bride-to-be. She was to be married in about a month when she came to see Felicity. The referral stated that she was fearful of her coming marriage. Now, Felicity thinks that everyone is, or ought to be, afraid of marriage. In his view, that may be the only realistic fear there is. Just to confirm that he was right about this, he checked Bierce's dictionary definition of Bride. He was right. There it was in black-and-white: "A young woman with a fine prospect of happiness ... behind her." Although somewhat dubious about the appropriateness of interfering with anybody's excuses for avoiding marriage, he agreed to see her. Natalie was excited and ecstatic about her coming marriage. Seeing her thus transfixed, he could not doubt that 'love is a temporary insanity, curable by marriage'. Only one thing marred the prospect of this day above all days. She feared that her hand would tremble visibly during the toasts, and that she would spill her drink. Now Felicity was not disposed to abandon her to spoil that part of her day for herself. It hardly seemed fair that the one part of the day that ought to be fun should be riddled with fear. Either none of the day, or all of the day, should be terrifying.

So, instead of sending her away, Felicity reluctantly got Natalie relaxed – using a quick relaxation procedure with some sub-hypnotic induction instructions. While she was relaxed, he asked her to review the entire sequence of the wedding day, starting with the moment at which she opened her eyes in the morning, and ending as the married couple entered their room for the night. He suggested that she leave anything after that out of her imagination for the present as she was with a stranger, and anything else would be personal and private. Felicity was proud of his thoughtful propriety. However, he really knew that he had asked for that part to be omitted because he was a prude and would likely feel embarrassed by thinking about her thinking about the nuptial bed.

During a single two-hour session, Natalie got sufficiently relaxed and reviewed the whole wedding day twice from beginning almost to the end. Being relaxed, she was aware that her hands and arms were nice and limp, and that they were not trembling at all. In her imagination, she raised her glass calmly in her hand, held it comfortably while the imagined toasts took place, and sipped her champagne happily and contentedly after each toast. In fact, she reported afterwards that she had imbibed so freely during the imagined events that she felt a little tipsy. But she added that her new husband was amused by her light-headedness. There was no further treatment. A few weeks after Natalie's marriage, Felicity received a Thank You note, as if he had given her a wedding gift, indicating, with gratitude, that the wedding had gone smoothly, and she had not even remembered to think about trembling.

<u>An Encopretic Enuretic</u>

Nathan's case was not as easy as the others presented in this chapter. Like another patient, Neil, who had been treated successfully by Felicity at an earlier time, Nathan was unable to urinate in a public washroom. In fact, he even found it hard to urinate at home with the washroom door unlocked. But in a public place he just could not do it – the stream would not start and he was on edge, looking furtively around to see and hear if anyone else was entering the washroom. Like most people with this sort of problem, as a child he had worried that his peers would laugh at the size of his penis, he had half-remembered fantasies (or memories) of being interfered with sexually by adult males, and he was anxious or guilty about nocturnal tumescence or emissions – that is, erections or 'wet dreams' at night. But the real problem was that he was afraid of urinating in any public place and his body would not allow himself to do so.

Nathan was half-heartedly interested in exploring the early experiences which may have led to his present problems. But he was definitely in a hurry to deal with his problem. He was a travelling salesman, and his problem was getting in the way of taking business trips any great distance from his home. His physician had tried him on all sorts of medications with no success. He now wanted results.

Felicity started him on a program of systematic anxiety desensitization using Wolpe's reciprocal inhibition therapy (RIT) method. Nathan was trained in the art of deep muscle relaxation. When sufficiently relaxed, he was asked repeatedly to picture a series of situations leading from the first sensations of bladder pressure when he was away from home, through urinating at home with the bathroom door locked, then unlocked. Then he was asked to picture himself driving to a restaurant, then walking into the restaurant to have a coffee, then going to the washroom to wash his hands. While washing his hands in the public washroom, he was asked to picture one, then two, then several men entering the washroom and urinating at the urinals. Finally, he was asked to picture himself urinating in a locked cubicle in a public washroom, then in an unlocked cubicle, then alone at a urinal, and then at a urinal with increasing numbers of others in the washroom.

With difficulty, over a long period of time (more than six months) he was able to feel comfortable imagining these scenes while relaxed. But he reported, "It pisses me off that I can't piss in the real situation." At irregular intervals, the desensitization treatment continued, with each new short burst of treatments addressing 'ideas' or 'insights' he had developed about the underlying nature of 'the problem'. Pictures were presented related to childhood experiences in the neighbourhood in which he grew up, related to present life irritants concerned with his wife and his son, related to work crises, and related to his own sleeping habits. While relaxing with Felicity, he was apparently able to experience these scenes in his imagination comfortably without interfering with his relaxation. But his anxiety about, and avoidance of, urinating in public washrooms continued.

He consulted psychiatrists who tried more medications and even some 'exploratory' psychotherapy to get at the roots of the problem. Finally, one of the psychiatrists accepted Felicity's suggestion and prescribed Anafronil. Almost all of Nathan's life changed for him almost at once. He felt calm and happy. He was comfortable at home and found he could tolerate his wife's 'peculiarities' and his son's 'odd habits'.

But he still could not, or would not, urinate in public washrooms. What was wrong? In fact, Felicity did not know – or he would have found a way to do something about it. However, it seemed to Felicity that all his efforts and those of others had been in vain due to two things. First, Nathan took his main presenting symptom (and, indeed, his whole life) much too seriously, as though dealing with his 'problem' was an urgent and important issue. Felicity's efforts to get him to 'lighten up' were to no avail. Felicity had hoped that the Anafronil would help lighten Nathan up. It did, but apparently not enough. Second, Nathan was almost constantly 'in his own head' worrying and thinking thoughts that kept him upset. It even occurred to Felicity that Nathan was not really imagining the scenes presented in the desensitization sessions, perhaps because his mind was somewhere else obsessing about something else. Again, Felicity had hoped to diminish Nathan's obsessive thinking with the help of the Anafronil. It seemed to have that effect, but it did not assist effective desensitization of the anxiety in the crucial washroom setting.

The solution to Nathan's problem remains undiscovered after five years of sporadic contacts. If Nathan contacts him again, Felicity will try once more to induce Nathan to try a number of options. He could try transcendental meditation (TM) to reduce his thought pressure. Assertive training might help him free himself of some of the 'buried' or inhibited resentments he harbours toward both his early and his current life circumstances. Flooding (intense exposure to the essential problem situation during which the person is immobilized and unable to escape) might be tried. In addition to some other procedures that have also been suggested and rejected in the past, covert sensitization (associating the symptomatic avoidance behaviour with a competing and unpleasant experience) might be used. Felicity agrees with Nathan that he's a 'hard nut to crack'.

Discussion – Phobophobic Phobia

It is not always clear that a phobia has been learned in the 'typical' phobic way – by avoidance (see chapter introduction). What is clear is that the avoidance perpetuates the phobia and, if continued through treatment, provides a powerful counter-therapeutic agent. But situation-related fears, or phobias, can be treated by a variety of quick and not-so-quick methods. And when they are successfully treated, a host of often apparently unrelated psychological symptoms may evaporate. This miracle is reported in quite a lot of the stories presented throughout this volume.

Since avoidance is a critical part of the phobic response, it is sometimes necessary to get the person to cease avoiding the phobic situation. In principle, this approach is called 'in vivo' (in real life) desensitization. The principle involved here is that it is impossible to maintain fear for very long in the presence of a feared but harmless situation or event. Thus, continuous exposure to the situation results eventually in respite or reduced anxiety. If reduction of anxiety is used as the signal to permit leaving the situation, the phobia must eventually clear. An example might help to explain this idea.

If you were to be frightened by the actions of another driver while you are driving along a road, you have two options. If you pull over, stop your car and get out of it while you are still scared, you will likely begin to settle down pretty quickly. You will also be starting yourself on the way to a fear of driving – a phobia. You would have 'set it up' that driving was associated with fear for you, and avoiding driving was associated with 'feeling better' and comfort for you. On the other hand, if you continue to drive, two things will follow. You will eventually calm down again, and you will not increase the risk of developing a driving phobia. Driving may be associated with getting upset, but it will also be associated with getting calmed down again.

There is another way to talk about 'in vivo' desensitization. If you are afraid of going out – say to the store – you will nevertheless not be afraid to go outside of your door, or at the very least toward your door. Of course, who would bother to do that? That doesn't get you to the store. It doesn't matter. Do it! Do whatever you can do <u>with comfort</u> . True, it won't get you to the store. But neither will doing nothing. If we 'cope' in any situation to the degree that is comfortable, we teach ourselves to do at least that much comfortably. If it would be comfortable for you to go ten feet from your home, do it! Next time, even a few minutes later, you might be comfortable going twelve feet away. Do it! At least that way you may eventually get to the store. Waiting for the fear to go away by itself will not work – it perpetuates the avoidance, thus the 'relief' from fear, and thus the anxiety about doing the act. So, do whatever you can do comfortably that leads you toward what you want to do in the end.

*Traumatic Anxiety – Self-Protection – Post-Traumatic
Stress Disorder – Traumatizing Trauma*

In some ways, post-traumatic stress disorder is a special case of phobia. However, being precipitated as it is in a dangerous (or at least apparently dangerous) life-threatening situation, the level of arousal is very high, the learned arousal is very high, and the associated stimuli (related to the danger or not) are imprinted in as few as one practice trial. This is because the perceived danger activates the 'hard-wired' autonomic nervous system whose main job is to learn to recognize and respond quickly to potential dangers.

A Slow Fall Snow Ball

When Felicity received a call from a psychiatrist describing Orville and referring him for assessment and any treatment which Felicity could figure out for him, Felicity decided that his reputation for treating schizophrenia must have been made. He was wrong. To be sure, the psychiatrist said that Orville was suffering from a schizophrenic illness, and the symptoms described sounded like those of schizophrenia. However, the treatment suggestion seemed to have been offered rather half-heartedly, and may have been offered as a kind of justification for referring a patient whose diagnosis was already clearly established.

Orville had been described and, upon contact, presented as a confused and troubled man, with little apparent emotional reactivity, except when he was trying vainly to talk about his hallucinations. With wide, staring eyes and dilated pupils, he talked wildly about huge snowballs rolling down hills and over-powering him, about alternating green and red lights which signalled doom, and about shattering noises which exploded in his head. He could hardly distinguish between real events he had experienced and awful nightmares where he was mutilated and injured or in which he was pinned helplessly in bed.

Felicity did the expected thing – he administered a battery of psychological tests to Orville to see if he could learn anything about the genesis of his schizophrenic disorder. To his shock, what emerged was an orderly and organized personality, with ample resources and compensations in the context of a rather pleasant disposition. The only scores which varied greatly beyond normal limits were those consistent mainly with traumatically-conditioned anxiety.

Felicity had not yet met Bart, so he did not have that memory to reference. But he had seen a number of Jewish survivors of World War II German concentration camps. Although these people's daily lives were often destroyed to a point far more severe than any others', the picture of confused dreams, both waking and sleeping, which referred to traumatizing experiences, were commonplace among them. Indeed, just the clinical contact with some of these people had been so intensely upsetting to Felicity that he, himself, had dreams, as if he was the victim. In these dreams, as if in order to work through his personal pain on behalf of these people, he had found himself constructing an intricate process of escape, followed by a kind of therapeutic review-from-a-distance in the dreams. But that's another story.

Was it possible that the schizophrenic-like clinical presentation displayed by Orville derived from post-traumatic anxiety or stress? Felicity could not obtain a clear story from Orville when he asked about any traffic accidents Orville might have been in. So he contacted the referring psychiatrist. The latter made some inquiries and phoned back to say that Orville had indeed been in a traffic accident in which he had been quite badly injured. The physician arranged for the automobile insurance company involved to supply Felicity with a description of the accident and of Orville's injuries in it. The story seemed to fit the pieces of the puzzle together rather well.

Orville had been driving in a little Volkswagen 'bug' through an intersection. He was proceeding through on a green light. A driver in a big white Buick driving on the intersecting road did not stop for the red traffic light that faced him. He came into the intersection and struck Orville's car on the driver's side. Orville was thrown out of his car. He fractured a number of bones in his body and was knocked unconscious. He was in hospital and in traction for many weeks following the accident. That was the report from the insurance company.

What had Orville seen? Well, for one thing, Orville was in no shape psychologically to report what he had seen until after the treatment was completed, when he reported what had taken place. Orville was a careful driver. As was his habit, while entering the intersection he checked again to be sure that the traffic light facing him was green. Then he glanced quickly at the traffic light for the intersecting road to confirm that it was red. Probably the 'alternating green and red lights that signalled doom' were the succession of retinal images of the green-red-green lights he looked at. Out of the corner of his eye, for a brief moment, too short to allow him to check or verify his perception, he saw a flash of something white (the Buick) which was rapidly expanding in apparent size as it approached. Presumably, as he was thrown by the impact, his mind was struggling to make sense out of what he had seen and what was happening. The only thing he could think of which was white and grew in size was a snowball rolling down a hill. And then he lost consciousness. When he returned to consciousness, after the great snowball had run over him, he was suffering great pain, and he found himself injured and confined, in traction, to a hospital bed. Intense physical trauma is often accompanied by what is called 'retrograde amnesia', in which the preceding half hour or so is unavailable for recall. But, as it turned out, all the disorganized pieces he had been raving about were represented in an orderly fashion in this story which he could not yet tell, and which he had vainly tried to explain to others as the basis of his intense distress.

Felicity treated Orville in almost exactly the same way in which he later treated Bart. If, as Felicity concluded, the anxiety underlying the schizophrenic-like symptoms was traumatic in origin and phobic in nature, it could be treated with Wolpe's method for systematic anxiety desensitization (RIT). Orville was taught the art of deep muscle relaxation. When he was deeply relaxed, he was asked to picture in his mind a succession of traffic scenes. These started with him picturing himself sitting in his car parked in his driveway looking around inside the car. They proceeded to scenes of Orville driving his car up and down his drive, then in a vacant parking lot, then on an empty country road. Then he was asked to picture a car parked ahead beside the country road, then a car approaching from ahead, then a car driving behind him. Then the scenes involved the car passing from ahead and then from behind. The scenes then shifted to city streets devoid of traffic. Then there was light and later heavy traffic. Then there were traffic lights with no cars either way, first as he was stopping for the red light, then proceeding through a green light. Traffic was increased on his road at the traffic lights, and then on the crossroad. Finally, he was stopped for a light and a white Buick went across on the intersecting street, then it stopped while he crossed with his light, and then it came on through as he crossed on his light.

This long series of presentations was required because he was evidently very anxious about everything connected with traffic, and because Felicity approached each scene carefully in case Orville became too upset. However, as the traffic scenes progressed to city streets and traffic lights, his memory of the incident slowly clarified. Finally, he 'saw' the Buick in place of the snowball, whether or not he had actually 'seen' it in the original accident. From then on Orville was much less disturbed by the presentations, and the treatment progressed much more quickly.

It took about thirty-five sessions to complete this treatment – systematic desensitization is very effective but can be very poring for the practitioner! Following the treatment, Orville was asked to arrange to see the referring psychiatrist. The psychiatrist phoned Felicity in sheer delight affirming that Orville had completely recovered from his schizophrenia – although the psychiatrist was more than sceptical about Orville's explanation for what his schizophrenic ideas had all been about. The psychiatrist congratulated Felicity for having figured out the bright idea of replacing Orville's hallucinations and delusions with a simple and coherent delusion that permitted Orville once more to organize his life and get on with it. Felicity shrugged as he hung up the phone, deciding privately that everybody is bound to have his own ways of understanding things. Felicity liked his way better.

A Bridge's Umbrage

Felicity was almost more fascinated with Owen's case. Owen presented with sudden-onset searing, blinding headaches that occurred whenever he moved from a place with higher illumination to one with lower illumination or vice versa. He also complained of a general weakness in his arms and legs that particularly affected his driving. He was afraid that he would not be able to exert enough pressure on the brake to stop the car, or enough force on the steering wheel to control its direction. He was referred for skin temperature biofeedback treatment of vascular (blood vessel) function because he was thought to be suffering from migraine headaches. The strange addendum about the weakness in driving the car led Felicity to add an investigation into traumatic anxiety as part of Owen's psychological assessment.

Indeed, there was very little indication in the tests of visceral projection of tension or of neural irritability (which might have supported the migraine diagnosis), but there were high scores on the tests assessing traumatically-conditioned anxiety. When asked, Owen was able to date the onset of his headaches and of the weakness at about six months after a traffic accident.

He had been driving along a limited access highway. He was approaching an overpass on a bright, sunny day and was just pulling into the deceleration lane to exit. Without warning, his car was struck from behind by another vehicle that was being driven at high speed. So severe was the impact that the bucket seat in which he was seated was sheared off and deposited with its occupant on the back seat of the car. His inertia pinned him in his seat on the back seat, and he struggled in vain to reach the steering wheel and the brake to regain control of his car. Meanwhile the car was thrust forward under the overpass. Then, as he struggled forward to get back to the controls, the car emerged from under the overpass and sunlight washed his windshield so that he could not see where he was going. When he finally got control of the car and pulled it over, he was uninjured but quite 'shaken up'.

The intense and 'blinding' headaches, experienced when illumination levels changed, probably represented quite directly the physiological arousal of anxiety traumatically-conditioned to the immediate visual stimuli during the accident – the shadow of the over-pass and the blinding sunlight beyond it. The weakness of his limbs was likely a direct traumatically-conditioned expression of his kinaesthetically-projected sense of helplessness when he was unable to reach the brake pedal or the steering wheel. If these hypotheses were valid, it should only be necessary to desensitize his anxieties regarding traffic situations involved in the circumstances of the accident in order to rid him of his headaches and muscular weakness.

The method used, as with Orville, was Wolpe's systematic anxiety desensitization method (RIT). After Owen learned to relax, traffic scenes, similar to those used with Orville, were used as the presentations. The treatment program took twenty-five sessions. The weakness was gone by session twelve, and the headaches were gone by session eighteen. Owen was followed for only a couple of months after the treatment. His symptoms were gone, and he was driving comfortably – even enjoying driving.

An Unsimulated Simulation

And then there was Opal. She had been told that her problems were caused by a traffic accident. However, she could not remember the accident or what had happened in it [Not uncommon in accidents such as this. RR]. Her symptoms included word-finding difficulties and memory loss, stumbling and poorly coordinated movements, catastrophic immobilization when asked to do a simple organizing task (such as when she was asked to tidy up a desk), loss of planning ability (as in figuring out how to get from one place to another), and photophobia or discomfort looking at light. Her symptoms had already led to a diagnosis of brain damage having been made by the referring psychiatrist.

In his own perverse way, Felicity was delighted with her inability to help him figure out what traffic scenes might be used to formulate a hierarchy for systematic anxiety desensitization. So he decided not to use systematic desensitization. Instead, he checked to make sure that Opal had reasonably good ocular control – that just means that she could track something by moving her eyes back and forth without moving her head.

Then Felicity asked Opal if she would play a game with him, just for the fun of it. He understood that she couldn't remember anything about her traffic accident. However, she had all sorts of different ideas about traffic accidents other people might be in. He asked her to imagine 'a likely' kind of traffic accident which 'might be' like hers. She agreed to do so. He then asked her to become a professional movie camera-person, and to make a movie in her mind of the kind of traffic accident she had made up, having the movie start and end when the driver was safely at home. She played along with the game. She said she had made a movie of it in her mind.

Then the task was changed. She was asked to picture scenes from her possible past and future, and to locate where she saw them. In this way, she established her 'time-line' as running right through her from the past that was behind her to the future out in front of her. She was asked to float way up above her time line, and drift back until she was over the time when the accident might have taken place. Over the place, way above her 'time-line', she was asked to construct a movie theatre in which she was seated looking at a big screen with a still picture of herself on it.

Next, she was asked to leave her body sitting in the theatre and to drift up into the projection room above her. She was to look down through a window in the projection room at herself sitting below in the theatre. She was to keep looking at herself in the theatre below to watch how the (dissociated) 'she' in the theatre reacted and felt while the movie she had just made was being projected on the theatre screen. The movie was to be played through rather quickly in black-and-white and then to be rewound at fast speed in colour – so that everything would be happening backwards.

She said that the 'she' down in the theatre had been quite uncomfortable. She was asked to repeat the quick black-and-white forward and the fast-reverse rewind in colour, except that this time the 'she' in the theatre should be moving her eyes back and forth from one edge of the screen to the other while the film was running. She reported no discomfort in herself either in the projection booth or in the theatre. She then drifted down to the seat beside herself in the theatre and, still watching herself in the theatre to see how she reacted, ran the film in the same way, forwards and backwards. She reported some discomfort again. She repeated the procedure several times from that perspective while the 'she' that was watching in the theatre moved her eyes back and forth again. She reported no discomfort at all. To be certain, this step was repeated a few more times.

She was asked to drift back into herself and to watch the film herself while it was played forward and backward as before and she moved her eyes back and forth across the screen. She said she experienced no discomfort in this task. She was asked to repeat the task several times. Then she was asked to drift up into the movie and to become the driver while it was played forward and back as before. She reported no discomfort in several runs through the movie. Felicity asked her to role up the screen, close down the theatre, and return above her time-line to the present and drift down again into the present. She was asked if she enjoyed the game. She said she did.

She was seen a week later for her next appointment. She walked without any clumsiness at all. She spoke fluently without any difficulty in finding words. She said she didn't believe it, but her memory seemed okay. She recalled events she had formerly said she had forgotten. She even remembered the details of the accident – it still isn't clear whether it was the real one or the one she made up or, indeed, whether the two were different. She was delighted that she was able to find her way around town just fine. She was asked to look out the window at the sun-drenched out-of-doors. She described several things she saw out there. There was no squinting or other evidence of photophobia. She was asked to tidy up Felicity's messy desk, and did so without even the expected: 'What did your last slave die of, hard work?'

Felicity asked her to return to see the referring doctor. The psychiatrist later sent Felicity a copy of his consultation note to Opal's lawyer. In the note, the psychiatrist disparaged Opal, saying she had been malingering or simulating symptoms she did not have. The evidence he quoted for his belief was that she had exhibited classical symptoms of organic brain damage when first seen. Obviously, however, she had been carefully coached in these 'textbook symptoms' because barely a month later she had returned to see him devoid of any symptoms. He was annoyed at her for wasting the time of two busy health professionals.

Incidentally, Felicity never received another referral from that particular psychiatrist. But the cost in lost business was worth it. Felicity was overjoyed with the neatness of the method used. The method combined a Neuro-Linguistic Programming's (NLP) 'rapid phobia treatment' with an eye-movement rapid desensitization procedure which had just recently been described by Wolpe.

Discussion – Learning Learning of Learning

Traumatic anxiety (now called Post-Traumatic Stress Disorder or Reaction) is a bit tricky to treat. But it is even harder to recognize. The problem is both that its symptoms take so many different forms, and that the onset of symptoms is *usually* delayed from three months to a year after the traumatization. This last is due to the time needed for 'long-term consolidation' to structure the symptoms and to integrate them into the organization of behaviour that is called personality (also see George's story).

The 'long-term consolidation' delay in symptom-development makes it hard for the patient and for most non-psychologist professionals to recognize the relationship between the original traumatizing incident and the later development of symptoms. In fact, many patients and others simply reject out-of-hand the idea that a set of symptoms could be related to a much earlier traumatic incident. We are all too used to thinking of causality as based on contiguity between events in space and time. In the universe of psychological events, contiguity is often not all that good as an indicator of causality since learning is usually at stake, and learning nearly always requires consolidation time. Forty-eight hours, for short-term consolidation, commonly elapses before the first 'discomfort' symptoms may emerge. Multiples of six weeks, for long-term consolidation, may pass before 'organized' symptom clusters, or syndromes, appear.

Another interesting thing about traumatic conditioning is worthy of note in passing. Post-traumatic stress disorder may be one of the few (if not the only) kind of psychological disorder in which the 'initial' or antecedent cause (the only kind of cause recognized in the physical sciences) is manifestly the prime operative cause in the disorder. The traumatic events 'cause' the later effects through the arousal underlying the symptoms. In most other psychological maladies, while initial causes play a (frequently complicated and transformed) part, other kinds of causes, such as 'final cause' (or purpose) and 'perpetuating cause' (or habit strength or skill), seem to play much more important parts. And these other kinds of causes are often the only kinds of 'causes' available or susceptible to treatment interventions.

Panic – An Error Disorder – Titanic Panic

Lots of people experience panic. It comes about as a result of an intense self-protective preoccupation with how the body feels when a strong autonomic nervous system response is occurring. Panic can be produced in three main ways. (1) It can come about as a result of escalating terror of ambiguity, leading to over-generalization, leading to increased ambiguity, leading to increased fear – as a spiralling growth of fear. This reaction, called the 'catastrophic' response, occurs in some people who may also learn how to avoid it by 'muting' their reactions by a kind of inattention to the world around them. These events occur in some people who receive a diagnosis of schizophrenia. (2) It comes about most commonly as a result of a partly habitual error in the way normal bodily responses occur. Queeny's case will be used to illustrate this kind of reaction. (3) It can come about as a result of a kind of accidental learning. One of Felicity's own experiences will be used to illustrate this phenomenon.

A Miss Takes Mistakes

Queeny was a quiet, introspective lady in her early twenties. She was slim and attractive, and she was pleasantly conscious of her trim appearance. She was referred to Felicity by a psychiatrist she had consulted, for treatment of a resistant panic disorder from which she had suffered for years.

Queeny was experiencing panic attacks in spades. She had been experiencing bouts of panic almost daily, and sometimes several times a day, for about six years. Half facetiously, Felicity suggested she must be pretty good at doing them by that time, and he wondered if she could do one for him now. She did. There actually was a purpose for putting her through the experience. Most often, if a person can bring on symptoms voluntarily, he/she knows how they are produced and can stop producing them. Also, Felicity considered it important to have a first hand view of what she was doing so that he would be able to focus on the specific sequence involved – even although the procedure used is more or less the same regardless of the succession of events.

But Queeny could not reverse what she was doing and could not stop or prevent a panic attack. Their reported frequency and regularity, coupled with the fact that they occurred anywhere at any time of the day, meant there had to be something occurring beyond the usual triggers. The psychological tests Felicity administered were not helpful. But he did manage to zero in quickly on the issue during his inquiry.

The regularity of the occurrences was due to an error she had made about bowel movements. Felicity was reminded in this of Deryk whose story was gossiped about earlier. She had the idea that it was very important for health to keep her bowels evacuated. Consequently, she had developed the habit of having a bowel movement prior to every meal and before she went to bed at night. Had her bowel movements occurred after each meal, Felicity would have explored the possibility of food allergies or sensitivities, such as an allergy to a grain or a sensitivity to lactic acid. But having a bowel movement before meals was most likely to be habitual – as she, in fact, confirmed.

Felicity explained to Queeny the problem of too frequent bowel movements just as he had eventually done with Deryk. He asked her to repeatedly alter her bowel movement pattern to reduce her frequency by one bowel movement a day, maintaining each new reduced frequency for two weeks, until she was down to once per day. She had some difficulty adjusting to her new schedules, but she claimed to be doing so as the weeks rolled by. She also seemed to understand the reason for doing so, as though she knew that part of the panic-induction procedure involved tightening the rectal sphincter.

During the second session, after he had seen the results of Queeny's tests, Felicity suggested that she might profitably look up a Transcendental Meditation (TM) trainer in the phone book and learn and practice TM. Queeny was quite introverted. She tended to 'lock herself in her head' with her thoughts. This put her at the mercy of her own introspective thinking – riveting her attention on experiences from inside herself so that they tended to be reciprocally facilitated (that is, the experience and the thought about it each strengthened the other) and thus magnified. One of the many beneficial effects of transcendental meditation is that it tends, over time, to reduce the amount and the pressure of thinking in a person and to help the person feel in control of his or her thoughts. He thought it might have the effect of reducing the reciprocal facilitation of her panic by reducing her thoughtful attention to it.

As it turned out, as with a few other people Felicity has seen, the TM training increased her upset at first. She thought that if 20 minutes a day was good, and if 40 minutes a day was better, then sixty or eighty minutes a day would be even better. She started taking four 20 minute periods in which to do her TM. It seems likely that freeing herself from the control effected by thinking and its associated rationality occurred too quickly. As a result, she started to feel a strong release of rage and anger, and she began acting out at home, destroying her personal property in outbursts of feeling. Her trainer suggested she cut back to once per day, and the rages subsided.

Meanwhile, Felicity taught her the main means by which to stop or prevent panic attacks. The trouble probably began in Queeny when she was an adolescent. She wanted to look slim and beautiful, and one way she thought of to help this along was to hold her tummy in. She sucked her tummy in so well that the only way she could breathe was into her chest. While that may have helped her looks, it certainly didn't help her health. The diaphragm (which does normal 'stomach' breathing) is smooth muscle. It reacts slowly, but it can go on indefinitely without tiring out. But its slow reaction is undesirable under (real) emergency conditions when the body needs lots of oxygen. So, in an emergency, the body turns to the much faster-reacting striate or skeletal muscles of the chest wall. They quickly expand the chest cavity and suck air in to get the needed oxygen. That is, chest breathing occurs naturally in emergency-stress.

To understand how this works, it needs to be remembered that the chest cavity is a rigid structure formed by the ribs. It will expand a certain distance, but it will only contract by the same distance – the ribs coming together stop it from closing down any farther to blow more air out.

In normal diaphragm breathing, the out-breath is much longer than the in-breath, in the ratio from about 3:2 to 3:1. This means that the long out-breath slows down the whole breath cycle, resulting in relatively few breaths per minute. In chest breathing, the shortening of the out-breath to be equal to the in-breath (in a 1:1 ratio), speeds up each breath cycle, increases the number of breaths per minute, and thus increases the oxygen level in the blood stream very rapidly. That's good, right? Wrong!

In our engineered safe society, if we abide by a few simple rules (walking on the sidewalk, not jumping over protective railings), there is no danger. Since there is no danger to deal with, if we arouse the autonomic-emergency-stress response, there is nothing for us to do – there are no tigers to run away from, no predators to fight, and no food to be chased. There is no energetic activity (to use up the extra oxygen) for us to do when we are reacting with autonomic arousal. But this stress response still occurs in us – being hard-wired in us to recognize (mostly imaginary) dangers and to react to them. So we get all that extra oxygen in our blood streams and the resulting extra energy. And we do nothing with it. If the extra oxygen in the body, due to chest-breathing, is not used up by activity, it has several effects on the body.

First, to protect irreplaceable brain cells from getting burned out by too much oxygen, when the blood oxygen level rises, a reflex automatically activates constriction of the blood vessels feeding the brain. The resulting reduction in the volume of blood feeding the brain, even although it is oxygen-rich blood, reduces the amount of oxygen the brain has available to it (anoxia), and the person feels 'woozy', 'zonked out', or dizzy. And that experience scares most people.

Second, the muscles receive an increased oxygen supply. This lowers the metabolic threshold of the muscle cells, and they tend to tense up – the person starts feeling 'up tight' or tense.

Third, the striate muscles of the chest wall react quickly, but they also tire out quickly. Very soon, their resistance to responding may make it feel to the person as though he/she cannot breathe. He/she may feel some muscle pain and perhaps interpret it as a heart attack. These events may scare the person even more.

Fourth, the sympathetic response is stronger (steeper) than the parasympathetic response of the autonomic nervous system (remember the slopes of 'avoidance' and 'approach' gradients discussed previously. In normal diaphragm breathing, the long out-stroke (controlled by the parasympathetic system) has time to neutralize the 'anxiety' created by the shorter in-breath (which is controlled by the sympathetic system). But in chest breathing, the relative shortening of the out-breath does not give enough time for the strong sympathetic response of the in-breath to be neutralized by the weaker parasympathetic response of the out-breath, and the person becomes more and more anxious and feeling under acute stress – anxiety or stress builds higher and higher. So chest breathing quickly makes the person feel worse and worse, especially if the person is conscious of the bodily experiences occurring – as when the person is introverted or very introspective. The result is a panic attack.

To control or prevent a panic attack, all one has to do is to reinstate diaphragm breathing for about a dozen breath cycles. This can be done in several ways. The physician, concerned as he is primarily with the body chemistry, may suggest the person breathe for five or so minutes into a brown paper bag. That results in the person breathing his own carbon dioxide back in and not increasing the oxygen intake. This lowers the oxygen level with some benefit. But it does not reinstate diaphragm breathing. And who would want to breathe into a brown paper bag in public?

The old saw speaks of 'whistling in the dark'. Most of us would think this is just a way to 'buck oneself up' or to scare ghosts and hobgoblins away. Actually, it makes sense. Most of us whistle only on the out-breath. That means the out-breath gets extended and chest breathing is made harder while whistling.

But the obvious thing to do is just to make long out-breaths – this is **NOT** to say do ‹deep breathing›. Let›s be clear on how to do this best. First, do **NOT** interfere with the **IN**-breath – let it happen as it wants to so that you can feel confident that you are getting all the oxygen you need. Just *time* the in-breath in your mind. Second, having timed the in-breath in your mind, make the **OUT**-breath two, or three, or four, or five times longer than the in-breath. It's easy to do. And, if you do it, the only way it can be done is to reinstate the action of diaphragm breathing to keep pushing out the air after the chest wall has collapsed as far as it will go. Third, do these long *out*-breaths for only about three or four breath cycles at a time, interspersed with uninfluenced breathing for another about three or four breath cycles. The reason for this last stipulation is to ensure you don't bring the oxygen level in your blood down too quickly, before the corrective vasodilation of the blood vessels in the brain has time to occur. If you drop the blood oxygen level too quickly, while the blood vessels in the brain are still constricted, you may feel even more dizzy due to increased anoxia (less oxygen still for the brain), and that may scare you more. But the basic trick in dealing with panic is bursts of three or four 'long **OUT**-breaths' and that is all.

Felicity gave Queeny this explanation. She practised long out-breaths a few times in the office, and she agreed to practice them several times every day and to use them if she started to become panicky. Yes, even breathing has to be learned, but mainly because we have taught ourselves how to do it in an erroneous way. If you have mastered normal healthy breathing, and can remember to make long out-breaths when you are anxious, you can avoid ever having another panic attack. And you have also mastered a way to make yourself less anxious and uptight at any time. Felicity added a last reminder: "Remember, Queeny, I did **NOT** say to take *deep* breaths, **NOR** did I say to stop breathing. Let your in-breath occur as it wants to. Just time it in your mind, then push OUT your out-breath so it is two to five times as long as your in-breath was. And do these long out-breaths in groups of 3 or 4 at a time only."

Queeny has been in touch with Felicity from time to time across the intervening ten years. She reports that she has not had a panic attack since she consulted Felicity. Basic panic is about the easiest thing there is to deal with in psychotherapy, even although the subjective experience is about as severe as any.

A Delusional Illusion

But panic can come about in another way. It can come about as a result of learning an idea or meaning. Quinsey was referred to Felicity for treatment of his 'cardiac neurosis'. What this means is that he was terrified that at every moment he was dying of a heart attack. In Quinsey, as in most people who develop cardiac neurosis, the problem developed as a result of two things happening at the same time. The two things are usually 'palpitations' and hyperventilation or chest breathing. The 'palpitations' are interpreted by the person as his heart 'acting up' – a heart attack. And the tightness of the chest and the difficulty in breathing, from fatiguing of the chest wall muscles after a time of chest breathing (hyperventilation) are interpreted as further verification that a heart attack is in progress.

In fact, 'palpitations' rarely involve an experience of the heart working. Except occasionally in some very skinny people, nobody can feel his or her heart beating in his chest. As far as one can tell, essentially all 'palpitations' are muscle spasms of the muscles of the chest wall (although people call them 'heart palpitations'). Very occasionally, the speed of the muscle spasms may mimic the person's pulse rate, so that the following test doesn't always work. But in almost every instance, when one has 'palpitations', it is easy to prove that it is not the heart beating by taking one's own pulse. Since the rate of the 'palpitations' will usually be different from the pulse rate, they are *not* heart activity being experienced. They are insignificant muscle spasms.

The way that tightness and pain in the chest can happen in chest breathing has already been explained in Queeny's case. But chest breathing and palpitations occurring together can be pretty scary to the person experiencing them and, once the expectation is established, the habit of becoming scared is hard to shake off.

Quinsey had experienced his 'cardiac neurosis' for some three years before he was sent to Felicity. Consequently, information alone was not about to correct the fear – nor did it. Felicity suggested that Quinsey and he undertake a program of systematic anxiety desensitization using Wolpe's reciprocal inhibition therapy (RIT) method, and Quinsey agreed. The thirty sessions were difficult for both Quinsey and Felicity. Quinsey learned to relax quite well. But he was prone for quite a time to bursts of rapid chest breathing. Felicity has always tries to talk on the patient's out-breath during relaxation instructions and imagery presentations – in order to help the person maintain and deepen relaxation. So Quinsey's unexpected bursts of chest breathing meant that Felicity had to remain vigilant and to change his own breathing patterns from time to time to suit Quinsey's. This meant that Felicity couldn't relax himself during the process of the treatment while both Quinsey and he were imagining the same presentations.

What happened was that Quinsey lost his cardiac neurosis, and Felicity picked up the lost neurosis for himself. That's right, Felicity developed the fear that at every moment he was dying of a heart attack. And his panic grew every day.

On the strength of an old adage that 'the psychologist who has himself as a client has a fool for a therapist', Felicity consulted a psychiatrist friend for help. This friend decided it would be better if someone else treated Felicity and so he referred Felicity on to another psychiatrist – a psychoanalyst. Fortunately for Felicity, the analyst was not available to see him for six months. Meanwhile, Felicity visited another friend and colleague, Fortunato. Fortunato listened to Felicity's story and then delivered himself as follows: "Why, you silly ass! I have paid you often to come into my practice to share what you know with my staff and me. You have convinced us all that the evidence is satisfactory that psychoanalysis doesn't work. Now, you have a problem and you go for psychoanalysis!? You unspeakable jerk!" I'm informed that many friends talk to each other like this.

Felicity hadn't even considered the question of results. Of course, nobody ever accused Felicity of being too bright. However, he took Fortunato's words to heart, returned home to his own practice, trained one of his psychometrists to treat him, was treated with Wolpe's systematic desensitization (RIT) method, and he recovered.

And he learned yet another lesson about care that needs to be taken both in providing treatment *and* in seeking it.

And he learned first-hand what it felt like to achieve a panic attack, and to be a patient – it actually wasn't that bad either this time or the several other times Felicity was in treatment. Panic is a great disorder to induce in yourself. It's so easy to fix. Be happy if panic is the thing you do to yourself. Felicity hated his, didn't fix it for himself and even almost got himself stuck with it as a permanent fixture. But then, we already know about Felicity's smarts. A patient once told Felicity that if he had just….

CHAPTER 6

ANGER! TERRITORIALITY: THE INTOLERABLE EXCITEMENT ...

Maddeningly Madly Mad

Some of us are motivated by anger. But where does anger come from? In other yarns, people are described who experienced anger or rage as a result of electrical short-circuiting within the brain that accidentally stimulated the 'rage' centre. Does all anger come from this source? It does not. Anger comes from several sources, and each seems to result in quite different ways of experiencing or expressing anger.

Most of us tend the think that by far the majority of our experiences of anger are caused by others and what they do. This is simply not so. Of course, there may be some instances of anger, which Felicity has not yet encountered, that are 'caused' by someone else. However, in Felicity's experience, all anger is caused by the angry person him/herself. OK, go ahead and get angry at that, if you like.

Some anger occurs when the person feels frustrated or prevented from doing something he wants to do. But who says that anybody should be able to do anything he wants to do? How about getting angry at gravity for preventing us from leaping about in the sky like Superman. Natural restrictions act on us and we accept them – or else we make ourselves angry because we're unwilling to accept them. But by far the most frequent thing that prevents us from doing what we want to do is our own thoughts, attitudes, and beliefs. These internal events evoke much of our anger.

Some anger comes from feeling attacked or in danger – that is, from autonomic arousal, the 'fight or flight' response. But who decides we are 'being attacked' or are in danger? If you are unexpectedly bumped from behind while walking on the sidewalk, will you necessarily feel angry? Suppose you turn around and it is a ten-foot tall monster man with a club in one hand and a gun in the other, and he's looking down at you. Fear, rather than anger, is probably the main emotion of the day. Sorry, I was wrong. When you turned around it was a frail little elderly lady on crutches who fell over and bumped into you. Concern for her well-being, and not anger, is likely your predominant feeling. Moreover, in our engineered safe society there is really very little to be afraid of – including the image of prevalent danger on the streets fostered by the highly selective reporting of rare events by the media. The need to attack angrily when fearful is really only there when escape is believed to be impossible or when the danger is thought to be real – all beliefs belonging to the person.

Probably, most anger comes from our own expectations which are not met by others – the other person wasn't considerate or friendly or didn't do the task the way it 'should' have been done. But who has the right to make rules about how another 'should' conduct him or her self? It is by having expectations that we set ourselves up for disappointments. And when our expectations are not met, we are likely to make ourselves angry. Nobody, including you and me, is in this world to live up (or down) to another person's expectations.

It's true that there is always a stimulus involved in anger. The stimulus may serve to evoke arousal, or it or the arousal may serve to evoke a thought. But both the arousal and the thought are reactions of the aroused or thoughtful person – the stimulus is just there. In these terms, the basic sequences (sometimes called 'equations') involved in the activation of anger are either:

1. Stimulus –> Autonomic Arousal –> Thought –> Anger, or
2. Stimulus –> Thought –> Autonomic Arousal –> Anger.

Either of these sequences involves certain kinds of thought and arousal to evoke anger. In the scenario just mentioned, the surprise of the unexpected bump from behind created *autonomic arousal* (not anger), and turning around to find out what happened provided a 'meaning' or the *thought* that determined the resulting kind of feeling (sequence #1). In other situations, a *thought* (for example, the meaning Felicity attached to being told he was like a lawyer), may contradict attitudes of personal importance or worth, so that we 'get up on our high horses' (autonomic arousal), and think (tell ourselves) we are justified ("How dare he insult me!?") in becoming angry at having been, for example, insulted (sequence #2). Some of these thoughts and the ways in which we arouse ourselves are illustrated in the stories which follow.

Chronic Hostility – Closeness Intolerance

Introduction to "The Love Test Tube"
In order to measure the strength of your 'love' feelings, imagine a test tube into which you have poured all of your loving feelings and your needs for closeness, dependency, and relationship with others. Actually, the original total amount of these feelings and needs probably doesn't differ much from person to person.
But now we're going to spoil the nice love-filled picture. The infant, lying in its crib, gets hungry. It starts to cry. The mother is out in the garden and doesn't hear the baby. The baby cries louder and more insistently, kicking and waving its little fists. This additional

activity indicates that the autonomic-stress-anxiety nervous system is being activated and that the baby is becoming anxious. Each time this happens, a bit of anxiety becomes conditioned or learned to be associated with the external stimulus most related to the feelings being experienced at the time – in this case, with the mother whose presence is desperately needed. This learned drive of fear increases the motivation of the person to avoid or prevent *expression* of the love feelings by a certain amount, and it also increases or intensifies the poignancy of the (love) feelings to which it becomes attached by the same amount.

Let's represent this learned fear drive, which is added to the love feelings in the test tube, as a kind of sticky wax poured in on top of the love feelings. It increases the amount of feeling or drive as measured up the side of the test tube, and it prevents the love feelings from bubbling up and getting out (being expressed).

Other events add their own layers of wax to seal in the love feelings and to intensify them. The child feels lovingly toward the father and wants to climb on his knee, but dad is too busy for that, and the child feels the pain of rejection – as more wax to 'cork' and to be attached to its loving feelings. The child tells a secret to a friend, who then blabs it all over the place. And more wax is added as the child learns to fear trusting another. The child has a crush on a child of the opposite sex, but the other child likes and goes off to play with someone else. And another waxy cork of fear is installed over the love feelings to keep them down.

In those for whom the 'love test tube' has become a problem (which is almost everybody), long before adulthood the wax build-up over the love feelings has become quite thick, raising the 'amount of feeling' to a much higher level than the love feelings alone. Now something or someone stimulates the love feelings – the person meets someone he or she likes. If the aspect of the emotion felt is the 'love' part of the substance in the test tube, the experience the person has is no longer one of 'I love'; it is the feeling called possessiveness – the feeling that the *other* must love *more* (or it will be unsafe to care). If the aspect of the emotion felt is the 'fear' part of the substance in the test tube, the experience the person has is one of jealousy – the fear that the *other* person will not love *enough* (and will care for another soon). If it is the wax seal or 'inhibitive' aspect of the 'waxy' substance in the test tube of which the person is aware, the experience the person has is one of defensiveness or self-protection. The kind of self-protective defence used when ‹love' feelings are anxiety-loaded is most often experienced as 'I do not trust' the other, or as a kind of psychological 'distancing' to prevent the other from 'getting too close' (since that may result in hurt feelings).

Having worked this reverse alchemy of converting love feelings to possessiveness, fear to jealousy, and inhibition to the self-protective act of keeping others at a distance, we can go a step farther. We can look at the picture from another perspective to learn some more about how love converts to hostility. Instead of looking at the test tube from the side to measure the amounts of feelings and inhibitions up its side, we might look down through the throat of the test tube. If we do that, the picture changes. What we see now is a small circle of 'love' feelings at the bottom of the test tube. It is a small circle because it is at the greatest distance, seen through the waxy substance. Around that circle are lines representing the somewhat closer 'waxy' substance of the 'fear'. Around these lines is a larger circle, representing the top of the inhibitive or corking wax.

The little circle in the middle represents the 'core' of at least one of the personality's conflicts. If it represents 'love' feelings, then the larger circle of defenses maintained by the surrounding lines of anxiety or fear are psychological 'distancing' defenses whose job it is to prevent close emotional involvement with others. Distancing defenses are used to prevent loving feelings from being expressed and close involvement from happening, so that the fear about loving is not aroused. There are several available and commonly used types of defenses for 'keeping others at a distance'. The first one is the 'cognitive' defence of deciding 'not to trust' others. Another one is to become very 'intellectual' or 'rational' – who can relate emotionally to that sort of behaviour? Another is to be 'cold' and 'aloof', defying others' attempts to relate. Still another is to be 'demanding' and 'complaining' – who can relate to that sort of thing? Finally, one can be just plain 'nasty' and 'aggressive' – that should keep others away pretty well. Now, if you think about it, all of these defenses to push others away at a distance are basically 'hostile' defenses, acting in ways almost guaranteed to 'put people off'.

But why is this kind of hostility 'chronic hostility'? There are at least three reasons why. First, since the person acts in a 'distancing' way (pushing others away defensively), others are apt to react in an appropriate fashion – namely, staying away. The person's focus of attention tends to be on the behaviour of the other. So the defensive person, who is 'pushing others away', is less likely to notice what he or she is doing, and more likely to notice what the other person is doing. The 'staying away' response of the other is apt to be interpreted as 'rejecting'. The things other people do *to us* are then used to 'justify' how we react *to them* – of course, nobody does anything *to* us (they do what they do for their *own* reasons, even though we may be the recipients of their behaviour). However, once the inference is made that the other's actions are 'done to' the 'closeness intolerant' person, the latter's vengeful (hostile) thoughts and 're-'actions (which may be seen by others as 'paranoid') maintain the mutually 'rejecting' cycle, and keep the hostile feelings alive – and chronic.

Second, when in conflict about almost anything, most of us are inclined to focus our attention on and notice any 'negative' events which occur, and to ignore the 'positive' or desired events. We notice the occasional/*few* instances when others fail to act as *we* imagine they should (if they truly loved us or were trustworthy). And we ignore, the *many* events in which others are friendly, loving, accepting and trustworthy. This makes it impossible for others to 'prove' that they can be trusted or that we can love safely, even if they wanted to, which means that every day brings new events for the afflicted person about which to fume, fret, and feel furious.

Third, it is important to notice that, when there is love *and* fear in the tube, the increased amount of 'feeling' measured up the side of the test tube tells us that the person›s intensity of 'feeling' is greater than that from the 'love' feelings alone. That is, if the person experiences any of the feelings involved in the 'love test tube', he or she feels an increased strength of 'feeling'. This means that the desire for close relationships, and the loneliness generated by their lack, is intense and constant. And so the 'hostile' defence used to prevent expression of the fearsome 'love feelings' is also fairly constant or 'chronic'.

It's true that this sounds pretty contradictory and self-defeating. And, of course, it is. But that's the nature of conflict. The fear part, coming from survival needs (autonomic nervous system), is stronger than any other feelings. So it tends to 'drive' the person away from what he or she wants to do. In this case, it drives the person to push others away, particularly when the person feels most lonely and most in need of others.

You may notice that there's something wrong with this idea about the nature of this conflict. How can the 'fear' part alone be stronger than the fear-increased 'love' part? Although there probably are some differences between people and rats, we might use an experiment with rats to illustrate how this works.

Imagine a tunnel with a 'goal-box' at one end of it. Every time rat 'Alex' is put in the goal box, it is given a painful shock. Now it is put in the goal box (with or without shock) and a spring-operated scale is attached to its tail. It doesn't like being in the box where it was shocked (and was scared) repeatedly, so it pulls like crazy to run *away* down the tunnel. If we measure the 'strength' of its pull away from the goal-box at various places down the tunnel, we find it pulls very hard when it is near the goal-box, and less and less hard the farther it is down the tunnel.

In contrast, every time rat 'Bobby' is put in the goal box it is fed. Now it is put into the tunnel at various distances from the goal-box with the spring-operated scale attached to its tail from the far end of the tunnel. It wants to get to the goal-box to get food. So it pulls like crazy to run down the tunnel *toward* the goal box. If we measure the ‹strength› of its pulling at various places down the tunnel, we find it pulls very hard when it is near the goal-box, and less and less hard the farther away it is down the tunnel.

We can plot on a graph the 'gradient' or slope of the strengths of the pulls toward or away from the goal-box at various distances from it. When the 'approach' and 'avoidance' gradients are plotted, the 'avoidance' gradient is always steeper (higher at the beginning near the goal-box, and drops off quicker) than the 'approach' gradient. That is, at or near the goal-box, fear is the stronger of the two drives – even if the rat is very hungry, that is, even if it is also 'anxious' to eat.

But that's not all we can learn from our rats. When rat 'Connie' is put in the goal-box, it is alternately shocked and fed – it is fed one time and shocked the next. Later, when it is put into the tunnel with the spring-loaded scale attached to its tail, rather characteristic things will happen at various distances from the goal-box. Since the 'avoidance' gradient is steeper than the 'approach' gradient, if the rat is put in the tunnel near the goal-box it will pull *away* from the goal-box. If it is put in the tunnel at the far end from the goal-box, it will pull *toward* the goal-box. If it is put into the tunnel at the point at which the two gradients cross each other, since the 'approach' and 'avoidance' needs are equally high at this distance from the goal-box, the rat doesn›t know what to do and it runs around in circles or back-and-forth – pulled toward and pushed away with the same intensity.

How does this help us to understand the 'love test tube'? When any 'closeness intolerant' person is close to or with another person, fear is the predominant feeling, and the psychological 'distancing' defenses are activated – the person feels and/or acts in a 'distancing' or 'hostile' way. When the same person is far away from other people (is alone), the need for closeness is intense, and the person feels lonely and isolated – pulled toward other people (loneliness is a motive to drive us to be with other people). When a 'closeness intolerant' person is alone, but is thinking about other people or contemplating physical proximity (i.e., bringing others in close while at a distance), the person doesn't know what to do, and runs around and around in his or her mind – ruminating about the pain of needing others when they are so rejecting. You know, in some ways, rats *are* a lot like people.

The commonest source of what is usually experienced as anger, strange to say, may be love. That's mad, right? Perhaps it is. But let's listen in to Ingrid's story to see if we can understand or feel how that happens.

A Beloved Hatred

A pretty young lady in her mid-twenties was referred to Felicity by a colleague. She complained of depression and a feeling that there must be something wrong with her because nobody liked her. In Felicity's business, everybody reacts to the word 'depression' as though it were a diagnosis, verified by the fact that the patient has affirmed it. Perhaps doubting our competence, sheep-like, we often allow ourselves to be led blindly by those who, being unable to see into themselves, need the help of someone else to sort them out. This time Felicity was not impressed with the 'diagnosis'. The lady looked much too anxious and uptight to fit that label well.

Ingrid complained that she had never had a real boyfriend. What was the matter with the men out there? Besides, she believed that she had never had a girlfriend or experienced what friendship was like. Daylight dawns slowly in Felicity's mind. Nevertheless, eventually he began to realize that Ingrid had to be talking about her own expectations about friendships which far exceeded what anybody would ever be willing or able to fulfil. What was she expecting of others? Perhaps Ingrid had a part in rejecting those men and women who might have shown an interest in her. How had she seen them – as being too ... what? He waited.

She described a history of felt isolation, abandonment and rejection. Her father had died when she was very young, and she thought that the resulting lack of a father left her ill-prepared to interact with other men. Her mother had worked and, after school, she was relegated to lonely isolation in a room at the home of a relative (not adding 'until the mother came home' – that might have implied a positive time). She had tried to make friends with the other girls, but they had rejected her because they were too involved in their own cliques and, besides, her clothes had not been purchased in one of the stylish stores. The boys had never liked her because of ... her nose, or her teeth, or the shape of her face, or the quality of her skin, or ... Wall to wall, she laid out a carpet of life riddled with rejection. Nor could she see any contribution to her plight from her part. Everything Felicity suggested had already been tried by her without success.

Maybe she *was* depressed. Certainly, the world seen through her eyes was a melancholy, joyless, and failure-filled place without any happiness or even relief. Ingrid wept. Felicity could not understand her tears. Considering the recent upsurge of support for the country's government and the recent huge profits of the major banks, Felicity thought Ingrid deserved high praise for being able to cry about anything else. And he told her so. The psychological tests Felicity had administered to Ingrid confirmed a pattern of 'chronic hostility' rather than the depression of which she was complaining, so he preferred that she be confused rather than sorry for herself. She responded to his jovial comment as he had hoped, by 'coming out of herself' and staring at him as if trying to read his mind. She failed to penetrate his attentive stare. She smiled and relaxed.

In varying degrees almost everybody participates in the experiences that shaped Ingrid's approach to daily living. The picture of 'closeness intolerance' ('the love test tube') certainly fit Ingrid. She regularly affirmed that there was nobody in the world to whom she could relate, that she hated everybody, and that she had no friends. She had a lengthy array of criteria that people would have to fulfil (hoops they'd have to jump through) before she could trust or relate to them. She found extensive evidence that others hated or rejected her in the most trivial occurrences, such as the ways in which they expressed themselves or the tone of voice used, or even her own interpretations of what people meant in mildly ambiguous statements. If challenged with contradictory evidence, for example about the friends she had, she had reasons by which to downplay the 'reality' or genuineness of the friendships. She obsessed all day and well into the night about minor interpersonal incidents with the help of which she demonstrated to herself that others rejected or didn't like her. She was angry all day, every day. She hated the world and everybody in it for letting her down. No wonder she was as melancholy as she said she was.

The problem at core was that, on the inside, she felt intense need to be dependent and close to others. But the anxiety associated with that need was so strong that it became essential in her mind that any relationship she had be absolutely and completely engrossing and close (safe) – at least on the part of the *other*. However, she could not tolerate any such closeness and so had to find ways to keep everybody at a distance. She was quite clear that she required any man she met both to be absolutely perfect according to her exacting standards, and to be utterly attracted and committed to her from the very start. Of course, such expectations could never be met, and so she suffered and hurt all the time. She also found ways to revenge herself on others either in her own mind or, preferably, in some verbal attack on their vulnerabilities at least equivalent to that she had felt on hers.

Felicity was at a loss. He tried everything in his bag of tricks to see whether he could penetrate any part of the intricately woven armour with which Ingrid defended herself. Ingrid put forth an heroic effort to try to confound her defenses, but she could not let them down enough to allow herself a chance to get beneath them. She seemed to understand the problem clearly enough, but that didn't help her to resolve it. Part of the problem, of course, was that she didn't really believe that she was pushing others away. It was 'they' who were rejecting her.

For once, Felicity was sorry that he was not permitted to prescribe medication. There were a couple of medications, Ritalin and Anafronil, which he would dearly have liked to use from time to time. At Felicity's suggestion, through her physician, Ingrid obtained some Anafronil. On it she felt calm, comfortable, and actually happy. Its psychological effects seem to include the tendency to reduce obsessional thinking and this, in turn, permits the person to calm down and look around at the pleasant things in life. But Ingrid did not want to achieve an 'artificial' effect from a drug, and was fearful of having to remain on a medication for life – fearing, among other things, that having to do so would mean that she had a 'chronic disease'. So she didn't stay on the medication for long – just long enough to convince herself that it could have an effect and that she actually could feel happy.

Although Ingrid repeatedly complained that there was no solution to her problems (she seemed to think there should be one thing which would 'fix' all of her life), she was really unwilling or unable to commit herself to the idea of changing herself. If the people around her didn't do the changing, it meant to her that they didn't love her enough for her to 'feel safe' in caring about them. In time, it is possible that Felicity may be able to get her to lessen her fear of her 'love' feelings, by procedures such as the visual 'squash', systematic anxiety desensitization, or encouragement to 'find the good in others and in events'. Only time will tell if he can find the keys to unlock Ingrid's defensive doors so she can let in some joy.

A Loving Hostility

It was easier with Ian. In his early thirties, still not having had a relationship lasting more than a month, he was referred to Felicity for treatment for his anger at the world of people around him. Ian was also afraid of loving others. However, even although he too saw the world as a vile place with everybody out to take advantage of him, he was conscious that the basic problem was his own unwillingness to let go and to trust others. He received a series of systematic desensitization (RIT) sessions in which he was taught to relax and then asked to picture scenes in his mind. The scenes had him talking to other people, and then expressing positive feelings about nature, then about a third party, and then about the person with whom he was talking. Finally he was asked to picture himself expressing loving feelings to the other. In addition, he undertook some assertive training to foster expression of his feelings to others. Before his thirty sessions were completed, he was courting a lady. He was married a year later. He asked Felicity to 'stand up with him' at his wedding, as if needing encouragement at the final point of making a commitment.

Across the years, Felicity has treated quite a number of Igors and Imogenes who felt hostility or hatred toward most of the people they knew. Each complained that there was nobody out there to whom they could relate or who cared about them. With some of them, Felicity set out to 'cut off the waxy cork' of fear about loving by desensitizing or de-training the anxiety they felt about their own 'love' feelings. With some, he tried to 'drill little holes' in the bottom of the 'love test tube' to 'let off little bits of loving feelings' (not strong enough to evoke inhibitive fear) by means of emotional responses training (equivalent to assertive training). With some, he asked them voluntarily to 'remove the cork of not trusting' for just a few moments at a time so that they could express happy or caring feelings briefly, coping with their feelings and taking the chance they might feel anxious or fearful. As the fear of closeness or loving feelings was reduced, the need for the distancing defenses evaporated. Now the 'reverse alchemy' of the 'love test tube' could reverse itself and become 'true alchemy'. Instead of being bothered by how he or she inferred the *other* was feeling, the ‹new› person began to notice (mainly) his or her *own* feelings. Freed from the anxiety or fear 'cork', the original form of the 'love' feelings was reinstated, and the person›s experience became one of 'I love', and not 'Does he or she love?' Of course, most of us would think that this idea sounds wrong. It›s also important that the other loves us back, or it's 'no good' loving another. Actually, this almost universal attitude is probably wrong. It is just fear talking or, if you prefer, it is the evidence of our fear about loving another.

In each case, as treatment progressed, Felicity always thought he could 'feel' the person's growing freedom, trust, and 'yummy' warmth. At this point it seemed as though the walls of the person's world opened up and Mister or Miss Right emerged from the woodwork. The miracle which made others 'available' to them seemed to be that suddenly they were emotionally 'available' to others.

Rage – Energy Intolerance – Anti-Social Pro-Sociability

If 'hatred' is the extreme experience of 'closeness intolerant' hostile people, then 'rage' is the extreme experience of 'energy intolerant' angry people. However, there is an additional event which occurs in the 'energy intolerant' to convert their anger to rage – an event that is described in a later chapter. Meanwhile let's look at the main source of this kind of experience of anger.

Picture a test tube – don't worry, this test tube is a little different from the last one. Into the bottom of this test tube, pour all of the body's energies. By energy is meant here the sum total of what the body does; the body is little more than an energy-producing machine. Each type of cell produces its own kind of energy for the body to use. Bone cells are rigid and produce energy in the form of resistance against compression or bending – to allow the bone-supported parts to bear weight. Muscle cells produce contractile energy – pulling across joints to allow movement of body parts. Nerve cells produce electrical energy – to allow transmission of messages from place to place in the body, allowing the executive functions of the brain to coordinate what the rest of the body does. Skin provides tensile energy to stretch as may be needed. Some organs and glands are chemical factories to produce chemicals that release their energy in bodily chemical interactions. Everything in the body produces energy.

Having said that, the most visible kind of energy produced by the body is that of the muscle cells which create motion. It is this energy that probably best represents what was intended when you were asked to imagine pouring all of the body's energy into this test tube, to measure its amount up the side of the tube.

Across the years of growing up, a funny thing happens. The child feels energetic, exuberant and boisterous. In a big deep voice, the father orders: 'Don't you raise your voice to me!' Something wrong with using energy in forceful activity? And a waxy cork of fear becomes attached to the energy, covering it with a film 'to keep it under control'. The child comes in from playing in his/her Sunday best on a rainy, muddy Sunday. The mother looks horrified and screams at him/her. He/she doesn't know anything about laundry or about the mother's concern with cleanliness. He/she was just having a good time and being energetic. Something wrong with energy? And another waxy cork of fear is laid over his/her energy 'to keep it down'. He/she runs energetically through the house, and the mother anxiously warns about bumping into the furniture and the precious ornaments. He/she doesn't know the value of such things. Is there something wrong with energy? And another waxy cork is installed to foster carefulness. He/she is energetic and restless in school, and the teacher thunders: 'Sit still and pay attention!' Something wrong with energy? And another wax cork is implanted over energy. He/she is wrestling with a little friend from down the block and the mother, who is worried what her neighbours will say if their child is hurt, stops them with anxious alarm. Something wrong with energy? And another cork of fear is learned to be associated with or to inhibit energy.

As the child grows up, these corks of fear, learned to impede the use of energy, build up in the test tube. Now in adulthood, or much earlier, if the energy is stimulated a strange transformation has taken place. If the person is aware of the 'energy' part of the fear-increased arousal potential, the experience he/she has is one of 'anger' – anger is just energy called by a bad name because of the bitter taste of fear. If the person is aware of the 'fear' part of the feeling in the test tube, the experience is one of 'anxiety' or 'uptightness'. If the person notices the 'corking' effect of the fear over the energy below it, what is experienced is the effort at 'self-control', to hold back or to try to 'be good'.

But let's extend this picture a bit more. Suppose the person gets the idea, either by him/her self or through training, that 'anger' is the worst kind of feeling – after all, it may lead to violence and do harm to others. If this happens, he/she is likely to add his/her own additional 'cork' of 'intellectual' or 'philosophical' or 'reasonable' control on top of the existing cork. This part of the 'cork' is felt as 'guilt' or the fear of doing wrong. Certainly, this should increase the sense of 'having to be in control' – the corking effect. It may even add enough to the 'fear' part to convert the uptight anxiety to 'panic' or 'terror'. But it does much more. It also increases the intensity or amount of the feeling measured up the side of the test tube, so that if the person's experience is of the 'energy' part, the feeling may become one of 'rage' or even violence.

The majority of rage, and the violence it may evoke, comes about as a result of fear. Most murders are performed by Mr/Ms Milktoasts (including drug abusers, fearful of postponing an urgently felt drug need) who fear their own anger, and who have held it in until a 'final straw' triggers an outburst, maybe eventuating in the harm they most fear.

Again, it might be instructive to change our perspective on the test tube, and look from above down its throat. What we will see, in the distance, is a small circle of 'energy'. Around it will be radiating circles of the cork of fear whose job it is to keep away possible stimulation of the core of 'energy'. Around the top is a larger (closer) circle representing the top of the waxy cork – whose function it is to avoid, control, or defend against use of the feared 'energy'.

What kinds of 'defenses' could be used to inhibit or block the use of energy? Of course, the general type of 'defence' is the effort to 'control'. But control can be effected in several ways. One way is to 'be reasonable' – 'let's not get excited; let's talk this out; let's be reasonable about this thing'. Another way is to maintain fearful and vigilant 'caution' or 'care' – for example, not to hurt anybody's feelings by saying the wrong thing, according to whatever rules of conduct the person has learned. This last effort at cautious control is the familiar approach that advocates taking 'precautions' to prevent lawlessness (the externalized or projected aspect of the fear of energy or anger) in the community – for example, to inhibit crime in the service of keeping the peace. Another way is to be helpful to others, or to get into sports – both use up energy in 'safe' ways. Another way is to become depressed (the extreme result of energy or anger inhibition) – how can you get angry if you are just too tired or exhausted, if your mood is too low to allow you to get going, and if your energy level is depleted? In fact, most depression is a way of preventing or defending oneself from becoming angry.

The 'reasonable' or other 'corking' defenses used to hold energy down in the 'energy test tube' involve the exercise of control, which also adds to the quantity of energy feeling while fostering the conversion of energy to anger. Control works quite literally as a 'cork' to 'bottle up' the energy that we call anger.

A Core-Topping, Cork-Popping Just Joust

Jack was a man in his mid-twenties who was referred to Felicity because he was depressed and periodically became either destructively angry or suicidal – the so-called 'episodic' personality. In particular, he would become explosively angry, even violent, when he imbibed alcohol. The referring psychiatrist intended to begin psychotherapy with him in about six months, at which time Jack could be accommodated into his schedule. He indicated that there was much unresolved conflict in Jack's early background which would probably require several years of psychotherapy to work through. However, he felt that Jack could benefit from a bit of behavioural therapy in the meantime to tide him over until the real treatment was to begin – in six months, when his schedule permitted it.

Besides, Jack was seriously depressed. And the psychiatrist wanted the depression monitored and any needed emergency therapy made available to him while he was still on the waiting list.

Felicity didn't mind being a makeshift means for temporizing. Still, he thought he ought to earn his fees while he was supplying supportive contact until Jack could obtain the real psychotherapy. Accordingly, he thought it might be a good idea to do some tests – as a temporizing measure, of course. And the psychological tests might turn up something that could usefully be addressed in this behaviour therapy substitute for the real thing.

The tests presented a picture of a fairly severely depressed, 'nice' man who only wanted peace and tranquillity in his life. He had always wanted to be a 'good' person, and he had learned all the rules of conduct that he had been taught. He was almost compulsively careful as he navigated space in anybody's place – to the point where he was often tensely awkward in his movements so that he would actually knock something off a table as he attempted to avoid doing just that. He was a 'reasonable' and rational person who used these means to exercise firm 'control' over himself and his actions. One could almost hear him singing Professor Higgins' role in My Fair Lady – particularly the part about having 'the milk of human kindness by the quart in every vein'. He also had a great deal of 'bottled up' anger. A picture of the 'energy test tube' popped into Felicity's otherwise vacant mind.

Any disinhibiting agent is likely to help 'the cork to pop' and a flood or explosion of anger to occur. An obvious disinhibiting agent is alcohol. Jack certainly reacted strongly and angrily when he imbibed, as his 'bottled up' anger was freed or disinhibited. But 'justifications' for anger may also serve as 'disinhibiting agents'. If something happens by means of which the person can justify anger, he may well 'blow up', become angry and even escalate his angry feelings as they are released even to the point of violence. This too happened with Jack from time to time.

Of course, the tests Felicity administered to Jack also revealed some of the things from his developmental history that the psychiatrist thought needed to be addressed. Jack felt criticized and the brunt of fault-finding. This seemed to be the content around which a high level of guilt feelings had developed. He had always tried to be a 'good boy', but always felt he fell far short of what he should have been in his parents' eyes. He felt used and abused by his supervisor and his fellow employees at work. His good-natured ways set him up to be asked to do extra work and, although he thought he was doing the job better than any of his co-workers, he felt he received nothing but complaints and negative feedback from his boss. Although he considered all this to be thoroughly unjust and unfair, most of the time he was unwilling to acknowledge, or unable to experience, any anger at all. It was true that he frequently thought of killing himself, and he had made several attempts at doing so, including cutting at his wrists and looking down the barrel of a loaded gun.

Felicity felt set-up. It was as though he wasn't allowed to treat this man, but he had to live with the risk that Jack would commit suicide while under his care. Felicity's thought made him chuckle as he realized that he had just let himself fall into the same trap that Jack was using – he felt inhibited in the use of his energies for the task, and was feeling hard-done-by as if someone else was setting him up to feel guilty. Of course he could treat Jack. It's just that he had been asked to do so by behavioural rather than psychotherapeutic (same thing) means.

There are at least three alternative approaches to treatment for people exhibiting the 'energy test tube' problem. The 'cork' can be removed by the person temporarily to allow him to find ways to use his energy, 'giving up' control voluntarily but only from one moment to the next. The methods for this purpose are generally classed as cognitive therapies or cognitive behaviour therapies. These methods may range from examining and changing 'self-talk' or thoughts to ones which have 'better' outcomes for the person, through deciding or telling oneself to trust his brain's good programming just for now, to 'playing the game of anger' and enjoying it – but only when not angry. The last approach is analogous to Erickson's attempt to control epilepsy by learning voluntarily to produce 'mini-seizures'.

Or 'little holes can be drilled' in the bottom of the test tube to let off little bits of energy, not sufficient to arouse anxiety. The methods for this purpose are commonly classed under assertive training. They may include practice in handling recurring situations by rehearsed responses that are slightly stronger than the person's usual responses, by learning to make brief affirmative statements, or by learning to express personal feelings in place of angry attacks directed at others.

Or the 'fear' feelings that have become conditioned or learned to be associated with the use of energy can be unlearned or desensitized to reduce the intensity of anger and return it to its original nature as 'energy'. The methods for this purpose are generally classed under systematic anxiety desensitization methods, some of which are described in other stories presented here.

Given Jack's 'normal' level of conditionability (speed of learning new emotional habits), Felicity calculated that, in the six months allowed him, he should be able to complete work in all three of these areas. He gave Jack a self-administering and self-scoring test to allow him to estimate his participation in a number of common 'errors of thinking' by which we all upset ourselves. He gave him a self-administering, self-scoring test of 'assertiveness' to help him to locate some of the ways in which he was under-assertive or not standing up for himself and his personal rights. And Jack also completed a Fears Survey Schedule and a few self-administering anxiety tests to help him identify stimuli of learned anxiety and fear to which he was inclined to react with undue arousal. Dutifully, Jack completed the tests as he was asked.

The tests showed that Jack regularly upset himself by making nearly all of the most common 'errors of thinking' identified by Ellis. He rarely asserted himself to a 'normal' degree in any common life situation. He had learned to over-react with anxiety in ambiguous situations (where his 'rational' controls could not work well); in dealing with authorities; in being judged or criticized; in any situation evoking guilt feelings; in situations involving dirt or disorder; in feeling anger of any kind; and in losing control. The picture could hardly have been more appropriate to what the 'energy test tube' would suggest as a way to understand Jack's problems.

On the cognitive level, each of his 'errors of thinking' was carefully examined, alternative ideas, attitudes, or beliefs were considered, and he was assigned homework to test out the effects of thinking different thoughts (or telling himself different things) if only for just a moment. He quickly became adept at recognizing other self-demeaning and depressing thoughts that were passing through his mind in all sorts of situations where he felt depressed or put upon by others. He even began to notice momentary flashes of anger in some situations at work and while interacting with his parents. He took to logging in a diary all sorts of thoughts he had in a wide range of his life situations. He was impressed both with his own very considerable accomplishments in this task, and with the lift in his mood accompanying changes in how he talked to himself about what was going on, who he was, and what he was doing.

In the behavioural area, he was quick to learn to use 'I' statements to replace his former, feeling-hard-done-by 'You' statements. He mastered and began to use the 'three-part statement' in dealing with others, in which he first stated what he had understood from what the other had said, then gave expression to how he felt about it, and finally indicated what he proposed to do about it. He found that he related better to those around him, and that he was able to say what he felt, what he wanted, and what his needs were. At first, he was concerned about how he and others would react to what he thought of as 'aggressiveness'. But he soon discovered that others did not seem to get annoyed with his assertiveness, that instead they seemed to respect him for it, and that he himself did not feel scared by his apparent 'aggressiveness'.

He also began practising 'in vivo desensitization' of his reactions to a few repeating life situations. As repeating life situations which upset him, he chose 'being always the one in the family expected to wash the dishes', 'being asked to do extra work in his job', and 'being criticized by his boss'. He prepared a list of about sixteen different responses he might use in each situation, grading the responses carefully from the most aggressive to the most under-assertive (doormat-like). He committed the three lists of responses to memory. Then, when the situation recurred, he paused, in his mind ran quickly through the list of responses to that situation, picked the level of response which he thought he would be comfortable giving, stepped down one item on the list (in the under-assertive direction, to be sure he would be comfortable giving the response), and delivered that response. In these initiatives, too, he was delighted to discover that his mood seemed steadily to be improving along with increased energy and vitality.

Meanwhile, Felicity set about to do systematic anxiety desensitization with Jack, using Wolpe's method which has been described previously. He was trained in deep muscle relaxation. When he was sufficiently relaxed, he was asked to picture scenes in the categories of anxiety that had been identified in the tests mentioned earlier. Scenes were presented such as forgetting his watch and not knowing the time while on his way to an appointment, being called on the carpet by his boss, being criticized by his parents, walking up to a dusty window sill and running his fingers through the dust, experiencing others' anger towards him, feeling angry, and losing control in public. They worked steadily through the hierarchies of anxiety stimuli, presented in slow progression from the least to the most anxiety-provoking. As this work progressed, the obvious tension and fear vanished from Jack's demeanour, his mood lifted and he started acting in a normally decisive and forceful way nearly all the time.

At the end of the six months, Felicity terminated his contact with Jack and transferred him back to the referring psychiatrist for the real psychotherapy. Jack attended the first session with the psychiatrist. After the session, the psychiatrist phoned Felicity clearly confused. He demanded to know what had happened. Felicity indicated that he had fulfilled the referral request and had undertaken some behavioural treatments with the patient. Felicity described his findings and how they had approached the treatment task. The psychiatrist said that he had seen Jack, that he could find nothing to treat, that as far as he could tell Jack had recovered, and that he was no longer planning to treat Jack.

Jack also phoned. He reported that he and the psychiatrist agreed that he required no further treatment. He asked Felicity if it would be all right to contact him in the future, corrected himself to say he would be contacting him if he felt the need for further help, thanked Felicity and hung up. That was the last direct contact with Jack. But there have been indirect contacts. Jack has referred several of his friends to Felicity. Each has indicated that Jack is doing well and that he sings the praises of Felicity as a non-psychotherapist. This last word reassures Felicity that Jack has not yet sunk back into under-assertiveness or depression.

A Spirited Spirit

Some years later, a professional lady in her mid-thirties was referred to Felicity for anti-stress treatment. June suffered chronically from bronchitis that was complicated by a number of respiratory allergies and repeated bouts of sinusitis – all apparently perpetuated by her high level of bodily stress. The referring psychiatrist was continuing his psychotherapeutic contact with June, exploring her emotional distress referable to her early developmental life.

Certainly, June was physically weak when first seen. And she was obviously depressed. She spoke very quietly and used precise speech and highly literate language. She was creative and sensitive, delicate and restrained in her movements and very concerned that she do 'the right things' at all times. She was easily brought to despair by criticism, and was quick to respond with guilt-motivated apologies or silent attentiveness. In order to avoid criticism, she wanted to achieve perfection – if she could only find out how. She was in all respects the image of the 'perfect' woman from the point of view of most men. And yet she had never been married, and she had a restricted circle of friends composed about equally of men and women.

Felicity administered some psychological tests to ensure that he understood what was going on in June. The expected findings associated with anxiety and guilt, energy/anger-inhibition and perfectionism were present. But the Rorschach inkblot test produced a most unusual pattern of responses. On this test, she demonstrated a pattern of responding that would suggest a widespread defensive vigilance, as though every area of her life was replete with conflict and guilt, requiring constant self-protective caution. This vigilance did not appear to be merely a result of her perfectionism. Instead, it seemed to represent an early-learned helplessness in the face of any stressor, which almost forced her to exercise cautious control, through crippling preoccupations with minor issues, so as to avoid coping directly with life's situations. In theory, this should result in an inability to cope with stressors, thus maintaining high stress levels and thus continuously depleting her stress resources. This would somehow have to be dealt with before therapeutic changes could be achieved.

This highly efficient, perfectionistic woman felt she was always at fault for not knowing or not following ‹the rules›. Her interactions with her father, in particular, caused her great pain. She wanted to do the right thing, but she thought that everything he said to her was critical, and that he was always right and infallibly able to spot the 'errors' she made. But she felt no anger at all.

It seemed likely that her respiratory disorders and her quiet speech merely expressed her attempt to 'choke herself off' so that she could not answer back, contradict, or express any anger. The therapeutic task was seen as involving several successive elements. First, it would be necessary to reduce some of the anxiety that maintained her vigilant defensive posture. This was addressed by means of systematic desensitization using Wolpe's **RIT** method. Her creativity and sensitive imagery both facilitated and impeded this process. On the one hand, she was able to create bright and emotionally-meaningful images for herself. On the other hand, their intensity tended to evoke too much anxiety so that progress had to be particularly slow and careful. The latter trend finally worked against this approach to therapy since she became sensitized to the procedure itself and wanted to terminate it.

Second, she would have to be helped to find ways to stand up for herself in a modestly assertive fashion. This initiative was started early in the treatment process and continued for a long time. Progress in this procedure was slow. Relabeling of responses and feelings was attempted along with some standard assertive training procedures. At the same time, her very carefully chosen language was examined repeatedly with her. She was surprised to discover how often the words and phrases she chose confirmed and justified for her the self-defeating attitudes she had adopted. They often confirmed her beliefs that her father was always right, that there were absolute rules of conduct and order which she must discover and apply, that she was in error, that she should feel guilty when she failed to follow the rules, that she must be governed by others' views, and that she was destined to be weak, vulnerable, and ill. As this process developed, she had brief periods of improved health and robustness.

However, each time she seemed about to blossom forth in health and strength, something happened as if to verify that she was destined to be frail and vulnerable. She fell off a piece of furniture she was standing on; she was involved in a traffic accident; she developed a resistant infection; or she lifted something heavy and 'injured' her back. The sequelae of each of these sorts of incidents had to be managed as a priority. It did not occur to her that an accident is an inevitable occurrence due to the action of immutable natural laws of which she might have been aware, i.e., that she was accident-prone. To face that idea would lead her to feel responsible for these accidents, so that it would be incumbent upon her to feel additional guilt.

Third, it would be necessary to diminish the power of the inhibitive guilt (her self-judgements). That would be a hard task as she did not want to address any feelings at all, and in particular those associated with her father – as the main focus of her guilt feelings. However, she was able to find in herself an image of her father as a huge, foreboding shadow approaching her as she lay helplessly on her bed – as a representation of the guilt she felt, quite apart from anything else it might represent. She also found in the back of her mind an image of her father thoughtfully nurturing her development of knowledge in a garden – as a means by which to represent innocence for herself.

These two imaged 'parts of herself' were pictured as being brought out of herself and placed one on each of her hands. She talked to each of these parts of herself in turn, asking it (externalized so that she would know the parts of herself to which she was talking) to tell her what its highest intentions for her were. Her guilt part wanted her dead. But why? So that she would not be a disgrace by making mistakes. But why did it want her not to make mistakes? So that she would be perfect. But why did it want her to be perfect? So she could be happy – she could hardly believe she had said this last thing. And what of the other part of her – her innocence? It just wanted to make her happy.

The two opposing parts of herself ultimately had the same intentions for her!?. Perhaps they could talk to each other to find means by which they could cooperate and reunite themselves into one 'whole' part of her. Her two hands came together to represent the re-uniting of the two parts in one (using the NLP 'visual squash' method). But the best integration of the two parts which emerged involved uniting the figure of her father with his shadow behind him, such that the shadow was almost hidden from view by the form of the man. However, there was apparently enough resolution in this 'protection from guilt' image that, for the first time she could recall, within a number of weeks, she was able to shout with rage at her father after he had shouted a succession of critical remarks at her in his powerful, angry voice. The process of treatment was a long and complicated one. In order not to activate a countervailing force, it was necessary for Felicity to refrain from an obvious initiative here and to settle for a sometimes time-consuming and only partly-related input. Nevertheless, movement toward health, if slow, has been fairly steady, and it seems inevitable that June will eventually 'grow up' (as she put it) and take on the determination and guidance of her own life. To do this she will have to be able to assert herself firmly in all areas of her living and not allow her guilt to govern her life.

June is not yet recovered. She is conscious of the advances she is making, and she can see a time ahead when she will have recovered her health and her vitality. But the final move in this direction is also impeded by a defensive sadness, depression in fact, which mourns the coming loss of her youthful reliance on those around her to guide her ways. She can feel some of the anger that has been lying dormant for so long, but she is still very afraid of that anger. Yet she seems to know that she will have to experience it before her energy and vitality are finally freed to allow her health and peace.

It is painful indeed to sense the fear, even the terror, of a patient who believes she cannot hold back forever the great tidal wave of anger which she feels may roll over her at any minute. In many such people, drinking alcohol may seem as though it absolves them of the responsibility for eruptions of anger disinhibited by the alcohol. But the pressure within remains, draining resources, and fought in dark depression even to the cost of life itself.

It is not too surprising that Freud believed his patients' ideas of demoniacal forces acting within them, such that he described their attempts to prevent themselves from acting out as 'defenses' – implying thereby an internal danger against which they must protect themselves and others. There is no danger other than that bred of fear itself. It is just energy pressing for use – energy which, exchanged for that of others, is the reason and glue that keeps people living and working together in communities as social beings. That's right. The energy which is at the root of much anger is the very essence of what draws people together to live in mutual cooperation in societies. Far from being a destructive force, it is a constructive force. It may only be fear that converts it to a form that has traditionally been viewed as destructive.

Interjected Irrelevant Irreverence – How to Insult Your Shrink

Let's take a break from the 'seriousness' of cases and have a little fun. We have now addressed the main topics needed for this purpose. So, if you would like to return the favour done you by your therapist in 'giving you a diagnosis', you might like to know how to do it. It's quite easy.

First, you should realize that a psychological 'diagnosis' shared with a patient is at once a useless and a destructive act. One of its consequences is that it tends to impede progress and to make therapeutic change more difficult, if not impossible. When it is given, it marks the person giving it as a master of the argumentum ad hominem (name calling) ad nauseam. Why not 'turn the tables', if you like. Or, if you'd rather, you could just skip this section and move on to the next.

Behaviourally-oriented therapists, such as Felicity, are inclined to be energy intolerant people, who may episodically get angry and who may use their energies in work to propitiate their guilt feelings or to achieve a kind of redemption from their imagined unworthiness. Felicity would say that, in his case anyway, the unworthiness may be more than just imagined.

Psychoanalytically-oriented therapists are inclined to be closeness intolerant and inference-prone people. They tend to use their love feelings to bond them to those with whom they cannot have a relationship on equal terms, while bitterly resenting perceived slights and rejection by those with whom they might have real relationship.

Then there are those people who seem to sit in between these poles in their approach to psychotherapy. It is possible that either closeness intolerance or energy intolerance lies at the 'core' – the deeper level of their personality. Then the 'defence' used by the person may itself become anxiety-loaded – hostility in the closeness intolerant, or dependency in the energy intolerant may feel uncomfortable. So the person may erect another layer of defence over his defence – passivity to defend against chronic hostility, or 'distancing' to defend against dependency. The result can be a person who feels pretty emotionally empty and joyless – the extra 'onion skin' of defence prevents feelings.

And then there are psychotherapists whose sexual drives are anxiety-loaded and in conflict. They are inclined to imagine that everything people do is motivated by sex. Could Freud himself have been one of these people? The psychotherapy pool into which they gaze shows them reflections of their own inhibited or troubled sexual drives.

Isn't it funny how psychotherapists can find something wrong with almost everything, including each other? Traditionally, psychotherapists, along with most psychologists, psychiatrists, archaeologists, and detectives have been thought of as 'paranoid', chronically hostile people, well-practised in finding faults in others. Other psychotherapists have been thought of as 'empty' people who can live life mainly vicariously through reflections from the lives of others seen in the pool of psychotherapy clients. And then there are social workers and fire-fighters who delight in 'doing good' and fail in the process to notice the harm they do.

See how easy it is to make anything that is good and worthwhile seem dark, foreboding, ominous, and nasty? But then you should also remember both that this is a chapter on a nasty thing called anger, and that anything is possible in make believe – including enjoying the imaginary state of being nasty, of which we both know you and I are incapable.

Rage – Restraint Intolerance – Restraining Restraint

Felicity used to be privileged to listen in to conversations among groups of little, frail schizophrenic ladies in which they would often argue competitively with each other about two kinds of things. The one common argument was about which of them suffered from the worst 'head tension'. Felicity always thought he should be the winner in that one. But then they were better than he was at making up telling arguments. And, anyway, they wouldn't listen to what he had to say.

The other common competition among them was about the number of big, burly cops required to restrain them while they were being transported to the hospital for enforced care. The most skinny and frail lady could boast that eight police officers were needed for this task. What made it necessary for an entire police force to line up to deal with such a tiny package? Part of the answer, of course, is that the police recognize that the person is upset, and so they try to treat her gently while still achieving the restraint required. But the other part of the answer is that restraint breeds panic and rage, and these extreme forms of human emotion generate an energy level far beyond normal expectations based on a person's apparent size, strength, and vitality.

Restraint breeds fearful arousal. The arousal grows as the felt restraint remains unabated. If the restraint continues, in the service of breaking free, the arousal becomes rage. Rage uses energy, bred of the fearful arousal, in a way that appears angry and aggressive but is really aimed at terminating the restraint. This sequence of events must lie deep at the primordial root of all living creatures in the service of survival. Beyond the safety of civilization, the most likely form taken by restraint would be in the fangs of a predator. If this is true, it becomes easy to understand that every ounce of all available resources might be called upon, as if to maintain life, when restraint is experienced – especially if the restraint experienced comes from a source that cannot be understood or which is not perceived as in some way benign or temporary. Fortunately for Felicity, most of the little, frail ladies seem to have considered him to be benign and temporary – that is, benignly and temporarily insane, and therefore no threat to them as a source of confinement – a point of view which he has always been pleased to acknowledge and to foster.

However, most restraint comes from within, rather than at the hands of another. And most frequently the source of internal restraint is a product of introversion. The way in which it grows comes from the fact that introverted people are not as active and restless as others. This means that, as children, they found it easier than the average child to halt or impede an action upon command or instruction. As a result, they do not do many of the things that might result in direct experiences with the world. And they rely heavily on words (verbal instructions) to mediate their experience. Both introversion and words are sticky and restraining.

Moreover, introverted people are inclined to take life very seriously. The average child discovers that situations and reactions of those around them differ and change from time to time and place to place. Introverted children are likely to take adult instructions, information, and 'words' much too seriously. This, coupled with the importance they are likely to attach to the normal 'good boy' stage of moral reasoning development (during which they are likely to be rewarded amply with praise), fits them to adapt particularly readily to verbal instructions. Adults tend to interact using verbal instructions, and therefore they tend to interact particularly easily with these children, and to approve of their verbal facility and compliance. Thus, introverted children tend to develop a rule-governed, dependent, dependable, reasonable, and verbally-mediated approach to daily living. And, of course, this approach tends to earn them 'good boy' Brownie points from the adult world, especially from teachers to whom they relate well.

But the increased verbal mental activity impedes action – thought and action tend to be reciprocally incompatible. And two other factors also tend to perpetuate inactivity and cautious avoidance of anticipated harm. One is the 'good boy' (level of) morality that they tend to carry into adulthood. The other is a conditioned avoidance of situations where they come to believe there is danger. This results in the development of phobias, in which the fear is increased as a habit by the mild relief experienced in each avoidance of the feared situation. These two factors also serve to perpetuate inactivity and cautious avoidance. The plethora of thought produced by their inward-looking inactivity, and their dependent unwillingness to make simple decisions, creates confusion and intensifies obsessive preoccupations in them that may effectively make them unable to address issues or complete tasks.

Meanwhile, of course, like anyone else's body, the bodies of introverted people are producing energy – which is not being used up while they temporize, hold back, and think, although some of their energy does get channelled into mental activity. The unused energy, unable to find expression in activity, creates pressure to increase thought even more. The inhibiting effect of thought is experienced as a kind of inability to act – enforced, for example, by the 'rules' and the 'reason' with which they govern their lives. As the self-inflicted inhibition becomes uncomfortable and even intolerable, they begin to feel the panic and the rage of anyone who feels restrained. They often have destructive or other (to them) 'bad thoughts' which they dare not act out or express (adding to their sense of restraint) and which make them feel guilty (which, yet again, adds to their sense of restraint). Inside, they may come to feel a raging inferno that, in the most obsessive, includes fantasies of absolute and total destruction of the universe, and themselves with it.

This is the experience of rage referred to earlier in speaking about the 'energy intolerant', only here it is magnified by their sense of being restrained far beyond the simple limits leading to depression. But why don't these people suffer depression? Well, they do. But it is a different kind of depression from that of other energy intolerant people. It develops in a way that makes life seem flat, empty, and useless. This magnifies their negative and joyless view of the world, which their exceptionally refined critical judgement has re-created in experiences coloured in unrelieved tones of grey.

As an aside, part of this rage is secondary to the joylessness of life and the world as these people perceive it. The problem is that introverted people are 'in their heads', and they believes that the thoughts to which they are paying attention must be very important. Why else would they be paying attention to them? This view magnifies the importance of words and ideas to the point that ideas are likely to become ideals – idealized images formed by abstracting the best from among the elements of a class of events and combining them into non-existing but 'perfect' examples of that class. Now the person makes a leap of faith, believing that the 'ideal' things are the way the world is 'supposed to be'. Then, when he compares each external event with the 'ideal' in its class, of course everything falls short of how it is 'supposed to be'. Repeated experience with the short-falls of events from the ideal is the best way known to humankind to suck the joy out of life and to make the world around seem utterly 'inadequate' – inadequacy that is not created by or in the world, but only in the person's own head. And the belief that the world is 'supposed to be' the imagined idealized world seems to justify rage at the world which is seen not to 'live up to' the fabricated (ideal) standard set by these people in their own minds.[5]

But the main source of the rage experienced by them comes from the sense of frustration and confinement they have as a result of the self-imposed introversive and rational restraints with which they keep their actions 'in control' in the prisons of their own minds. These people assume that self-control is absolutely necessary and almost

---

[5] This is probably the basis for much of the radicalization, both Islamic and Christian, that we are seeing in the world these days. RR

cannot conceive that control may be excessive, let alone that it may be unnecessary.

A Benighted Knight

Kevin was referred by a psychiatrist for behavioural treatment to moderate the anxiety that supported his impenetrable obsessive defenses. His psychotherapy had not been progressing sufficiently quickly to satisfy either Kevin or his psychiatrist. The man who appeared at Felicity's office was a tall, nervous, bearded man in his late thirties, whose face was covered with blemishes. He carried himself in a tense and awkward manner. He spoke in a slow and deliberate way, with much hesitation and uncertainty. And he looked as though he would rather be anywhere else, quite alone and free to preoccupy himself with his own thoughts.

Kevin had three or four doctoral degrees in various 'hard science' and applied fields. He turned out to be as brilliant intellectually as anybody Felicity had ever met. But he was employed as a technician doing laboratory work with little or no primary responsibility devolving on him. What a waste! If it were not for the fact that Kevin was also an extremely 'nice' person, Felicity might have considered beating him about the head with a large club to try to get him to take on some of the responsibility for which his training had prepared him. But that thought could only be harboured before Felicity got to know Kevin and the immense burden of restraint under which he laboured.

Where did Kevin's 'restraint' come from? Like nearly all of the restraint that people feel, it came from within himself. He had started off in life as a very introverted child – and, now in adulthood, he measured way off the bottom of the Extraversion scale on Eysenck's test. Again, what introversion means is that the person mediates most of his experience in life with thought, in words. Although it seems possible that introversion may have an element in it from genetic inheritance (certainly Kevin's father was also a very introverted person), it is likely fostered by introverted parents, and it grows easily as a result of some life experiences.

Kevin maintained steely control in the prison of his mind. He was proper and polite. His malediction repertoire wasn't worth a tinker's dam (we would call it a 'damn'), except at himself for having made some dreadful mistake such as putting his pen in 'the wrong' pocket. He was precise and perfectionistic. He could not tolerate the idea of making a mistake. Of course, that was why he had to maintain himself in employment where his mistakes could be checked by somebody else and where he had no responsibility in case he made 'the wrong' decision.

Felicity saw that he would have to do several things if Kevin was to grow out of the cage in which he had put himself. The first thing he had to do was to arm himself against falling into the 'red herring' traps which are common among obsessives. They often try to focus on issues that they think will interest others, often believing that these issues are of central importance or that they lie at the root of their problems. However, nearly every thought they have is likely to serve as a defence against addressing things central to their personality problems. By themselves, they are unable to detect what is at root in their problems. Consequently, much of what they want to talk about amounts to 'blind alleys' or 'red herrings'. Felicity kept this knowledge firmly in the forefront of his mind.

Indeed, Kevin tried almost at once to direct conversation into 'the real' issues of his life. He had the idea that psychotherapy was supposed to address sexuality. Having had no girl friends, he was sure that the problem had to do with repression of his sexual impulses, and he began talking about the problems lying in the way of freeing his sexuality.

Now Kevin was clever, and so Felicity decided he would have to play the magician to get them on course. Felicity suggested that they do some tests to have a look at what was under the defenses Kevin was already talking about in a rather intellectual way. But before doing the tests, Felicity said that it might be fun to do some mind-reading. He told Kevin he thought he knew what Kevin's basic life values were – partly focusing on values as a different topic to absorb Kevin's mind. Kevin looked incredulous and amused. He agreed to the testing, but he wanted first to hear just how 'far off the mark' Felicity would be about Kevin's values.

Felicity said that he thought Kevin's main life values probably involved things like Intelligence, Precision, Efficiency, Reliability, Effectiveness and Power. Kevin's mouth fell open with shock. "How did you know that!?" he gasped. "Easy", Felicity chuckled, "you see, those are the values that adults seem to espouse for children and that 'good children' take on as though they were the appropriate and correct values to have. And here's the real kick in the head. They aren't really values at all. They are measures or evaluators by which we can evaluate how we are doing in achieving the things we are 'supposed' to achieve as we grow up. In a way, they are also some of the means available to measure how we are doing in pursuing our 'real values'." Kevin was clever, and he saw at once there might be a whole range of possibilities about how things were put together in him that he had never considered. Thereafter, it was fairly easy to draw him back from any 'red herrings' he was pursuing.

The tests presented the kind of picture commonly found in obsessives. Felicity got writer's cramp trying to record the lengthy Rorschach. He got bored out of his skull waiting for Kevin to finish the Differential Diagnostic Technique (DDT) with his interminable caution and rigid efforts at control. Since both tests are scored for everything the person produces, the task of scoring them took Felicity the better part of a day, and left him blind and bleary-eyed at the end. So trying was the whole experience on one who was temperamentally opposed to work that Felicity nearly forgot why he had done the testing in the first place. The findings of the tests were not at issue. They seemed to Felicity to be a foregone conclusion. He had wanted the tests as a means by which to shape the direction and form of treatment – naturally in a sneaky way.

He interpreted the tests to Kevin in a straight-forward and honest fashion, but perhaps intentionally with a lot of jargon. Unfortunately, Kevin was clever and verbally facile enough that he understood most of what Felicity said. However, that turned out well because it did allow Kevin to grasp the essence of the results. He was able to understand the series of treatments Felicity planned to use. In fact, his ability to follow (even to anticipate) where Felicity was going was such that the ensuing interactions were exciting in their detail and progressed at a speed which Felicity had no right to expect.

The treatments Felicity planned involved a series of steps. He began by using Wolpe's method for systematic desensitization (RIT), employing relaxation. The imagined situations involved dirt, uncertainty or ambiguity, social interactions leading to angry verbal behaviour on the part of others and then of Kevin, and external and then internal restraints acting on Kevin. This work was introduced intermittently throughout the course of the treatment, with a couple of sessions employing desensitization followed by a couple of sessions doing other things.

Then Felicity began a program of assertive training with Kevin. This started with the conventional training in 'I' statements and the 'three-part statement' (mentioned earlier in Englebert's treatment). This was followed by some 'in vivo' desensitization of assertiveness (as described in Jack's story). Then came an examination of the language Kevin used in talking about himself and his life experiences, both to others and (in his thoughts) to himself. In this latter initiative, the main issue pursued was an attempt to get Kevin to break free of his reliance on justifications, reasons, and rules as the 'causes' or excuses for his attitudes and conduct. He was asked to consider the motto: "Never explain. Your friends don't need it, and your enemies won't believe it anyway." The attempt was being made to get him to recognize his own role and responsibility in 'causing' what happened in his life – in effect, placing him 'at cause'. He found this very difficult to do, and it remained for the next part of the process before he could grasp what Felicity had in mind.

Fourth, he was asked to examine the role of control in his life. At first he was able to 'see' it best in relation to his father. His father had to read the papers and listen to the news every day in order to ensure that world events proceeded smoothly – he saw his father as fearing that if he did not keep his finger on the world's pulse, errors might be made by the world's leaders. He then could see that he had adopted a similar attitude toward others by insisting that they abide by 'the rules' so he could feel that their actions were being adequately controlled. Then he could go the next step to see that this meant they were 'controlled' by him. Only then could he begin to see himself 'at cause' in insisting that rules be followed, and then to see that he was not at cause at all since he was governing and being governed by impersonal rules and principles. At last he could see how he had caused the extreme control he exerted over himself.

Fifth, Felicity described the role of uncertainty and ambiguity in Kevin's life. Kevin was quick to grasp the many elements of this issue. He could see himself as a microcosm of the rest of the world. As the world had developed language, science, and philosophy as means by which to cope with uncertainty and ambiguity (the most universal stimulus for fear) in life, so he had devoted his efforts in mastering the 'hard sciences', in being reasonable and in becoming 'rule-governed', all as means by which to cope with uncertainty and ambiguity in life. He grasped the idea that his high level of introverted and abstract thought had developed as a childhood means to help him 'organize' himself and his life to cope with uncertainty. He saw that the increased range of options of understanding, which developing thought had given him, increased the amount of ambiguity with which he had to contend. And that increased his difficulty in knowing what to do and in making decisions. He could see that his efforts at reasoning put him increasingly at the mercy of rule-governed living and reliance on thinking. And at last he understood that his thoughtful maintenance of innumerable options of understanding each event in life, with his consequent indecisiveness, merely increased the ambiguity in his life. This, in turn, increased his stress which, in turn, increased his need to rely on his old thought-focused ways, once more to increase his indecisiveness and stress. In all of this, Felicity sought to encourage Kevin to trust the already existing beautiful programming of his brain to respond appropriately at once, and to make instantaneous decisions and thus actions – even, if possible, intentionally to make mistakes, and to enjoy them.

Sixth, Felicity used a self-administering, self-scored questionnaire to examine Kevin's participation in some common mistakes of thinking that Ellis had identified. As expected, he made most of those particular thinking errors, and 'in spades'. This allowed some work to be started in re-examining thinking errors carried from childhood into adulthood by which Kevin managed to upset himself. Although this was intended as a minor initiative, it turned out that Kevin took on the task of re-examining a host of his attitudes and beliefs on his own. He found that most of them, brought up with him from childhood, were in error (at least from the perspective of adult life) – and might well be changed. He was delighted with this exercise. It used his best resource, his brain power. And he could enter the task as a game. It provided, not only new insights into himself, but also real substantive changes in his feeling life. It allowed him to adopt different approaches to living and freed him to do things he had not felt he could do in the past.

Seventh, Felicity addressed Kevin's sense of rage. At first, Kevin would not acknowledge any rage within him. He judged violence to be an unacceptable, even terrible thing. As his guilt feelings subsided, however, he began to talk about the 'bad thoughts' which came into his mind (as if from some external source) and which scared him. He had to fight off the wish, that he repeatedly found in his mind, for the world, perhaps the entire universe, to blow up in one devastating explosion, taking the whole thing with him to its final destruction. He feared that if he did not fight off this fantasy, his wish for it would 'cause' it to happen. Felicity teased him mercilessly about this fantasy, asking him to enjoy the whole idea, and building images for him to extend and supplement the fantasy, laughing uproariously at each added feature. At first, Kevin was shocked at such destructiveness on Felicity's part. Indeed, had this initiative been introduced at an earlier stage of the treatment, Felicity's behaviour would have driven Kevin out of therapy. As it was, by this point Kevin had developed some trust in Felicity, and he eventually joined the game with good humour.

Eighth, this development allowed Felicity to introduce 'playing the game of anger'. Kevin was asked to play the game of anger, at least with Felicity even if he could not with others. The basic 'rule' of the game was proposed as: only play the game of anger when you are not angry – in case the game makes you feel anxious about your pretended anger. The idea was to exaggerate everything way beyond any reasonable proportions. If another were to say, 'You don't like me', the answer might be something like: 'How could anybody possibly like you? After all, you must realize that you are the vilest, the most horrible and unspeakable person that ever walked this earth. In all of human and animal history there has never been anything as low as you. Heck, Adolf Hitler didn't have a patch on you for vileness'. The crazy thing is that nobody can believe that degree of vileness in himself, and he is therefore apt to take such extreme statements as an expression of love. Of course, Kevin was clever enough to see at once that this method was not only intended to allow him to 'use' his up-to-now-restrained bodily energy by having a sense of 'safe' impact on those around him, but also to provide him with a way to diminish his own negative, self-depreciating, guilt-ridden self-judgements.

These initiatives were introduced as a series of 'doors' that needed to be opened slowly. As they were opened, changes occurred in Kevin's life. Noteworthy among them was the development of a courting relationship with a young lady – a relationship in which he progressively was able to take on a decisive and, later a leadership, role. He was delighted.

Ninth, it became necessary for Kevin to develop his life according to his own rules. A goal-finding program was introduced in which he was asked to find and develop two kinds of goals. The first kind were 'achievement' goals in several areas of living – including work, property, special relationship, family, leisure use, community contributions, and values development. These goals were assembled, boiled down to highly abstract and almost inconceivably 'big' goals. Then a method of management of life by objectives and results was structured in which he would have to accomplish a series of sub-goals toward the achievement of each main goal area. For each goal he would have to educate himself, do a 'market analysis', design his final product, get it into production, sell himself and his design to others, and expand his activities and perhaps extend the original goal. For each of these sub-goal areas, he defined a series of objectives necessary to complete that task and, finally, a series of action plans to make it possible for him to complete each objective. He did well with this detail.

But the 'real' intention of the goal-finding program was to get Kevin to develop and pursue another kind of goal, namely, 'personal development' goals. He was asked to list all the qualities or characteristics of his 'ideal self' – all the personal qualities he would like to have as part of himself. He was encouraged to include 'outgoing' to compensate for his introversion, 'spontaneous, emotional, and free' to compensate for his habits of excessive emotional control, 'assertive, decisive, forceful' to compensate for his energy inhibition, ambiguity-intolerance, and indecisiveness, 'happy, joyful' to compensate for his flat and joyless depression, 'fair and irrational' to compensate for his wish to control others with the force of reason, and 'loving, gentle, and considerate' to ensure that he would like himself as he adopted these new qualities. Of course, he doubted that even the extreme exercise of his will would ever permit him to acquire these qualities – which led to the second stage of this 'personal development' goals program.

Having completed the list of the personal development qualities he wanted for his 'ideal self', he was given a statement to explain how these qualities might be achieved. Felicity said that the way in which we became the way we are is because all through our lives, whether or not they were conscious of it, others have had goals for us. Mother, father, brothers and sisters, teachers, friends, colleagues, maiden aunts and the local cop all have constantly been rewarding us for acting in the ways which *they* considered to be appropriate. That would be fine except that they all have had different goals for us, and each has pulled us in a different direction as these others reward or approve, or even just notice, our behaviours. No wonder we are so confused about who we are by the time we grow up. But now, as grown-ups, we are free to decide for ourselves who and what we want ourselves to be – and we are free to ignore others' attempts to train us to fit their images of us. The only remaining question is How?

The answer to this question depends upon another explanation. We tend to believe that the things we do come from the way we are. It is as though we believe there is a 'happy' centre in the brain so that when we are happy we smile and laugh and act in lively ways; or that there is a 'sad' centre in the brain so that when we are sad we cry, turn down the corners of our mouths, and stoop as though yielding to gravity. Phrenology notwithstanding, there are no such centres in the brain. It is not true that we cry because we are sad, or that we laugh because we are happy. What is true is that the actions come first. From its internal proprioceptive sensory (kinaesthetic muscle sense, temperature, and pressure) receptors, the brain receives information about what the body is *doing*, and it interprets the actions as though the body felt 'happy' or 'sad' or whatever. As William James indicated, we are happy because we laugh and sad because we cry, not the other way around. To develop any qualities we want within ourselves, all we need to do is, first, to decide which qualities we want, second, to decide and list which behaviours or actions are involved in each quality (defining each quality in terms of the behaviours we think are involved in it) and third, to set out to reward ourselves for each, even momentary, spontaneous occurrence of any approximation to a behaviour from the list.

After completing his list of qualities of his 'ideal self', Kevin was given a Behavioural Dictionary in which each 'personal quality' was provided with four examples of possible behaviours to define it, to help him with the next step of the task. He was asked to choose any particular quality that he wished to have, and about six associated observable behaviours exhibited by people who seemed to have a large measure of that quality. This would afford him a list of behaviours for which he could reward himself. Rewarding each occurrence of each behaviour listed would increase its habit strength until he was satisfied he had achieved his personal development goals.

Once the list of behaviours was developed, it was checked by Felicity to make sure each really was a 'recognizable' or observable behaviour. Kevin was then asked to read over the list of behaviours every morning in order to remind himself of the behaviours for which he was to be vigilant. Then, throughout the day, any time he observed himself, even for a fraction of a moment, spontaneously doing *any* approximation to *any* of the behaviours on his list, he was asked to reward himself, under his breath if necessary, by walloping himself on the back and congratulating himself warmly. He was cautioned not to use his characteristic perfectionism in this task – for example, by waiting to reward himself until he had done the action 'just right'. An example was given to illustrate how to approach rewarding himself, using one of the most crucial qualities for him – namely, 'outgoing'.

Suppose he had 'defined' the quality 'outgoing' for himself with behaviours such as, for example, 'approaches others', 'smiles on approach' and 'starts conversations'. Now he is walking along a sidewalk. There are people walking towards him, as he is walking toward them. So he is doing one of the behaviours – approaching others, even if not because he is being 'outgoing'. Since he is doing one of the behaviours, for *every* person he is approaching he should be walloping himself on the back and being pleased with himself. If he does this long enough, eventually his pleasure with himself might result in a smile of self-satisfaction. Whoops! Now he is doing two of the behaviours – approaching others and smiling on approach. So he should start walloping himself on the back with two hands and being doubly pleased with himself. Now, the first person walking towards him, seeing a mad man approaching (that is, someone walking along the sidewalk and smiling), might move as far away as possible from Kevin to pass him by. But the second person, seeing a pleasant, happy, smiling person approaching, might smile back. That's nice, and it probably makes Kevin feel pleased, so he smiles more broadly – of course, qualifying for a heavier pounding on his back and more pleased self satisfaction. A sixth person might actually greet the smiling Kevin with a ‹Hi›. By the twentieth smiling passer-by, Kevin might even feel motivated to say 'Hi' to him/her. Whoops! Now Kevin is doing three of the things on his list – approaching others, smiling on approach and starting a conversation. He had better grow a third arm to wallop himself on the back three-fold and be triply pleased with himself. In this way, slowly over time, various behaviours could be trained to increase and, in concert, to result eventually in the full-bloom of each quality (such as 'outgoing' to moderate his introversion) in himself which might have been a personal development goal.

Eventually, Kevin followed the plan fully, and blossomed into the very kind of person he had defined as his ideal-self. He also grasped the idea that he could change his mind in the future and become any kind of 'new' person he might want to be at the time. Having said this, it needs also to be said that there was some resistance to carrying out the program at first. The idea seemed too much of a commitment to change on Kevin's part. To help Kevin to get over this initial resistance and participate fully in the program, Felicity thought it might be fun to try something else. In the face of all reason, he did.

He asked Kevin about the 'zits' which covered his face – they were blotchy red marks like a host of pimples. Kevin said that they were a neurodermatitis, and that they had been with him from childhood. Many physicians had been consulted about them. They had tried everything, and nothing had worked in the smallest degree to get rid of the blemishes. Felicity asked if Kevin would like to get rid of them. With scepticism approaching scorn, Kevin said he would like to, but surely Felicity was not stupid enough to imagine that he knew how to deal with a physical problem that physicians had been unable to cure. Felicity chuckled with mock embarrassment, but suggested it might be fun to try something if Kevin was willing to do a rather long and boring task. Now, that sort of a task was still Kevin's strong suit – he could keep at the boring, the irrelevant, and the immaterial for donkey's years, as he had already demonstrated by getting himself all the degrees after his name.

Kevin was asked to spend two-hour blocks of time staring at his face in the mirror. The 'rules' were that, although he could blink his eyes to lubricate them as needed, he was not to look away from his face for anything, even for a fraction of a second. He must continue to stare at his nose (the centre of the face) for the full two hours at each sitting. Of course, he wanted to know what that would do. Felicity said he didn't know whether or not it would have the desired effect, but it ought to result in extinction of Kevin's habitual perceptual 'self-image' by using 'conditioned inhibition', essentially fatiguing it out – this idea will be explained more fully in some stories fabricated in the section on schizophrenia.

Since Felicity was not particularly reassuring or detailed in what the effects of this homework might be, it seemed at first that Kevin would not participate. Of course, Felicity took the opportunity to congratulate Kevin warmly on his assertiveness in turning down this request. However, Felicity did say that, just in case Kevin decided to do the task, Kevin ought to be warned that he would probably experience some strange perceptual phenomena while staring in the mirror. Although Felicity did not know what these might be, after about thirty minutes, and thereafter at about ten minute intervals, Kevin would likely experience some strange changes in what he saw in the mirror – his face might seem to disappear, it might look distorted, and it might look absolutely weird or even terrifying. However, it would 'correct' itself back in a couple of minutes if he just 'rode out' the experience. That did it. Kevin had to try this thing out to see if Felicity was or was not at least within arm's reach of sanity. If such strange things could happen, Kevin had to experience them. If they did not happen, he would at last be sure that Felicity was the quack Kevin was beginning to think he was.

Kevin's curiosity having been captured enough to keep him at the task, he reported that his face did change every so often, and at about the intervals Felicity had suggested. At first he could not see his face. Then his face became grossly distorted, although he was at a loss to describe just how. But he was fascinated with the kaleidoscope of images through which his face changed during these periodic intervals in each mirror gazing episode. He even began to look forward to each new interval to see what it might bring. And he enjoyed the anticipation of using his verbal skills to try to tell Felicity what he looked like in each.

After about ten of these two-hour 'mirror gazing sessions', Kevin observed that the 'zits' on the upper half of his face, for the first time in his memory, were disappearing. Felicity examined them and confirmed that indeed that was what was happening. Kevin expressed puzzlement that they were vanishing in the upper half of his face only – from about half-way up the nose and upwards from there. Felicity was puzzled too. Suddenly, Felicity 'knew' what the problem was. "You silly old ass", he said, "I know what's wrong. You're so much 'in your head' that your gaze has probably shifted upwards to look at the centre of your forehead instead of remaining on your nose". Kevin looked thoughtful and then, with a burst of embarrassed mirth, agreed that he had indeed been doing just that. He wondered what difference that should make. Felicity told him to focus his eyes on his nose and see what happened.

Kevin affirmed thereafter that he kept his eyes firmly fixed on his nose. As if to confirm his report, by the end of the next ten mirror-gazing sessions, the red, blotchy 'zits' were gone from all of his face. This experience removed all Kevin's resistances. He got to work designing his personal development goals and the list of behaviours for each, and rewarding himself for the actions on his lists whenever they occurred spontaneously.

What purposes did all these stages in Kevin's treatment serve? Were they all really necessary? Felicity doesn't know whether they were or not. He had developed the stages from attempts to treat a large number of obsessive people across the years. Each stage in the treatment seemed to be required in order to deal with particular kinds of issues encountered in several cases. Felicity had come to the belief that, in these cases, it was necessary to open a series of 'doors'. At first he opened each door just a crack to let the person get used to the idea that there was something there to be addressed. It would then be possible to open the 'doors' fully to expose the person to the issues involved, so that treatment could be implemented to deal with them. Over the years, Felicity had put together a program for these kinds of people to treat an even broader range of issues than those addressed in the numbered steps of Kevin's program.

In each case, too, it seemed to Felicity that some particular unexpected thing had to be done whose results the person could see. This was to motivate the person to get past the resistances to therapeutic change that are so strongly built into these people. In Kevin's case, two such things were done. His values were listed for him as if by mind reading, and his 'zits' were cleared up. Obsessives are frequently considered to be the group of people who advance most slowly in psychotherapy. This may be due in part also to the self-defeating 'gains' they obtain from their obsessive symptoms that reward the persistence of their symptoms – the 'gains' come from their sense of safety in avoiding the risk of doing harm – by avoiding decisive action, and thinking instead.

A Uniform Unicorn

Before leaving this topic, it may be appropriate to note that there are cases where the 'gains' from the symptoms appear to be valued so highly by the person that no therapeutic movement can be achieved. Karl was just such a person. He had developed such an impenetrable view of his life that it approached delusion. But he was essentially very severely obsessive-compulsive.

Karl was encountered in the correctional system. He had been charged and convicted of arson. His offence had involved standing in front of a hospital that had refused him admission, soaking his arms with lighter fluid, and setting himself on fire. And this was 'arson'!? The justice system has some really hilarious ways of reacting to people's actions. It punishes some, and rewards others (lawyers) for being accomplices in crime. And its standard sexist, or more accurately genderist, propensities have even led it to incarcerate men for laughing – the charge is called mans-laughter.[6]

Karl saw himself as thoroughly joyless, bereft of all emotion and at the mercy of the world of human beings. He had a particular skill in playing the game of chess, which led him to conclude that he was very intelligent. And, having no feelings but only brains, presumably modelled after a character from Star Trek, he decided he was a non-human being in human form, displaced from somewhere else in the universe and abandoned here. Without the human resources to survive in human society, he was destined to live at the mercy of humans, depending on them for sustenance, but scorned and used by them for their sadistic joy in torturing him. What a 'model' of the world and of life! It certainly 'set him up' as a victim. It made it impossible for him to work to support himself, and it made it necessary for him, in his view, to live on social assistance and at the mercy of the 'professionals' on whom he depended. It explained for him why people reacted angrily towards him and rejected him. It made it seem natural that he would have to beg for any kindness. And it justified for him the intense rage he felt toward all those lousy professionals. Indeed, he repeatedly breathed out threats about how he was going to blow up, maim, kill, and otherwise brutalize the people and places he believed had assigned themselves the tasks of torturing and mistreating him.

So restricted was his life that he considered the sentence he served in the correctional centre to be, and later to have been, the best time in his life. But even although he enjoyed his incarceration time more than any other he could recall, that didn't mean he would forego any of his symptomatic gains while there. A wide variety of interventions was used to see whether he could achieve any therapeutic gains. There were no changes at all. If anything, his depression and anxiety measures worsened with each new treatment. He was constantly in crisis, and he would not yield to try out anything offered to help. He

---

[6]   Doug's worst joke so far.

suffered constantly. Of course, as a non-human, he had no feelings, according to him.

After his release, Karl maintained periodic contact with Felicity for years. He remained in constant crisis. He was willing to be admitted only to those hospitals having comfortable furnishings suitable for his care – nice rugs, chairs and the like. But he was outraged when an acceptable hospital would not admit him. The rejection was usually based upon his expressed threats to blow the place up or to murder the staff if they did not admit him. Of course, he considered these threats to be merely an expression of how he felt, and the 'reason' why he needed to be admitted to care. He would phone and utter dreadful threats toward those seen to be mistreating him. He was always on the verge of committing suicide – until too much time had elapsed without his having carried out his threats. He installed himself in a room, and supported himself on social assistance. His daily life was concerned solely with finding therapists, and losing them.

What were the 'gains' he obtained from his violent ideas and his constant search for people to 'look after' him? The answer seems to be that preoccupying his time with 'introversive' thoughts of these kinds allowed him to ignore his own responsibility for his rage (others 'caused' it) and for any self-supporting contribution he might be expected to make to society. His intense 'dependency' on others also prevented him from acting out his intense rage at those around him, even although they were seen as destroying him and his life. The 'gains' from his symptoms were that they served to screen him from any awareness of his role in his rage by justifying it to him, and of his responsibility to make decisions and to govern his life for himself. Given his ambiguity-intolerance (uncertainty terror), these effects of his symptoms helped him to minimize uncertainty or ambiguity in his life and thus to avoid accepting any responsibility for what happened in it.

Many people refer to some obsessive behaviour, such as that exhibited by Karl (and those who have convinced themselves they are at the mercy of others), as 'passive aggressive' behaviour. The trouble is that labelling it as 'passive' seems to contradict, and maybe to neutralize for the person, the 'aggressive' part of the phrase. Also, whatever it's called, passive aggressive behaviour is found in almost every kind of psychological condition. That is, the term is undiscriminating and its use may be counter-productive. But, perhaps because of its relevance to his own obstinate nature, Felicity, like many others, hasn't yet figured out how to understand or deal with 'passive whatever it should be called'.

Violence – Intolerable Irritability – Communal Communalities

OK, so this chapter interests you. See what was meant when I said that you would be revealing something about yourself in reading these pages? Now, hold it. This is NOT to say that you are violent. It is not even to say that you have any violent urges – even though you do. Doesn't everybody? Hopefully, the question you are asking yourself is Why do people have violent urges? Is it because it is in people's nature to be violent? In spite of the common intelligence on this subject, it is simply *not* true that it is in the nature of people to be violent. Then what makes people feel, and sometimes act, violently? Now that is a good question. And it is to the two separate parts of that question that we now turn.

Violent urges are one thing. We have all experienced in some measure at least some of the types of anger described in the foregoing stories – hostility or its extreme in hatred, anger or its extreme in violence, rebelliousness of guilt-intolerance or its extreme in criminality, and/or frustration or its extreme in rage. While experiencing such feelings we have often felt there was nothing we could do about them – 'I can't get mad at my boss, I might lose my job', 'I can't tell my friend off, I would lose his or her friendship', 'I can't express how I feel to my spouse, he or she would never understand and might leave me', and so on. Those are 'real' issues that force us not to express our anger, right? Wrong! They are restrictions we impose on ourselves by which we prevent ourselves from taking the risk of having to pay the cost of expressing our feelings. If we considered the cost of not expressing our feelings to be greater than the cost of losing our jobs, friends, or spouses, we would express our feelings. So *we* choose for ourselves which costs are greater, and which costs we are unwilling to accept.

For most of us, most of the time, the costs of expressing our feelings seem just too high, and so we refrain from expressing them. But when we do that, it is because we *anticipate* the horrible consequences we may endure if we were to express them. What if ... those consequences did *not* happen? Because they might not happen. It is the fear of the possible future consequences that determines whether or not we will express our feelings. Now comes the real point. Actually, the imagined possible consequences are merely the thoughts we use to help ourselves avoid the expression of our angry feelings. And the motivation underlying the need to thoughtfully impede our actions is the learned motive of *fear* – and the fear is really about our angry feelings. So it is our own fear of our own and other people›s anger by which we prevent ourselves from expressing our angry feelings.[7]

Preventing ourselves from expressing our feelings results in a sense of frustration – which we commonly believe comes from the outside world. But that frustration really comes from within ourselves. And it is important to realize where it comes from because that gives us back some control over our own lives by reminding us that it is we ourselves who block our expression of our feelings, especially of anger. It may be time to think back to what happens when we are anxious about our anger and/or feel the restraint that prevents us from using our anger or energy. The energy within us (which we call by the 'bad' name 'anger') presses more strongly (from the combination of energy and fear of it) and we feel more and more frustrated, more and more angry. And it may seem to us that the only way to relieve those self-generated feelings is to 'blow up' or even to be 'violent'. That is the way in which violent urges are created in people – and

---

[7]   Another reason, of course, is that we don't know how to express our feelings appropriately, since so many of us are not appropriately assertive. We don't know how to 'talk straight'.

created entirely by themselves and inside themselves. Think about what happens in the 'energy test tube' when we add our own 'cork' of fear because we believe we should not express how we feel.

But what produces violent actions? There are at least three different answers to this question. Some violent actions are caused by a loss of control due to an irritable brain. Leonard will be used to illustrate this situation. Some violent actions are caused by conditions in the person's life. Larry will be used to illustrate the effects of the use of a disinhibiting agent like alcohol – although it acted in a peculiar way on him. Some violent actions are caused by fear that is excessively high. Lonnie and Lucy will be used to illustrate this kind of reaction. There are certainly other causes underlying violence. However, the other factors are relatively uncommon, and they do *not* include the factors commonly advanced by the media – 'contract murder' or 'psychotic' violence, both of which are rare indeed.

A Rightly Wronged

One day, Felicity was having lunch and (for once) minding his own business, when a booming voice from the far end of the restaurant drowned out the usual ambient noise of lunchtime. The voice demanded: "Have you seen Clockwork Orange?" Felicity's unnatural curiosity got the better of him, and he turned to see who was being so loud, and at whom. He saw a great hulk of a man striding down the aisle between the tables creating a wake of people bowled over by his determined and forceful advance. And the person this powerful man was looking at and advancing toward was none other than Felicity. He reached Felicity's table and, glaring ominously down at the tiny child Felicity suddenly imagined himself to be, boomed once more: "Did you see Clockwork Orange?"

Felicity recognized the powerful man standing over him as Leonard, a patient he had seen at the mental hospital where he had formerly worked. While stammering out a weak "no" in answer to the question, Felicity fumbled through the dust-covered and yellowed files of his memory to retrieve what he could about Leonard.

Ah, yes, now he remembered. Leonard had been admitted to the hospital on many occasions, always escorted there by a dozen or so policemen, and always because of some violent act, usually involving a weapon, and frequently a knife. Fortunately, he had not yet killed anybody, but that was only because he was usually in a kind of daze during these episodes and was therefore unable to be accurate in his actions. Felicity tried to focus his attention sharply on Leonard to see if he was in such a daze now. True, his eyes were a little glazed, perhaps with anger, but otherwise he looked to be in full control of his faculties – as full control, that is, as Leonard could achieve.

Felicity remembered that he had been asked to do a psychological assessment of Leonard and that he had administered a battery of tests to him for that purpose. This had to be why Leonard had recognized him and was now talking to him in such an amiable and familiar way. Felicity ran through the ancient file in his mind to see what he had found. 'Oh dear, he was one of those!' The 'those' referred to demonstrated a high, negative differential index of control on the Differential Diagnostic Technique (DDT). To Felicity, this meant that Leonard was subject to periodic 'blind' rages as a result of a complex seizure involving the 'drive centre' in the old brain – a condition which has been fabricated in several of these stories, including those about Chester, Chuck, Harry, and Hector. The possibility that a 'blind rage' was just developing with Felicity as its prospective target did not escape Felicity's steel-trap mind.

Leonard continued. "Well, you had better see it for your own safety's sake," he thundered. Felicity tried to appear brave. "Why?" he asked tremulously. The booming voice seemed to be right inside his ear and Felicity could almost feel the prick of a knife in his side. "Because you people don't know what you're doing in screwing up other people's minds," he shouted. "You give those shock treatments to people and it takes their minds away. And then they blame us victims because of what you've done. For your own safety you had better see Clockwork Orange! Get it!?" The immense expanse of

Leonard's face blotted out the light as he peered closely at Felicity to see if he had comprehended his instructions. Felicity looked back into the face trying to look properly humbled, penitent, and empathic and, having no voice left with which to speak, he nodded as if with understanding and acquiescence. Leonard seemed satisfied that Felicity would seek to further his education by seeing the movie in question. He pulled himself up to his impressive giant height, scowled at Felicity, delivered a great "Harrumph" and, in leaving the place, stamped huge holes in the concrete floor with his, it must have been size 20, boots before he crumpled up his monster frame to duck through the restaurant door.

For an instant, Felicity felt a great sense of relief at having so narrowly escaped with his life. Then he remembered he was in a restaurant. He didn't know where to look or how to hide. He was sure that everybody in the restaurant was glaring at him as the most dreadful, abusive criminal there ever was – to have so mistreated this poor man. Besides, perhaps everybody there would consider it an indictable offence that he had not seen Clockwork Orange. In a moment of desperate hope, he almost blurted out that he had heard about Agent Orange – in case that degree of unrelated education might compensate for his sin of omission. He restrained his announcement long enough to consider that he might be subjected to the third degree of a torturous inquisition if he made such a claim. That thought stopped him cold since he realized he didn't know anything about Agent Orange other than the name. He was afraid to look around to confirm his suspicions. And he was afraid not to look around in case the entire horde of former abused patients, obviously having collected in this one place, were about to descend upon him to make him their lunch dessert – he had seen a movie in which people became cannibals under some conditions, and he was sure the conditions were right here and now.

Leonard had left behind him a wide empty corridor as his immense frame had ploughed its way to the door. If he acted quickly, Felicity might take advantage of that escape route. By way of a diversion, to distract the multitude of his pursuers, he piled enough money on the table to cover his bill and a healthy tip for everyone in the place, and hurried out of the restaurant as if to catch up with Leonard in order to make amends or to do his 'doctor thing'. He had been careful to see which way Leonard turned on the sidewalk, and Felicity hurried off in the other direction. Felicity never went into that restaurant again.

A Frenetic Histamimetic

Larry was admitted to the correctional centre where Felicity worked. He was a slim man of average height. He was in his mid-fifties. He was serving a sentence for sexual assault of a child in which he had inflicted some physical harm to the child both in his sexual molestation and, afterwards, in his attempts to ensure the child's silence about the event. His record was shocking. He had been admitted to the facility to see if treatment might work. Nothing else had deterred him from violence across many years.

Larry had served time for innumerable assaults, some sexual but mostly occurring during bar fights. He claimed that he was in bar fights almost every night when not in jail. He had been incarcerated for many break-ins and thefts. And he had spent a long stretch in prison for murder, in which he had kicked a man to death. He was indeed a dangerous and violent man.

His persona in jail, however, was absolutely the mirror image. He was friendly and accommodating to everyone, staff and inmates alike. Everybody liked him. He had a wonderful sense of humour. Nobody seemed the least bit afraid of him. He was just about the ideal image of the good neighbour next door.

Shortly after Larry was admitted, Felicity visited Larry's living unit to conduct some business. Larry approached Felicity, waited respectfully at a distance until Felicity had finished talking to everyone else who approached him, and then managed to arrest Felicity's flight before he could escape. Larry said he needed desperately to talk to Felicity whenever he might have the time. Felicity asked what it was to be about. Larry said that his record was full of all sorts of violence, but that he must be like Dr. Jekyll and Mr. Hyde because that was not like him at all, except when he was drunk. He wanted very much to find out what was wrong with him and to get it treated.

For a moment, Felicity wondered what Larry was trying to 'con' out of him. But looking into the earnest, desperate, and despondent face which confronted him, Felicity could not doubt his sincerity. So he made an appointment to see Larry. At the appointment, Larry recounted the history of his dreadful actions, expressing deep remorse about his crimes. But he did seem to want to avoid responsibility for them by affirming that they all occurred when he was drunk, and that he was unable to stop his alcoholism. Then he pushed the right button in Felicity's mind. He said that there must be a devil inside him that made him act that way, because that was just not the way he was put together or felt inside.

Felicity arranged for a Differential Diagnostic Test (DDT) to be administered to Larry. Familiar findings emerged. The test suggested that Larry might be subject to periodic 'short-circuiting' in the region of the old brain containing the 'drive centre'. That is, he may have been subject to 'partial' or 'complex' non-convulsive seizures. But there were two atypical features in the picture. Other than depression and alcoholism, the history of this case did not reveal any of the features commonly associated with the by now familiar DDT syndrome. He had not done badly in school. He learned reading and arithmetic as quickly as the other children. He had not been hyperactive, nor had he exhibited any signs of attention deficit disorder. There were no childhood bouts of rage or tantrums. There had been no over-eating or under-eating. There had never been any sleep disorder or serious panic attacks. And, aside from when he was drinking beer, there were no indications of sexual offenses, aggressiveness or violence. The other feature was that his score on the DDT didn't quite reach the cut-off point at which one would infer that he was, in fact, subject to 'complex seizures'.

Felicity inquired into his history of alcohol use. It turned out that Larry had imbibed every kind of alcoholic beverage and, having reached 'skid row', had also abused a host of substances that are used as substitutes for alcohol. Only one kind of alcoholic beverage had any effect on him at all. That was beer – the one drink he craved all the time. On other kinds of alcoholic beverages, which he would substitute for beer when he couldn't get it, he would have a 'normal' happy high. But with just one or two beers inside him, he was transformed into a vicious brute, looking for fights and needing to find outlets for the dark rage within. Larry had no way of understanding why this happened. Felicity did.

A couple of digressions are needed here. First, any bodily tissue can react as if it is allergic. The allergic response merely involves inflammation (swelling with fluids) of the cells in the affected area. This kind of inflammation is the first part of the body's immune response by which it protects itself from 'dangerous' material that enters it. That is, the body reacts to the allergen (the material which stimulates the allergic response) as if the allergen is a real 'danger' to the body's health. The thing that makes an allergen different from other kinds of poisons, infections, or foreign matter is not the way the body reacts to it. It is the fact that the allergen is *not* a real danger or threat to the body – evidenced by the fact that other non-allergic people do not produce the immune response to an allergen, and do not suffer any illness or other harmful consequence from it. Thus the allergic response is an *unnecessary* immune reaction to an unreal danger.

One kind of bodily tissue that, like any other, can respond with the (immune) inflammatory allergic response is nervous tissue, i.e., the nerves – particularly those in the grey matter of the brain, which are not insulated by the myelin sheath that protects the nerves of the peripheral nervous system. Does alcohol act as an allergen and produce the inflammatory response in some people's nerve tissues? Almost certainly not. Certainly not in Larry's case. He could drink all sorts of alcoholic beverages with no effects at all on him. What the alcohol in beer probably did in Larry's case was mainly to serve as a 'transmitter' substance to hurry itself and its allergenic contents through the blood stream to get its contents to the 'target' organ – in this case, the 'drive centre' in the old brain.

A second digression is necessary to explain how nerves work to produce and conduct their electrical charges. Nerve cells perform the task of a 'sodium pump'. Sodium chloride, or salt, in the nerve is ionized, or separated into its sodium and chloride ions (or parts). The 'sodium pump' pushes the sodium ion out of the nerve to the outside of the nerve's membrane. The nerve is now 'charged' and ready to transmit a signal. It waits for a stimulus. When a suitable stimulus contacts it, the membrane's permeability or penetrability is increased, allowing the sodium ion to re-enter the cell and de-ionize its chloride partner. The de-ionization creates an electrical current. This current serves as a stimulus to increase the permeability of the surrounding membrane, allowing the next sodium ion to enter and de-ionize its chloride partner. The succession of de-ionizations passes along the nerve fibre and creates the electrical charge transmitted along the nerve's length. This is what happens under normal conditions.

But if something happens which interferes with the ability of the membrane to become consistently penetrable at all points, some of the sodium ions may not be able to re-enter the same cell. They may then pop over to visit neighbouring cells, de-ionizing some of their chloride ions and starting current passing along the lengths of neighbouring cells. This amounts to a sort of short-circuit, epilepsy.

Now let's get back to Larry. What in the contents of beer could be allergenic (prone to create/mimic the allergic response)? Presumably, it was the thing that makes beer different from other alcoholic beverages – the grains in it. If this formulation is valid, then what follows? The grains in any beer consumed by Larry arrived quickly at the site of the brain target, carried there by the alcohol (which enters the blood stream very quickly). The nervous tissue in the drive centre reacts to the allergenic grains mimicking the usual allergic immune inflammation. The inflammation *decreases* the permeability of the nerves membranes. This prevents some 'pumped out' sodium ions from de-ionizing within their own nerve. In turn, this leaves an ionized electrical potential which may 'jump' over and de-ionize a chloride ion in a nearby nerve fibre – thus starting the neighbouring nerve fibre going with an active electrical charge moving along it. In Larry's case, the only thing that seemed to trigger off this 'short-circuiting' epileptic-like activity was a response mimicking the histamine/allergic-inflammatory reaction to something (presumably the grains) in beer. Without the presence of the allergen in beer, Larry was a really wonderful human being – that is, he never had any epileptic-like activity affecting his behaviour. Presumably, without the allergic response to beer, Larry's brain was capable of producing enough 'neural inhibition' (described elsewhere) to prevent 'short-circuiting'. With beer, his brain could not produce enough to block the short-circuiting effects of the allergic response, the rage centre was triggered and he became violent.

But why should the allergic response occur specifically in the 'drive centre' area to create this rage response? The answer is probably that there were at least two 'drive centre' areas affected by the allergic short-circuiting response. It is likely that the rage centre was implicated to evoke the violent responses, but it is also likely that the so-called 'reinforcement centre' was involved which provided reinforcement or reward, and thus strong learning. But what was he learning? He was learning both the habit of responding in an allergic fashion to the grains in the beer (yes, there is other evidence too that allergic responses can be, and usually are, learned) *and* the habit of seeking and drinking beer – becoming addicted to beer. That's right, addictions are mostly learned habits, and not a result of some sort of physiological or chemical imbalance).

Now, you must surely be aware that the kind of fiction that has just been offered is quite plainly mad – and that Felicity is obviously nuts, not only for having dreamed up such nonsense, but also for being dumb enough to try to tell somebody else about it. That's not how the body works, right? And it's particularly patently false that allergies or addictions are learned. Everybody knows they are chemical and physiological events having no relevance at all to psychology. Well, let's see how the rest of the story unfolds, just for the fun of it.

If Felicity was right, then by training Larry's brain to increase its production of 'neural inhibition', it might be able to produce enough to prevent 'short-circuiting' when he ingested beer. He should then, over time, stop his addiction to beer – since each future use would be an 'extinction trial', being un-rewarded due to failure of the prevented short-circuiting to stimulate the 'reinforcement centre'. And, even if drinking beer, he should not react to it with rage or violence – due to prevention of the short-circuiting stimulation of the 'rage centre'. Out of pure perversity, Felicity decided to try an experiment.

Larry agreed to be treated in the biofeedback lab. EEG electrodes were attached over the C3-C4 sites on his scalp (as described in Chester's story) and a whistling 'reward' was given when and while the EEG was recording sensorimotor rhythm (SMR) activity from those sites, i.e., brainwave activity of about 13 cycles per second. At the same time, galvanic skin resistance (GSR) electrodes were attached to his right hand and, as described in George›s story, for every 1,000 ohms of skin resistance increase (less sweat, more 'calmness') the slide he was watching was changed as a ‹reward› for becoming physiologically more calm. These procedures, called SMR and SCARS conditioning, have been described already in several other stories.

Now anybody can see that this 'treatment' is about as useless as boobs on a gander. Yes, Felicity actually had this poor man hooked up to EEG and GSR electrodes. And the entire treatment was just some whistling sounds whenever a particular kind of EEG activity was occurring, and change of some boring slides whenever the GSR moved upwards by a thousand ohms of skin resistance. You and I know that this would accomplish nothing at all. What is Felicity trying to do, compounding idiotic fiction about the cause of this man's condition with manifest lies about the causes of illnesses such as allergies and addictions, and then trying to insult our intelligence by offering this trite and meaningless activity as though it was a treatment for anything? Maybe he's trying to tell us something, but we're certainly not going to buy into it, right?

For about two weeks around the 18th to 20th of these half-hour sessions, Larry reported thinking repeatedly and continuously the thought, 'skid row, skid row ...'. He was not disturbed by the thought, but he could not stop it. It stopped itself as suddenly as it started. Having received, from other patients, similar reports about obsessional thoughts occurring at around the same relative time in this treatment, Felicity felt reassured that treatment was progressing 'as it should'. Moreover, the percentage of time within each session during which Larry was producing SMR activity in his EEG increased fairly steadily over successive sessions, growing from about 15 to 20 percent at the beginning of treatment to as high as 65 to 70 percent toward the end.

Larry was released from this sentence about ten years ago. Felicity has been retrieving his cumulative correctional file at regular intervals. The file is always a thick one, revealing an immense number of charges, convictions and sentences, all of which stop abruptly following his release from that sentence ten years ago. Of course, it's always possible that Larry died, or that he moved out of the jurisdiction. It's also possible that he has been doing all sorts of violent actions but hasn't been caught. Who knows?

A Ground Mound

Lonnie was also encountered in the correctional system. He was in his mid-teens. He and his brother were terribly close. Of the pair, the older brother was the leader, and Lonnie played the role of a rather timid follower. He never said 'no' to anyone, especially his brother. He loved his brother dearly but was also somewhat afraid of him.

One day, the older brother suggested to Lonnie that they go hunting. Without anyone else's knowledge, they slung their rifles and went out to the woods. In a small clearing in the woods, the brother sat down and started to clean his gun. Lonnie was looking into the woods when, suddenly, he was startled with fear at the report of a gunshot right behind him. He spun around to find his much-loved brother lying on the ground writhing in pain from an accidental self-inflicted wound in the leg.

Lonnie was panic-stricken. He didn't know what to do. He could feel in sympathy an exaggerated degree of the pain his brother must be suffering. This created even more confusing distress within him. He could think of only one thing through his panic – a movie title, *They Shoot Horses, Don't They*. He aimed his rifle and shot his brother.

He was in greater panic still seeing his brother lying still and dead. He was in a worse state of confusion. He dug a shallow pit, buried his brother in it under a heap of soil, and rushed home to hide his own gun and to get busy as if he had been doing something alone all day.

This sad tale, almost better than any other, illustrates the root of most violence. It is fear. The learned drive of fear, like any other drive or motive, cumulates with other drives to add to the intensity of each. In Lonnie's case, fear of being angry or even assertive had been a life-long pattern. Fear of his brother may have increased his fear in his brother's company. In this incident, fear from the startling effect of the loud noise when his brother's gun accidentally went off undoubtedly added to this. Seeing his much loved brother suffering must certainly have added even more fear. The sympathetic pain he felt probably increased his arousal even further. Now his brain was in a whirl with fear so that he could not think clearly, and that probably increased his fear even more. The upsetting event devolved into the violent discharge of a gun, and left his confused mind to react to his extremity of fear, almost by hoping it had never happened – which didn't keep him from being convicted.

A Shifty Shafting

Anyone knows that's not what violence is about. But then there was Lucy. Lucy was a gentle and loving lady in her mid-thirties. She always did as she was told, and she did it at once. She was terrified that someone might not like her or, worse, that someone might get angry and even attack her.

She did not adopt the solution to her fear taken by Linc, another of Felicity's patients. Linc was a big, well-built young man in his early twenties. Out of fear that he might be attacked by others (Felicity never learned any event to justify this fear), he had gone into body-building and the martial arts. He had invested so much effort in the martial arts that he had become a black belt and a trainer in his own right. He remained terrified about others' anger and the possibility of being attacked.

But Lucy did not go the route of self-defence training. She married a big strong man partly so that she could feel 'safe' under his protection. But then she became fearful of his size and strength, fearing that he might get angry with her and attack her. To protect herself from this risk, she made herself utterly subservient to him.

One evening, her husband returned late from work. He was very drunk. He picked a fight with Lucy and, presumably sensing her fear and vulnerability as she cowered in front of him, he began to beat on her. He continued the beating for some time, and then, half in fatigue and half in alcoholic stupor, he fell back on the bed and went to sleep.

She was already in a panic and was feeling a great deal of pain from the beating. She feared he would wake and begin to beat her again. She looked desperately around for some means to placate him. The first thing that caught her eye was the iron sitting on the ironing board. Doing the ironing might pacify her husband. She picked up the iron. But she didn't know what to iron. So, to remind herself that she was doing this work for her husband, she put the iron down on his stomach [and if you believe that story, I have a bridge in Brooklyn that you might like to buy. RR]. Then she went to the closet to get one of his shirts, put the shirt on the ironing board and plugged the iron in. Her attention was drawn back to her husband again as he emitted a snort. She thought he was waking up and she became panicky again. In her panic, she forgot what she was doing and she cowered in a corner.

By the time her husband was awakened by the searing pain on his stomach, the slowly heating iron had produced fairly severe burns. He threw it off, leaped up and started once more to beat on Lucy. In time, the effort tired him out and he fell back once more exhausted on the bed. Her blind, traumatic panic aroused Lucy and she repeated the same action she had been doing just before the traumatizing attack. She put the iron back on her husband's stomach, plugged it in once more and then returned to cower in her corner. The iron had been pulled out of the wall when it was thrown off by her husband, and it had time to cool down again while he beat her. So when her husband was again awakened by the searing pain on his stomach he had even more severe burns. Once more he started to beat upon Lucy.

This cycle of events continued through the night. Finally, a neighbour was awakened by the commotion and phoned the police. When the police arrived, they found Lucy's husband suffering from extensive burns over most of his abdomen. And they found Lucy badly bruised and bleeding all over from the beatings she had received, and in a state of utter exhaustion. They admitted her husband to the nearest general hospital for treatment of his burns, and they admitted Lucy to the mental hospital to get first aid and to deal with her advanced state of exhaustion.

Felicity does not know what triggered Lucy's husband to his violence. He never met the husband. But he did meet Lucy, and there seemed little doubt that fear was the motive underlying her 'blind' violent acts. These were hardly acts of self-protection. One might imagine that they were acts of revenge. However, after her fears were moderated by a program of systematic anxiety desensitization using the RIT method described earlier, in Lucy's mind, the only motive she could identify as underlying her actions was nothing more than fear. This fear 'switched off' judgement and 'switched on' a series of automatic actions which, as it turned out, repeatedly had rather self-defeating results.

Surely these cases do not represent violence as it occurs in the real world. Perhaps not, but neither do the media stories in the newspapers or on television. The latter represent real fantasies of real fiction, and not the real world. Most frequently they are made up by even more fertile imaginations than Felicity's. And those that are reported as news are typically exaggerated, selected for their sensational and meaningless value, and presented without any appreciable understanding of the human qualities of those involved. Contrary to the fictional world according to television, contract murders and violence between strangers are rare indeed. Most violence springs from passion, and most often from the passion and the extremity of fear.

However, it is true that another kind of violence has been appearing in urban centres worldwide. This is the violence of riot and vandalism. Is that due to fear? Probably not. Activity (performed or witnessed), colour and noise have the automatic effect of arousing the autonomic nervous system. Colour and activity rivet attention to their sources, and noise scatters attention and thus self-control. Add to these stimuli a crowd of people to be mimicked and to augment excitement, and the conditions are ripe for riot. Although opportunism may play a role in looting, if the crowd's actions become destructive, the major factor causing vandalism seems to be the sense of the crowd's power. The individual that feels he participates in the group's power as if it were his own. This, coupled with any helplessness perceived in non-participants, can evoke sadism with its possibly destructive consequences.

CHAPTER 7

PHYSICAL HEALTH PROBLEMS

Physical Dis-ease

Here's where you can really get confused and have lots of fun. There are so many varieties of this sort of problem that it is hard to know where to start. In this set of tales any old order has been adopted to talk about a range of possible events. The main thing to note is that the types of health problems addressed are likely to stretch your credulity almost to the limit (the stories about madness will stretch it all the way to the limit, and some stories after that will go beyond the limit). But buck up, don't let your fancy flag – remember that all of this is pure fiction.

Let's start by being entertained at Felicity's expense. He's a pretty strange bird with his own problems – which, of course, like everybody else, he will try to blame on everybody else.

An Out-Grown In-Grown

In-grown toenails? That's right, Felicity had to suffer from that indignity. I know, in-grown toenails have almost nothing to do with psychotherapy. But the story may be instructive in its own way.

One day Felicity was limping around work. A friend asked him what was wrong. He complained about his in-grown toenail. His friend suggested he consult her podiatrist. He did so. The podiatrist examined the toe and said: "Yup, in-grown toenail."

When asked what he could do for it, the podiatrist said he would remove half the toenail and hope it would grow back in straight. That sounded to Felicity like surgery. So he went to see his physician to inquire about podiatrists since Felicity knew nothing about them. His physician told him to stay away from podiatrists – they were quacks (which, of course, only means a non-physician). He looked at the toe and said, "Yup, in-grown toenail," and referred Felicity on to a surgeon friend of his.

Felicity consulted the surgeon. He looked at it and said, "Yup, in-grown toenail." But he did add something helpful. He said it was a 'clubbed' toenail. Felicity asked him what that meant. He said that the toenail had become thick so it wouldn't lie flat any more. Felicity asked what he could do about it. The surgeon said there was only one thing to do about it. He would have to remove the entire toenail back behind the root so that it would never grow again – as it would just grow back in clubbed. Felicity looked appalled and suggested the ground would be awfully uncomfortable. The surgeon agreed: "Oh, you can't leave it like that. I would cover it with skin." Felicity asked where he would get the skin from, his bum? The surgeon said: "Oh no, it's got to be skin from the end of the toe." Felicity was dubious: "There isn't enough skin there – it won't stretch." "Oh, I know that," the surgeon smiled, "I'll have to cut off a bit of the bone to shorten the toe to get enough skin to wrap over it." "You want to do what!?" Felicity reacted, "Then I won't be able to get shoes to fit and I'll be lop-sided for the rest of my life." The surgeon shrugged with apparent indifference.

Thoroughly amused by the barbaric ideas of this strange surgeon, Felicity returned to his physician to share the joke with him. The physician listened to Felicity's light-hearted account of his visit to the surgeon. Then the physician affirmed that the surgeon had been right, and that such was the 'conventional medical practice' concerning in-grown toenails.

Now Felicity had had enough experience with physicians to know that the phrase 'conventional medical practice' is a hallowed one in medicine. It, not science, is the physician's final 'court of appeal'. Anything, other than what physicians in common are taught, is considered improper and, worse, sheer quackery. Felicity left, shaking his head and mumbling: "Quack, quack, quack!" Parenthetically, the word 'quack' is always used to refer to one whose point of view you do not share – unless the user is one duck speaking to another.

The next day, Felicity was talking with his psychologist friend – the one who had first stated the Principle of Perversity (Introduction). Felicity was laughing about his experience. His friend looked at Felicity thoughtfully. "If the problem is that the toenail is too thick," he said, "why not make it thinner with a nail-file?" (That sentence was the psychotherapy in this case.)

Felicity stopped laughing, went to the store and bought himself a nail file. He filed the surface of the offending toenail until it became a bit thinner. The next day he was gratified to notice that the toenail was now lying flatter and was no longer so in-grown. But that's not the end of the story.

A while later, Felicity was in a hospital for observation – surprisingly not a psychiatric hospital. He overheard two nurses talking. One said, "I see Mrs. Jones is back in the hospital again. She was in just a while ago for the in-grown toenail surgery, wasn't she?" The other replied, "Yes, now she's in for gangrene in that foot." Felicity was shocked. For want of a nail-file, the foot was lost!

<u>An If It Is Id [8] ...</u>

But psychotherapy does have greater relevance to Felicity's own life, if not to his in-grown toenail. In fact, Felicity has put himself through and has been put through psychotherapy quite a few times during his career. A couple of these experiences are relevant to the topics in this volume. One of them might be entertaining at this point. But first, what is this section about?

This small section might have been titled after one of the Songs of Couch and Consultation: 'Shrinker man, shrinker man, set me right if you can. Free me of my tics and twitches, disconnect my latent switches, shrinker man'. However, a title that long wouldn't fit on the one line it would be granted. The title aside, this section has to do with muscle anomalies.

Some people like to knit. Others like to watch sports. Felicity likes to type. Of course, since his fingers don't coordinate like any normal person's, so that he has never been able to learn to play the piano or type with all his fingers, he types using the 'pick-and-peck' method. One finger of his right hand types, while he uses two fingers of his left hand, one for the space bar and one for the shift key. In spite of the awkwardness of this method, he has worked his speed up until his right hand flies all over the keyboard at a seemly rate.

Now we get to the place where he blames everybody else for his own difficulties. The trouble is that whoever invented the keyboard put the 'i' at one side of the keyboard and the commonly associated 'd', 'f', 's' and 't' at the other side. Felicity used to complain that his left hand on the space and shift keys got in the way of his quick-draw right hand. Although there is probably another explanation for it, his problem was that if, for example, he wanted to type: 'if it is id ...', he would end up typing 'id id id id ...' Then he would be embarrassed if he didn't notice the error – his embarrassment probably revealing the real motivation underlying the typing error.

---

[8]   "Id" is German for "It," the term that Freud chose for the unconscious desires that "live" us, that govern so much of our behavior.

Well, he finally decided he had to do something about this embarrassing error. So he spent a great deal of time at his favourite pursuit in front of the typewriter consciously typing, 'id id id id', as though he was pretending to type 'if it is id' (There was probably another reason for doing this exercise, though you may be sure he wouldn't admit to it). Eventually, he achieved two effects from this 'psychotherapy'. First, he was finally able to type 'if it is id' accurately – to his relief, joy, and immense pride. Second, his sex drive, which was never very high, declined somewhat. But so much for personal revelations for now. Onwards to the interesting stuff.

An Idealistic Tic

Passionato was a sitarist (the sitar is an Indian guitar) of some renown in the area of India where he lived. He was seen at a clinic where Felicity was working as part of an assignment with the World Health Organization (WHO? World Health Organization, that's WHO). Actually, Felicity went to India in order to make sure the place really existed. He considered it possible that India might be just a figment of Rimsky Korsakov's fertile imagination. Does it exist? It does. Of course, that's just another affirmation in this book of lies. So, if you want to check out Rimsky-Korsakov's allegations in the Song of India, you'll have to take the trip yourself. Incidentally, this is not the same Sergei Korsakoff whose drinking habits made him renowned enough in medical circles that a condition was named after him. The latter's first name, in contrast to the former's last name, seems to be a matter of complete indifference to most people.

Anyway, Passionato was a sitarist who played beautifully at one time, but would not perform any more. The problem was that his playing arms (those were the arms with which he played, and not any other arms he might have possessed) hurt too much. Felicity was shown a taut band of muscle running down the inside of each forearm. It looked liked a tightened sitar string running just under the skin. It was chronically tight and terribly painful in spite of

Passionato's many efforts, on his own and with help, to relax these painful impediments to his ability to give pleasure to others. Felicity was being asked what could be done to treat this malady.

Have you ever tried to conduct psychotherapy through an interpreter? Well, don't. It's hard, although it is interesting. Even Felicity noticed a couple of things about this man. The first thing he noticed was that Passionato's sad face had a 'set' about it that involved some tense angularity of the line of his jaw. Felicity had seen that angularity (in place of a smooth curve) of the jaw line before in both homosexuals and obsessives. It seemed to his untutored eye that the angle was formed by chronic tension of the jaw muscles, as if the person was chronically clenching his teeth. At first, that reminded Felicity to think about the common apparent association between homosexuality and the selection of the performing arts as a vocation. But then he remembered the same morphology (look of the body) in non-homosexual obsessives. He remembered that what they often have in common is a certain level of unexpressed anger – although they often think of the targets of their anger quite differently. That reminded Felicity that people who are tensely angry often talk through clenched teeth as if to try to prevent opening their mouths and getting really mad.

The second thing Felicity noticed came from the interpreter. During the initial conversation together, while Felicity and Passionato were becoming acquainted, the interpreter rendered what Passionato said on three occasions using the English word 'contaminate'. Now this word is rather rarely used in ordinary social conversation. Felicity had heard that word used much more frequently by obsessives than by any other group of people. Consequently, the second time it was used by the interpreter, Felicity stopped him and asked him the Tamil word for 'contaminate' that Passionato had used. The interpreter gave a word. Felicity asked what the literal English translation of that word was. The interpreter was clear that it meant 'contaminate'. Later, just to confirm that the obsessive pathology did not belong to the interpreter, Felicity asked a couple of other Indian friends what the Tamil word meant. They agreed it meant 'contaminate'.

Now Felicity was really interested. Could it be that something in a particular psychological habit system could result in a kind of idea which is common across cultures, and which results in a common word usage to express the idea regardless of the language used? Who knows? Felicity certainly doesn't.

Felicity wondered if there were two interacting processes going on to maintain this man's muscle symptom. Could he have developed self-doubts about the perfection of his playing, or have felt resentment that his work wasn't appreciated enough, so that he was frustrated or angry enough to resist performing? And could he be trying too hard to relax as a way of 'fighting off' any anger or frustration he might be feeling – to keep his feelings under control? Both ideas would tend to fit with how obsessives react. Of course, these 'brilliant' psychological interpretations didn't help Felicity to figure out what to do. They were just further examples of thoughts Felicity had which didn't interest him.

Felicity tried something he realized could well risk his already shaky reputation with his hosts at the clinic. He asked Passionato to tense his fist, hand, and wrist in various ways in order to increase the tension of those painful bands of muscles. He watched as Passionato tried every way to tense every other set of muscles and to stretch or relax the tight band. Through the interpreter (who may have feared interpreting correctly), Felicity tried to shape Passionato's efforts toward tensing the very bands which were already much too tense. At first, it didn't work.

Then Felicity turned Passionato's attention to his jaw muscles. He asked him to tense them. He could do that easily. He asked him to pay strict attention to how he was tensing his jaw muscles and to see if he could reverse the process. He could do that almost to the point that the jaw line reverted to a smooth curve. He then asked Passionato to hold his jaw as tense as he could for as long as he could. He encouraged him to keep it tight. Minutes ticked by. Twenty minutes elapsed. Suddenly, Passionato's jaw started to tremble and twitch. Then it fell open. Through the interpreter, Felicity kept encouraging Passionato to tense his jaw muscles. After about two minutes the sharp angle of the law line re-appeared. It held for about ten minutes before it started trembling and then fell open again. There was more encouragement. After about a minute the sharp angle of the jaw developed again. This process was continued for another twenty-five minutes, during which there were three more minute-long periods of twitching and sagging jaw activities.

Meanwhile, Felicity kept watching the tense bands along the forearms while this focus of attention on the jaw was going on. They were steadily becoming less apparent. Felicity asked Passionato not to move in any way, and then asked him just to look down at his forearms. Shock registered on his face and on the face of the interpreter as they stared at the smooth forearms. Then the tight bands in the arms grew once more as if stretched by the fixed stare of the two men.

Felicity asked Passionato to tighten up the bands as much as he could now. He did. He was asked to practice that exercise of tightening them and letting them go over and over again to feel what it felt like to control both actions from inside himself. He was seen again the next day. He was strumming cautiously on his sitar. Felicity asked him to 'put that thing away'. The intended result was achieved. He seemed offended and he stared at Felicity as though the latter had just made a perverse and profane demand. However, he did as he was asked.

Felicity now had him tense and hold his shin muscles by pulling his feet up into a sharp acute angle. He did so for a while, and the bands in his forearms slowly let go. Then Felicity asked him to let go his shin muscles and to tighten up his forearms so the bands would re-appear. Passionato did so, and Felicity asked him to hold that position as tightly as he could. Passionato complained that it was very painful to do so. Felicity feigned sympathy, but affirmed that it was necessary.

With genuine courage and continuous encouragement, Passionato held the forearms in tight flexion, keeping the bands standing up tightly for an hour and a half. It seemed likely that his willingness to try was predicated largely on the magical things that had happened when he followed Felicity's directions with his jaw muscles. About fifteen minutes after he started the tensing of his forearm (the shorter time presumably being due to the fact that the muscles had already been held pretty tensely while he was practising on the sitar), the wrist and arm muscles started to twitch and then they simply went limp. He was encouraged to tense the arm again. He managed to do so after about a minute had elapsed. He held it again for about eight minutes before the twitching and flaccidity re-emerged. The process continued for the rest of the 'session', with about eight minutes of tenseness interspersed with one minute intervals of twitching followed by quiescence. Passionato was impressed with this effect on the muscles of his forearms. But he was more impressed when Felicity said he could rest now and stop the tensing. Almost immediately, the tight bands along his forearms let go and the forearms recovered their normal smooth, fleshy tone.

The interpreter continued the exercises with Passionato for two weeks while Felicity was away on tour. When Felicity returned, the clinic was buzzing with excitement. Passionato had recovered, and he had just given the staff a concert on the sitar.

He gave Felicity a private concert before leaving to return home. Not having much couth, and thus not being much of a connoisseur of any music including that of the sitar, Felicity sat listening absolutely riveted and entranced. He was watching Passionato's forearms. The muscles in them rippled easily as he played and there was no special band of muscles visible anywhere. The sub-dermal sitar strings were gone, and the muscle action was smooth and painless. Even Passionato's jaw line was smoothly curved and at peace as his face was transported to a mystical world in which the harps of heaven played gently and lovingly to him.

A Realistic Tic

Perry was referred to Felicity for treatment of his severe spasmodic torticollis. That means that the muscles at the back of his neck and shoulder kept tensing suddenly, twisting his head sharply around to the right through almost 90 degrees of rotation and his chin was pulled down and his head tilted backwards. Some of the time, if he wanted to see where he was going, he would literally have to walk sideways. Besides, it was painful. His condition was sufficiently severe that his physician had said that if he could not soon get rid of the torticollis, they would have to cut the nerve feed to the affected muscles surgically so that he would be partially unable to turn his head in that direction any more. What a barbaric thought! I suppose that when you only have a hammer, everything you see looks like a nail.

Now Felicity knew of an instance in which treatment using EMG-feedback had made a case of torticollis worse. EMG stands for electromyograph, which is the recording device for measuring muscle potentials. That big word reduces to 'electro', meaning the measurement or recording of electrical potentials, from the 'myo' or muscle cells. The muscle cells are activated by the electrical potentials of the motor nerves that feed the muscles. These electrical potentials are recorded on a 'graph' to display changes in them. How do you like that for a complicated statement about something quite simple?

Fortunately, Felicity also knew the mistake that was made by the psychiatrist in using the EMG-feedback in that other case. A big complicated instrument called a polygraph (literally, a unit containing many channels for graphing from many electrode pick ups) had been set up to record several EMG channels. Electrodes, to pick up EMG signals from the muscles, had been stuck on the patient's shoulders and upper back. The idea was to detect and record the amount of tensing of the muscles involved in the torticollis over long intervals of time. The polygraph had been set up in advance with threshold filters, so that when a strong EMG signal was detected by the machine it could switch off something else – in this case a record player. When there was little or no activity recorded from the muscles, the record player would be switched on again. The recorded music was to serve as 'feedback' so that, as it was switched off and on by the polygraph relays, it would tell the patient how he was doing – hopefully to help him learn how he could relax the muscles involved in his symptoms.

The idea was an elaborate one and not bad in its essential conception. But nobody listened to Felicity when he pointed out that a basic mistake was being made. The patient loved classical music. So did the psychiatrist. The psychiatrist assumed that the patient's love of classical music would result in her receiving pleasure, and thus 'reward', while the music was on. This was the only instance in which Felicity's general and uncouth view that music is just unwelcome noise was right. Many people would understand this idea if it referred to the gentle melodic refrains of contemporary music – which combines the mellifluous tones of jack hammers, pile drivers, dentists' drills, cannon fire and ricocheting bullets, all recorded in a tin can, and played at peak volume for the benefit of the stone deaf. Few would accept the idea that Felicity's views apply equally to classical music. But, whether pleasant or not, all music is noise and, especially if it is liked, it is arousing – it gets the person tense. So turning on the music when the patient was relaxed made her tense, and turning it off when she was tense was calming. It was her symptomatic tension that was being rewarded or reinforced, and so the method taught her to increase her symptoms and their strength.

Now the psychiatrist who had done this experimental EMG-feedback procedure with this lady was Dr. Asch. So when Perry was referred to Felicity for treatment of his torticollis, Felicity got an interesting (to him) idea. He decided to repeat the experiment, but to 'reverse the contingencies' in order to be able to do the same experiment Asch-backwards. He connected EMG electrodes to Perry's skin over the muscles near those involved in the torticollis. He arranged for varying electronic sounds, including static (the only cognate for music he recognized), to be fed to a single earphone in Perry's ear. These sounds were switched on while there was above-threshold (tense) activity from the muscles and switched off when there was below-threshold (non-)activity from the muscles.

Meanwhile, he sat with Perry and taught him the art of deep relaxation of all the voluntary muscles in his body. The procedure was continued after Perry had learned to relax well, with Felicity shifting to what is called 'differential muscle relaxation' – the skill of relaxing separate muscle groups separately when they are not being used, even if other muscles are being used.

Perry's spasms soon began to occur less and less frequently and, when they did occur, they started to be less and less severe. Within twenty-five sessions, there were no visible occurrences in his daily life of the torticollis. There were still some mild spasmodic EMG activity from the affected muscles. The procedure was continued for another five sessions until the EMG no longer recorded any spasms even when he moved shoulder or arm muscles on either side voluntarily – except, of course, for the EMG activity associated with the movements.

Felicity told Perry he did not know whether the effects would last indefinitely. He encouraged Perry to make contact with him again if the torticollis returned at all, saying it would likely require very few sessions to reinstate the calm habit. Perry was delighted with the results and assured Felicity he would be in touch if it happened again. That was twenty years ago, and Felicity has heard nothing more from Perry.

A Ticklish Tic

But who can afford to set up a complicated EMG device with relays and feedback systems built in to deal with other cases of torticollis? Few can, especially since these cases are quite rare. But there is a less rare situation that is, in some ways, an analog to the problem presented by torticollis. These are the hyperactive children and young people of the world.

Now, one should be very careful about interpreting hyperactivity as 'just' that. We can easily be misled by noticing the obvious. A couple of examples might be instructive.

A mother brought her five-year old son to see Felicity. She was at her wits end. The child was not yet toilet trained and would urinate night or day in his pants. Now Felicity is not fond of young children and he didn't relish having a kid hanging around wetting on his furniture and dribbling on his rug. So he thought he might just turn the task back to the mother – poor thing. He asked the mother how old her child was. She said he was five. Felicity asked how old she thought of him as being. She said she thought of him as five and, frankly, she was worried about how the other children at school would take to his wetting himself. Felicity asked her whether she would be as worried about it if the child was two years old. She said she would not. Felicity asked what she would do about the problem if the child was two. She said, she would toilet train him. Felicity beamed. "Wonderful," he said, "so why don't you take him home, think of him as two years old, and toilet train him." He added that it would be nice if she would phone him in a couple of weeks to let him know how she was doing. She did. And she reported that she had successfully toilet trained him and he was no longer wetting himself.

But that refers to the effects of a simple expectation. Here is another story that is even more instructive and more serious. A young person in his late teens was admitted to the old mental hospital where Felicity had worked. The presenting symptom was 'head banging'. Everybody assumed he must be mentally retarded, doing as many mentally disadvantaged people were known to do, namely, to rock and to bang their heads on the wall fairly continuously. Still, there was a risk that the concussion from the head banging might do harm to his brain, his skull, or the retinas of his eyes. So the staff thought something ought to be done about this symptom. Felicity was asked to see him.

Psychologists do psychological tests, right? So Felicity administered an intelligence test to the patient to confirm that he was mentally handicapped. The patient did not like the testing, and he winced repeatedly when Felicity asked him questions. But the intelligence test score was well within the 'normal' range. Ouch! This young person was not mentally retarded. So what was the matter? Felicity hugged the medical staff to check him out. Finally, they did. He was found to have an abscess in the middle ear. It hurt like hell, and he preferred to distract himself from the earache with the pain from the head banging. It's not a bad idea to find the cause of something before you spend too much time trying to treat the symptom(s).

But Philip was just a restless, hyperactive boy in his mid-teens. He had been hyperactive all his life. In his mid-teens he was assaulted by a group of boys who pounced upon him unawares. His parents feared that he may have been traumatized by this incident. And certainly the scores on the tests seemed to confirm that he was suffering from traumatically-conditioned anxiety of fairly recent origin. Felicity decided to try to get rid of the anxiety by means of Wolpe's reciprocal inhibition therapy (**RIT**) and, when that failed, by means of Quirk's stimulus conditioned autonomic response suppression (**SCARS**) procedure (described in other stories). Neither method worked.

The problem was that Philip could not, or would not, sit still. As a result he could not relax for **RIT**, and no stable **GSR** measure could be obtained to allow conditioning in **SCARS**. Felicity had already found a way to deal with this accessory problem in some other similar cases.

A friend and colleague had an organization working with him. One part of that organization designed and built electronic equipment to specifications. Felicity got a friend to arrange to have an 'immobility conditioner' built for him. The equipment they developed required a neon light bar on one side of the subject, shining its light across the surface of the reclining person's body. On the other side of the person was a stand on which was the immobility conditioning unit. It was a little box with a photo-sensitive (light-sensitive) electronic sensor on it pointed across the subject toward the light. There was a knob on the box with which Felicity could adjust the threshold response so that sound either was or was not emitted from the speaker in the box. Then the volume knob was turned up full. If the unit was adjusted just right, any time the person moved just a bit, thus changing the light or shadow pattern reaching the photo-sensor, the unit's oscillator switched on and a loud, shrieking sound was emitted by the speaker. As soon as the shadow or light pattern returned to its former state, the sound would stop. This little unit proved very effective in stopping restlessness and hyper-activity during treatment sessions, thus allowing desensitization procedures to be undertaken.

It worked very nicely with Philip. Once he had stopped moving about on the reclining chair, he learned quickly to relax, and the RIT method for desensitization was completed in 15 sessions. Of course, all Felicity had done was to use a cheaper and simpler procedure than the analogous EMG-feedback procedure to do much the same thing. No doubt, people who like to spend money on TV's, computers, and other electronic systems would be able to achieve the same result using an interesting pattern on a monitor (for the subject to watch) controlled by any of a number of types of devices for detecting muscle potentials or movements.

A Mortified Mortician

At the other pole, there was Peter. Peter phoned to arrange an appointment to see Felicity. When he entered the office, Felicity became genuinely alarmed. He feared Peter had come into his office to die. The man he saw was in his mid-thirties. He was emaciated and pale. He looked like a ghost, or like death not yet warmed over. The man had bones and he had skin, but there was hardly any flesh at all. That's right, he looked like a skeleton with some pasty white skin stretched over it. Felicity marvelled at the fact he was walking at all. What could he possibly want with Felicity? He ought surely to be living in a hospital.

And he had been living in hospitals undergoing tests of all kinds to find out what was wrong with him. Finally, some physician had decided that he must have an ample dose of thanatos (death wish) and had referred him to a string of psychiatrists, and finally to Felicity. Felicity was fascinated with the idea, but he didn't know what to do about it. So he did the same thing each of the physicians had done in the past. He took a history.

Until his early twenties, Peter had been a robust, hardy and athletic young man. At about twenty-five, his physical condition started to decline. He felt sick to his stomach all the time and he often had cramps and diarrhoea. There was no accident near that time or before it to help account for the change. He had not been sick at all prior to that. Felicity was not satisfied with that report and he pushed for a detailed history of illnesses. Peter had paid a visit to Mexico in his early twenties and he contracted 'Montezuma's Revenge'. But he got that under control quickly.

Felicity asked how he had got it under control. He said he had gone to a physician in Mexico who had prescribed antibiotics for him and he had started taking them. Felicity asked what kind of antibiotics he had received. Peter said he didn't know, but they were nicely flavoured lozenges which were available across the counter. Pressed for more details, Peter said he knew he couldn't get these things at home and so, since he liked their taste, he brought bags of them home with him. Had he used them? He had. In fact, he enjoyed them so much he ate them like candies, and he had a big enough supply of them to last him for almost a year.

Felicity groaned a sigh of understanding. He asked Peter if he drank much milk. Oh yes, his doctor had told him to drink lots of milk for its good nutrients to try to build his body back up again. Felicity scowled and bit his tongue. "OK," he said, writing down a list of names on a slip of paper, "I want you to go to a health food store and make a purchase. Buy the first product I have listed and try it for two weeks. If you feel no change, try the second product for two weeks, and so on down the list. And I want you to come in to see me to monitor how you're doing every two weeks. And phone me if you feel there is anything unusual or wrong." A psychologist giving a prescription? Preposterous!

Peter was astonished too. He asked Felicity what the pills he was being asked to buy were. Felicity agreed he owed Peter an explanation for this unexpected development. He pointed out to

Peter that antibiotics do not just kill foreign bugs that attack the body. They kill any kind of bugs, both good and bad. Now, there are flora and bacteria in the intestines which are there to maintain the health of the body. One set of these healthy and normal flora are called lactobacillus acidophilus. Their job is to help in digestion of the lactic acid in milk. If these healthy flora were killed off by the long-term use of antibiotics, then Peter would be unable to digest milk products. The lactic acid should produce the very kinds of intestinal symptoms he had reported, and the associated intestinal activity could easily prevent the digestion of other foodstuffs he ate. The pills that Felicity was suggesting were various brand names under which lactobacillus acidophilus is sold. He thought the first on the list was the best, and so he had suggested Peter start with it. Through the mask of his stretched facial skin, Peter looked as though he was completely confused, but he said he would try it out as nothing else had worked. He said he would phone if anything seemed to be going wrong.

When Peter appeared for his next appointment two weeks later, Felicity gave a double and triple 'take'. Felicity's reaction was not lost on Peter and he smiled and chuckled with pride. Where was the ghost? The man who presented himself at Felicity's door had colour in his skin. The pasty look was gone. There was even a little fullness in his cheeks. The deeply sunken, hollow eyes seemed almost alive in contrast to their former appearance. In place of the stooped posture and the laboured movements that had seemed to exhaust him, he stood erect, almost as though he had some liveliness. He reported that he had experienced no cramps, no diarrhoea, and no sense of feeling sick to his stomach. His appetite had improved radically. He had recovered his good mood and some sense of energy and vitality. Felicity bantered with him. "No, you can't do that to me," he complained, "How will I ever survive in business? You get feeling awful at once, do you hear," and the like. Peter was absolutely delighted with himself.

He was seen for the next two months on a fortnightly basis. He began to put on weight as the flesh filled up under his skin. His appetite was excellent, and he began talking about the huge lunches or suppers he had eaten. The bony look of the skeleton disappeared, and a slim but robust looking body was building.

When it seemed there was nothing left to do and Felicity was about to send him back to see the referring physician, Felicity received a call from the physician asking whether Peter had yet made contact. There was a tone of concern in the physician's voice that vanished when Felicity said that Peter had indeed made contact. Felicity asked why the physician was concerned. The physician replied, "If you've seen him, you'll know what worries me. I don't know how much longer he can survive." Felicity said that he thought Peter was doing pretty well, and that he was about to ask Peter, who was with him right then, to have a check-up with his physician. The physician took this as reason for concern and he said he could see Peter right away. Since Felicity's office was in the next building, perhaps Felicity could bring him right over.

Felicity had a break in his schedule and he agreed to do so, thinking that the physician might have some intelligence to share with him face-to-face. The physician was standing in his waiting room as Peter and Felicity entered. The physician greeted Felicity, looked out the waiting room door as if trying to find someone else, then turned and looked at Peter while enquiring of Felicity if Peter had not been able to make it over. Peter emitted a bright laugh and said, "Hi doc. Don't you remember me? I'm Peter." The physician stared at him in disbelief. Then he sank in mute and utter shock into one of the waiting room chairs. The receptionist, who had been listening to what was taking place, rushed out of her room into the waiting room, stood in front of Peter and stared at him. She almost screamed at him: "Peter, are you in there!? What happened to you?" "I got better," he replied.

The physician got up and ushered Peter into his office, calling back over his shoulder to Felicity, "I've got some more patients to refer to you." Of course, he never did. Felicity was used to the fact that in this business, if you 'invent a better mouse-trap' people will avoid you like the plague.

Peter came to see Felicity two weeks later for his next appointment. He said that the physician had examined him and declared him recovered. Then the physician had wanted to know what Felicity had done to him. The physician probably thought that Felicity must have used hypnosis to achieve this miraculous cure. When Peter told him about the lactobacillus acidophilus, the physician was reported to have snorted something like, "Is he practising medicine without a license?" Felicity shrugged. They both chuckled a little. Then Peter made his way off into the sunset, but not on a white horse – his own legs were quite strong enough to support him now.

A Tubal Trouble

The state of the body is not only understood by looking at its outside. It can often be experienced from the inside. Of course, sometimes the inside condition can't be experienced directly. Phoebe was such a person. She was referred to Felicity by her obstetrician and gynaecologist. Phoebe and her husband wanted to have a baby, but there was something wrong. It was discovered that Phoebe's fallopian tubes were too tight to permit an ovum to pass through into the uterus. While air pressure could be used to demonstrate the tubal constriction and also to create temporary expansion of the tubes, it did not help to keep the tubes open. The physician thought it possible that some hidden conflict in Phoebe's unconscious might be causing Phoebe to tighten her tubes. Perhaps Felicity could unburden Phoebe of this conflict.

Felicity thought it was an interesting challenge. He had (and has) no idea how the tubes might get tightened up, and he was far too impatient to wait through years of psychotherapy for the patient to be unable to unravel the mystery for him. So he decided on the basis of the psychological tests that the problem was merely that Phoebe was too anxious and uptight, and that uptightness for her had a visceral target. Perhaps reducing her anxiety arousal generally might turn the trick.

He selected Quirk's stimulus conditioned autonomic response suppression (SCARS) as the method of choice for the desensitization. There was nothing clever about this decision. He simply reasoned that using the galvanic skin resistance (GSR) as the response through which to train anxiety reduction would be more relevant to how the insides of the body functioned than using relaxation training of the skeletal muscles (as in Wolpe's RIT method). Since Eysenck's Extraversion score suggested that she conditioned at an average rate, he set out to do thirty-three half-hour sessions (the average number) of SCARS.

Now Phoebe and her husband had been trying to get her pregnant for about six years without success. The 33 sessions took about eighteen weeks to complete. By session twenty she reported that her period was late. By the time they had finished the treatment program, her pregnancy was confirmed and she was well on her way to having the hoped for baby. She phoned Felicity as soon as the baby was born. He was in good health and she was ecstatic. Who knows what happened? Certainly not Felicity.

A Crohn's Cronies

One day, a friend, Penny, phoned Felicity. She asked if she could see him on a professional basis. When she arrived, she looked depressed and distraught. Felicity was alarmed and asked her what was the matter. She said she had to come to grips with her mortality as her doctor had just told her she was going to die.

Felicity felt like using some obscenities. He refrained and asked her please to fill him in. She said she had been suffering acute pain in her lower abdomen and she had consulted her physician about it. He had run a series of tests on her and then had called her in. He had informed her that she had Terminal Ileitis.

Felicity asked her what that meant to her. She said that, as far as she knew, 'terminal' meant it would result in death, and she understood that 'ileitis' meant the dread killer was Crohn's disease.

Felicity asked Penny what else her doctor had told her about this condition. She said he had told her that she would be started on cortisone, and that if the disease progressed she would have to have, possibly repeated, surgery to try to halt the progression. Felicity was unable to contain himself any more. He swore using some 'street' invective. Then he apologized to Penny.

He said: "I'm truly sorry you got in the hands of a twit, Penny. Let me explain what all that is about. The phrase 'terminal ileitis' refers to swelling or inflammation (-itis) of the part of the body called the 'terminal ilium'. The terminal ilium is the last little part of the small intestine before it connects with the large intestine or colon. It is called 'terminal', in healthy people too, because it is the last little part of the ilium. Terminal Ileitis, or swelling of that part is called Crohn's disease. It is not fatal. Crohn's disease, for the patient, is a source of pain and anxiety. Crohn's disease, for the surgeon, is a wonderful source of income. What may make Crohn's disease dangerous, and perhaps even fatal, is the treatment it receives from the physician.

"The chemotherapy is usually cortisone. Cortisone is a naturally occurring stress hormone produced by the adrenal cortex, and its effect is, among other things, to settle down arousal or activation of the immune response of the body. When it is given as an exogenous substance (as a medication) it tends to lull the immune system. That reduces the irritability of body tissues, usually reduces the swelling (or '-itis') and thus usually reduces the pain. Over long maintenance use, it also lulls the immune system such that it may not respond well to infection. Infection may then spread, and that can be dangerous.

"If the medication is not working well enough, the other choice available to physicians is surgery. The surgeon may go in and cut out the affected (*not* infected) part of the small intestine. If the pain recurs, he may go in again and again to cut out more and more of the intestine − if the patient allows him to do so. Of course, as the intestine is thus shortened, it becomes harder and harder for the body to retrieve nutrients from the food it receives, and that may make the person weaker and weaker, and less able to cope in a robust way with the strains of living. Also, each time the surgeon cuts into the body it represents a serious and stressful insult to the system, as well as causing injury to which the body may react with other kinds of conditions.

"So what am I saying to you? Don't do it! Let's, please, think this thing through together." For reasons Felicity never understood, Penny had always liked and trusted him. She was shocked at her misunderstanding of what the physician had told her. She was relieved by what she now had heard. But she was fearful that on this occasion Felicity had things wrong. She pleaded for some confirmation of what he had told her. So, together, they looked up some medical texts to be sure Felicity was right. Once she felt she had confirmed and understood the information she had received, she asked what they could do about her condition.

They started with 'the basics'. Inflammation or swelling of any tissue occurs when the body's immune system identifies a substance or object as being foreign. For example, some respiratory system cells can react to environmental substances (allergens) as if they were dangerous when they are not; some skin cells can simulate the reaction of becoming infected, and thus may form pimples; and some intestinal cells can produce a reaction to some kind of food or substance in the intestines, as in Crohn's disease.

There are several parts of the immune system's reaction. Fluid is pumped into the area, causing swelling, which may be painful. The blood vessels dilate or expand, causing redness or inflammation and allowing an increase in the number of white cells that can get at the area to attack and kill any infection. The suffix 'itis' refers to the swelling and inflammation.

The immune system is activated by the autonomic nervous system, which stimulates and orchestrates it. The autonomic nervous system, in turn, has been activated by the brain, which has identified some 'danger' within the body, the system that it regulates and controls. The brain and autonomic nervous system, being nervous tissue, can learn to recognize and react to dangers, apparent or real. Similarly, they can be taught to stop reacting to unreal dangers.

Is there any real 'danger' there for the body to react to? Perhaps, but it is more likely there is none. If there was something there which really threatened the body's survival, either the danger would have been dealt with by the immune response or, within at most weeks, the uncontrolled danger or infection would have spread pretty widely and the person would be dreadfully sick or dead. By the time the inflammation has been there for, let's say, six months, something other than an active or infectious agent is 'causing' the continuation of the symptoms. What could that something be?

Although some kinds of chronic diseases seem to travel in families, any genetic factor involved tends to provide only a weak pre-disposition to 'react' in the way defined by the disease. The effect of a weak genetic link rarely insures the development of the illness – although this is not always true, witness a straight hereditary disease like Huntingdon's Chorea. But let's talk about the emergence of a disease as if it were the overflow from a cup. There may be some sediment filling the bottom of the cup from a genetic factor. Then there is some amount of 'fill' in the cup from the amount of the irritating substance (poison, infection, or allergen) available to the person – too much may fill the cup because the system can't deal with it, although that too is rare. The third, and last, thing which is poured into the cup is the available 'reactivity' of the target kind of tissue – this is usually a general bodily 'reactivity', but it may be specific to the particular tissue. This 'reactivity' is probably best represented by the reactivity of the person's immune system or, which is the same thing, the reactivity of the person's autonomic-stress nervous system. If these three things added together produce 'enough' total reaction, the cup may over-flow or the threshold of the illness may be exceeded, and the illness develops.

Now, we can't easily alter the person's genetic inheritance. But by living under reasonably sanitary conditions we can usually control the amounts of poisons or infections getting into our systems – that's what public health is all about. But the thing we really can control is the 'reactivity' of our stress systems. That is why cortisone is used to treat so many immune diseases, like Crohn's disease. It damps down and lulls the immune reactivity. But it also suppresses the immune response making it hard for the body to rally to fight off infections. There is another way.

The other way is to help the immune system to get some rest. That not only lulls it a bit, but it also keeps it fresh and ready to deal with poisons, infections, and allergens if it needs to. This other way, unfortunately, is not generally understood by physicians. It involves training the autonomic nervous system into a peaceful and restful state. The standard ways to do this are called stress or anxiety desensitization methods. And there are several of them. To deal with a physiological response within the body, perhaps the best method is Quirk's stimulus conditioned autonomic response suppression (SCARS) method (described in several other stories).

Penny decided to try SCARS. Galvanic skin resistance (GSR) electrodes were attached to her right hand. She was shown sets of slides related generally to the classes of anxiety that she reported on a Fears Survey Schedule. Every time her GSR response increased (less physiological arousal as indicated by less palmar sweat) by at least 1,000 ohms, the slide she was looking at was changed to serve as a 'reward' for her body having 'calmed down' by a small amount. There were thirty-five half-hour sessions. She was on cortisone at the beginning of this treatment program, so that it was impossible to tell when the inflammation stopped. About two-thirds of the way through the SCARS programme, she stopped using the cortisone. There was no pain, nor has she had any more bouts of pain in the fifteen years since this treatment was completed. It seems to have terminated her terminal ileitis.

A Pyloric Re-tread

And then there was Paul. Paul had developed kidney failure. A suitable donor was found, and he had a kidney transplant. Unfortunately, the body's immune system identified the donated kidney as foreign tissue and started to attack it. That is, organ rejection started to take place.

His physicians did the usual thing. They put him on quite massive doses of cortisone to lull the immune system, hoping the transplanted organ would start to be recognized as a personal belonging after a while. The organ rejection continued and the cortisone levels were increased.

At this point, Paul consulted Felicity. He asked whether some method of psychotherapy might help to limit the organ rejection. Felicity agreed it wouldn't hurt to try. They started on a program of SCARS, as described with Penny just now. By half-way through the program, the indications of organ rejection were weaker and the cortisone was cut back. By the end of the program, the indications of organ rejection had stopped and Paul was off all cortisone. He remained healthy during the next five years of occasional contact.

Did the cortisone finally turn the trick? Did the body just stop trying to reject its new organ? Did the SCARS treatment help? Felicity doesn't know. Whatever position (belief) you happen to hold, the SCARS method was at least like chicken soup – it may not have helped, but it couldn't hurt.

A Misplaced Plaque

Priscilla collapsed one day at home. She was taken to the hospital where, after a number of tests, she was diagnosed as having Multiple Sclerosis. Cortisone was prescribed to help her body function more effectively, and she was released home. But then she began to fall down and lose consciousness. She was subjected to a C.T. Scan and an EEG. The C.T. Scan showed that the plaques on her nerve fibres, which were thought to represent the underlying pathology in Multiple Sclerosis (MS), had progressed to her brain. The EEG results showed that she was subject to epilepsy. The events in which she fell and lost consciousness were diagnosed as grand mal epilepsy.

Dilantin and Phenobarb were prescribed to deal with her epilepsy. However, even although the dosages were increased greatly, the seizures continued. She had to be admitted to hospital from time to time, both due to MS 'episodes' in which she lost control over her body and could not move, and due to injuries suffered in falling during her epileptic seizures.

The neurologist was concerned because the seizures could not be controlled with medication. So he referred Priscilla to Felicity to see if he could reduce the rate of occurrence of the seizures. The referral and the case appeared to be a fairly straight-forward task of seizure frequency reduction. So Felicity used Sterman's SMR training method for the purpose. He connected EEG electrodes to Priscilla's scalp near the C3-C4 sites, and began training Priscilla's brain toward an increased production of sensorimotor rhythm (SMR). This was done by providing whistling 'feedback' contingent upon SMR production – this means the whistle was turned on when SMR was present and off when SMR was absent. This procedure has been described in several other stories.

There were twenty-five sessions of SMR training. The seizures stopped a quarter of the way through this training, and they continued to be absent when the anti-convulsant medications were withdrawn. This was all that had been expected or hoped for. But something else happened too. Although the losses of functioning – in vision and muscle coordination – did not reverse themselves, there were no more of the attacks or 'episodes' by which MS typically progresses, and there was no further deterioration of her physical and mental functioning. Fifteen years later she remains able to function at the same relative levels at which she was functioning at the end of this treatment. And there have been no further seizures or MS episodes, although she has remained off the anti-convulsants and the cortisone. How come? Felicity can only guess, since these stories are entirely anecdotal and in no way represent scientific studies.

A Nervous Nervosa

In a way, Pam presented a treatment problem similar to Priscilla's. Pam was a pretty young lady in her early twenties. The only thing that marred her beauty was that she was terribly skinny – emaciated, in fact. The trouble was that she was afraid to eat. When she was referred to Felicity she had been diagnosed as suffering from anorexia nervosa.

Like so many so-called diagnoses, anorexia subsumes a lot of different kinds of conditions. The risk with most of them is that the patient will become dehydrated or starved and will die. Pam had spent a great deal of time in hospital where the main effort, other than investigating her, had been to keep nutrients going into her to prevent her from dying. There was still no satisfactory way to account for her anorexia.

Felicity did his usual thing of administering and scoring a number of psychological tests. Once more, the Differential Diagnostic Technique (DDT) provided the main useful information. This test was described in Chester's case, and has been referred to often in the foregoing. The test showed that Pam had a particular problem in perceiving visual angle, seen in handling straight-line as compared to curved-line figures. And the size of the discrepancy was such that it could not properly be accounted for on the basis of commonly recognized personality problems. It occurred to Felicity that the problem in the perception of visual angle implied by these test findings suggested that Pam had an irritative focus in her brain, in the area of the 'drive centre'.

Although you might think this finding is becoming a bit boring, in this case it seems likely that the part of the 'drive centre' implicated in Pam's partial seizures might be the satiety centre. That is, if electrical short-circuiting was repeatedly triggering electrical activity in the satiety centre, Pam's body would constantly feel as though it had already eaten, was satisfied, and required no food. If this strange hypothesis was valid, then using Sterman's method to train her brain to increase its output of sensorimotor rhythm (SMR) might prevent the short-circuiting so that she would no longer feel as though she was stuffed with food and she might start eating. The idea at least warranted a test.

Pam went through a total of twenty-two half-hour sessions in which she received a whistling sound whenever her EEG showed any SMR activity from the C3-C4 sites, and silence when there was no SMR activity there. Her time-integrated SMR production rose from about 8 percent during the first sessions to about 50 percent during the last sessions. By the fifteenth session she had started eating and was recovering some weight. By the last session, her weight was approaching a normal weight (for her height) of about 115 pounds. She reported that her appetite had returned and that she enjoyed eating again. What happened? Is EEG-SMR training a way to develop aesthetic sensibilities to create one who appreciates good food?

A Vascular Vagary

Pat was suffering from intense headaches. The referring physician said that she was having migraine attacks. Felicity checked out the other possibilities to account for her headaches. There was no reason to suppose she was having sinus or tension headaches. Certainly she was having the visual disturbances and the nausea that often go along with migraine; and besides, she had already been seen by her physician.

Migraine is supposed to be a vascular disorder – affecting the blood vessels. What is supposed to happen is that the blood vessels start to spasm – to tighten closed and then loosen open quickly, like a tremor of the muscles of the blood vessel walls. Although, in principle, the dilated or open condition of the blood vessels is generally the healthy way for them to be, the pain of migraine is thought to come from the rapid opening or dilation of the blood vessels in this 'tremor'. To achieve a healthy state, the task is to get the blood vessels to remain relaxed and open.

Now, in a standard temperature environment, the only thing that alters the skin temperature is the volume of blood in the peripheral blood vessels (just under the skin). If the blood vessels near the skin dilate, the volume of blood flowing through them and getting near the skin surface increases and the skin temperature rises. Among other things, this allows the body to release heat from the skin surface to the environment, and it is why some people have warm skin. If the blood vessels near the skin contract or tighten up, the volume of blood reaching them and getting near the skin surface is reduced and the skin temperature declines (gets lower). Among other things, this allows the body to conserve its heat, and it is why some people have colder skin.

The only way to increase skin temperature is to increase the volume of your blood near the skin. This can be done by training the peripheral blood vessels to dilate and to remain dilated, as in a method developed by Green as a specific treatment for Migraine and for Raynaud's disease (patches of cold skin). If a person who is prone to migraine can do that, the migraines usually stop.

Pat agreed to try a bit of skin temperature biofeedback training. She had a thermistor (a temperature pick up) affixed to the palmar surface of the middle finger of her right hand. This allowed her skin temperature to be monitored continuously on the biofeedback unit. In the usual procedure, the person is asked to listen to a continuous tone that varies in pitch as the skin temperature varies. Usually, the biofeedback machine provides lower pitch tones as the skin temperature increases, and vice verse. The continuous analog feedback of the tone allows the person to 'find out' what thoughts and the like help to raise the skin temperature. Then, if a migraine aura (indication that an attack is about to happen) occurs, the person can think the relevant thoughts, raise the skin temperature, and prevent the migraine attack. That is, training with continuous feedback results in discontinuous voluntary self-regulation whenever it is required.

But Pat wasn't aware of any aura to warn her that a migraine attack was about to occur. And once it had begun, she forgot everything she had learned and was 'locked into' her headache.

Voluntary self-regulation was not likely to work well for her. Instead of giving her continuous feedback, she was given discontinuous and contingent feedback. Contingent feedback means that she only got the 'reward' of feedback if and when her skin temperature did what it was supposed to do – in this case, when it rose. Contingent rewards for any kind of response tend to increase its habit strength. The result is that suitable kinds of discontinuous and contingent feedback eventuate in continuous production over time of the automatic learned response. This seemed to be a more satisfactory approach to Pat's problem – that is, to train her in habitual and automatic re-regulation rather than in voluntary self-regulation.

A digital counter was placed in her view while she was attached to the skin temperature unit. She was told that Felicity did not want to disturb her relaxation by talking to her. So every time a new count appeared on the digital counter, that was to be his way of saying 'good for you'. Felicity monitored the silent skin temperature unit. Each time Pat's skin temperature increased successively by one-tenth of a degree Fahrenheit, Felicity pressed the remote counter control and increased the count by one. If the temperature dropped down again (for any reason), Felicity waited until it had recovered by at least a half degree and then he started again pressing the counter button to give her counts for temperature increases. The number of counts and the starting and ending skin temperatures served as the treatment record.

During the first few half-hour sessions, Pat's skin temperature started at about 70 to 75 degrees Fahrenheit, and it remained under 80 degrees. She would get as many as sixty to ninety counts as the skin temperature fluctuated up and down. By half way through the 20 sessions, she would start at around 75 to 80 degrees and her skin temperature would rise to 90 to 95 degrees. Her counts tended to run up around two hundred counts in the session. By the last few sessions her skin temperature started around 90 to 95 degrees and would increase to 95 to 99 degrees, and her counts declined again to about sixty to ninety in a session.

As training progressed, the skin temperature rose more and more during successive sessions. In addition, her initial skin temperature, recorded at the beginning of each session, began to rise steadily over time. That certainly suggested that her skin temperature habit was being established upwards. Meanwhile, her migraines simply stopped. None were reported after the third training session. She reported no further headaches when Felicity met her some three years later. And when he shook her hand it was warm.

A Gnarled Knuckle

Felicity has not yet been privileged to treat a patient with cancer. Other psychotherapists, such as the Simonton's and Mahrer, have had that opportunity, with remarkable recoveries reported. It makes perfectly good sense that cancer ought to be both preventable and curable with properly devised psychotherapy. This statement is based on a number of reasons related to the non-viral causes of cancer. However, to talk about that without any stories to support the talk would surely tax your credulity beyond the point of its survival.

But then, there is arthritis. Like cancer patients, few arthritics will pursue treatment by a psychologist. After all, with both cancer and arthritis, you can see and feel the physical swellings of the body parts. There are 'real' physical things there, so how could 'the mind' have anything to do with it? Of course, this way of thinking has very little to do with what psychotherapy and Psychology are really about.

The so-called body and the so-called mind are really not separate parts of the person at all. They are one. The body refers to the anatomy and chemistry of the body, and the mind refers to the way they work. Perhaps you could say that the mind refers specifically and particularly to how the brain works – but then the brain controls and regulates how everything works and everything the rest of the body (and itself) does. Psychology has to do with the living (functioning, doing, reacting) body. In contrast, the anatomy and chemistry are virtually the same whether the body is alive or dead – which is why physicians can be trained, and post-mortems undertaken, on cadavers. For present purposes, let's pretend the body is still living.

Patrick was referred to Felicity because of a stomach ulcer that was flaring up repeatedly. The referring physician thought he might be unduly anxious, perhaps due to psychological traumatization from a traffic accident in which he had been involved. There was some traumatic anxiety identifiable in the tests the psychometrist administered, and Felicity thought that it might be worth treating. But he was more interested in seeing if the ulcer could be healed.

Then he met Patrick and he was no longer interested in either of those issues. Patrick's hands were absolutely deformed by arthritis. He could do almost nothing with them. The direction of his fingers was at about a forty-five degree angle with the plane of his hand. His knuckles were swollen to easily twice their normal size. He did not bother to comment on his arthritis to Felicity. After all, what could a psychologist do about that?

Now Felicity understood Patrick's point of view and did not even try to contradict it. Heck, even the research on arthritis seemed to suggest it was not a psychosomatic disorder. In fact, Felicity knew that in one study by a psychiatrist it had been shown that the swelling experienced in arthritis occurred before, and not after, the pain. So, the study was used to conclude that the swelling caused the pain (an assumption in itself), not the other way around. And so, at best, arthritis was seen to be a somato-psychic disorder and not a psychosomatic disorder. Makes sense, right? It does not.

Nobody in his right mind would think of the pain in arthritis as causing the swelling. That is not what makes arthritis a psychosomatic disorder. The psychological causes come long before that. Although this is not necessary, the process usually starts with some kind of injury – from a fall or whatever. The injury results in a sensation of pain at or near a joint. Every time the person moves, the joint moves and the person hurts some more. Since nobody likes to experience pain, the body starts at once to do whatever it can to stop pain. If the pain comes from a joint, the body protects itself (automatically) by trying to stop the joint from moving – to reduce the pain. (Among other things, that's what creates a limp – limping prevents quick joint movement.)

Now, the best way to keep a joint from moving, other than tying a splint across it, is to tighten the muscles all around the joint to hold it still. Muscles pull across joints, and when they are tightened all around it they compress the joint somewhat. But the person keeps moving around and the compressed joint keeps moving too (even if only a little). That creates more pain, which results in tighter muscle tension. Eventually, the lubricating fluid between the bone surfaces of the compressed joint may be squeezed out, and the two bones start rubbing together. This produces more pain – and possibly joint degeneration from the friction of rubbing the two hard surfaces against each other.

Notice that the pain from the original injury has probably stopped long ago when the injury healed (probably in days, months at most). But the pain is being perpetuated as a result of the muscles around it having become defensively or self-protectively tensed or tightened. The self-protective tensing of the muscles around the joint is the 'psychological' cause of what is to follow.

When the brain experiences pain (whether from the original injury, or from the tense muscles, or from the friction between the joint's surfaces), it automatically activates the autonomic nervous system. That, in turn, automatically activates the body's immune system – the brain assumes there is an injury requiring both attack on any infection and repair of the injury. The immune system pumps fluid into the area of the joint, creating swelling and thus more pain – and more defensive muscle tension. Now the joint becomes swollen and therefore more painful, and arthritis may be diagnosed. But that's not all it does. The immune system also sends growth hormone from the brain to the affected site. Its job is to stimulate growth of the (assumed to be damaged) tissue.

If there is no damage to the tissue, but the body's immune system keeps acting as though something is wrong (e.g., if the poison nicotine keeps attacking the lungs without actually damaging them), the continuously stimulated cell growth may eventuate in cancer. If there is some damage that the growth hormone cannot reach (as when the joint surfaces are compressed together) it may stimulate growth of cells around the area. Bone cells are living tissue too, and bone spurs may be stimulated to grow around the affected joint – causing more pain (and so forth). That is, the body's immune system does several things, all having consequences.

If one can simply train the muscles around an affected joint to relax, the lubricant and the growth hormone can get between the bone surfaces, lubricate them and stimulate bone surface growth for re-generation to occur. Of course, when the muscles relax, the reduced muscle tension and pressure on the joint surfaces reduces the pain experienced, and this helps reward the learning of muscle relaxation as well. At least that's Felicity's theory.

It seemed clear to Felicity that Patrick needed some anxiety desensitization. First, he needed it to be rid of the anxiety traumatically-conditioned in his traffic accident. Second, he needed it to reduce the viscerally-projected anxiety and tension which might be keeping his ulcer going. And, third, he needed it to reduce the autonomic reactivity that might be keeping his hand muscles tense and the immune system trying to fight the supposed injury in the knuckles. But which kind of desensitization should be used? The visceral projection of tension (which did seem to be occurring according to his Rorschach) affecting the ulcer might suggest the use of the galvanic skin resistance (GSR) mediated method of stimulus conditioned autonomic response suppression (SCARS) that has been described elsewhere. However, the involvement of the skeletal-striate muscles in the arthritis might suggest Wolpe's reciprocal inhibition therapy (RIT) method since it uses trained relaxation of the skeletal muscles. Felicity decided to go the latter route.

He trained Patrick in deep muscle relaxation, taking special care to focus on relaxing the hands gently. Then he asked Patrick to picture a variety of scenes in his mind while remaining relaxed. The scenes were presented in pairs, with each pair followed by the request that Patrick raise one of his fingers, one to four, to indicate whether discomfort had decreased, increased, remained the same or been absent across the two items of each pair. At successive sessions, the hand used for this finger-raising signal was alternated to allow both hands to be exercised in this way. The scenes Patrick was asked to picture included the usual sequence of traffic images that have been described in other stories. He was also asked to visualize scenes in which he became impatient, irritated and, finally, angry (to address the usual factor underlying ulcers), and scenes in which he felt mild and then severe pain, became ill and was finally admitted to hospital (to address autonomic function).

Felicity had no choice. He had to watch Patrick's hands to await his finger signals. That allowed Felicity to examine the arthritic swelling carefully at each session. There were forty sessions. By the twentieth session, there was some reduction in the knuckle swelling and the fingers were twisted to a noticeably smaller angle. By the end of the treatment, no ulcer pain had been reported for a long time, the fingers pointed straight out from the hand, the knuckles looked to be only slightly thicker than 'normal' knuckles would be, and Patrick was beginning to use his hands almost normally, even for quite fine finger work.

Felicity saw Patrick on several occasions for non-professional reasons over the next three years. His hands looked normal, and he seemed to be using them in normal ways – and he said they were fine. But, presumably considering the effects on his arthritis to be a result of 'spontaneous recovery', Patrick's physician did not refer any other patients at all to Felicity. Was Patrick the only case of arthritis Felicity has treated? He was not. However, the few others Felicity has seen did not exhibit visible changes except for the fluidity and ease of their movements. But, then, their arthritis was not something Felicity was privileged to examine or treat directly. In Patrick's case, his hands could be seen.

A Racked Back

Felicity can't count the number of people he has seen with back pain. In almost every case, simple relaxation training relieved the pain, at least temporarily. The point is that almost all back pain is a result of self-protective muscle tension. That's what supports chiropractic and a large part of massage therapy – the body's defensive tension is temporarily altered and the person feels better for a while. But the pain returns when the person re-establishes the defensive muscle tension. In Felicity's practice, if the defensive muscle tension is relieved, and then is perpetuated as a new habit by being connected to associated stimuli, the pain does not seem to recur. Consequently, if Wolpe's systematic anxiety desensitization (RIT) was used, the back pain usually vanished for the remainder of Felicity's contact.

But what of conditions such as degeneration of the vertebrae? Pierre had suffered from back pain for years. His physician had X-rays taken which showed that a couple of his vertebrae were severely degenerated. He assumed that this condition was permanent since bone substance had been lost. Therefore, he was extra careful with his back, ensuring that he never strained it by any heavy lifting or other hard work. Felicity could certainly understand the wish to avoid any work, heavy or otherwise.

But Pierre had consulted Felicity on another matter. He had a phobia about flying. This posed a problem for him as he had a good deal of travelling to do associated with his work. He didn't want to drive because that would mean sitting for long periods of time in one, rather tense, position. He wanted to feel comfortable flying to his various destinations.

Wolpe's systematic desensitization (RIT) method was used to deal with his flying phobia. Pierre was taught the art of deep muscle relaxation. When he was deeply relaxed, he was asked to picture all sorts of scenes associated with flying. The scenes started with him at home thinking about phoning to arrange a flight, then phoning to arrange it, then packing for it, and then calling a taxi. He was asked to picture himself in the taxi at various distances from home on the way to the airport. He was asked to picture arriving at the airport, checking in at the flight counter, walking to the waiting room, waiting, and then boarding the plane. He was presented scenes in the plane involving finding his seat, sitting down, strapping himself in, looking around inside the plane, and looking out of the window at the airport activity. He pictured the plane moving out to the runway. Then he was asked to picture arriving at his destination, with the plane approaching the field for a landing, then landing, then rolling up to the terminal. Finally, he was asked to picture the original take-off, and various stages in the flight.

This long series of presentations took some thirty-five sessions. By the time he had learned to relax, he reported his back pain was gone. It remained absent. Toward the end of the treatment program, he arranged to have another series of back X-rays taken because there had been no back pain for a long time. He was worried that the spinal degeneration had progressed to the point that he could no longer 'feel' the injury to his back. The X-rays showed that nearly all of the spinal degeneration was gone, and that the vertebrae were re-generating themselves. He had another X-ray some six months after the desensitization was completed, and there was no longer any degeneration visible. And he had remained free of pain throughout that period of time.

If pain remains longer than six months, it is not due to a physical injury, as such. Body tissues simply renew and regenerate themselves when that which is keeping them 'injured' is removed. In most cases, the thing that 'keeps' them that way is defensive or self-protective muscle tension.

A Sore Eye At Sis: Psoriasis

How about psoriasis? Patsy had had patches of scaly, dry, itchy skin all over her body for as long as she could remember. Every kind of pill and ointment had been tried with no noticeable benefit. She was referred by her psychiatrist for behavioural treatment for her social anxiety. She was always embarrassed around people, and she tried to stay away from others as much as she could. On inquiry, it was clear that the main reason for her social embarrassment was her appearance. She thought other people would be disgusted by the look of her psoriasis and, anyway, from her point of view it marred her attractiveness – so what was the use? While talking with her psychiatrist, they had concluded that, since nothing could be done to get rid of the psoriasis, it would be best to deal with her social problem as though it was a social anxiety.

Felicity thought he would be pretty self-conscious too if his skin looked like Patsy's. The skin condition was too widespread over her body to be susceptible to the mirror-gazing procedure, described elsewhere, to condition inhibition of self-image. He didn't know much about psoriasis, and his attempts to find useful literature on it suggested to him that few other people knew much about it either. However, it had to be some kind of an immune response so that moderating the autonomic nervous system's reactivity ought to influence it somewhat. And that approach would also be consistent with the anti-anxiety treatment he was being asked by the patient to undertake with her.

He connected galvanic skin resistance (GSR) electrodes to the palm and back of her right hand. For half-hour sessions, he showed her pictorial slides selected to represent the areas of phobia or fear depicted in her responses to a Fears Survey Schedule. Each time her GSR level increased (less sweat, more 'calmness') by at least 1,000 ohms, the slide she was watching was changed as a 'reward' for getting more physiologically comfortable. The procedure used was stimulus conditioned autonomic response suppression (SCARS) which has been described in several other stories. There were thirty-five treatment sessions in all.

By half-way through the treatment, Patsy was reporting an increase in the itchiness she felt, but the patches of psoriasis were a little less noticeable. By three-quarters of the way through the treatment, the itchiness had diminished, some of the scaly skin was pealing off and fresh, pink skin was visible at the sites. By the time the treatment was terminated, although Patsy claimed to have a couple of small patches of psoriasis (which also seemed to be healing) in places hidden by her clothing, none were visible. Moreover, she did not appear self-conscious, she reported feeling comfortable around people and she had joined a couple of recreational groups with other women.

Was this a cure of the psoriasis? Who knows? Felicity has not seen Patsy or the few other people he has treated for psoriasis since completion of their treatments. Since all had claimed that this was the first time in their adult lives they had been free from psoriasis, it seems likely to Felicity that they would have returned to see him if the psoriasis had recurred.

An Anti-Histaminic Auntie-Body

It was mentioned earlier in this chapter that allergies are a product of three things: perhaps a genetic predisposition which, if present, is immutable [the predisposition, not it effect. RR], the availability of the noxious substance or the allergen in the environment, and the stress-related reactivity of the target cells that react to the allergen. There is little that anyone can do about a person's existing genetic inheritance and, aside from living in an environmentally controlled glass house, there is little that can be done about the seasonal presence of allergens. In fact, the allergists' and homeopaths' use of diluted doses of the allergen to desensitize the sufferer's allergic reactivity is really an 'in vivo' process of stimulating a limited, sub-clinical reaction to allow the body to habituate non-reactivity. That's right, they set out to unlearn the immune-allergic reaction. Unfortunately, this method does not work all that well with many people for a number of specifiable reasons.

Felicity has treated several people's allergies by systematic desensitization (Wolpe's **RIT** or Quirk's **SCARS** method) or hypnotic procedures. Since you have heard about these procedures before, they may be boring. A story about a person treated by a more 'modern' (NLP) technique might be more interesting.

Primula had suffered from hay fever and asthma for many years, sometimes accompanied by itchy skin. These were reactions to cats, house dust, and tree or grass pollen. She was uncomfortable inside or outside, or anywhere near cats – which she adored.

Felicity pointed out to her that there was no real 'danger' from any of her three allergens. She acknowledged that, but said she nevertheless reacted to them. Felicity pointed out that, since there was nothing dangerous about them, her brain must be making a mistake in maintaining its vigilant readiness to react to their presence with reactivity of the target allergic cells in her body. She agreed. He asked her how they might get her brain to react to these allergens as though they were harmless. She didn't know.

He asked Primula to tell him, if she knew, what it was about cats that she sensed or received and reacted to – any picture of what it looked like from the recesses of her mind would be fine, no matter how 'silly' it may seem. She said she imagined that what she reacted to about cats looked like little spirals – like curly hairs, except they spiralled to a point like a cone. They were black, and the point on their ends would catch onto skin or mucous tissue and irritate it by tickling. Felicity was pleased, and he asked her to put that image up on a shelf. He then asked her what else she could think of that was small, looked like that, but had no unpleasant effect on her at all – in fact, she liked it. After some thought, she said she thought of tiny cone-shaped sea shells which had black mother-of-pearl all over them. Felicity was delighted and he asked her to put that image up on the shelf too.

He then asked Primula what particles of the house dust that afflicted her looked like. The image was of little irregular black things with hairs coming off them that could stick to tissue and irritate it. The similar but pleasant and non-irritating image was of particles of smooth black coal dust from a particular fireplace that she had liked as a child. Those were put up on the shelf. Then he asked about tree and grass spores. They looked to her like tiny green balls with little spines out from them that would stick into tissue and irritate it. The similar but pleasant and non-irritating image was of little green sparkles that one might spray on a Christmas tree and that would stick there to make the tree bright. Those were also put up on the shelf.

She was asked to close her eyes and picture herself in a room divided in half by an impenetrable, transparent Plexiglas screen stretching from ceiling to floor and from wall to wall. Closed doors from a common hall accessed each half of the room. She was asked to watch from her partitioned off half of the room while little black, cone-shaped spirals from a cat were released in the other half of the room. How did she feel? "Fine." She was asked to arrange for a frame, like a picture frame, to be put around the area containing the spirals. Then she was asked to compress the frame with its contents to the size of a picture frame, and then to push the picture frame and its contents back against the far wall. She accomplished this image. Then she was asked to arrange for a whole lot of tiny black, cone-shaped, mother-of-pearl covered seashells to be flung lightly into the frame with the spirals of hair. As the seashells moved toward the frame, air currents sucked the air out of them so that when they reached the frame the spirals of hair were sucked into them and gobbled up. She said she could really see that happening and had already anticipated that occurrence.

When the spirals of hair were thus imprisoned, she was asked to watch herself entering through the door into the other half of the room, pausing and looking around. She was asked to say how the she in the other half of the room appeared to feel. She said that she appeared to feel just fine. She was asked to watch herself in the other half of the room walk up to the frame to look closely at it. How did she feel? She felt OK. She watched herself in the other half of the room, as she reached out, touched, and caressed the black things in the frame. How did she feel? She reported no feeling at all. She was asked to walk into the other half of the room, join herself in there, and do the same things. How did she feel? No feeling at all was reported. Felicity was delighted. He suggested that she take a handful of the black shells, put them in her purse and take them home with her as a souvenir. She giggled as she complied in her mind with that idea.

The same procedure was then done, first using the black spiny house dust neutralized by the black shiny coal dust particles, and then using the green spiny spores neutralized by the green shiny sparkles for the Christmas tree. She claimed no distress at all while picturing herself in the other half of the room after each of these exercises. She even said she had fun doing the procedures.

In the year that has elapsed since this procedure was undertaken, Primula claims never once to have suffered from any allergic responses, neither hay fever, nor asthma, nor itchiness. This has been true although she has spent a lot of time in houses with cats, in dusty houses, and walking outside on the grass and under trees. Was this a 'cure'? In the case of allergic responses, Felicity is inclined to believe that it was 'a cure'. The method seems quite directly to correct the error made by the brain in reacting to the allergens as if they represented danger.

The problem many people might have in accepting this as a real treatment method is likely to be that the brain would be thought to be incapable of detecting the presence of the allergen consciously. How, then, could it learn to react differentially to the presence of the allergen? The problem here is that most people assume that the brain is only capable of learning responses of which it is conscious. The error in this idea is demonstrated by observing that a cat (only) allergy responds to a cat but not to a dog, even if the person cannot detect consciously whether there is a cat or a dog in the house. The body makes the discrimination, mediated by the brain which triggers and orchestrates the immune reaction.

A Dietetic Diabetic

Of course, diabetes is a horse of a different colour. It is also said to be a chronic disease for which there is no cure. All the term 'chronic disease' means is that it does not yield to 'initial cause' analysis – the only kind of approach to people's problems physicians are trained in or understand. That is, for medicine, it is 'chronic' and has no cure. Fortunately, these days we are not restricted to medical means for treating problems. So, what physicians are unable to understand and cure, may well be cured by methods used by other disciplines. Moreover, Felicity is one of those people who, if you tell him there is no cure for something, he will not rest until he has found at least one cure. And, if there is one cure, there will almost certainly be more than one.

So, when Paula came to see Felicity saying she had diabetes, he immediately began to ruminate about how he might find a way to cure it. Of course, that wasn't why Paula had come to see him. She had accepted, as if it was fact, what she had been told by her physician, namely, that there was no cure for diabetes. What she came to see Felicity about was her stress reactivity. She had been told by her physician that the reason why she was unable to control her blood sugar, in spite of good dietary habits and energetic exercise, was because she was suffering from chronic stress. Perhaps a psychologist could help her to reduce her stress reactivity, and thus help her to control her blood sugar.

Paula pushed the right button in Felicity's soul. She spoke of the strict diet she had been given, and with which she had been complying. All of Felicity's sympathies were aroused. Some people like to taste good food. Felicity is ravenous about it. He takes the time to pass it quickly over his palate so that he can get to the next delicate morsel as soon as possible. And the thought of skipping desserts and sugary goodies is quite unacceptable to his gluttonous view of life. So he had to find some way to get Paula over her diabetic disadvantage. But how?

Her diagnosis was Diabetes II. Like her father and her grandmother, she developed her elevated blood sugar in her late fifties. She had been told that there was a strong genetic link in Diabetes II, and so she assumed that her 'disease' was an inherited one. That seemed to be an end to the question about whether or not it could be cured – it could not. Now, Felicity knew that all the genetic factor would do would be to create a pre-disposition to the development of the condition. He realized that it was possible that excessive use of sugars might potentiate the pre-disposition. But a pre-disposition to what?

Unlike Diabetes I, where insufficient insulin is produced and exogenous insulin (medication) usually has to be taken, the problem in Diabetes II has more to do with the utilization of the available insulin at the level of the cells. The insulin production may be low, but there is enough present that, if it could be utilized to help the cells metabolize sugar, there would be no problem. How was it that the body could not utilize its insulin?

He noted that Diabetes II, or late onset diabetes, usually starts at about the time of the involutional period – the time of life called the menopause in women. Now insulin is a hormone. At that time of life a lot of bodily hormones tend to become less available to the body in both genders. Moreover, the production and utilization of most hormones tend to be triggered and facilitated by other hormones. The idea that a reduction of hormonal stimulants, to maintain the effects of other hormones, might be a relevant issue seemed justified by the observation that the other main time during which Diabetes II tends to be stimulated is during pregnancy. During pregnancy, the body's hormones undergo major changes. Felicity asked Paula to have her physician obtain assays on various blood hormones.

Although the hormone assays showed that several of her hormone levels were well below normal, her physician was unwilling to prescribe hormone supplements to see if they might have any effect on her insulin utilization. Felicity was not discouraged. Paula's body used to utilize its hormones adequately. How could it be induced to produce and utilize enough of this hormone again?

The master endocrine gland, the pituitary body, is located in the brain. That suggested that the triggering sequences for most of the endocrine system might be capable of being re-regulated habitually by the brain. For this reason, and to address to the referral request, twenty-two sessions of Quirk's stimulus conditioned autonomic response suppression (SCARS) were used. Her subjective sense of stress and anxiety declined appreciably.

But that might respond to only half of the problem. The endocrine organs are chemical factories that produce chemical hormones. It might be necessary to provide the body with some of the chemicals needed to produce the required substances. That suggested the probability that nutritional supplements might be needed. Felicity poked around in the nutritional literature.

Paula started taking 200 micrograms of chromium – replacing that with magnesium when the chromium started making her 'feel sick' – which, as in many people, seemed to bring her blood sugar down somewhat and to help stabilize it. The literature suggested the use of a number of other substances (such as an amino acid, arginine, to stimulate insulin production and aid fat metabolism) which were unavailable. He did manage to locate one of these substances for her, called Vanadyl Sulfate. Like most diabetics, she was monitoring her blood sugar daily. Whenever her blood sugar started to rise, she took a couple of the Vanadyl pills. In this way, she managed to keep her blood sugar from fluctuating too greatly and only moderately above 'normal' limits. But her blood sugar level was not yet normalized.

At first Felicity was annoyed that he was unable to find out what would happen if Paula's diminished hormone production were increased by medication. Then, while listening to Paula talk about her life, something she said kept running through his mind. She noted that her sexual appetites were lower than in the past and that her sexual activity had declined to the point of virtual non-existence. It occurred to him that reduction of sexual activity might itself reduce the stimulation of at least the sex hormones. He asked whether her sexual activity could be increased. Later, she reported that although her husband had accepted the idea of increased activity at first, the activity remained sporadic. In response to a question about how that might be corrected, she thought she might regulate it herself and increase its frequency and consistency. Within a few weeks of commencing daily self-stimulation activity, she reported that her blood sugar had stabilized itself within the upper limits of the 'normal' range.

Was this a 'cure'? Felicity doesn't know. The above results having held for several months, Felicity's contact with Paula ceased and he does not know whether the effect remained. Sadly, learning about how the body works and how its conditions can best be treated is slow since most of the available research funds tend to be gobbled up by medical studies. Oh well, perhaps some day ...

CHAPTER 8

A QUICK LOOK AT BRAIN DAMAGE – IMPAIRING IMPAIRMENT

This is a volume about psychotherapy. So what on earth has brain damage to do with that? The answer you might expect is that some psychotherapists try to help people 'live with' impairments resulting from their brain damage. Of course, Felicity won't do anything normal or expected – probably intending to exercise his temperamental obstinacy. So, just for the fun of it, let's look into whatever lunacy he has in store for us now.

A Wobbly Wonder

While walking down the wide hospital corridors, Tracy staggered so much that she bumped into both walls within any stretch of ten feet. Her psychiatric diagnosis was also schizophrenia. That wasn't the problem. She was brain injured. Of course, 'organicity' (I suppose that's a city made up of organs, though it doesn't say what kind of organs) was added to the diagnosis to represent the neurological condition. The history she was able to give offered no clear indication about her past or about any injuries she might have suffered. But there was no doubt she was a 'mal-coord'. Felicity thought it might be fun to try to treat this schizophrenia with a strange method too.

About the time that Tracy was admitted to the Behaviour Therapy Unit, Felicity happened to get lost down in the outpatient department. While trying to find his way out, he opened a door and looked into a room. The room turned out to be one of those observation rooms with a one-way screen. Sitting on a table in front of the screen was a funny-looking board on which there were 100 push-buttons arranged in 10 rows by 10 columns. There was a wire from the board to a twenty-pen recorder. Felicity's sharp mind needed only ten minutes of cocked-headed contemplation of this contraption to deduce that it was probably an interaction recorder for group therapy – where the observer could hold down a button, for example, in row 6 and column 3 (causing appropriate deflections in two of the recorder's pens) to indicate that, for the period of time of the pens' deflections, person 6 was talking to person 3. The thing that interested Felicity most about this equipment was that it had about a half an inch of dust collected on it. It took only another five minutes of what for Felicity passes as thought for him to figure out that the equipment had not been used for at least a short time.

So it was that when, several days later, he was interviewing his new patient, Tracy, he put her mal-coordination together with the equipment he had so recently seen and he beamed a triumphant smile toward the not-too-attentive-looking hapless lady he had just received under his tender care. After doing a few tests to document her impoverished coordination and gleaning what little information she could afford him, he dismissed her back to the Unit and hurried off to try to find the outpatient department again.

By chance, he found it. By chance also, he found someone there who looked about as lost as he was, asked this person (probably a patient) if he could borrow the interaction-recording device and, receiving the person's permission to take anything he wanted, he scooped up the equipment and ran back to his office. Once there, he locked the door, dusted off his wonderful new 'borrowed' property, and hid it under his desk. The days passed and he was unable to discern any posse out to catch the miscreant. So, looking as though he was doing something completely normal, he secreted his ill-gotten gains under his arm and ran it up to his nurse's room. He abandoned it there so it would look as though she had stolen it if anybody came looking for it. The next day, he purloined his family's metronome on the way to work and added it to the pile, to complete the equipment that would be needed for Tracy's treatment.

Felicity asked the nurse to sit with Tracy for two half-hour periods each day, morning and afternoon, to help Tracy with the task he wanted her to do. The nurse was a much nicer person than Felicity had any right to expect. She accepted the new imposition on her time with amazing grace. At first, the metronome was to be set at a very slow rate. It was to be speeded up slowly at each new session only if Tracy was able to keep time with it fairly accurately. Tracy's task was to push on just one of the buttons in time with the metronome and, as if it might be a reward, to watch the deflections of the associated pair of pens on the pen-recorder. She would be able to see how evenly she timed the pushing of the key, and both the nurse and Felicity would be able to evaluate later how she was doing by looking at the lengths of the lines between pen deflections on the recorder's paper tape.

The treatment began, and Felicity kept track of how Tracy was doing by looking over the paper tape after each session. He could see both the regularity of Tracy's button pushing, its accuracy (from the pens which deflected – showing which button had been pressed), and the speed of the tapping she was doing (from the distance between pen deflections). As soon as she was doing as well as he thought she should, he asked the nurse to get her to push two side-by-side buttons, alternating back-and-forth between them, starting again at a slow beat from the metronome.

Tracy was about as clumsy as expected at the beginning of this task, but she slowly improved and she improved all over again at each new setting of the metronome. When she had mastered an even and rapid tapping between the two buttons, Felicity asked the nurse to get her to tap around a triangle of three buttons, again starting at a slow beat of the metronome. The nurse became a little edgy at this point, remarking that she felt a bit like the person beating the drum to set the rowing rate for the slaves in a Spanish galleon. Nevertheless, she did continue with the task.

As it turned out, it seems that the triangular motion afforded the level of complexity needed by Tracy's brain. As she began to master this intricate three-button manoeuvre, Tracy's overall coordination began to improve. She started walking the halls on legs about as steady as those of a person mildly drunk. She could help a little in combing her own hair. Her speech became less slurred. She had much less trouble finding her words in conversation. And she was able to eat with the rest of the ladies on the Unit, since she became almost accurate in transporting food to her mouth most of the time.

Finally, she satisfied Felicity that she had mastered the triangular movement at a reasonable rate of speed. By this time, her gait no longer looked at all drunk, she was eating with some delicacy, she was combing her own hair with modest success, and she was even seen to clap her hands just like a normal person in response to some entertainment she was watching. She seemed like any ordinary person. However, Felicity had learned to doubt his own judgement about people's normalcy. The question in his mind was whether her schizophrenic symptoms were now more clearly visible, being less masked by her 'organic' mal-coordination.

At Felicity's request, she was presented at conference [a common medical teaching procedure. RR]. Those attending the conference were asked to determine the symptoms most needing treatment at this time. The conference concluded that she had recovered from her schizophrenic illness and her 'organicity' and that she could be discharged. While sharing farewells with her when she was leaving the hospital, Felicity felt robbed of the opportunity to treat her schizophrenia. But she didn't seem to share his disappointment. Felicity could never understand people.

Follow-up interviews were held over a period of only six months since she planned to move out of the vicinity. However, during that time she remained well-coordinated and appeared to function adequately without medication or continuing psychotherapy. Did

Tracy recover? And, if she did, how? Was she putting on an act? Only a person living in some remote place can answer these questions, and perhaps she doesn't know either.

An Uncertain Certainty

Trina was a girl in her mid-teens who had been blind from birth. Her parents brought her to see Felicity because, as they put it, 'she was afraid of the darkness in which she lived'. Felicity had to meet this girl! "How," he thought, "can a person fear the dark when it is the only thing she has ever known?" His question was answered as soon as he saw Trina. She was markedly uncoordinated, presumably related to cerebral palsy (CP).

A blind person has to organize the world in which he/she lives by organizing her movements (kinaesthetic muscle sensations) and her contacts (tactile sensations) with it. Trina's lurching and poorly coordinated actions would necessarily create highly unpredictable contacts with the things around her and thus an image of unpredictable relationships among those things in space. The result would have to be a high level of uncertainty and thus ambiguousness in her world. And ambiguity is the universal source of fear – everybody experiences at least some fear in ambiguous situations.

Felicity did not know what he could do to help her to feel less anxious since his methods used visual images. But he thought he might be able to diminish the spasticity of her movements. The hypothesis he had was that irritability of her brain (see later) might account for her spastic movements. If that were true, then reducing the brain's irritability might correct the spasticity of her movements. She might then be able to organize her world better by means of movement and touch, and the fear of 'her darkness' should subside. Actually, Felicity had previously tried, with some success, to reduce the spastic movements interfering with Tom's life – another CP patient Felicity had treated a year or so earlier.

Sterman's biofeedback treatment method, which had been used with Tom, was started with Trina. Two EEG electrodes were attached near the C3-C4 sites on her scalp. Then, every time any sensorimotor rhythm (SMR) was recorded in the EEG, a whistling sound was turned on automatically, and it lasted as long as there was SMR activity being recorded from the sites. There were about ten half-hour sessions, during which Felicity observed some learned increase in the amount of SMR activity in Trina's EEG.

After about the tenth session, Trina reported some strange sensations. Her mother took her to her physician. He examined her and declared to them that Trina could now 'see' – that she had 20/200 vision (meaning that she could see at 20 feet what the normal person can see at 200 feet). Everyone was shocked at this unexpected development. But the expected joyous consequences were not to be. Indeed, it looked as though this silver lining was little more than a cloud.

Trina had been told she could see. Therefore, she concluded, it was no longer necessary for her attend the school for the blind. But she could not see. Her eyes, never having been fixated by light, roamed randomly around in their sockets. It is true that, as they passed any particular patch or shape of colour around her, she could distinguish the patch of colour – as different from another patch of a different colour or shape. But her eyes had not imprinted the skills of fixation on an object, tracking an object, focusing on an object, or even accommodating to the amount of light – skills learned in the first weeks of life. And now, not having had these skills imprinted at the early 'easy' age, they would be hard, if not impossible, to learn at this age.

Moreover, if Trina had been fearful of the darkness in which she lived before, she was now even more fearful of Felicity who had done this thing to her. She would not continue to visit Felicity to see if her eyes could be trained to perform their normal functions – which would permit her not only to have vision, but also to see. And she was in her mid-teens, an age at which young girls tend to begin to become independent of their mothers. She only felt a more intense need to rely on her mother, thus increasing her sense of inner conflict.

All Felicity could do under the circumstances was to feel a great sense of remorse for his having created the new distress this young lady was experiencing, and to instruct her mother in methods by which to train her daughter's eyes to serve her in the task of seeing. Since there was no further contact with the family, Felicity has remained remorseful but, hopefully, wiser for his part in creating fear in her.

This story can hardly be left without some kind of an explanation. Is it intended to imply that some magic or a miracle occurred? It is not. Although the following 'explanation' can hardly be stated as having established validity, it does provide a kind of plausible understanding of the events described.

First, some definitions are needed. Focal epilepsy refers to epilepsy affecting a specific area or group of nerves in the brain. Non-focal or general epilepsy refers to epilepsy affecting a wider area or a large number of nerves in the brain. Status epilepticus refers to a fairly constant state of epileptic discharge or of 'short-circuiting' in the brain. It is possible that a general form of status epilepticus might be occurring in Trina's brain as a result of the widespread nature of her CP symptoms, perhaps due to a birth injury. This could well be initiated from a focal discharge affecting a specific set of nerve tracts, such as those leading to the visual cortex from the eye. This, in turn, might continuously interfere with the transmission of nerve impulses, such as retinal impulses, thus effectively preventing vision. This might happen, for example, if the foetus came equipped with, or developed, weak access to neural inhibition for at least that specific area of the brain. This might be one way to account for blindness in some people whose eyes and optic nerves are intact but who are said to suffer from 'nerve blindness'.

If this explanation is valid, then trained increase in sensorimotor rhythm (SMR) in the EEG might result in increased access to neural inhibition throughout the brain. This, in turn, might prevent the uncoordinated brain activity underlying the CP symptoms. At least, that was the idea Felicity had in starting out to treat the CP symptoms with EEG-SMR training. What may have happened before the desired effect was achieved, however, is that the threshold amount of neural inhibition, required to prevent the focal epileptic activity on the optic tract, could have become available to block the irritative interference with visual tract transmission, so that vision was no longer prevented. If this latter effect were to be achieved, vision might develop, even if for the first time.

It will be noticed that the above story is replete with 'ifs'. That was intentional. It is rather hard to verify exactly what is going on in the brain in its moment-to-moment functioning. Since its functioning is mainly comprised of invisible electrical activities which, unlike engineered electrical circuits, cannot be controlled to observe what happens under varied conditions, it is hard to specify exactly what is taking place at any given moment. The only way yet available to discover what might be going on within the brain is to find ways to control the stimuli going in through the sensory tracts and to observe the effects on the system in the resulting behaviour. The abbreviated interval of time available in Trina's case, along with the occurrence of an unpredicted event (vision), prevented any effective test of the above hypotheses. How's that for science fiction!?

A Magnificent Magnification

Terry was seen at a hospital. He was referred for a psychological assessment to measure his degree of impairment and disability. Several years prior to this contact, he had been in a serious traffic accident. His skull had been crushed in the impact and the neurosurgeons had cut out some of his damaged brain and had inserted a steel plate to replace the crushed section of the skull.

When he appeared at Felicity's office, he was limping heavily with his right leg, and his right arm hung limply at his side with the wrist and fingers bent slightly inwards. His conversation was slow and laboured since it was hard for him to find the words he wanted to use. He could not read any more, at least not well enough to do any questionnaire tests. He wrote in a clumsy way with his left hand, but he made so many spelling mistakes that what he wrote was hard to understand. There was only rather patchy sensation from the right side of his body. And he was subject to frequent grand mal (losing consciousness) and petit mal (fleeting sensory or motor events) seizures. He was clearly putting out massive efforts to continue to function at all.

Terry's brain was damaged beyond repair. He was suffering a severe loss of function as well as periodic debilitation from his epileptic seizures. Felicity wondered why it had been necessary for Terry to be referred to him for the assessment. Dutifully, he undertook some neuropsychological tests with Terry to quantify the impairments and disabilities. Then he phoned the referring physician to provide a preliminary report and to inquire about the reason for the referral – which would help determine how detailed his report should be. The physician said that he had heard about Felicity and he was hoping that something in Felicity's bag of tricks might help this unfortunate young man. This was an unexpected turn of events and, taken completely off guard, Felicity agreed to see what he could do.

Lashley's Mass Action Hypothesis flitted through Felicity's mind creating a sense of despair. If the amount of impairment of functioning was indeed proportionate to the amount of damaged brain tissue, the massive loss of brain tissue should imply permanent and massive loss of functioning. Certainly, Lashley's hypothesis was accepted by psychologists and, besides, who could doubt such an obviously correct hypothesis. Felicity's 'mind' focused more and more on the word 'hypothesis' (which means 'guess'), and he began to run over in his mind the contradictory evidence that he had encountered. Lots of patients exhibited huge amounts of impairment of functioning with absolutely no 'visible' brain tissue damage – this was true in many epileptic cases, for example. Also, there were lots of patients who had large parts of their brains removed surgically without any particularly apparent losses of functioning.

Perhaps a more accurate reformulation of the Mass Action Hypothesis might be that loss of functioning is proportional to the amount of existing brain tissue whose functions are interfered with by continuing irritative (that is, epileptic) brain tissue. That formulation appealed more to Felicity than the earlier one. At least it might justify trying to do something for Terry.

As in Chester's case, Felicity started a biofeedback program with Terry, using Sterman's method to train an increase in SMR, in order to increase the availability of neural inhibition to his brain. Two EEG electrodes were attached to Terry's scalp near the C3-C4 sites – on the top of the head, about equidistant from each other and from the earlobes. The feedback EEG unit was set to recognize and respond with a whistling sound for all recorded occurrences of sensorimotor rhythm (SMR) activity – electrical activity from this brain site occurring at between 12 and 14 cycles per second and between 10 and 30 microvolts. The purpose of this whistling sound was to provide a 'reward' for Terry's brain for producing the desired SMR activity. SMR is an EEG activity effecting neural inhibition in the brain. Neural inhibition is one means by which the brain functionally insulates itself to prevent short-circuiting or epileptic or irritative activity from occurring. It was thought that if his brain could learn to increase its production of SMR, it might prevent both his epileptic seizures *and* any irritative electrical activity that might be interfering with the functioning of undamaged parts of his brain.

Meanwhile, galvanic skin resistance (GSR) electrodes were also attached to Terry's right (that's right, right) hand to measure changes in the amount of sweat of his hand. He was shown pictorial slides that were changed for each successive 1,000 ohms of increase in his GSR level. Quirk's stimulus conditioned autonomic response suppression (SCARS) method, which was described in Sally's case, was used here to train Terry to limit any intense autonomic-anxiety reactions. The purpose of this treatment was both to desensitize any traumatically-conditioned anxiety that might have been left over from the traffic accident, and to prevent the possibility of any autonomic storms occurring to erase any trained increase in SMR production which might be achieved. The EEG-SMR method and the SCARS method were used at the same time.

Terry learned rather slowly to increase both his SMR production and his GSR baseline. But he hung in there. At first he reported a declining rate of epileptic seizures. Then his mood started to lift. As treatment continued, his limp pretty well vanished, and Felicity noticed that he was using his right hand to do some simple tasks. Quite suddenly, Terry found that he could read as he had before the accident. Even more, his spelling suddenly improved. Then he began to write with his right hand so that, by the end of the treatment, he was writing about as smoothly with his right hand as he had learned to write with his left.

What brought about these changes? Again, who knows? It would be nice to think that the treatment served as a test of the revision of the Mass Action Hypothesis that had been offered. However, it is possible that the damage to Terry's brain did not account for the impairments of his functioning or for his epilepsy. Although this seems unlikely, it is possible that his epilepsy and his impairments were due to functional (psychological) ways of dealing with anxiety traumatically conditioned in the accident. If this had been true, then the use of anxiety desensitization (with SCARS) may have corrected the anxiety and thus removed the symptoms created by the anxiety. And, of course, this is mentioned really only to suggest that there may have been any number of other unknown reasons why this simple pair of procedures were followed by such radical changes in Terry's functioning and behaviour.

Still, in terms of the conventions of science, if a treatment is introduced under a given hypothesis, and if the treatment does as it was hypothesized to do, the hypothesis on the basis of which the treatment was undertaken is afforded increased credibility over other possible hypotheses. It may just be that some symptomatic consequences (mal-functioning or impairment of functioning) of some, even irreversible, brain damage may be modifiable or reversible given appropriate treatment procedures.

Still, who knows what happened or, for that matter, what is possible? Felicity doesn't. Perhaps due to his normally semi-conscious state, Felicity believes in the unconscious mind which, however, he designates as the, almost limitless, 'realm of the possible'.

Chapter 9

Madness! Exploring the Never-Never Land of Schizophrenia, the Bewildering Dis-ease

Why would one want to jump from telling fairy stories about physical illness into make-believe about schizophrenia? I asked myself the same question. The answer I gave myself was 'history'. The first jobs Felicity had as a psychologist involved working with children. During that trying time, Felicity developed the understanding that children are subject to those two dreadful diseases called Infancy and Childhood. The profound insight which grew from this understanding was that it is the job of adults, as quickly as possible, to wrench youngsters free from the grip of these unpleasant diseases to grow them into normal adults (like us). Then they could repeat with the next generation the same mistakes we made. Well, Felicity found the task of extricating youth from their dread conditions so unpleasant and so fraught with difficulties that he quickly abandoned that enterprise, leaving it, as he put it, to the more patient, more qualified and more tough-minded good graces of women.

Meanwhile, he had been working in private practice, and many of his clients in those days were people with sexual difficulties, often homosexuality. That is why some of Felicity's early practice in learning how to apply psychology to problems in the real world led him to begin his fabrications of stories about psychotherapy with fairy tales about sexuality.

However, when he stopped working with children, he started working in a state-run mental hospital which was old and run down, and which was probably indistinguishable from The Snake Pit. He began to try to come to grips with the people he found there, and thus to examine the nature of the 'disease' from which they were most commonly said to suffer, namely, schizophrenia.

So Felicity's personal history decrees that the topic of schizophrenia has also to be addressed here. If you happen to think that this mix of topics is inappropriate, Felicity would be pleased to join you in raising your voices in protest – addressed, of course, to the Inter-Governmental Office of Governmental Mismanagement, branches of which can be found in the government buildings and in the offices of the government leaders of every state and nation worldwide. If that initiative proves to be as ineffectual as expected, Felicity would be glad to join you in the ancient rite of a good old midnight howl at the ungrateful moon.

However, until those two appeals to higher authority fail, it will be necessary for us to accept patiently the vagaries of Felicity's history and to press on and to create some fantasies about schizophrenia.

Mistaken Diagnoses – Non-Schizophrenia – It's Sometimes Right to be Wrong

There is always an upside to everything. It's so nice that Felicity is wrong most of the time. If he weren't, he might be one of those insufferable know-it-all's who are so utterly boring, that is, who talk when you wish they would listen. Well, he does that too. Nevertheless, Felicity's habit of seeing everything wrongly has served him well from time to time. And, recognizing his own tendency to get things wrong has made him almost tolerant of other people's mistakes. Of course, it might be argued that it is Felicity who has been wrong in 'recognizing' error in other people's points of view.

Regardless of who is wrong, since this story is about Felicity's stories, we will just have to tolerate his judgements about others' errors, and accept for the moment that he is right. So, this chapter is about mistakes others have made in reaching some diagnoses. Of course, it may be that the whole volume is about somebody's mistakes of understanding.

Faintly Saintly

In the days of the old mental hospitals, people got locked up as 'crazy' for all sorts of crazy reasons. Ruth was one of these. Barely past her mid-teens, she found herself in the hands of a helping medical profession that had hoodwinked her loving family. She was consigned to a large, ill-kempt but sterile hall lined with cold, sparsely furnished bedrooms each shared among only six women – all of whose lack of consideration for one another and for personal hygiene would have put Attila the Hun to shame. The only sins for which she was afforded this punishment was that she was unduly concerned about her own personal hygiene, about the risk of hurting other people's feelings, and about expressing herself on anything for fear she might be wrong. She had only one simple goal in life – to be a saint. For this, of course, it was necessary that she be punished.

To be fair, this was not how Ruth was seen by the medical professionals under whose care she was placed. One of the young medical doctors was assigned the task of 'working up' this case. This doctor was serving his residency in psychiatry under the supervision of a full-fledged psychiatrist. Until he enrolled in his residency, this young doctor had received no training at all in the life science of psychology – and little after that – but had received extensive training devoted largely to the study of the anatomy and chemistry of dead bodies. Of course, the same was true of his supervisor before he had taken his residency in psychiatry. In accordance with his training, the young doctor approached his patient as though she was a piece of meat, undressed her and examined her to find that her body was flawless both inside and out. Since he was now learning to be a psychiatrist, he then examined her and her history under the microscope of sterile questions the thrust of which she could not begin to understand. He then referred her for the usual laboratory tests to be done by Neurology, Chemistry, and Psychology – in those days, psychologists were expected to do psychological assessments that nobody paid any attention to.

Felicity was the hapless neophyte in Psychology to whom 'the case' was assigned. He did the usual intelligence and projective tests that were expected of psychologists. He analyzed the tests and prepared a report for the great conference, called 'grand rounds', to be held concerning this patient. He came to the 'grand rounds', held in a huge amphitheatre, along with all the medical staff, psychiatrists, and specialists, psychologists, social workers, nurses and occupational therapists employed in the place. The room was packed. Felicity, presumably like most of the others present, was sufficiently over-awed by the impressive collection of 'big guns' that, sitting halfway back in the theatre among many other faces, he forgot to wonder how over-awed the patient was going to feel.

The young resident in psychiatry sat at the base of the amphitheatre clad in his white lab coat, trembling visibly in his boots and not daring to look up at the sea of white lab coats and white nurses' uniforms staring down at him. He was equally afraid to look over at the psychiatrist-in-chief, also in a white lab coat, who was sitting beside him.

The young resident fumbled through his notes and read from them his observations concerning this poor unfortunate girl. She could not pay consistent attention to the questions asked of her. She was often unresponsive to his probing questions and tended to talk off in a tangential direction when she did answer him. He had noted that she was not in control of her actions, being unable, for example, to extricate herself from her extended cleansing of herself in the bathroom. She made little sense in what she did talk about and the way she talked, was unable to complete sentences she started, and often 'blocked' in her thoughts about issues. Her movements were slow, restricted and executed with great difficulty, and if he placed her arm in a particular way, she would keep it there indefinitely. All these 'symptoms' added up, in his mind, to a classical case of catatonic schizophrenia.

The real psychiatrists began to ask him questions. Each wanted to be sure he or she made the most telling points or had noticed the most characteristic symptoms to be found in this schizophrenic patient.

Then various other reports were heard, including Felicity's psychological report. Felicity indicated that Ruth had 'normal' intelligence, which was really all the psychiatrists wanted to hear from him – at least they now knew that her manifest 'thought disorder' was not due to mental retardation. But Felicity also had the effrontery to suggest that the symptoms they had been talking about were not those of schizophrenia, but instead were those of a severe obsessive-compulsive neurosis. The psychiatrist-in-chief was briefly interested in that alternative possibility, even although it had come from a mere neophyte psychologist. It might have occurred to him for a moment that, like all psychologists, this one had completed at least seven years of university studies all concerned with psychology – the very field of study of the subject-matter of the conference. He may have remembered that this education had been followed by a year of internship in clinical or health psychology and that he had worked as a psychologist for a couple of years, even if it was only in a clinic for children. But then, psychologists were not physicians, so how could they be expected to be as clinically-insightful as real medical doctors, or as scientifically sophisticated (of course, psychologists' basic training is as scientists, in the basic science of Psychology). Anyway, Felicity's strange ideas were quickly thrust aside.

Then Ruth was brought in. She was supported by two stout nurses as she hobbled tensely in. She was seated between her 'doctor' and the chief of all the doctors – who was talking to her. She was sitting looking up at a sea of white-clad doctors all staring intently at her, apparently in cold, punitive scorn. Would she be drowned in that sea? She had heard about this terrible ordeal from other patients, and she knew it was the final court that was to seal her fate for all time. She expected to be taken from this court and cast into the back wards from which nobody ever returned. Time and time again, after being at this conference, patients from the reception ward had simply vanished never to be seen or heard from again. She listened intently for her sentence to be pronounced.

She tried to pay attention to the barrage of questions fired at her by the psychiatrist-in-chief, and then by other faces from that wall of white-clothed lawyers. But the questions came too fast, and she barely had time to process one question, let alone to respond with honesty to it, before two more questions competed for her attention and created dreadful confusion in her mind. She stammered and blocked. She did not complete her sentences. She tried to jump back to complete her answer to a former question accurately, thereby sounding very tangential and scattered in her thinking. And she 'split hairs' in her responses so that she sounded as bewildered as she was and quite unable to think in an orderly way. Finally, the psychiatrist-in-chief, himself, lifted her arm to the position in which he thought it should remain and left it there. She felt awkward holding her arm in that position. But she did not want to offend this important man, so she kept it where it was put. When she was told she could go, still holding her arm where it had been placed, she struggled in fearful tension to her feet and, trying to hold her stiff body 'just so', hobbled out at the pace of a very old and very tired turtle.

There was no question of the diagnosis. The notation in the records showed a final diagnosis: chronic catatonic schizophrenia. And the decision of the conference was that she would therefore be relegated to a bed on a back ward for the rest of her life.

There was only one dissenting voice. Although nobody was willing to listen to Felicity's diagnostic opinion, the chairman was willing to listen to any thoughts about the kinds of activity in which Ruth might be involved, given her youth. Felicity proposed that, since the conference was disposed to the opinion that Ruth had a chronic, intractable illness for which no specific treatment was to be undertaken, perhaps the conference would allow him to try out some 'behavioural therapies' with her.

The idea was outrageous. Psychologists didn't treat patients. They did psychological tests to provide psychiatrists with one type of laboratory investigation of their patients. However, perhaps in deference to Felicity's youth and inexperience, and the need for Felicity to have a solid learning encounter to discover that you couldn't cure this kind of patient, the chairman graciously gave Felicity permission to 'take on this case' for a little harmless 'behaviour' therapy.

Felicity, of course, already knew what was wrong – at least in his mind. It was a severe, but simple, neurosis and not schizophrenia at all. And some neuroses were being treated in those days by a new method devised by (psychiatrist) Joseph Wolpe called Reciprocal Inhibition Therapy. Felicity knew that a psychologist friend of his had treated a patient with this method. He contacted his friend and asked him how this treatment was done. The friend gave him a curt description of the method over the phone, but had no time in which to teach Felicity any more about it. Felicity got hold of Wolpe's book and worked his way through it. On the basis of the resulting slight acquaintance with the ideas, he began to treat Ruth. No change at all was occurring. Felicity tried out all sorts of things to get Ruth to relax. She could not do it at all. Her body was as tense as a board, and her muscles were like stretched wire springs.

In sheer frustration, Felicity went to visit the colleague who had used the method and begged for some help in undertaking the procedure. The friend at last confessed that he really didn't understand how to use the method well, and that the outcome he had obtained in his case was a result of blind luck, and had only been temporary anyway. Together, they arranged for their local psychological association to organize a workshop with interested professionals, and to invite Wolpe to give a training session. Felicity was delighted with what he learned in the week-long course, and he returned to treat Ruth with renewed vigour and commitment.

About a year after the conference in which she had been given her life sentence to the back ward of the hospital, Ruth was once more conferenced at Felicity's request. The surroundings were the same. She was once more confronted by the wall of white-draped 'lawyers', and she was once more seated at the front with her 'doctor' and the psychiatrist-in-chief. But there was her friend Felicity sitting in the middle of the third row. She talked to him in answer to the questions put to her. Finally, she was asked what was the main thing that she thought accounted for her recovery. Felicity felt a mixture of intense joy at the last word uttered in the question, and of embarrassment at the answer. Ruth burst into girlish giggling and said it was the 'laughing sessions' they had shared together. All Felicity's pride and self-importance, felt in his mastery of this new behaviour therapy, and in his success in curing this incurable disease, crumbled at his feet in what he considered to be a trivialization of his accomplishment.

But it served Ruth well. Since the mere psychologist had really done nothing more than a comedian could have done, it was acceptable to the conference to graciously grant that it had made a mistake in the original diagnosis, and that the patient had recovered and could return home once more.

But the conference, unbeknown to itself, had done something else. True, it had affirmed on this occasion that it was not an infallible tool by which to achieve 'the final diagnosis'. But it had also vacated a bed that had been consigned in its collective mind to a single person for perhaps fifty years into the future. This fact did not elude Felicity's groping mind. Following the conference, in the fresh blush of his acknowledged success, he went to see the psychiatrist-in-chief and brashly remarked that, by the chief's own calculations, Felicity had saved the hospital one bed for at least forty-eight years. Having allowed that idea to be implanted firmly in the chief's mind, Felicity added that he thought it only just and fair that he, Felicity, be granted a unit of twelve backward beds, and a nurse to service them, in which he could experiment for, say, four years with the applicability of behaviour therapy to schizophrenia. The psychiatrist-in-chief looked benignly at Felicity, laughed uproariously, said he understood now how 'laughing sessions' worked, and granted the dumbfounded Felicity his request without amendment.

The rest of these tales about schizophrenia are possible because, for the next six years, Felicity was in charge of the treatment for twelve in-patient beds which were (it's almost unthinkable to say) surrendered to the care of a wild-eyed, rebellious, impulsive young psychologist and his regular-days nurse. Now everybody who is anybody knows that these sorts of things could not have happened, and certainly not in those days. So, unfettered by the demands of reality, these tales can be told.

A Dream Team

We've had a story about a non-*catatonic* non-schizophrenic in the person of Ruth. Although we're not done with schizophrenia yet, it might be refreshing, even silly, to tell a yarn about a non-*paranoid* non-schizophrenic. Rosemary was just such a person. Rosemary was admitted to Felicity's Behaviour Therapy Unit bearing with her a diagnosis of conjugal paranoia. She was a very attractive married woman in her early thirties. She had a husband who adored her. The only blemish on their marriage was that Rosemary had been living in the hospital for about four years suffering constantly from jealousy about her husband. If he mentioned another woman or looked in passing at a calendar with a picture of a female on it, Rosemary was consumed with jealousy. She was sure he no longer loved her, that he really wanted to be with the other woman, and that he was about to leave her. She would remonstrate with him hour after hour about any and all such events. Finally, to obtain some peace of mind and some rest for both of them, it was decided that she would take a vacation from him in the hospital. It was also hoped that the hospital vacation would rid her of her jealousy. However, the vacation was extended rather longer than planned due to the discovery by her psychiatrists that she had a mysterious mental illness called conjugal paranoia.

To be fair, the hospital psychiatrists had inherited this diagnosis of her condition from the psychiatrists who had been treating her for years in the community. She had started going to psychiatrists in her late teens, and the psychiatrists to whom she had been referred were psychoanalysts. Rosemary had become very well indoctrinated in the mysteries of psychoanalysis. She knew what her role as the patient was. Consequently, after she was admitted to his Behaviour Therapy Unit and was given appointments to see Felicity in his office, she came in, sat down and, without further ceremony, began to recount in precious detail all the events which went to make up the contents of her nocturnal dream life.

Nor could Felicity dissuade her from this well-habituated activity. She simply ignored his attempts to draw her into other more productive therapeutic pursuits. It was as though she felt duty-bound to educate Felicity in the correct therapeutics and process necessary for psychotherapy. She was unwilling or unable to notice that she had already tried that approach to treatment and that it had yielded no benefit for her at all. Felicity began to think that Rosemary might indeed be suffering from a schizophrenic illness given her imperviousness to his presence, interventions, and obviously impeccable logic. "Perhaps," Felicity thought, "since she isn't listening to what I am saying, I ought to listen to what she is saying." Now how's that for a shockingly different idea!?

Most of Rosemary's time was spent describing a recurring dream in which she saw her husband in the company of two women, involved in any number of wondrous and tantalizing acts. The one woman was a white woman dressed all in white. The other was a black woman dressed all in black. It was evident that Rosemary was trying to sort out in her mind what her unconscious was telling her about her good and her wicked sides – or perhaps it was her husband's good and wicked sides. Felicity had never been much of a judge, and it troubled him when people were judgemental. Besides, damn it, he just was not interested in triangles; he knew he was a square But her tales sounded as if they were scripts for soap operas.

He was upset by the lack of progress in this 'psychotherapy'. It bugged him that Rosemary wanted to tell him about the intricate and intimate details of these two women's actions and their contrasting attires, and he was often confused about which woman was which. It occurred to him that he would be happier if he had to keep track of only one woman. He wondered how that might be achieved.

No less to his shock than to yours, he remembered one or two things he had learned in his undergraduate psychology classes. He thought it might be fun if he could make use of that learning to combat the complexes created in Rosemary by her psychoanalysis. Skinner had suggested that whatever is rewarded tends to increase, and whatever is unrewarded tends to be reduced or extinguished. Felicity turned his back on Rosemary and started to ignore her. He wrote up notes, doodled, hummed, and even made phone calls while she detailed the black qualities of the black girl or the white qualities of the white girl. One day, Rosemary mentioned a white quality of the black girl – the black girl was said to be wearing a white belt. Instantly, Felicity swung around to face Rosemary, leaned excitedly toward her, and delivered himself of a breathless "wow!" She seemed unperturbed by his interruption of her tale, and she continued to talk about black features of the black girl and white characteristics of the white girl.

But her recurrent dream began, ever so slowly, to transform itself. Changes were erratic and somewhat random at first. However, the reported dream contents changed in successive sessions as Felicity continued to "uh huh" enthusiastically, as if he was trying to reward her for every mention of a black element of the white girl or a white element of the black girl, and to ignore both Rosemary and what she was saying the rest of the time. The black girl was increasingly reported to be wearing white accessories and then white clothes, and the white girl was reported increasingly to be wearing black accessories and then black clothes.

Then came the day when Rosemary came in for her usual psychotherapy appointment and, without any apparent surprise, recounted dreams in which her husband was seen with only one girl – a white girl in a black dress with some black and some white accessories. The dreams contained the usual wondrously sensual activities – the nature of which will be left to you to imagine, since your mind is certainly possessed of a much more salacious imagination than Felicity's. The dreams with the one white girl dressed in black and white continued to be reported at the next session that week.

As usual, Rosemary went home that weekend to spend some time with her husband. For the first time in his memory there were no recriminations of a jealous nature. Tucked away in a closet, she found a calendar with a picture of a scantily clad woman. She looked at it, asked her husband in an off-hand way whether he liked the way the woman's hair was done, shrugged when she received no reply, rolled it up and put it away again in the closet. Her husband had not answered out of sheer shock at her response. As he put it, the wind from a feather waved near him would have knocked him off his feet.

Rosemary spent the next couple of weekends at home. She seemed delighted to be with her husband. She continued to act as though she was no longer jealous on shopping trips. She no longer grilled him about what he had been doing during the week since her last visit. Their sex life was reported to be greatly improved. It seemed that she and her husband were happy together at last. Meanwhile, the dream reports, to which Felicity was now fairly constantly attentive and reinforcing, continued to present her husband with one white girl dressed in black and white elements, and there was a happier tone in her voice while she reported them.

Felicity arranged to have Rosemary presented at conference. The opinion of the psychiatrists was that she had recovered, and she was discharged home. During the two years of periodic follow-up interviews with Felicity, Rosemary continued to present herself and her relationship with her husband as happy and satisfying. Her husband certainly seemed delighted with her and with their relationship, and said that there was no longer any jealousy between them. She required no medication nor any continuing psychotherapy, and was receiving none.

If this was schizophrenia or one of its sub-categories, namely, paranoia, it was apparently remarkably responsive to simple reinforcement of the contents of her thoughts. You see, contrary to the myths we have all been told about the symbolisms in dreams, the contents of dreams come about rather simply. They are largely taken from events, including thoughts, in the person's life of the preceding day, tinged with a flavour from the things about which the person is most afraid or upset. It is true that dream contents are chopped up and distorted. However, that seems to be mainly a result of two factors. Firstly, during sleep, the person is disengaged from the 'driving' effect on the sequence of events afforded by the 'orderly progression of stimuli' from the world presented to the senses in daily waking life. And, secondly, the 'organizing' effect of reason, regulated by the cerebral cortex in waking life (and lulled in sleep), is absent. So, if a person's habitual patterns of thinking are modified, as by simple operant conditioning, the thoughts with which the person is preoccupied may change, and thus the person's dream contents may change.

Of course, a cynic might want to suggest that all that happened with Rosemary was that she learned not to talk about the paranoid jealousy that was upsetting her – after all, Felicity ignored that kind of talk and rewarded less 'paranoid' talk. If that is indeed what happened, Rosemary, her husband and Felicity were all gratified by the outcome. And it is possible that Rosemary's happiness in not talking about her jealousy may have served to reward and thus maintain her inhibition of such ideas.

It turned out that there was nothing particularly novel about what Felicity did with Rosemary. Other psychologists reported similar methods with similar results. Felicity found a paper by Ayllon in which he reported use of simple operant conditioning of behaviour (reinforcing or rewarding the 'desired', non-symptomatic actions) in schizophrenic patients, following which their symptoms vanished. The technically neat element in that work was that nurses were trained to do the reinforcing of the desired behaviours on the ward as a daily routine.

In the usual case, nurses, who are caring people, are taught to inquire into and observe symptomatic behaviour of patients. Of course, this tends to reward such behaviour with attention, and thus may increase the occurrence of the undesired symptomatic behaviour. Ayllon got the nurses to reverse their natural and caring habits, to ignore any symptomatic behaviour and the person producing it, and to reward with their attention any kind of non-symptomatic behaviour.

A Depressing Mania

No account of non-schizophrenia would be complete without at least passing attention to the other major mental disorder, manic-depressive 'illness' – now called bi-polar affective disorder. Rachel was subject to this disorder. Rachel was a heavy-set, even rotund, woman in her mid-forties. She had been re-admitted to the old mental hospital at least a couple of times every year for some sixteen years. Each time she exhibited a mixture of manic pressure of speech and depressive affect (feelings), sometimes separately, and sometimes at the same time. She was admitted to the Behaviour Therapy Unit just to give that Unit its turn at trying to deal with her hard-to-manage behaviour.

Felicity was more impressed by the depressive features Rachel exhibited clinically and on her psychological tests than he was with the (apparently 'defensive') flights into mania. He concluded from the tests that the main psychological problem underlying both poles of her disorder was her intense need for clinging dependency. She needed to hang on to attention from others and to acquire others' efforts to lift her mood and help her to feel better.

He tried a number of different means by which to train her in independency and in assertiveness. She was stubbornly resistant to any of his obviously brilliant and impressive ideas and efforts. Felicity was not used to treating a patient for longer than a few months without seeing some benefits from his work. Accordingly, when no change at all could be demonstrated in almost six months on the Unit, he was forced to do the unthinkable – he had to think about her. As if that was not enough of an indignity, he found his muddled brain was not sufficient to the task of finding any decent solutions to the problems posed by Rachel. The one thought he had seemed inappropriate and demeaning to the patient.

He consulted Rachel's psychiatrist and, in order to illustrate how devoid he was of any good ideas, told her about the one inappropriate thought he had. The psychiatrist thought it was a good idea, and encouraged Felicity to try it. She even offered to serve as a security guard during the 'treatment' in order to keep other staff away in case they might feel they had to intervene. Her support of what Felicity thought to be almost an improper idea was just another instance in which people astonished Felicity and made him feel like an innocent square. The 'treatment' was to take a full half-day, and it was scheduled into both of their timetables for a whole afternoon – in case it lasted longer than planned.

On the appointed afternoon, Rachel was summoned to Felicity's office. When she arrived, Felicity told her that he had a terribly important task that had to be done as quickly and as precisely as possible. He said that, since Rachel was possessed of immense energy and was such a nice and accommodating person, he had decided to ask her to help him. She looked properly puffed up with her importance and agreed to do whatever it was he needed her to do. He took her into an adjoining office containing only a desk and a chair, asked her to seat herself, and put a paper and pencil on the desk for the task she would be doing. The paper was a test answer sheet covered on both sides with little circles. Felicity told her that he needed to have each of the circles filled in with dark pencil marks as soon as possible, but without any pencil marks extending outside of any circle. She said she could do that, and she buried herself in the task.

Every few minutes, Felicity hurried into the room 'to see how she was doing' and 'to encourage her' to hurry up with the task. Each time, as he left the room, he spluttered out an audible giggle as though he could not restrain his laughter until he got back into his own office. At first, Rachel seemed oblivious to his mirth. So he smiled and chuckled behind her back as he entered the room. She began to detect that there was something about his behaviour and her task beyond what 'met the eye'. She examined his face suspiciously each time he entered the room. He allowed his face to register feigned seriousness while holding his stomach and fighting off a feigned smile of amusement. Eventually, she concluded he was laughing at her, indeed that he was ridiculing her. She asked him directly what was happening, and whether he was trying to play a joke on her. As if he could no longer contain himself, Felicity broke down in gales of laughter, pointed his finger derisively at her and nodded his acknowledgement that he had indeed been playing a practical joke on her.

Right on schedule, Rachel let out a scream of rage and leaped at Felicity trying to beat at him with her fists. Being ready for just this reaction, Felicity caught her arms, turned and pulled her so that she fell forward. He let her down gently on the carpeted floor, face down. Then he sat down on her. Rachel kicked and screamed in absolute fury at the dual indignities of the pseudo-task she had been given and the restraint of her position on the floor. Her own weight, augmented by Felicity's as he sat upon her, made her incapable of regaining an attack position. So she continued to scream and to thrash about all through the long hours of the afternoon.

Of course, the commotion brought innumerable staff running from all around the hospital. The psychiatrist, manning the closed office door, turned them all away. Of course, everybody who came running to help wanted to know what was happening to whoever it was that was being murdered in there. Since she had to stand up outside the door, while Felicity was sitting comfortably on Rachel inside the door, the psychiatrist deemed it only right and fair to explain that it was only Felicity who was being attacked – so nobody need be too alarmed at whatever was happening. When Felicity later heard about this explanation, he could not fail to notice, to his chagrin, that it had apparently satisfied all the staff who had inquired – as if they felt that murder would be a just and fitting reward for him.

After about three hours of kicking and screaming, Rachel tired of the exercise. She finally asked to be allowed to get up. She said that she was ready to settle down. But Felicity was not quite finished. As he let her up, he congratulated her warmly for being so wonderfully assertive and thanked her for providing him with such a nice comfortable seat on which to sit all afternoon. The Banshee let out another blood-curdling scream and attacked again. Felicity caught her flailing arms, pulled and swung her and let her gently back to the floor again. He resumed his perch on her back. This time the screaming and kicking lasted barely another hour.

With surprising suddenness, the noise and activity stopped. She was quiet for about a minute. Then she started to laugh. Felicity let her get up. She was almost doubled up with laughter for a full five minutes. Hearing this, the psychiatrist entered the room. Rachel looked back and forth at her two doctors, pointing at each in turn and laughing uproariously. They joined in the mirth. Finally, Rachel's laughter subsided. Through sporadic giggles, she thanked both Felicity and the psychiatrist, gave them each a warm hug and asked if she could now go for supper. It was agreed that was a superior idea and, arms linked, the three of them sauntered off to the dining room.

Rachel was presented at conference the following week and was discharged as recovered. It's true that she was re-admitted periodically after that to the hospital. However, there were no re-admissions for slightly over a year, and each admission after this 'treatment' was for a brief few days 'for a rest'. Each time, when she was ready to conclude her 'rest' cure, she would make contact with Felicity or her psychiatrist. As soon as she met either one of them, without other words, the two together would break into gales of laughter for a few minutes. Rachel would then affirm that she was now ready to be discharged.

Was this a treatment for anything? Felicity certainly wouldn't affirm that it wasn't. On the contrary, he took to referring to this incident under the title of Mis-Treatment Therapy, or the M-T (empty?) Therapy. He was grateful to Rachel for her good-natured response to his attempt to get her angry at two people who were 'important' to her so that she could discover it was not necessary to be 'nice' and 'clinging' in order to have people like her. From Felicity's perspective, the important indicator of therapeutic benefit was her laughter, by which she seemed able to dispel her depressions.

Dementia – Varieties of Schizophrenia – Untranquillized Tranquillity

In eight years of working in the old mental hospital, Felicity requested the purchase of quite a few fairly expensive items of equipment to permit him to do some of the things he needed to do. However, during that time he was gratified to be granted only one $30 expenditure for the purchase of a 'electrical shock stimulus' device. Not one of *that* kind. He didn't want to do 'shock treatments', which are actually called Electro-Convulsive Therapy, or ECT. No, he wanted to use 'tickle shock' to the fingers to deliver a mild discomfort. If he were going to knock people out, he would have used a two-by-four – that was about as sophisticated as he knew how to be.

It's true that ECT and a shock stimulus have a couple of things in common – they are both used in treatments of some psychological disorders, and they both help people to 'live better electrically'. But Felicity wanted the 'shock stimulus' for the Behaviour Therapy Unit, to be used daily by the nurse, morning and afternoon, with all of the twelve patients on the Unit. He wanted it for a treatment method he had read about in Wolpe's book called anxiety-relief conditioning. It provided a kind of 'psychological aspirin'. The patients took to calling the procedure the 'Be Calm' method. Indeed, it was intended to provide a psychological tranquillizer for the patients since they were taken off all medications when they were admitted to the Behaviour Therapy Unit.

Oh, you didn't know that? Oh, yes, by prior agreement with the psychiatrists, all the patients were taken off all psychotropic medications as soon as they were admitted to the Unit. Oh dear, you noticed another evidence of the fictional nature of these stories; oh well, let's press on regardless. Now, you may think that an arrangement removing patients from all psychotropic medications would be inappropriate. Surely, if patients are put on medications, they must *need* them. I suppose we accept that idea because we have heard about the wonderful drugs the pharmaceutical companies, drug stores, and physicians are constantly pushing. And we get used to the authoritative attitudes of physicians who seek ‹compliance with medical procedures› on the part of their patients. It is probably true that moderate use of antibiotics and of some supplemental drugs, such as insulin with some diabetics, *are* desirable and may be necessary to support life. However, many prescribed medications are not necessary, and some are probably inappropriate and even harmful.

The psychotropic (psyche or 'mind', and tropic or 'moving toward', thus, mind-bending) drugs, in particular, tend both to only moderate symptoms, and to be addictive. And they may even perpetuate some of the symptoms they are administered to treat. To illustrate this last statement, one of the consequences of taking patients off all medications when they were admitted to the Behaviour Therapy Unit was that a percentage of them recovered and were discharged before any other treatment could be introduced. And, in other settings, some patients undergoing psychotherapy while remaining on street drugs or psychotropic medications have displayed major delays in acquiring psychotherapeutic benefits, sometimes exhibiting no change at all until they have stopped using the chemicals.

Still, the common use of psychotropic drugs in health practice has created an expectation among patients that they should not have to suffer too much while in treatment. This expectation, of course, whether appropriate or not, had to be recognized as a reality by Felicity. Moreover, if only on humanitarian grounds, it seemed necessary to provide some means by which to effect some peace of mind among the patients if they were to be denied their expected tranquillizing pills. It was for this reason that Felicity felt it necessary to implement a program of anxiety-relief conditioning for the patients on the Unit.

Anxiety-relief conditioning involves a simple five-minute procedure. The index and ring fingers of the patient's right hand received ring electrodes attached, through a telegraph key switch, to the shock stimulus. The telegraph key switch was used both because it could not be left ON by accident, and because the 'release' action which breaks the circuit tends to be quicker than the 'press' action involved in pushing a button down on a switch. The output from the shock stimulus was protected with a $1/200^{th}$ ampere (5 ma) fuse so as to avoid emitting any dangerous shocks.

The patient was instructed, "At that moment at which you think that at the next moment the sensation to the fingers might become at all uncomfortable, give the verbal signal: 'Be Calm'." The person was told that as soon as the 'Be Calm' signal was given, the shock stimulus would be turned off.

When the patient had been instructed in that way, the voltage control potentiometer (knob) was set to zero volts, the telegraph key was pushed down (closed), and the voltage control was turned up ever so slowly. As soon as the patient gave the 'Be Calm' signal, the telegraph key was released (opened), the voltage value at which the signal was given was recorded, and the voltage control was returned again to zero for the next 'run'. Each treatment session involved twenty such 'runs', and took about five minutes. So, to treat all twelve patients on the Unit took a little more than an hour of the nurse's time when she arrived in the morning and again before she left work in the afternoon. The patients quickly started to look forward to their 'Be Calm' treatments.

This doesn't sound like it would do anything, does it? The way it works is fairly simple. The purpose is to train anxiety reduction to a voluntary (verbal) cue (in this case, 'Be Calm'). Most anxiety is 'anticipatory' anxiety – that is, it anticipates discomfort. To learn how to reduce such anxiety, it has first to be aroused in a controlled fashion *and* then reduced quickly and on demand. There are lots of ways of making a person anxious, but very few of them allow the anxiety to be reduced quickly and on demand. The electrical shock stimulus provides a way to create mild pain that can quickly be relieved by turning the shock stimulus off. But we don't want pain; we want anxiety to be aroused and relieved. So the instructions ask the person not to experience pain, but to give the verbal cue ('Be Calm') at that moment when he or she expects that the level of stimulation is *just about to become* uncomfortable – that is, when discomfort is *anticipated*.

So, every time the person feels anticipatory anxiety, and then gives the verbal ('Be Calm') cue, the body discovers (from the many practice trials) that it feels a reduction in its discomfort or anxiety. After a while, every time the person gives and/or hears the 'Be Calm' signal, whether or not attached to the shock stimulus, the body reacts by reducing its anxiety. Apparently, it learns that the 'Be Calm' cue signals that the anticipated discomfort is about to be reduced.

The method conditions or trains anxiety-relief. That, in turn, provides a means by which the person can calm him or herself down at any time during the day, and also provides a means for the nurse to create non-chemical calmness in her patients twice a day during the regular anxiety-relief conditioning sessions.

This program was an important one on the Unit. A quick glance at each patient's recorded 'voltage tolerance' levels for the day provided Felicity with a simple and quick way of monitoring how each one was doing. If the 'voltage tolerance' (the point on the voltage scale at which the patient gave the 'Be Calm' signals) was unusually low, he knew the patient was probably feeling pretty depressed – she was apparently particularly sensitive to any felt discomfort, which is a major indicator of depression. If the 'voltage tolerance' was unusually high, he knew the patient was feeling particularly defensive, emotionally rather 'cold', and thus less vulnerable to discomfort. If the 'voltage tolerance' was increasing across the twenty runs of a session, he knew that the anxiety-relief response was conditioned and was working. That is, apparently, each 'Be Calm' signal was calming the patient down before the next electrical stimulation, so that she would be less uncomfortable for it and thus able to accept more voltage. Once this was established, anybody could help the patient to settle down by asking her to give the 'Be Calm' cue even though she was not attached to the equipment. The procedure reduced distress and arousal in each of the patients, and tended to prevent disruptive actions and interactions within the group due to distress.

Having told you this long story, what follows is bound to be a bit anti-climactic. You see, the usual anxiety-relief conditioning procedure was used in an altered way for both Susan and Shirley. Moreover, we are not going to start by talking about either one of them. Instead, let's pretend for a little while that the foregoing presentation of the anxiety-relief conditioning method might be relevant to something, such as the next story.

An Escapist's Escapade

Sadie was a pretty and skinny young lady in her early twenties. She was a patient on another ward. Felicity was asked to see her to determine whether anything in his bag of tricks might be of help. The problem was that she was thoroughly unmanageable. Periodically, she would start breaking things up on the ward in a frenzy of rage or excitement or panic – nobody seemed clear about what the problem was. She had been diagnosed as having a simple schizophrenic illness – "simple schizophrenia" being a diagnosis – and she was said to be unable to communicate what the problem was or why she acted out every so often as she did – 'every so often' being at least twice a day.

Sadie did have one remarkable talent. Unlike anybody Felicity had ever heard about, Sadie could slither out of a professionally prepared 'wet pack' within a minute or two. Now, a 'wet pack' was used (maybe it still is, for all I know) as a means to control unmanageable patients. The well-known straight-jacket merely confines the arms. A 'wet pack' involves a wet sheet in which the person is tightly and intricately wound so that arms, legs and body are not only confined, they are compressed, and in a supine position. The wet sheet is attached by another wet sheet to the bed. Of course, the wet sheet is sticky, and the wrapping is so tight there is no way of moving in order to slither out of the confinement. But Sadie could do it, although nobody seemed to know how. And she did it regularly. This, of course, made her that much harder to manage. The staff were at their wits' end.

If Felicity were asked to see this young woman today, he would put her through some elaborate psychological test procedures, make a brilliant formulation about the problem she had, and probably use some totally different procedure to treat her. But then he isn't seeing her today. This was many years ago, and he would say he was probably a lot smarter then.

Felicity went to her room to talk to Sadie. She looked at him as though he was the intruder he was, and demanded to know what he wanted of her. He didn't know what to say. But he must have looked as though he was going to break down in tears because she relented and agreed that he could talk to her as he was the second ugliest man she had seen all day. Having reached that pinnacle of pleasant cooperativeness, it might have been predictable that it would all be downhill the rest of the way. Fortunately, Felicity already had some tests that had been administered to her, and what he really wanted to do was to get a clinical look at her, and to see whether he would be privileged to be on the receiving end of one of her tantrums. He was. And the thunderbolt struck within barely two minutes of his appearance in her room.

Before fleeing the room, he was quick enough both to notice two things, and to duck whatever it was she threw at him. The two things he noticed were that, before she blew up, she was holding one of her wrists as if she wanted to choke it, and that the hand of the wrist she was holding had only the thumb and the index finger on it. Since he had nothing else to go on, he decided he must have made an important observation – the purpose of his visit.

He looked up her medical records to find out about her left hand. What he found out was that some years previously it had been suspected that she had cancer, presumably bone cancer, affecting some of the fingers of her left hand. Accordingly, three fingers of her left hand had been amputated. Now what? Felicity looked bleakly at the thin collection of questionnaires in her file. A strange prickly feeling spread over him. He recognized the feeling as the precursor, perhaps an aura, of what he was going to consider to be a brilliant idea – meaning it would be a half-baked guess that any kindergarten student of psychology would be ashamed to acknowledge.

The hypothesis was: What if this young woman was experiencing pain from 'phantom digits' – 'imaginary' pain as if it was coming from imaginary fingers which no longer were there? Phantom pain was not an unheard-of phenomenon. But Sadie knew the fingers were not there. So it might just be that she considered the idea of pain from non-existing parts to be too silly an idea to tell anybody about. That would account for why she was unable to communicate her 'problem' to anyone. Perhaps the pain was like a terrible toothache that just would not go away, or like an itch she couldn't scratch. That ought to create enough upset within her to churn her up to throw a tantrum from time to time. Felicity thought that if he had such a problem it might irritate him enough that he might throw tantrums too.

Felicity knew that nobody would accept an hypothesis as silly as the one he had just dreamed up. After all, that would be sensible, and this was a schizophrenic patient. So, rather than explaining his thought, he made up a story. He needed to find out, or so he said, what changes were occurring in her motivation. So he would administer tests to her repeatedly to see how her scores changed in relation to her tantrums. The staff accepted that plan because, after all, that's what psychologists did – they gave tests. But Felicity also pointed out that he might expect her to get pretty irritated at the repeated testing. And so he wanted it known that, if she became too upset, he might have to use some anxiety-relief conditioning with her to help her settle down. That plan sounded satisfactory to all the staff involved with the case.

Felicity arranged to have the Cattell Anxiety Scale (CAS) and the Pain Analog Measure (PAM) administered to Sadie twice a day at set times, but where the times could be varied so she was not being asked to do them while she was throwing a tantrum or (supposed to be) in a wet pack. This continued for a week, and Felicity was pleased to note that Sadie accepted this extra task with amazing grace. He then arranged for anxiety-relief conditioning to be done with her in the usual way (to the Right hand) twice a day. The only variation from the usual procedure (as described at the beginning of this chapter) was that she was asked to use the verbal signal, 'Right', as the cue to have the shock turned off.

The anxiety-relief conditioning to 'Right' was continued for twenty sessions (two weeks). By this time the voltage tolerance was increasing steadily over the runs in each session, indicating that the conditioning had worked and the 'Right' signal was calming her down. At that point, he discontinued the anxiety-relief conditioning for a week, but continued the ongoing testing.

Next, Felicity arranged for the anxiety-relief conditioning to be started again, but this time with the ring electrodes attached to the two remaining digits of her left hand, and using the verbal signal of 'Left'. This too was continued for twenty sessions (two more weeks). By this time the voltage tolerance was increasing steadily over the runs of each session, indicating that the conditioning had worked and the 'Left' signal was calming her down. Meanwhile, he had the ward staff record the time, duration, and intensity of each of her tantrums.

Now, what was all this about? First of all, a couple of notes are needed about the tests that were being administered twice a day throughout this period of time. The Cattell Anxiety Scale is a 40 question test which yields five sub-test scores on different aspects of anxiety, namely, (A) anxiety about feeling disorganized inside, (B) anxiety about losing control, (C) anxiety about what other people might think or feel about one, (D) anxiety of the kind experienced as guilt feelings and (E) anxiety about the pressure of uncomfortable feelings growing within one, such as anger. Felicity wanted to see whether any of these variables might be related to the timing and frequency of Sadie's tantrums. He was particularly interested in what might happen to the B, D and E scores.

And the results were quite interesting. The A and C scores remained the same throughout. The D score changed a little, but it was unrelated to anything Felicity could find that was going on in her life. The B score, and more particularly the E score, went up and down, rising quickly just before a tantrum, and falling off slowly after each tantrum. This was what Felicity had expected – that is, her anger drive and her anxious effort to control it both (1) increased as she was getting ready for a tantrum and then (2) subsided after the tantrum. Moreover, there was a slight reduction in the overall level of anxiety, and particularly in the E and B scores, during each of the two periods of anxiety-relief conditioning. And each successive reduction in anxiety, once established, was retained during the rest of the time she was undergoing testing.

The Pain Analog Measure (PAM) used a borrowed audiometer – a device that allows a tone of controlled pitch and volume to be fed to either ear or to both. In this case, it was fed to both ears through a headset. Sadie set the pitch and volume for herself, although she couldn't see the calibrations around the control knobs because the dials were covered. She was asked to indicate, by turning the knobs, both the quality and the quantity of any pain that she might be feeling in her body, but she was never asked to say where the pain, if any, was. She was asked first to turn the pitch knob to try to match or represent the *quality* of any pain she was experiencing, setting a relatively high pitch if the pain was sharp, or a relatively low pitch if the pain felt dull. She was then asked to set the volume knob to represent the *quantity* or intensity of the pain, with high volume to match or represent strong or intense pain, and low volume to match or represent rather low intensity pain. Felicity hoped that Sadie would be able to 'communicate' any pain she was feeling in this indirect way, even if she could not do so in words. The measures of pitch and volume were recorded as the pain 'scores' at each testing session.

Sure enough, the pain measures rose and fell, with the rises occurring in advance of a tantrum, and the drops occurring after a tantrum. But the pain measures often started to increase hours before a tantrum, long before the anxiety measures were increasing. And the pain measures fell immediately after a tantrum, and then fluctuated for a while before settling down. This pattern would be consistent with the idea that the accumulation of pain was triggering the tantrums.

Had Felicity's hypothesis been proved? It had not. All that was known was that Sadie felt increases in anxiety and pain associated with the approach of a tantrum, and reductions after the tantrum was over. Felicity knew that the test scores alone would not confirm his idea. The real question of importance was what might happen if the pain was modified? This brings us to the anxiety-relief conditioning and the differences between the methods used in the two sets of conditioning sessions.

The conditioning using the right hand and the signal 'Right' should, theoretically, have worked as anxiety-relief conditioning usually works – to reduce her anxiety – and the changes in the anxiety measures suggested that it worked as it 'should'. The electrical stimulation of the mutilated left hand (using the signal, 'Left') 'should' have increased the pain in her presumably already hurting left hand, and 'should' have reduced the pain following utterance of the new and different 'Left' signal. Thus, the second anxiety-relief conditioning procedure 'should' have produced a conditioned reduction of both anxiety *and* <u>pain</u>. If true, the measures of both anxiety and pain should have been reduced during and following the second (and not the first) anxiety-relief conditioning procedure. What in fact happened?

Actually, several things of note happened. First, neither of the Pain Analog Measures (quality/pitch or intensity/volume) showed any consistent changes until the middle of the second anxiety-relief conditioning procedure, except that they rose before each tantrum and fell after each tantrum. About midway through the second anxiety-relief conditioning (using the left hand and the 'Left' signal), both the sharpness (pitch) and the intensity (volume) of the pain being recorded on the PAM started to decline on average. Even when a tantrum was imminent, the PAM measures tended to be lower than they had been, presumably indicating that she was experiencing less pain as the 'pain focused' (left hand) anxiety-relief conditioning was proceeding. Of course, the pain may have come from somewhere else other than her hand.

Second, as if to confirm that Sadie was experiencing at least some pain (perhaps from phantom digits) in her left hand, during early sessions of the second (but not the first) anxiety-relief conditioning program (when the shock stimulus was connected to her left hand) she threw a tantrum *while* she was connected to the electrodes and undergoing the procedure. This happened not once, but on seven of the first twelve sessions – and each time her violent actions narrowly missed destroying Felicity›s much cherished $30 shock box. Apparently, the shock stimulation was being experienced by her as painful (as well as anxiety-provoking) when it was stimulating her left hand, suggesting that at least some of the pain she was recording on the PAM may have been from that site.

Third, the frequency and the intensity of her tantrums, as recorded by the ward staff, started to decline shortly after half way through the second (left hand) anxiety-relief conditioning procedure, although they had continued at a fairly constant rate and intensity up until that time. By the end of the second set of twenty anxiety-relief conditioning sessions, the tantrums had become quite manageable, and their frequency was down to about one every four or five days.

Unfortunately, this story does not have a satisfactory conclusion. Felicity went on a vacation for a month starting about two weeks after completion of the second anxiety-relief conditioning procedure. When he returned, he was busy for a couple more weeks with other duties and so he did not follow-up on Sadie's condition. When he finally got around to checking up on her, he was told only that she had recovered and had been discharged from the hospital. Work demands and other staff vacations interfered, and so he never did get around to finding out just what had changed in her condition, how it had changed, or on what basis the psychiatric staff had concluded that Sadie had recovered.

An Incomplete Perfection

In some ways, Susan's case was utterly unsatisfying. Susan was a round-faced, doe-eyed woman in her early thirties. Like most of the other patients, she was admitted to the Behaviour Therapy Unit with a diagnosis of schizophrenia. But Susan posed a unique problem. Far from being mute, she would talk almost incessantly. The problem was that she had a full, five-response repertoire:

(1) she would cry, (2) she would say: "Doctor, it all started when I had TB," (3) she would say: "Doctor, I've been thinking about committing suicide," (4) she would say: "I don't know what's wrong," and (5) she would say: "I don't know why nobody will listen to me." The order in which these five discrete responses were given was random – unrelated to events going on around her. Nothing would alter the pre-set course of her conversation, neither cajoling, nor authoritative demand, nor sympathetic listening, nor anything else that was tried.

Felicity was stumped. Each test administered was responded to with some sampling of the above five utterances. He could get no history. His subtle psychotherapeutic efforts were to no avail. Finally, all else having failed, in sheer desperation and as a last resort, he sat down to think. It seemed to his limited grasp of life that the restriction of Susan's response repertoire had to serve some defensive or avoidant purpose – that she was trying to avoid something. Since he could not divine what she might be trying to avoid, he concluded that the only course open to him was to get her to 'avoid avoidance'. But how could he do that?

The effort of thought must have made him sweat so that his brain got wet and swelled up to the size of a pea. The most recent thought in it about treatment had to do with anxiety-relief conditioning – the 'Be Calm' procedure the nurse was using twice a day with each patient on the Unit to serve as the Unit's psychological 'tranquillizer'. His momentarily enhanced brain power was turned to the task of discovering how he might use some modification of that procedure in order to train the patient to 'avoid avoidance'. In Susan's case, he did not want to use the aversion-relief as it was employed in the basic anxiety-relief conditioning procedure, since it might serve to reinforce any of her existing five responses further. They were already pretty well installed. She would not extend her repertoire to include the 'Be Calm' signal used in the procedure. She did weep a lot when the shock stimulus felt uncomfortable, so that the nurse would relent and turn the shock off – thus rewarding the weeping response.

Felicity got an idea, although he was sure it would not work. He would alter the anxiety-relief conditioning procedure to ask for a *different* response each time the shock was turned up, rather than always the same ('Be Calm') response. How's that for a novel, exciting, and radical idea!?

He got a sturdy stick and lashed it to his nurse's back to stiffen her spine. He instructed her to change the procedure by asking Susan to give a different response in a given class of responses each time the voltage was turned up, and not to turn off the shock until Susan gave a new response in the given category. Of course, Felicity is as much a jellyfish as anybody else, so he did suggest that the voltage control be turned up very, very slowly. Furthermore, when it was getting up to where the stimulus might become uncomfortable, the nurse should only make it look as though the voltage was being turned up. Also he suggested that the nurse might be satisfied with one or two or three responses in the given category at any treatment session. The categories used (and recorded) were neutral ones such as: "Each time I turn the shock up, I want you tell me a different thing you might ..." "... say about the weather," or "... say in greeting someone," or "... buy when shopping."

Since this was a different treatment, it was to be done only once per day, starting on a Monday. Following the Tuesday (second) session, Susan appeared at Felicity's office for her regular psychotherapy appointment, came in and gave him a complete history, with a full and normal response repertoire. Felicity was flabbergasted. Susan talked to everyone on the Unit using a normal response repertoire throughout the rest of that working week. Felicity had no idea what had happened, and so he cancelled the treatment during the next week. Having been off the treatment over the weekend, by Monday Susan was back to her five-response repertoire. The treatment was reinstituted on the following Monday and by Tuesday afternoon she was back to a normal range repertoire of responses. She was not treated on the Thursday or Friday. By Friday afternoon she was back to her five-response repertoire. This was just too weird. She was started on the treatment the following Wednesday, and had a normal repertoire on Thursday. She was back to five responses on Monday, after the weekend of no treatment. She was put back on the treatment on Tuesday and Wednesday, and had the normal repertoire on Wednesday and Thursday. On Friday, she was back to her five response repertoire. Felicity decided he would have to maintain her for some time on this strange treatment method, and the plan was to start it again on a regular and continuing basis on the Monday.

Unfortunately for this story, Susan eloped (that does not mean she got married; it means she walked out of the hospital) on the Sunday, and Felicity hasn't seen her since. Privately, he didn't blame her a bit. He thought he too would probably want to escape from such a chopped-up treatment program – probably suggesting that her therapists had not the slightest idea what they were doing, which was obviously true!

Since he had no hypotheses to check out in this case, Felicity had nothing challenging and intelligent to do about it except to wonder what to call the treatment method he had invented. At first he thought he would call it avoidance of avoidance conditioning. But he didn't like the acronym: AAC. He thought the procedure might have something to do with the person's response repertoire, so he called it conditioned acceleration of response repertoire acquisition, or CARRA. Actually, he preferred the name a friend of his gave it. The friend started using it with students who were trying to master various series of historical facts. His friend thought it was best termed Relief of Aversive Tactile Stimuli for the Acceleration of Semantic Signalling, or RATS ASS.

An Immutable Imitation

While Felicity's unnatural curiosity was not satisfied with the unknown sequel to Susan's story, it was destined to be glutted on the sequel to Shirley's. Shirley was admitted to the Unit because of a strange complication in her relationship with her psychiatrist. Her psychiatrist made her sick. Even if Shirley was in her dormitory, so that she could not see anything going on anywhere else on the ward, the instant her psychiatrist walked through a door onto the ward, Shirley would begin to retch wretchedly, vomiting up anything that happened to be in her stomach. Since the psychiatrist could not properly avoid going to the ward in the service of curing this particular patient, it seemed a superior idea to transfer Shirley to another unit. Since Shirley's diagnosis was schizophrenia that had not responded favourably to anything during her twenty years of residence in the hospital, and since her accessory symptoms seemed interesting, Felicity's unit was nominated as the one to be granted the privilege of Shirley's care.

Shirley was a skinny woman in her early fifties. The history showed that she had been raised a devout Catholic. She had the grey look of a nun lost in a trance, vacantly seeking a world whose image she had lost and in which she no longer had any faith. During her mid-teens, she had become pregnant on two occasions and, feeling deeply guilty, had brutal abortions both times – which left her feeling even more profoundly guilty. When she got married and had a son, her son was found to have a congenital heart defect. It was thought that she believed that this was punishment for her adolescent sins. It was assumed that the load of guilt she had experienced from this misfortune had proved too much for her weak or brittle ego so that she had regressed into schizophrenia.

Felicity did not want to make Shirley sick. He reasoned that the core of Shirley's schizophrenia and of her weak stomach must be autonomic nervous system arousal associated with her guilt – maximized in the presence of the psychiatrist to whom she had divulged her history. He thought it would be wise to reduce the arousal of her autonomic nervous system. At that time, the means available to him were through general de-arousal with anxiety-relief conditioning. It had no effect on any of her symptoms, although it did calm her down a bit when it was supplemented with de-arousal to specific stimuli using Wolpe's reciprocal inhibition therapy (RIT).

Starting on systematic anxiety desensitization (RIT), Felicity had taught her the art of deep muscle relaxation. She seemed to relax satisfactorily. He then started the gentle process of getting her to imagine stimuli that evoked mild anxiety, beginning with dusty windowsills, lower floor apartment balconies, and participation in small groups of people. Shirley reported no anxiety at all in picturing these scenes, nor was there any visible indication from her physiological responses (such as changes in breathing rates or patterns) in response to these images. He tried more intense anxiety stimuli. There was no anxiety response. He had her picture her psychiatrist walking onto the ward and coming over to talk to her. She did not react at all. Finally, he asked her to picture herself on the abortionist's bed having an abortion. She was unmoved. Felicity asked her how she felt when picturing the last scene. Shirley said she was surprised that he had asked her to picture it. Felicity was perplexed.

It was some time before he remembered that he had other treatments in his armamentarium. He decided blindly to bring out the 'big gun'. Since she was 'obviously avoiding' any anxious response to his varied anxiety-stimulus presentations, he thought she needed to be treated with avoidance of avoidance conditioning. He had Shirley started on CARRA – the method which had led to the dramatic changes in Susan's response repertoire. The procedure was started on a Monday.

On the Tuesday afternoon, Felicity was in his office involved in a conference with the psychiatrist-in-chief and Shirley's psychiatrist. A large 'Conference in Progress' sign was displayed on the outside of the closed door, and all the patients knew who attended these conferences. None would dare to interrupt, and particularly not the over-controlled, guilt-prone, authority-bound Shirley. Suddenly, the door burst open and in rushed the grey nun, flushed and sweating profusely. She tripped over her psychiatrist and flung herself over Felicity's desk to grab desperately onto his arms. She was hyper-ventilating rapidly and could barely gasp out her message. "Help me! You've got to help me!" she moaned.

The two other participants in the conference were dumbfounded. Mouths agape, they looked at Felicity as if he were a mixture of magician and devil. Felicity didn't mind the magician attribution, since magicians and psychologists are not much different – the one pulls rabbits out of hats, and the other pulls habits out of rats. But he didn't like the part of the look that seemed to relegate him to the infernal regions. He thought he had to do something brilliant to preserve his image of pristine simple-mindedness. So he did. He told Shirley, "OK, I'll see you in an hour, after the conference." When, with help, Shirley's racked and tense body dragged itself heavily out of the office, and when the door was once more closed and proper decorum had returned to the conference, the psychiatrist-in-chief asked Felicity, "What happened to your laughing sessions?" The tension in the air dissolved in hearty, if somewhat muffled, laughter.

An hour later, Shirley re-entered the office, was given the relaxation instructions, and relaxed tensely. Felicity had the rare consideration to remember Shirley's present delicate condition. Accordingly, he asked her to picture herself standing ten feet from a dusty windowsill, looking at a thick layer of dust on the sill. She began to hyper-ventilate heavily and tremble visibly. From that moment on, systematic anxiety desensitization (RIT) progressed in a smooth and usual fashion. Moreover, as expected, during the desensitization, she began to feel less and less anxious in scenes involving others looking at her, others questioning her, others criticizing her, and others angry at her, and in scenes involving her standing up more and more assertively to others. There was a steady decline in the signs of guilt feelings seen in her daily life on the Unit and in her conversations about herself and about her family.

About four months after the incident in the conference, another psychiatric conference was convened at Felicity's request to consider

Shirley's condition. The conference concluded that she had recovered from her schizophrenic illness, and that she could be discharged to her home. Shirley was seen in outpatient follow-up interviews for almost three years. And contacts between Shirley and other patients discharged from the Unit were reported to Felicity by these former patients over another interval of two to three years. Throughout that time, it was reported that Shirley was continuing to live a normal life at home, without further use or need of medications or psychotherapy.

In his own vague way, Felicity wondered just what CARRA should be called, and what it was doing to have the effects it seemed to have. "Oh well," he told himself, "someday I'll have to do some research to tear CARRA apart to see how it works and to see what it does. It does something, but it sure is weird. Oh well, someday."

A Tremendous Tremulousness

Sharon was admitted to the back ward Behaviour Therapy Unit under a pall of mystery. She was a short, stocky woman in her late forties, with a sort of a brusque hostility about her. She walked stiffly around with her right arm extended downwards, and her left arm crossing her body and holding her right arm tightly. On the psychological tests she exhibited a 'psychotic degree' of deterioration of emotional resources and a high level of anxiety and guilt-proneness. It was Felicity's friend, the institution's neurologist, who lifted the veil of secrecy. He explained to Felicity that the patient had a unilateral (right sided) masturbation tremor. Felicity had a hard time finding much literature on that condition. However, he did glean enough that it finally made a tiny bit of sense to him.

Masturbation requires movement of the hand and at least the wrist. When it results in sexual climax, the experience involves a very rewarding experience and a rapid sense of relief. These two consequences are contingent upon, and follow directly after, the hand and wrist movements. They, therefore, reinforce the hand and wrist movements, each time adding habit strength to what is apt to become continuous rapid movements of these parts. Hence the learned, unilateral (one-sided) hand tremor.

Sharon had been married for many years to a man who spent his days working hard at tiring labour, and who came home to eat and to go promptly to sleep. She had never worked, and she had no children to keep her busy. So she spent a lot of her daytime hours, and some hours at night, entertaining herself with the act of masturbation. This was before the advent of television.

She was probably vaguely (or clearly) aware of the cause of her tremor. Perhaps some physician had the indelicacy to inform her about it. Anyway, she felt acutely guilty about the tremor, and hence her habit of holding the offending arm as she moved about the ward.

Felicity was unable to find any other source or reason for the high level of guilt and distress that seemed to underlie the decompensation and regression which the tests had revealed. His primitive grasp of the world offered him no available solution to this lady's 'schizophrenic' problem – that is, other than finding a way to help her unlearn the habitual tremor. On practical grounds, the latter seemed like the easier condition to treat.

He found a report by Eysenck, which used Hull's hypothetical construct concerning the accumulation of reactive inhibition with continuous response evocation, as a means by which to measure motivation. And it was even suggested that the construct of conditioned inhibition could be used to account for the effects of negative practice on certain symptomatic habits.

These last two sentences translate into English as follows: The one guy (Hull) made up a guess that you get tired if you keep doing the same thing without rest; and the other guy (Eysenck) used that made up guess as a basis for measuring motivation (it doesn't say how). The second guy (Eysenck) also suggested that learning the habit of being too tired to do something you have done a lot could account for the fact that, if you keep practising forever a habit you don't want to do, it eventually stops happening. This idea sounded to Felicity like the very thing he was looking for.

Although the idea can be made to sound quite complicated, is really quite simple. If you continue to do anything without _any_ rest for a long enough time, your muscles will tire out. At some point in time you will no longer be able to continue the action and the action will stop. Now you may think it is the muscles which tire out making it impossible to continue the action. Based on the fact that fatigue of the nerve impulse occurs faster than that of the muscle response, Hull argued that it was the nerves (which coordinate the muscle response) that tire out. He called the resulting stoppage of the nerve output 'reactive inhibition'.

Of course, when something that is tired out gets rest, it recovers. Reactive inhibition stops the action from occurring and the nerves get rest. So, after a while, the person can begin the action again. Then, if she is made to continue and more reactive inhibition builds up, the involuntary inhibition happens again.

In addition, if a person is trying to produce a given action, there is some motivation present (i.e., the 'drive to respond). When the person is fresh (at the beginning), it takes a longer time for enough 'fatigue' or (same thing) 'drive-not-to-respond' to build up to create the inhibition than it takes after the action has been performed after the first period of inhibition and rest. And, as Eysenck argued, since the rate of build-up of reactive inhibition (fatigue) is constant, the time it takes for the first involuntary inhibition to occur is proportional to the original motivation (drive-to-respond), and thus can serve as a measure of that motivation.

Further, the involuntary inhibition (stopping the action) occurs when the fatigue or the (negative) 'drive-not-to-respond' exceeds the 'drive-to-respond'. Conversely, the action is possible only when the 'drive-to-respond' is greater than the 'drive-not-to-respond'.

But what has all this got to do with Sharon? Well, a drive (to be sure, it's a negative drive, the drive-not-to-respond) is reduced during each period of enforced inhibition. Now 'drive reduction' (of any drive) is the most important aspect of reinforcement or reward underlying most learning. So, _following_ each inhibition trial, the reduction of the drive-not-to-respond rewards what has just happened – namely, inhibition. That is, the inhibition is being learned – but only during the intervals when inhibition is being induced.

Let's try that again in English. If you want to stop an undesired action, if you can keep doing it continuously long enough that it keeps stopping against your will, the reduction of fatigue during the between-trials rest will serve as a reward and will train your brain in a new habit of not-doing the action. Think of that! But does it work?

It happened that a student nurse wanted to do something to help on the Behaviour Therapy Unit. Felicity asked her to sit for two-hour blocks of time with Sharon and (1) keep encouraging Sharon to try to produce the tremor, and (2) time the intervals when she could and could not do the tremor. Even although the student nurse was young and impressionable, she thought Felicity was as mad as the patients, and she said so in just so many words. After all, if the response would fatigue itself out by being done continuously, why didn't it just fatigue out while it was happening naturally? Felicity actually had an answer to this. However, he didn't give the answer for fear the nurse might tell the patient to stop holding her arm and thus make the whole treatment exercise unnecessary. The answer would have been that the habit of holding on to her offending arm was a 'neurotic' (in this case, guilt-motivated) habit that prevented the tremor, and thus prevented its fatiguing out. Fortunately, the student was sufficiently good-natured about the whole thing to do as she was asked, perhaps to have a good laugh at Felicity's expense.

But why use two-hour sessions? Felicity already knew that it would take about 30 minutes before the first complete inhibition would occur. It would then be 8 to 10 minutes between intervals of inhibition. The 'doing' of the tremor would basically be 'waste time' from the point of view of the treatment, since the only 'learning' of interest would occur in the inhibition intervals themselves – during which inhibition would be rewarded by the reduction of the drive-not-to-respond. If a one-hour session was used, the first half of the hour would be wasted time, and there would only be two or three learning trials (practice) of the inhibition to be conditioned, whereas one could get in as many as ten practice trials in a two-hour session.

Twenty of these two-hour sessions were planned. The student was asked to keep Sharon doing what appeared to be a rapid rotary movement of the wrist with the affected hand, and to time whatever happened. On average, the first full inhibition occurred about 30 minutes into the session. It lasted for 2 minutes, in the face of insistent demands from the student that Sharon continue the action. The second inhibition occurred about 10 minutes after the action was started again, and this inhibition lasted about 1 minute. Thereafter, the action was continued for about 8 minutes between successive inhibitions, which then lasted for about one minute.

When eighteen of these sessions were completed, while the student was delighted, Felicity was shattered. True, the practised rotary aspect of the action had stopped – it was not happening any more. But, Felicity must have observed the response inaccurately at the beginning. What remained was an action, mainly of the fingers, which looked like a beckoning motion. The student and Sharon began the long, boring task again, this time 'conditioning inhibition' of the beckoning motion. They were able to stop after the fourteenth session. The hand and arm were quiescent.

What has this to do with schizophrenia? Who knows!? Nevertheless, by the time the second block of treatments was completed and the embarrassing action had stopped, Sharon's clinical state seemed sufficiently improved that Felicity decided to present her at a case conference. There was no evidence of any schizophrenic symptoms in the opinion of the psychiatrists present, and so Sharon was discharged from the hospital as recovered. Of course, this had obviously not been a case of schizophrenia in the first place – although this time the psychiatric conference was not so sure it had been wrong in its original diagnostic determination.

She was followed in periodic outpatient interviews for the next two years. She maintained the appearance of normalcy throughout that time without need for further medication or psychotherapy. Consequently, contact was then terminated.

Having said all that, everybody knows that such a destructive, complex, and intractable condition as schizophrenia could not be based on such a simple thing as guilt, and that it absolutely could not be 'cured' by any such simple procedure as conditioned inhibition. But then there was Spring.

A Demeaning Meaning

Now Spring's name, and the hope inherent in it, could hardly have been more inappropriate. Spring had been the 'ugly duckling' in her family, and had always known she was. There was a character in Al Capp's comic strip, L'il Abner, who was named Lena the Hyena. Lena's front view was never shown in the strip and Al Capp explained that his reason for this fact was that viewing her face would make America sick. There were those who believed that Al Capp had been inspired to create his character of Lena after seeing Spring. To say she was unattractive would only faintly hint at the scope of her ugliness. It was perhaps no surprise that she loathed herself and, rather than realistically facing the facts of her appearance, had withdrawn into the flattened feelings, the bewildered confusion of awareness, and the faceless anonymity of 'schizophrenia'.

As has already been noted, Felicity is not very bright. It was perhaps fortunate, therefore, that Spring's features were sufficiently arresting that he was able to detect that there was something wrong that needed fixing. Although totally ignorant in such matters, he was informed on good authority that a lifetime of plastic surgery would not have sufficed to prepare Spring for public exposure. But Spring was on his unit, and he had to do something if only to protect himself from ravage through his own limited but delicate aesthetic sensitivities.

He was still puffed up with self-satisfaction about the success with Sharon and he was wondering whether he could use the same simple method of conditioned inhibition with somebody else. So, in his mind, he ran over Spring's face with that seemingly unlikely treatment steam roller.

He decided it might work. But could he get Spring to do what she would have to do? She would have to devote many sessions, each lasting for two hours, looking in the mirror at the object she most despised – her face. She might be willing to do so if someone sat with her. After all, Sharon had exposed her tremor to herself and the student almost indefatigably.

Another student nurse accepted the assignment. Felicity was unable to determine whether the student's willingness came from a fascination with the method bred of contact with the other student, or came instead from a private morbid fascination with the grotesque. Regardless of her reasons, he was grateful for her willingness to help. He preferred to preoccupy himself with his own private morbid imaginings about what strange perceptual events might occur during the periods of inhibition of Spring's self-percept (or self-image) during the mirror gazing activity.

The rules were spelled out for Spring and the student. Spring was to sit for blocks of two hours at a time staring at her face in the mirror, focusing on her nose (the centre of a face) without looking away even for an instant. Of course, whenever she had to, she could blink her eyes. Meanwhile, the student would encourage her to keep staring at herself in the mirror, and would time and record anything that Spring reported. Spring was asked to report from time to time what she was noticing, and particularly if what she saw changed in any way. She said she was willing to try this experiment if Felicity thought it would help, but she thought Felicity was himself cracking up.

The student's records showed that 'changes' occurred according on about the same time schedule as that reported during Sharon's sessions. But the 'inhibition intervals' were much more dramatic than those experienced by Sharon. Spring did report major changes in what she saw at the times designated as 'inhibition intervals'. To Felicity's relief, the first session's 'changes' were rather bland. Spring reported only that she could no longer see her face, or that she could only see an outline of her face devoid of any features. But this benign response was not to continue.

In following sessions, aberrations in her appearance, which she reported during the 'inhibition intervals', far outstripped those that resided naturally in her face. Her eyes and mouth were seen to take each other's place. Her nose resembled her two ears glued to each other with nothing between. The contours of her face became liquid and flowing, as if seen in motion in grossly distorting mirrors. Her hairline started just below her nose and her chin protruded, upside down, above it. Then some of the images she saw defied description. Her natural appearance was not quite as deformed as these images might suggest. And it is an immense tribute to her incredible courage that Spring was willing and able to face staring at herself in the mirror for such long blocks of time. Her willingness to continue looking at such incredible distortions of her already detested features must have required courage almost beyond belief.

Spring and her student sat through twenty of these two-hour mirror-gazing sessions. It will not be claimed here that at the end of that time Spring was a raving beauty. But three things did happen which warrant comment.

First, her appearance did change. People who had not seen her for a while and who knew nothing about her treatment, not only expressed amazement at her pleasant, even attractive appearance, but some did not recognize her at all. Her appearance had improved beyond simply being a 'plain Jane' to the point where it was quite pleasant to look at her. Most importantly, Spring was delighted with her appearance, and she took to using make up and getting her hair styled as an expression of her delight.

Second, barely weeks after completion of the mirror-gazing treatment, her clinical condition had improved enough that Felicity arranged for her to be presented in conference. The conference concluded that she had recovered from her schizophrenic illness and could be discharged. This time, there was not even any discussion about the earlier schizophrenic diagnosis. It had been the correct diagnosis, and she had recovered. The only confusion expressed in the conference was on the part of some of those who had known Spring before her transformation. They expressed doubt that this was the same woman. Spring was followed with outpatient visits for two years before termination of contact, and she remained free from symptoms without requiring medication or psychotherapy.

In her mid-forties, for the first time in her life, she found a boyfriend. It is true that her choice turned out to be to her financial detriment, as he stole a number of things from her home to sell in order to support his alcohol addiction. Almost exactly the same thing happened with her second boyfriend. However, after she absorbed the idea that she might have implicitly been 'asking for' such treatment in her felt desperation for a relationship, she began to expect that she should be treated with the respect she had developed for herself. And the next man in her life turned out to be a polished gem.

Was this woman suffering from schizophrenia? The psychiatric conference certainly believed she was – even after she had recovered. Even Felicity's sometimes obstructionist tests initially confirmed schizophrenia consistently across tests. It might be argued that Spring's contorted features, which had apparently created her 'ugliness', were either a defensive way of withdrawing herself by keeping others away, or a direct reflection in her features of the high intensity of distress and morbid ideation that she had experienced from early in life. Felicity did not know which, or even whether, either of these explanations was appropriate. There used to be a radio program called 'The Shadow' in which the signature statement was something like, 'Who knows what evil lurks in the hearts of men? The Shadow knows' – delivered, of course, in a deep sepulchral voice. That association was about as far as Felicity's understanding took him.

Still, the thing that had been done as 'treatment' for this woman, who had lived for about twenty years in the back wards of the hospital, was to 'condition inhibition' of a habit – the habit of how she perceived or 'saw' herself. There are probably those who would argue that all that was done was to force this poor woman to look at her face long enough that it no longer bothered her, and that consequently she could relax her features enough to produce a reasonable appearance. Perhaps she was just being desensitized to her main anxiety (that about her appearance) using the method of desensitization called 'flooding'. Perhaps, or perhaps not.

A Miraculous Mirage

Sherri was admitted to the Unit because it was the Behaviour Therapy Unit's turn to have her. She had been on almost all the female wards in the hospital, and everybody just wanted to get rid of her. She was the most disliked patient in the hospital in the minds of patients and staff alike. She was a crotchety old woman of fifty-nine who exhibited the flat affect and thought disorder of schizophrenia, the delusions and hostility of paranoia, the fussy repetitive actions of compulsiveness, the interminable hair-splitting and justifications of obsessiveness, and the unhappy complaining and clinging dependency of depression. To say Sherri was a total pain in the butt was only weakly to express the extent of her interpersonal talent in disturbing others. To make matters worse for herself and the various classes of inhabitants of the hospital, she had been a resident in the hospital for forty-five years, since the age of fourteen. Her arrival on the Unit was greeted with a community-wide moan of despair.

Not knowing what to do with her, Felicity had a series of psychological tests administered to her. All five of the already noted psychiatric conditions were clearly represented in Sherri's test results. She also displayed high levels of anxiety in her tests. By now, Felicity thought he knew how to treat anxiety. So, in addition to the anxiety-relief conditioning, which all the patients on the Unit were receiving twice a day, he decided to use Wolpe's method for systematic anxiety desensitization (RIT) to treat Sherri.

Now anybody who knows anything about Wolpe's treatment method knows that it works for phobic anxiety, but not for other more diffuse types of anxiety, certainly not for complex neuroses, and absolutely not for the schizophrenias. But, then, either Felicity didn't know or had forgotten about all those bothersome limitations of the method. And it certainly didn't get through to his vacant mind that this method simply could not work in such a case. Besides, he didn't know what else to do. So, he started treating Sherri with systematic desensitization.

He revised Wolpe's original Fears Survey Schedule – the questionnaire by means of which areas of phobic anxiety could be identified. He extended it to include some of the kinds of fears that Felicity's limited experience told him were common among schizophrenic patients. He added items to represent fear of ambiguousness or uncertainty, of penetrability of body boundaries, of condensations of unrelated events, of perceptual distortion, and of losing control, to mention a few.

He administered the extended questionnaire to Sherri, and he thought he could pretty well understand the resulting picture of her fears given the psychiatric disorders from which she was suffering. He then behaved in a completely irrational way. He reversed the logic of his own conclusions. If he could understand her expressed fears as expressions of, or as caused by, her psychological disorders, he wondered if could he understand her psychological disorders as expressions of, or as caused by, her fears. Even he knew that was stretching his credibility somewhat, so he omitted to mention the idea to any of his fellow staff – preferring not to be locked up with the patients.

He trained Sherri in the art of deep muscle relaxation. Then he began to ask her to picture various scenes in her mind, and to indicate to him by raising her finger whether her discomfort was increasing or decreasing across the several presentations of each scene. He started with mild dirt scenes (to get at 'schizophrenic' sensitivities), mild scenes where others noticed or watched her (to tackle paranoid concerns), mild scenes of confusion or uncertainty (to address her obsessive worries), mild scenes of others being annoyed with each other (as an approach to her depression) and mild scenes of leaving daily tasks incomplete (to fix her compulsions). As time passed and she became comfortable with these scenes, the presentations were changed to pictures which, according to her initial report, would have evoked stronger and stronger anxiety responses in her. The anxiety evoked by these situations also subsided with repeated presentations.

It turned out that it was often necessary to return to scenes that had already been desensitized and to repeat them after some time had elapsed. This fact was not particularly surprising. Wolpe had conceived of the process of working up through a hierarchy of anxiety stimuli, from low to high anxiety images, as representing movement along a stimulus generalization gradient from the 'tail' of the generalization distribution toward and to the central position. This sort of language is supposed to make sense to psychologists. The sense it made to Felicity related to Mednick's suggestion that one of the problems in schizophrenics was that they tended to exhibit a particularly wide stimulus over-generalization gradient or distribution. Could it be that, in people with schizophrenic symptoms, the tendency to stimulus over-generalization might result in re-sensitization of the formerly desensitized stimuli from other events on the generalization scale not yet desensitized? Whatever all this means (it actually makes sense, believe it or not), it was because he anticipated this phenomenon that Felicity kept going back to test out Sherri's reactions to situations to which she had already been desensitized.

Felicity worked on this desensitization task with Sherri for a long time. About a year and a half after they got started in this work, in a moment of blind trusting impulse, Sherri confided to Felicity that she still did not trust him at all. In spite of this cautious restraint of her part, two years after starting this program, the task seemed to be approaching an end, and so Felicity arranged to present Sherri at a psychiatric conference.

Having at one time or another been on every female ward in the hospital, Sherri knew everybody at the conference. She entered the room as if she were at a party with old friends. The conference participants were shocked to be greeted by a pleasant, cheerful lady of 61, who answered questions directly and concisely, who talked with a simple and appropriate logic, who exhibited no signs of confusion, withdrawal, delusion or obsession, and who everybody thought a particularly likable person. The conference concluded she had recovered from all five illnesses and could now be released.

Released! But where would she go? For forty-seven years her only home was the hospital. Obviously, she could not just be pushed out onto the street [Note: This was before the civil rights movement demanded that people not be locked up when they had committed no crime, and the provincial government jumped on the discovery that they could save a lot of money by discharging "crazy" people to the street, whether it was in the patients' best interests or not. RR]. The social worker was away on vacation at the time and so things would at least have to await her return. After the conference, Felicity told Sherri of the conclusions reached, but assured her that she could reside in the hospital until arrangements could be made for her in the community when the social worker returned. Sherri seemed to take all this in her stride – which gave Felicity some concern.

Two weeks passed before Felicity met Sherri again in the hall. He remembered he had to speak to the social worker on her behalf and told her so. Sherri asked why. In a very condescending way, as if talking to a very young child, Felicity told Sherri that somebody would have to arrange for a place for her to live in the community. In a matter-of-fact way, Sherri said she had already done that for herself. Realizing that she probably didn't know that people had to pay for their accommodations, Felicity offered that arrangements would have to be made for her support. Sherri replied that she had already arranged for welfare support by herself. Now completely at a loss to know what to say, Felicity stammered that, well, they should arrange for something for her to do to keep herself busy. Sherri informed the thunder-struck Felicity that she had already arranged for a training course with a community rehabilitation service and had also arranged to serve as a volunteer in one of the general hospitals in the community. Felicity's self-importance flew away with his gesture of resignation, and Sherri bade him farewell and glided gracefully down the corridor and out of the hospital.

Two years later, still on no medication and receiving no further psychotherapy, Sherri graduated from her vocational training course and landed her first ever job as a clerk-receptionist – at the age of 63! Felicity continued for a while to see her in periodic follow-up interviews, and after that to hear about her from other patients discharged from the Unit. Sherri found two older surviving sisters, now both retired and quite reclusive, who had not visited her in the hospital for forty-seven years. She moved them in with her and became the centre of their social lives – taking them out and around the town, and inviting friends in as company. Felicity has no idea how Sherri learned normal adult socialization. It must have been dormant in her across the years, masked by the overlay of psychopathology and freed to be expressed as her psychopathology lifted. It would seem that almost nothing is impossible.

One of the many lessons Felicity concluded he had learned from Sherri was that it was possible for the most severe and debilitating conditions to be predicated on a complex array of anxieties and fears. Moreover, it might be possible to unlock the confines of even the most severe types of psychopathology by desensitizing the underlying anxieties and fears. Perhaps anxiety was not only the common core of the neuroses; perhaps it was also the common core of the psychoses. He was certainly going to keep treating schizophrenia by means of anxiety desensitization.

A Re-Mented De-Mented

Another opportunity was already waiting for him. Sally had been admitted to the Behaviour Therapy Unit in a florid schizophrenic condition. She was doing all the right things. She was obviously hallucinating – she talked to thin air, seeing and hearing things nobody else could see or hear. She was withdrawn, isolating herself from others and staying near walls or in corners. When she did talk to other people she used words in strange ways so that one could be sure what she was talking about. When she spoke, her voice had a monotonous tone, except when she became excited while talking to the air.

During their first interaction, Felicity noticed that Sally pulled back from any close contact with him. She spoke of her panic when she had recently been in a crowded elevator. Felicity's mousetrap mind concluded that there was a claustrophobic element in Sally's make up. Fortunately, Felicity had read a book once. It was by Fisher and Cleveland, and it talked about how some schizophrenic patients felt their body boundary was 'permeable'. This scholarly background helped Felicity to grasp what he was being told when Sally's psychiatrist patiently informed Felicity that the problem in the elevator and in face-to-face contact was not really one involving claustrophobia. Rather, Felicity was told, the problem was that Sally was terrified that, if she happened to have any physical contact with another person, some exchange of skin or flesh might occur so that she might acquire some part of the other person and be left with this grafted-on part, losing some part of herself forever in the process. (Note: Which, of course, is true, if you believe modern physics, but that is a story for another time. RR]. Felicity almost understood that the prospect of such an event might be a trifle upsetting.

Nevertheless, not knowing what to do about this anxiety about the permeability of the body's boundary, Felicity (being Felicity) decided to adopt his own first misunderstanding of the case, and to treat Sally as though she were in fact claustrophobic. He never did grasp the dull-witted nature of this choice.

So he went about the task of training Sally in deep muscle relaxation. When he thought she was probably sufficiently relaxed, he decided to test to see how limp her body had become. He explained that he was going to lift her arm slightly and drop it, and asked her to keep relaxing and not to 'help' him. Gently, he took her wrist intending to lift the arm about an inch and then drop it back to the armrest of the lounger chair in which she was sitting. The wrist and forearm were as stiff as boards, the elbow bent as though it had a rusty hinge, and the dropped arm returned to the armrest with slow deliberation. Felicity had two thoughts – more than at any other single time. He concluded that she was not yet relaxed, and he thought that just possibly the psychiatrist had something after all – perhaps the tight arm reflected Sally's fear of exchanging flesh with Felicity's fingers.

After further futile efforts to get Sally to relax, Felicity decided he would just have to forego relaxation with her. But he was still too bull-headed to give up on his single-minded course of action with her. English is a wonderful language. It has so many irregular verbs in it. For example, the verb To Be Stubborn declines as follows: I am Strong Willed, You are Stubborn, He is a Pig-Headed Old Fool. Anyway, in his 'strong-willed' mode, Felicity decided that it might be all right if she wasn't relaxed, as long as she stayed absolutely still. At least she would not be defensively avoiding 'exposure' to the ideas and pictures he wanted her to image while relaxing ... err ... sitting still. Of course, he failed to remark that her 'catatonic' status meant that she was nearly always being still, and thus nearly always not avoiding what was going on around her (except by means of the activity going on in her head).

So, having given her time to get relaxed, he started to ask her to visualize a 'presentation' for him. He asked her to picture herself standing in the wide hall by the elevator, watching some people entering the elevator. Instantly, she reacted as though she was in panic. She hyper-ventilated sharply, her already tense body stiffened up, her eyes popped open, and her pupils dilated widely. Felicity asked her what had happened. She told him that she had done as he asked, and that she had pictured herself hanging on by one arm underneath an elevator as it shot up in a very tall building. At first, Felicity wondered whether there was something wrong with her ability to receive his succinct communications. However, after trying a couple more innocuous presentations with equivalent results, it occurred to him that he did not know the language Sally was using. He thought he might do better if he avoided English or any other language and instead had her look at pictorial images of his presentations to her.

At this juncture, Felicity ran across Quirk's account of stimulus conditioned autonomic response suppression (**SCARS**). The paper didn't offer much useful information, but it did suggest to Felicity that it might be possible to use pictorial slides to represent scenes for patients to think about. It also suggested that the galvanic skin resistance (GSR) might be used as a means to monitor anxiety in response to slide-presented pictures. It suggested that slide change might be used as a reinforcer for GSR increases. And it even made a brief reference to the idea that it might be possible to treat 'psychotic' patients using SCARS.

Felicity took photographs of the scenes he wanted to present to Sally, brought his slide projector from home and projected the pictures one at a time on the wall. He was gratified to notice that Sally sat still (of course, catatonics tend to do that a lot), looked at the pictures and gave no outward signs of being upset.

But he wasn't really interested in the presence or absence of outward signs of distress. He wanted to know what was going on inside her while looking at the pictures – how she was feeling inside. That is important because, during anxiety desensitization, if the person is appreciably anxious, even if it doesn't show on the outside, the person can be learning to be more anxious rather than less. And even Felicity grasped the idea that increasing the person's anxiety might be counter-therapeutic.

To find out how she was feeling inside, Felicity asked her to think of the situation in her life where she felt the most upset, scared, and anxious she had ever felt, and to assign the value or number 100 to that degree of feeling anxious. Then he asked her to think about that situation in her life where she felt the most comfortable, calm, and at ease she had ever felt, and to assign the value or number of 0 to the good feeling she had then. On that scale of 100 Subjective Units of Discomfort, or SUDs, he asked her to say how she felt right now. Her answer, 90, sounded about right to him since he had instructed her about SUDs when she had just arrived from the Unit for a session.

He then wanted to use the SUDs scale to help him monitor how she was feeling while she was looking at the slides and sitting still. The first time he asked her to say what her SUDs level was while she was looking at a slide, he was reassured when she said she was at 20. About thirty seconds later he asked her again. She now said she was at 140. There was no apparent difference in the outward signs of distress so he thought he must have heard her incorrectly. He asked her again about a minute later, and she said she was at 0. A minute later, when asked again, she reported being at 520. This time Felicity had heard her correctly. He tried for several sessions to explain the SUDs scale and to get Sally to estimate her distress on it more accurately. He was unable to get any more reliable or meaningful estimates. Perhaps this was just another illustration that they were not talking the same language.

Felicity remembered that the Psychology Department at the university he had attended had some obsolete equipment that was not being used. He visited the department and obtained the loan of an old galvanic skin resistance (GSR) device to see if Quirk's idea had any merit. He thought he could measure changes in the sweat on her hand (actually in the amount of electrolytic activity in the sweat cells) as a way of keeping track of her changing levels of anxiety. Sally accepted the electrode rings on the index and ring fingers of her right hand, and Felicity began to monitor her GSR while she was watching the slides during her next session.

She was now sitting still instead of relaxing, looking at pictorial slides instead of imagining the scenes, and being monitored by means of the GSR instead of monitoring her own subjective state. And it seemed to Felicity that the method was working. During the first two sessions, every time he showed her a new slide, the GSR device recorded a fairly sharp drop in skin resistance – that is, her palms were sweating a little more. Then, as she kept looking at the same slide, the GSR showed a steady rise (i.e., less sweat) until it had recovered to its former 'base line' level. He would then change the slide, and the GSR reaction would repeat itself. He thought: "Good, since the GSR is reacting as I'd expect with each new anxiety stimulus, it must be monitoring correctly the state going on within her."

But then came the third GSR-monitored session. At first, the same reaction occurred to each new slide. Then the pattern changed. There was no drop in the skin resistance with each new slide. Instead, the GSR continued to rise slowly at each slide change, and it continued to rise while she looked at the slide. Felicity thought

Sally must have gone to sleep. But, no, her eyes were open and she was scanning the picture in front of her. He thought she must have adopted her usual defensive approach of 'fogging out' or muting her response to everything around her. But she seemed to be focusing on the pictures and scanning them rather than staring vacantly at them. He thought she must be increasing her tolerance to or 'getting used to' watching slides and so was not reacting with anxiety to each new one. In successive sessions, he tried pictures that he thought 'ought' to be more upsetting for her. The increases in the GSR with each new slide only became greater. Besides, she was reaching levels of skin resistance that seemed to Felicity's limited experience to be much too high to be her ordinary base line levels. He was not unhappy that she seemed to be getting 'more comfortable'; he just did not know what to make of what he was seeing. She 'ought' not to be desensitizing that well since she was not relaxing and since she was passively looking at scenes rather than actively picturing them.

The fog cleared when Felicity remembered Quirk's observations about slide change working as a reinforcer to train GSR increases. He noticed that he was changing the slides *only* when the GSR had recovered and was rising. Was it possible that the act of slide change, being made contingent upon successive GSR increases, was serving as a reinforcement or reward to train the GSR in the ‹comfortable› (upwards, less sweat) direction? Was he actively training desensitization? Only time would tell. He almost felt annoyed at Sally for making it necessary for him to think.

He was sure there had been no therapeutic benefit from the first dozen or so sessions during which he had been trying to get her to relax, had been trying out imaginal presentations, and then had been trying out the use of pictorial slides – all with a remarkable lack of success. Now, as he persisted blindly in this simple exercise of asking her to sit still and watch the slides while he changed the slides for each successive 1,000 ohms of GSR increase, he began to notice and to hear about changes in Sally's clinical condition. She seemed to be recovering from her schizophrenic symptoms. Surely this could not be merely a random or temporary fluctuation in her psychotic state.

She had been a resident of the hospital for some fifteen years without any record of any noteworthy variation in her condition.

Sally and Felicity completed about thirty-five of these GSR and slide change sessions together. Felicity had met with her for only half-hour sessions from the start, fearing he would not be able to maintain her attention for longer intervals of time. After these thirty-five half-hour sessions, Felicity was absent from the hospital for about two weeks on vacation. When he returned, the nurse asked him to see Sally to find out what was wrong. She seemed very different from the other patients. When seen, Sally was lively, vivacious and normally responsive. She exhibited a good range of emotional responses and no thought disorder.

What had happened? Felicity waited for several weeks to see. To be sure, there was a period of about ten days during which Sally was obviously very upset and anxious. But even during that time she exhibited no signs of concern when Felicity shook hands with her or took her arm to 'help' her up some steps, and there were only very weak signs of confusion and withdrawal.

Felicity arranged for a psychiatric conference about Sally. Once more, the conference concluded that she had recovered from her schizophrenic illness and that she could now be discharged home. Again, she was followed with periodic interviews for the first two years after her discharge. She remained functioning in the community, without the help of medication and without further psychotherapy, apparently content and happy with her life, her friends and her work.

But what had brought about the change in her? Some might want to argue that she just grew out of her illness, or even that she did not have a schizophrenic illness at all and had finally tired of putting on the act. Felicity, perhaps out of sheer naivety, was impressed with the value of this wonderful new treatment he had happened upon almost by chance. He decided to adopt Quirk's method as having full status in his treatment armamentarium.

Was this case just a fluke? After he had operated the Behaviour Therapy Unit for some years, Felicity was able to replicate Quirk's original findings. He found eighty cases that had been treated almost exclusively with one form or another of anxiety desensitization. In forty of these cases, he started by using Wolpe's RIT method and, in the other forty cases, he started by using Quirk's SCARS method. Seventy percent of the RIT cases had recovered using RIT alone, and eighty-five percent of the SCARS cases had recovered using SCARS alone. Actually, ninety-five percent of the total group of eighty cases recovered, since some received both procedures, using RIT and SCARS as 'back-up' methods for each other. In the cases where both methods were used, he made sure that at least a month elapsed after one method had been tried before the other was instituted – just to be sure that the first method tried had not worked. But perhaps this group of patients were mostly pretty benign cases? Maybe they were. However, all had schizophrenia as at least one part of their psychiatric diagnoses, and their average length of continuous residence at the hospital prior to admission to the Behaviour Therapy Unit was 9 years. Felicity still uses SCARS when it seems appropriate to do so, and he has treated several hundred people using that method.

What do you think? Could such a silly method work? Felicity heard about one young psychologist who, when he heard about the method, argued that all that was happening was that the GSR electrodes were being polarized. Quirk's reply to this suggestion was, "Hey, that's great. If polarizing electrodes cures schizophrenia, I'm going to do lots more electrode polarization."

Felicity's curiosity was churned up. With both Sherri and Sally, he had set out to desensitize their anxieties. If that was what had been done to modify their 'illnesses', it seemed to him to support the idea that the 'illnesses' might be accounted for by their anxieties, and not the other way around. The effort of trying to think around this matter regularly gave him a headache.

A Simply Simple Simplicity

In Felicity's opinion, Sabrina did not seem like 'a schizophrenic'. The referring psychiatrist said she had a schizophrenic illness, simple type. Certainly, she was a simple person who seemed sort of helpless, indecisive, unmotivated and dependent. But Felicity imagined he had met quite a few women in their early forties like Sabrina. Perhaps, in the community where he lived, Felicity had failed to recognize psychosis or to anticipate that people he met were destined to be certified as mentally ill on the very day on which he met and interacted with them. But, then, we already know how sharp Felicity isn't.

At least in Sabrina's case, Felicity had the good sense, not seeing 'anything wrong with' her, to get a series of psychological tests administered to her. The test results were generally consistent with those from the Rorschach, and the Rorschach yielded evidences of a psychotic degree of deterioration of functioning and of difficulty in perceiving and communicating the way most others do. However, the only specific 'active' symptom in the Rorschach was a general lack of differentiation in Sabrina's emotional responses. Felicity had no idea at all what that might mean, nor any idea what to do about it or about her regardless of what it might mean.

He puzzled for a long time about Sabrina's condition. He kept trying to reformulate for himself the idea of emotional responses that were undifferentiated. He thought he had read something which seemed to sound like that, but he couldn't recall where. His thoughts were always scattered, and one day it occurred to him that what he was trying to think of had something to do with what psychologists call phenomenology – which is different from what psychiatrists call phenomenology. He found a book of his on phenomenology (not phrenology) and browsed through it. Wham! There it was. In an article by Snygg, he saw the basic postulate that: "Phenomenological differentiation is consistent with control of behaviour."

Felicity had no idea at all what the word phenomenological referred to in that context, and only a faint idea about how psychologists use the term differentiation. To make it easier for himself, he changed the words around to suit himself. He formulated the hopefully equivalent statement that 'perceptual discrimination is consistent with the control of behaviour'. He hoped that 'behaviour' included emotional responses, and that 'control' included the idea of differentiation.

On the strength of this clear-thinking analysis, Felicity tore a number of pictures out of magazines he was about to throw out and arranged them in an order, from the simplest to the most complex. Starting with the simplest picture and working down the series, and using only one picture in each twenty-minute session, Felicity asked Sabrina to describe in detail what she saw in each picture. The first one happened to be a picture of a plate on which was a tomato with a stem and one leaf. Sabrina began by saying it was a juicy tomato. Felicity asked her where she saw the 'juicy'. She said she didn't. She was asked to stick with what she saw. Each time she gave a concrete or factual item, Felicity congratulated her. The pictures became more complex, but each took about the same amount of time as Sabrina became more adept at the task.

After about twenty sessions, Sabrina failed to keep her next appointment. Felicity called up to the Unit to find out what she was doing. The nurse said that Sabrina had just been discharged from the hospital by her psychiatrist. In justified wrath at having his tender toes trod upon, Felicity phoned the psychiatrist demanding to know why the patient had been discharged. The psychiatrist replied that he knew Sabrina had been getting treatment from Felicity and that, since she had recovered, he thought it only fitting and proper that she be released to return home. Felicity was taken aback by this unexpected outcome, so he mumbled something and hung up the phone. It seemed that he had not only been unable to detect the schizophrenia in the first place, he had also been unable to detect the recovery from it. On the other hand, to Felicity's mind that did seem somehow only consistent and right.

This method, called either Perceptual Discrimination Training or Fair Witness Training [see Heinline's novel, *Stranger in a Strange Land*. RR], was promptly adopted as another method in Felicity's armamentarium. It turned out to be a 'slick' little procedure for use with those schizophrenic patients where anxiety desensitization alone was not enough, or with whom, like Sherri, their tendency to stimulus over-generalization fostered re-sensitization to anxiety stimuli to which they had been desensitized. After the idea of 'perceptual discrimination' had lodged firmly in Felicity's mind, it was an easy step to the application of the method in these last types of cases.

The general psychological means by which the range of stimulus generalization, whether too wide or not, is narrowed is termed discrimination training. It really might have been more accurate to call the method perceptual differentiation training since it may be the perceptual response that is being discriminated, and the term differentiation is used when responses (as opposed to sensations) are being refined.

A Rainbow Rainfall

But the experience with Sabrina opened other doors too. One of these doors led to another procedure that had been developed for Sarah. Sarah was involved in long-term, intensive psychotherapy with her psychiatrist. She was not admitted to the Behaviour Therapy Unit. Felicity became involved in an accessory way after he obtained a strange finding when asked to do some psychological tests on Sarah. The strange finding may be worth describing first.

In response to one of the Rorschach cards, Sarah did a very unusual thing. She displayed a response pattern that would suggest that she was particularly prone to be defensive in responding to the reality of the real world. At the very least, this finding would suggest that she was experiencing some conflict about handling the reality of the real world, defensively becoming preoccupied with 'less than real' events or things. Even Felicity understands that this kind of psychological mumbo-jumbo, although it ought to mean something, wouldn't make much sense to any real person. Nevertheless, he had seen this type of reaction in Rorschachs occasionally in the past, each time from a patient who was thought to be schizophrenic but did not exhibit the usual signs of 'deterioration' of functioning over time.

When Felicity went to talk over his findings with Sarah's psychiatrist, he was not sure he would be able to make much sense out of them. He bumbled through various ways of trying to say what he thought it was he was trying to say. The psychiatrist, a remarkably sensitive person, brightened almost at once when Felicity started to talk. When she got a chance to get a word in edgewise, she said: "I think you're right. For Sarah, fantasy *is* reality, and reality is fantasy." The Rorschach reaction could hardly have been expressed better. Of course, the question was not one of how to express the problem, but one of how to treat it.

The problem the psychiatrist had in her psychotherapy with Sarah was that Sarah was unable to trust her psychiatrist. She had continuously been subjected to sexual abuse as a child, and she had become preoccupied with a destructive idea about sexuality as the primary motive in others. If others were friendly, she *knew* that they had salacious motives toward her. If they were unfriendly, she *knew* they were out to destroy her. There was no middle road that the psychiatrist could adopt in order to establish a therapeutic relationship with Sarah.

Felicity puzzled long and hard over this one. He recognized that his thought processes were following a similar course to those he had gone through with Sabrina. He was trying to formulate in words a way to conceive of the problem Sarah presented. The problem was that she perceived, as though it were something 'real', the salacious or destructive intentions of others. That was like a delusion, but it had a more 'perceptual' character to it rather than 'conceptual' (as in a delusion). It was as though her fantasy life was 'getting in the way of' her perceptions of the world, and as though the fantasies were over-generalized to all people. He decided it would be necessary to 'correct' her ambiguity-intolerant, over-generalized, and pathological way of perceiving and conceiving of things. That sounded to Felicity like a good name for whatever kind of procedure he might dream up: generalization, ambiguity, and pathology extinction, or GAPE. Okay, now it had a name, what would the treatment method involve?

One of the occupational therapists had a lovely talent for drawing. Felicity explained his problem to her and asked her to draw a long series of 'representational' forms ranging from some which clearly represented something specific and concrete (the first one was a picture of a coat-hanger), through some which were moderately ambiguous (could be a rising or a setting sun), to some which were really quite ambiguous and could be almost anything.

Felicity realized that Sarah might not react well if he, as a male, undertook the treatment program with her, so he arranged for his female psychometrist to do the task. A lamp, operated by a foot switch controlled by the psychometrist, was set up under the desk at which they would be working. The lamp could be turned off or on, and when it was on it could shine either a red or a green light up the wall behind the desk. Felicity was sure that Sarah found the colour red disturbing and aversive based on how she had responded to the Rorschach. The task for Sarah was to be to 'handle' the stimulus ambiguity (to respond quickly), the stimulus generalization (to respond at an appropriate level of abstraction or generality), and her own pathology (to give a response which was appropriate – that is, similar to responses others gave to a drawing). If she managed to accomplish these tasks well enough, the red light would be turned off and the green light turned on for a short time (as both an aversion-relief and a positive reward).

Of course, both the 'meanings' of the cards to other 'normal' people (in this case, staff) and of the red and green lights as possible rewards (for Sarah) had to be tested first. A lot of staff were helpful in giving their 'meanings' for the pictures until the psychometrist felt she knew the range of 'acceptable' response to each. And a brief 'test' exposure to the coloured lights with Sarah quickly showed she hated the red light and quite liked the green.

Treatment was started. During the first many sessions, only one criterion was applied to her responses in order to warrant the reward of turning off the red light and turning on the green – speed of responding (handling ambiguity) *or* concreteness of response (handling generalization) *or* common responses (handling her pathology). As she mastered each criterion separately, the task was made more difficult by requiring two out of the three criteria to be met for the light to be changed. Once she was adept at that, the task was changed so that she had to conform to all three criteria to have the light changed.

With the help of the insistence of her psychiatrist, Sarah persisted bravely in attending the sessions and in solving the riddles posed to her by the psychometrist. About half way through the program, it was reported that Sarah had suddenly taken to watching anxiously out of one of the ward windows in the mornings to see her psychiatrist arriving at work. As soon as she arrived, Sarah gave every evidence of relief and was able to go about her daily activities. Soon afterwards, Sarah gave strong evidences in her psychotherapy of an intense dependency on her psychiatrist. At last, that allowed the psychiatrist to use the developing relationship to therapeutic ends, and she began to discover a number of remarkable features of Sarah.

Everybody knew that Sarah walked around looking down at the floor. But nobody was aware that Sarah had not seen a human face since the age of six when she had taken to avoiding looking at others out of sheer shame and guilt. Nor did they know that she recognized people from their shoes. Nor had she ever to her knowledge raised her eyes to see a rainbow. It was wonderful indeed to see Sarah suddenly exploring her newfound world with excitement and fascination – reading about rainbows and other wondrous things of her world, and raptly exploring the intricacies of the human face in precious detail. She was like one, blind from birth, who suddenly had vision. Many of the staff wept with joy to see her newfound freedom. Felicity joined joyfully in the flood of tears.

Sarah progressed well in her psychotherapy until, after about a year following the introduction of the GAPE procedure, she was discharged from the hospital as recovered. She was followed for a couple of years by her psychiatrist as she took courses, obtained employment, established a group of friends and, finally, met a man and later married him. The bright-eyed, happy smile on Sarah's face each time she was seen visiting the hospital or in the community spoke more clearly than words about her obvious recovery and the joy of discovering normal life at last.

Risking Rigidity

This is a series of fantasies about psychotherapy, right? What has lobotomy to do with that? Well, it does have something to do with it. You see, quite a few schizophrenic patients, in addition to the disadvantages they experience from their symptoms and from the 'diagnostic' labels they are given, also have to contend with the results of some of the treatments which have been tried to relieve their symptoms. Among these treatments, the one that seems to have had the most permanent and irreversible effects is a surgical procedure known as lobotomy. In this procedure, burr holes are drilled in the patient's skull and a knife inserted to cut some of the nerves connecting the old brain (diencephalon) and the new brain (cerebral cortex). A related procedure was called leucotomy.

By the time that Suzy was admitted to the Behaviour Therapy Unit, she had already been given a trial of LSD to treat her schizophrenic illness, and had then been lobotomized. Suzy had been a bright professional woman in her mid-thirties. She was married and had a supportive husband. However, she looked at life through rather darkly tinted glasses, saw little to give her joy in it, and at some point had felt no longer able to perform her duties at work with her former level of perfectionism. So she sought psychiatric help. In her terms, she had suffered a nervous breakdown.

Although Felicity had heard that phrase often, he had never been able to understand what it meant. The nerves don't break down, neither do they get exhausted – at least not so they don't recover almost at once. Felicity felt he had to understand what had been wrong with Suzy if he was going to be able to fix it. But he could only get a limited number of possible explanations of the phrase he had so much trouble understanding. It might mean that the person's functioning had broken down and that this had been due to some 'nervous' (in the colloquial sense) cause. It might be one type of schizophrenic language phenomena in which two unrelated ideas were condensed into one phrase for purposes of non-communication by the physician. Or it might just be another case where Felicity's thinking was too concrete for him to be able to understand ordinary communications. Finally, he gave up in his effort to understand these 'diagnostic' words.

He did know that the psychiatrists thought Suzy was suffering from a schizophrenic illness, that his tests seemed to confirm that diagnosis at least in terms of psychometric measures, and that she had been lobotomized. Moreover, he knew that studies of the effects of lobotomy had shown no definable benefits from the surgery, but only the disadvantages of increasing the patient's rigidity of thinking and thus intractability, and of increasing the patient's tendency to be impulsive. But then a lot of the surgery that was still being done was known to be pretty useless.

Of course, the 'reasonable' thing to do is to use whatever is known about something to try to fix it. However, the fact that lobotomy had already been performed, suggested that there was nothing else known that could be done to treat Suzy. But Felicity knew that, as a group, physicians are generalists, trained mainly in the anatomy and chemistry of the body, and not in how the body works. Moreover, after fulfilling the demands of 'conventional medical practice', they often do not do much by way of thinking outside of the medical box. So, the ancient item of wisdom, possibly dating from Confucius, may be worth considering after all: 'When all else fails, follow the directions'. That is, it may be wise to try everything else first, before the last resort of following existing 'conventions'. If that sounds unreasonable and inappropriate, that sounds like Felicity.

He put Suzy through the usual procedures for schizophrenic patients on the Unit, including anxiety-relief conditioning and systematic anxiety desensitization, first with SCARS and then with RIT. Although she was improving with both of the desensitization methods, the progress was painfully slow, and much slower than her measured conditionability would suggest.

He started to meet with her for conversational psychotherapy in addition to the standard procedures. He worried that his sense of shame about the surgery she had received made him overly solicitous with her and may have been impeding her recovery. However, during these conversational interactions he was shocked to discover just how resistant she was to any kind of change. He had worked with many people with strong obsessional characteristics, but he had yet to grapple with the intensity of the rage often felt by such people. And, anyway, he thought that much of her lack of resiliency was due to her lobotomy.

Sensing Suzy pretty intense anger, Felicity set about doing some careful assertive training with her. But he was off-track, thinking she was enraged at something specific such as the lobotomy, so the assertive training went badly. But it only went badly in that Suzy started to unleash her wrath mainly at Felicity and all the professionals like him. Nevertheless, the focus she adopted allowed her to release much of the inhibitive pressure within her, and suddenly the desensitization procedure started to work at about the expected rate.

About nine months after she was admitted to the Unit, Felicity arranged for a conference to consider Suzy's progress. Once more the conference concluded that she had recovered and could return home. But this time, the post-discharge follow-up did not go well. Almost as soon as she returned home, Suzy began to drink heavily. Within six months she was a full-fledged alcoholic. By some magical kind of thinking, Felicity felt responsible, so he continued to see her on an outpatient basis for the next two years, treating her for her alcoholism. It became clear that the disinhibiting effect of alcohol on her inhibitive, obsessional qualities, the tranquillizing effect of alcohol on her remaining strong anxiety, and the euphorizing effect of alcohol on her dysphoric and sullen depression, all had a reinforcing (rewarding) effect on her and had increased her habituation or addiction to that substance. It became necessary for Felicity to treat her introversive-obsessional (verbally mediated) characteristics and the rage accompanying them. It was necessary for Felicity to continue the systematic desensitization work to moderate her anxiety further. And it seemed necessary for Felicity to address her sullen depression with more non-specific assertive training, rational-emotive therapy, and cognitive behaviour therapy – all of which were methods that had been appearing in the psychotherapy literature in the recent past.

Slowly, Suzy recovered from her alcoholism, and she started to attend Alcoholics Anonymous to ensure that she remained "on the wagon." Meanwhile, unfortunately, her marriage relationship decayed and she found it necessary to redirect her vocational training and to find work by which to support herself. Felicity maintained contact with her through this additional hard and rather bitter time of her life. In the long run, it was her tenacity, which had almost made treatment impossible, that served her well. She worked hard at her treatment, participated actively in A.A., and struggled intensely with her re-education. Her persistence earned her the victor's garland when she finally pulled herself together and launched herself into a new and sparkling career.

An Antiquated Antic

It may seem that Suzy was a unique person (as she was) in having overcome the disadvantages of her illness and her lobotomy. But she was not alone. Samantha had also been lobotomized for her schizophrenic illness long before she was admitted to the Unit. In addition to the disadvantages of having been lobotomized, she had also suffered a stroke that had paralysed her left side. Her left hand functioned as a hook on which she could hang her purse if it was light enough, and her left leg allowed her only to hobble along with a slow shuffling gait. But she also had a great advantage. She was a temperamentally cheerful and positive person.

Samantha demonstrated to Felicity that lobotomy need not pose any insurmountable problems to treatment or to change. She was treated with the standard anti-anxiety program used on the Unit, including anxiety-relief conditioning and systematic anxiety desensitization (RIT), and she recovered in barely three months time. The psychiatric conference congratulated her on her recovery and discharged her home. She was followed in occasional visits for the next two years, and she remained happy and functioning well, without further need for medications or psychotherapy. Oh, you might be pleased to know that the neurological consequences of Samantha's stroke pretty well cleared up, too. When she was seen for the last time there was hardly any visible limp and, as she left the interview, she picked up her purse with her left hand, swung it by the strap over her shoulder and sauntered out.

CHAPTER 10

CRIMINALITY

Guilt Intolerance

Felicity would almost prefer to leave this chapter heading all by itself without further comment. It may be one of the simplest capsule phrases there is to capture a whole area of human enterprise. That's right, most crime is motivated mainly by guilt. The trouble is that the person who is going to be a criminal feels so uncomfortable about guilt feelings that he will not tolerate them or the 'guilt trips' that he thinks others lay on him. Feeling guilt or being put on a guilt trip leads him to feel angry. And he may even act in such a way that others might think he 'ought' to feel guilty – partly to prove to himself that he has made himself impervious to feeling guilt. That's what is meant by 'guilt intolerance'.

It's true that there are other motives underlying criminality. These include: inferiority or failure intolerance, disturbance or distress intolerance, sensitivity or empathy intolerance, closeness or interaction intolerance, conformity or introspection intolerance, regulation or discipline intolerance, intolerance for internal or external controls, and even such mundane things as greed. Subcultural values and self-enhancement needs may also underlie some crime. But if there is one basic theme subsumed in all the factors underlying crime it may be intolerance for internal or external controls, which is probably most often brought on by guilt intolerance.

Since Felicity has only recently started to come to grips with some of these ideas in his treatment work, he is not yet ready to tell stories to illustrate what he has not yet learned about the real factors underlying criminality in general. Some of his cases involved in particular forms of criminality have been described in the foregoing. However, in addressing criminality in general, it seems most appropriate to refer to the work of a pair of researchers named Reynolds and Quirk, who have taken the gist of Yokelson and Samenow's writings on the criminal personality to heights of clarity and empirical understanding not even guessed to be possible by the original writers in this field.

Felicity is ready only to remark that the intolerance of guilt manufactures a quiet raging anger, sometimes expressed as rebelliousness. The function of rebelliousness seems to be to deny and damn all self-depreciating guilt feelings and to generate a new more active feelings by converting the emotion felt in guilt into a destructive force against all that might induce guilt in the person. Society has tried to re-convert the anger back into the guilt from which it came. This has been attempted by demeaning criminals as people unable to feel guilt, and it has relegated them to penitentiaries where they may languish until once more they can feel (but do not) the penitence of guilt – which society (wrongly) believes will impede criminal conduct.

Having just made all this up, and not yet having had time to dream up any cases or treatment based on this clearly brilliant, correct, and modern view of what crime is about, Felicity prefers not to spin any yarns about cases involved in this kind of anger – the anger bred of an intolerance of guilt. Now that's integrity!

CHAPTER 11

A FLAKE'S MISTAKES – ERRORS OF UNDERSTANDING AND ACTION

Of course, no discourse is complete, or even meaningful, without some at least passing reference to mistakes and errors. Some of the most carefully-engineered machines exhibit up to a 1% error. Certainly, in the human services area, at least that amount of error is to be expected. But *not* much more. Psychotherapists are prone to allow or excuse 'a lot more error' than a machine is to be allowed. But how much more? When we are dealing with humans and their lives, can we allow ourselves even as much error as a machine can be allowed to make? Granting that we are all fallible humans, and that in the service of human rights and liberties we need to have some leeway, what amount of error is the limit when dealing with people?

Years of struggling with this matter have led Felicity to the view that we psychotherapists can perhaps not be expected to achieve much better than ninety-seven percent effectiveness – that is, expecting at least a three percent error. In some types of situations, we might even have to allow ourselves up to twenty percent error. This is usually due to the fact that there is measurement error involved in assessment or diagnostic procedures, and this source of error in initial understanding has to affect the selection of treatment procedures and thus their outcomes. However, if we can anticipate that degree of error because of the particular diagnostic tools we have to use, we probably ought to inform our patients of the expected amount of error, or else that we are not up to standard in that area of practice. Some therapists might react to these figures with disparagement, suggesting they are unrealistic. If so, Felicity would argue that those psychotherapists are (1) not in a position to compete adequately with the average sixty to eighty percent success rates obtained with medications, and (2) not maintaining close enough evaluative quality-control over their work, and have not examined and learned from their failures adequately.

Assessment Errors – Errors of Measurement – Assessing Assessments

Psychotherapy is a responsible enterprise, and failures not processed through 'post-mortem' are just not acceptable. Here we are concerned with some of the sources of mistakes which all of us make. Since mistakes in psychotherapy would be expected to start with mistakes of understanding on the part of the therapist, it seems right to start this discussion with an explanation of some of the more obvious complexities involved in assessment, thus in reaching an understanding of the person and, in turn, selecting an appropriate means for treatment intervention.

A Tearful Scream

A recent immigrant by the name of Ursula, in her early thirties, was admitted to the old mental hospital. She was irritable and very complaintive, frequently screaming in apparent rage about how badly she was being tortured. She was manifestly hostile in an abrasive and contemptuous way about the mistreatment which she felt she was receiving from the various hospital staff. She was unwilling or unable to divulge much about her history and was extremely guarded about giving any personal information. She seemed unable to accept the logic of information given her, and it was felt by staff that she used an idiosyncratic logic in many of the things she did and said. She wore two pairs of slacks and two to four dresses at the same time, in a manner jarring to the eye.

Ursula was interviewed by two extremely astute psychiatric diagnosticians, and both concluded beyond a doubt that she was suffering from a paranoid schizophrenic disorder. Since paranoid schizophrenia was one of the conditions being treated on the Behaviour Therapy Unit, she was transferred to that unit for treatment. Her behaviour on this unit gave every indication supporting the diagnosis, and so the behavioural treatment being used for paranoid schizophrenia was implemented with her.

Only the gentlest of methods were employed. But for six long months of intensive treatment, Ursula continued to scream of the abuse and torture to which she was being subjected. At the end of six months there was no change in her clinical condition.

Felicity was disturbed by the lack of progress. In considering what could have gone wrong, he noticed that the clinical condition had been so apparently consistent with the initial diagnosis, that no psychological assessment had been undertaken upon her admission to the Unit. For the sake of completeness, a battery of psychological tests was administered. The test results were startling. Ursula's test scores, far from confirming the inferred paranoid schizophrenia, were consistent only with a diagnosis of endogenous depression. Ursula was transferred back to the admitting ward with a recommendation for electro-convulsive therapy (ECT) or ‹shock treatment›. Three ECT treatments were administered on the Monday, Wednesday and Friday of the next week. By the Monday of the following week, she was considered to have recovered and was discharged home. She had stopped screaming and complaining, the strain in her face was gone, and she started wearing only one dress and no slacks beneath it.

Ursula was followed at widely scattered intervals for the next ten years. She continued to be a cheerful and very pleasant person with no evidences of any adjustment difficulties. She got married and she and her husband had a family. She had certainly recovered.

In retrospect, there was a clue in the clinical presentation which, if considered differently, might have changed the manner in which the rest of her symptoms were understood. It turned out, as she later was able to explain, that the reason why she had worn several layers of clothing was that she was cold – a primary symptom of endogenous depression. It seems likely that her appearance prejudiced the interpretation of her other symptoms. It is probable that what the staff were taking to be evidences of confused logic or thought disorder were merely reflections of her relative lack of facility in the English language as a recent immigrant, and that her apparently inappropriate actions were simply reflections of habits from her culture of origin. Her screaming complaints were now understood to be the equivalents of depressive weeping, except that, being on her own in a foreign country, she felt she had to be 'strong' and not to cry.

One lesson that Felicity learned from this case was that 'things aren't always what they seem' [as Gilbert and Sullivan observed, "Things are seldom what they seem; skim milk masquerades as cream." RR] It is the last case in which Felicity failed to obtain at least some basic psychological assessment data to confirm a clinical diagnosis before proceeding with treatment.

An Unforesightful Foresight

In his early twenties, Ulric was referred for anti-anxiety treatment because of an agoraphobic reaction. He felt extremely fearful that some catastrophic event would occur if he were alone, particularly in driving anywhere. His family was exceedingly closely knit, and the family members had adjusted their schedules to make it possible for one of them to drive him wherever he had to go, and to be at home when he was there. The onset of these symptoms dated from an occasion when he was driving alone and experienced a panic attack for no apparent reason. He stopped the car and got out of it for a few minutes until he had settled down. Thereafter he feared being alone in the car, or being alone anywhere.

At the first contact, in addition to the administration of a standard battery of tests, a subjective units monitoring device (SURE) was administered to Ulric. This monitoring instrument was administered just before each treatment session throughout the course of treatment. The treatment that was undertaken was systematic anxiety desensitization (using Wolpe's reciprocal inhibition therapy method). There were twenty-one hour-long sessions in the treatment program, mostly concerned with imagery progressively increasing his independent action, especially in driving, and increasingly while alone.

The monitoring instrument employed amounted to an extension of Wolpe's method for estimating anxiety on the Subjective Units of Discomfort (SUD) scale. In this method, the person is asked to remember that circumstance in life in which he/she felt the most anxious, uptight and scared ever, and to assign to the feeling experienced in that situation the value of 100. The person is then asked to remember that circumstance in life in which he/she felt the most calm, relaxed, and at ease, and to assign the feeling experienced in that situation the value 0. The person is then asked to divide up the subjective or felt distance between these two points into a hundred equal units, and then to estimate on that scale how he/she feels now. At all future subjective rating times, the person is asked to maintain the same standard 0 and 100 reference points or situations.

Felicity has used a series of other subjective scales, distributed in a manner analogous to SUD, to permit the monitoring of a number of subjective dimensions, so as to estimate changes associated with ongoing psychotherapy. A wide range of scales can be laid out to be rated in the ME/SURE (Monitoring Estimates: Subjective Units Rating Ergometrics) device. In any given case, some scales will be relevant to expected or targeted therapeutic changes, and some scales will be irrelevant. The inclusion of therapeutically irrelevant scales provides a means by which to determine whether ratings of change on relevant scales are or are not meaningful.

The ME/SURE procedure turned out to be reasonably satisfactory during the first few treatment sessions with Ulric. However, it soon became evident that the ratings were becoming truncated by the scaling method. In fact, it developed that Ulric was soon feeling better than he had ever felt, and it was impossible for him to record his subjective state on the scales. Accordingly, it became necessary to re-design the scales in such a way as to provide tails extending the measures (in equivalent units) at both ends to allow Ulric to represent changes in his subjective states.

As he improved, Ulric pointed out that the scales were inadequate to allow him to represent how he was feeling on the scales. In previous cases, it is likely that the real amount of improvement had not been measured by these scales. An analogous difficulty probably affects most clinical tests. Most clinical tests are set up to measure pathology or troublesome symptoms. As therapeutic changes occur, the symptoms tend to vanish. But provision is rarely made to include in tests items that represent improvement, let alone those that represent a better than normal state or those concerned with variables that predict maintenance of therapeutic benefits. Consequently, determining the point at which treatment ought to be terminated is commonly very difficult. Sometimes, treatment is completed long before it is terminated.

The last two cases to be reported here are concerned with lack of foresight in the assessment process. In the first case, Felicity forgot to perform an initial assessment, with damaging results. In the second case, Felicity forgot to make allowances for the expected changes that would occur in psychotherapy, and this resulted in a loss of important information – thus unduly extending the therapy. But most of the mistakes made in the assessment process have to do with the process of measurement and of deriving inferences from the measures taken. It is time to turn to these kinds of issues.

An Error Terror

Psychologists are very conscious of what they are doing, and about the pitfalls they may encounter in developing and using measures of behaviour and personality. There are all sorts of conventions and 'rules' concerning mental measurement. There is even an authoritative set of published standards about the development and use of psychometric devices. Two of the things that are of greatest concern about such devices have to do with 'validity' (or the extent to which the test measures what it is supposed to measure) and 'reliability' (or the extent to which the test is precise and dependable in measuring whatever it measures).

Various types of 'validity' are recognized. 'Face' validity concerns the extent to which the test items look as though they are related to the thing being measured. 'Concurrent' validity refers to the extent to which it provides a good measure of other related measures. 'Predictive' validity is about the extent to which it predicts something which has not yet happened. And 'construct' validity addresses the extent to which it relates to the concepts in the theory from which it is derived. Notice that all of these types of validity are concerned with the specific relevance of the test to what it was intended to measure. [On the other hand, it might be argued that a test is always valid, the only question being "Valid as a measure of what?" And it takes a psychologist to answer that question. RR]

The most widely used test in North America is the Minnesota Multiphasic Personality Inventory (MMPI). As a whole, this test has a good deal of 'face' validity, as the questions it asks are generally the types of questions one might ask in a clinical assessment interview. However, as a whole, it has very little of the other kinds of validity. Actually, this makes it a truly wonderful test. Literally hundreds of research studies have been done, for example, to find 'scales' comprised of sets of the MMPI items useful in predicting or measuring a wide range of variables – uses for the test never dreamed of by its originators. Each scale includes only some of the test's items, and it may be highly valid (or not) whether or not the test as a whole is,

There are also several different types of 'reliability' which are recognized. 'Retest' reliability defines the stability of the test over repeated applications with the same people. 'Split-half' reliability estimates the extent to which the test is comprised of parts that are internally consistent with each other. 'Item-scale' reliability addresses the extent to which the items consistently contribute to the measurement of the same thing. And 'standard error of the mean' reliability is concerned with precision or the extent to which the measures consistently create equivalent measures among the same types of people. It would certainly seem that concern with reliability features of a scale would be useful and important. And they are.

However, things aren't always what they seem. Of course, Felicity had to learn about the various aspects of validity and reliability when he was receiving his training at university. And, in the case of validity and reliability, he believed what he was taught. One result of his belief was that it took him a dog's age to find ways to measure change in psychotherapy – so he could keep track of how well he was doing and adjust what he was doing to suit the realities of the people he was treating. You see there are all sorts of problems that come from following the old adage, 'When all else fails, follow the directions'.

Take the case of trying to measure psychotherapeutic change in treated criminal offenders. There is a traditional view among mental health workers that 'nothing works in corrections'. Indeed, it has been very hard to demonstrate any changes in offenders following treatment. Like everybody else, Felicity was using the MMPI as one of the measures of change in treated offenders. One reason for doing this was that among the so-called ten 'basic clinical scales' of the test, one which appears to have particularly good reliability and validity is the 'Pd' scale. The Pd scale is known to provide a pretty valid measure of a person's criminality or of his susceptibility to getting involved in crime. This fact seemed to justify the use of that MMPI scale both as an initial measure of the person's pre-treatment 'degree' of risk of criminality (not a bad use of it), and as a measure of change in that quality of the person following treatment. The latter use sounds pretty sensible. The trouble was that the Pd scale would not record changes. So it was often concluded that no changes were taking place in treated offenders.

Then, bless their souls, Blanchard and Scapinello took a look at the item composition of the several MMPI scales, including the Pd scale. What they found was that, although there seemed to be a kind of 'face' validity for the items contributing to each scale, many of the items contributing to all the scales were 'historical' items. That is, once the person had given a particular answer to a question, that same answer would have to be the answer he gave in the future, at least if he were answering honestly. For example, if the person indicated at one testing that his parents fought a lot, or that he didn't get along with his teachers, he would very likely give the same answer at all future testings. One's history doesn't change, and so historical items do not permit one to measure change when it takes place in a person. That may permit one to identify a problem history and thus the problems the person may have now, but it does not allow change to be measured. The point in all this is that, although most of the MMPI scales are comprised of many historical items, a *majority* of the items contributing to the Pd scale are historical – a higher proportion than those comprising the other scales. No wonder it was so difficult to record treatment effects with offenders! New tests, free from historical items, had to be devised to make it possible to demonstrate that treatment can work with offenders too.

But that's not the end of the problem. If you start using a test that has good 'retest' reliability, it may be so 'stable' that it will not record the full amount of change which may have taken place. One way to achieve retest stability is to have lots of historical items. Another way is to get 'too' psychometrically sophisticated and create a scale that keeps asking the same question in more-or-less the same way (as in the some of the so-called 'state-trait' scales) – thus not covering enough of the field in which changes may occur. Actually, the same applies to scales having good 'split-half' or 'standard error of the mean' reliabilities. Some measurement instability is needed in order to permit a test to measure change associated with treatment.

Then there's the problem of practice effects in repeated uses of a test to measure change. At one time, Felicity needed a means by which to monitor changes in mood and energy during treatment. Monitoring measures ought to have what is called a 'motor skills' no-growth curve over repeated applications. This means that the test produces almost a flat, no-growth picture if it is used over and over again. Most psychological tests don't work like that. People learn something during the first testing, which they apply in the next testing – so their performance changes.

Felicity asked a group of volunteers he had working with him to find a test for him with a 'motor skills' curve to monitor changes in mood and energy. This was just another example of the wonderful benefits he has obtained from volunteers working with him. These volunteers went off and experimented with all sorts of monitoring devices. And they found one that worked. It was Tiddly Winks. That's right! The person presses down with a large plastic disc on the corner of a small plastic disc so that the small disc jumps up and forward – in this case toward a 'target' bowl. After a very small amount of practice, the person masters a certain level of skill in the task. Thereafter, the person will tend to under-shoot if depressed and lacking energy, to over-shoot if elated and energetic, and will have a good 'hit rate' if he/she feels 'normal'.

An Unresponsive Responsiveness

In assessment procedures, it is important that the stimulus conditions are applied in a standard fashion, and that responses are recorded in a standard way. If these conditions are met, except for the relatively narrow limits of measurement error, the major source of assessment error is likely to derive from errors in the communication process.

The Minnesota Multiphasic Personality Inventory (MMPI) was administered on a routine basis to Una while she was incarcerated in a correctional institution. There had been no indication from the correctional staff of any problems identified in this woman, nor did she appear to Felicity, during a brief interview, to manifest any major psychosocial adjustment difficulties. However, the MMPI profile suggested very considerable and intense psychopathology. She exhibited extreme scores on the clinical scales, with a jagged pattern of wide variations. What was the matter with the test or with Una?

At first glance one might have thought that she was severely disturbed. However, the L and F scores ('validity' scales) were also extremely high, and she was asked whether she had any difficulty in understanding any of the questions. Una claimed to have had no trouble understanding the questions, and said that she had responded to the items with care and honesty.

A few of her responses were reviewed with her. She now gave the opposite responses to the responses given originally. Felicity was about to infer the presence of an extreme bi-polar affective disorder, when the inmate, as if sensing something was wrong, said, "You asked for Xs on the answer sheet, so I put Xs to indicate the wrong answers, as you asked." It took a full twenty seconds for the import of this cognitively dissonant item of intelligence to sink into Felicity's slow brain. He then arranged for the MMPI to be keyed in once more, this time entering the blank answer box as the response. The resulting profile was quite satisfactory, and seemed to reflect Una's personality reasonably accurately. For Una an 'X' could only mean the wrong answer, and she was communicating, with the requested 'X' response, the response pole which did not apply to her.

Fresh from this experience, Felicity encountered another case with the same kind of jagged, high scoring MMPI profile, also with radically elevated L and F validity scale scores. Accordingly, he met briefly with the inmate to determine the nature of the response set adopted. The inmate stated that the 'X' had been used to indicate the response pole that applied, indicating thereby that there had been no communication difficulty at the response end. However, on consulting the inmate's test file, no reading test could be found. It was discovered that the inmate had appeared late for the group testing session, and that no reading test was administered. The reading test was administered, and the inmate was found to be reading at the grade 4.5 equivalent level. Had this been discovered prior to the administration of the MMPI, the MMPI would have been administered orally. The difficulty in the validity of the MMPI profile in this case was due to communication difficulty at the stimulus end – the inmate simply could not read well enough to understand the questions being asked.

Within a week, another inmate provided an MMPI performance yielding extremely high L and F scores, suggesting an invalid profile. In this case, the reason was marked clearly on the profile by the computer input clerk. While entering the inmate's True and False responses into the analysis program, she had detected a rhythmic pattern of responses, which changed from T T F F, to T T T F F F, to T T T T F F F F, to T F T F. Clearly the inmate had elected not to take the time to read or to understand the questions asked, and had responded essentially at random. Part of the task of understanding the results from a test include reaching an understanding of any difficulties of communication between the client and the test questions and instructions.

A Mind Matter

Felicity is very human. Very often, he can't make up his mind. It's not entirely his fault. You see, any clinical event is by its nature a 'rare' event. On any scale, both the extreme (rare) events or scores or people, and the rest of the not-unusual events or scores or people, are part of the whole population. Due to anticipated errors of measurement, some of the extreme cases will tend to score toward the population mean, and some of the rest of the population will tend to score toward the extremes.

This results in an area of overlap between the 'real' extreme cases and the rest of the population – an area of overlap that typically includes many more of the 'rest of the population' than of the extreme people. If there are 100 people in the real 'extreme' group, and

10,000 people in the 'rest of the population' group, then if there are 10 people from the 'extreme' group in the area of overlap, there are probably about 1000 people from the 'rest of the population' contained in the area of overlap. This means that any selected 'cut-off score' will be unsatisfactory. For example, if the middle of the area of overlap is selected as the 'cut score' beyond which individuals will be construed clinically as having 'problems' or as being 'extreme' on the scale, about 40 'normals' might erroneously be identified as 'extreme', and about 3 (or 3%) of the real 'extremes' might be misidentified as being 'non-extreme' (normal).

The more we try to capture correct identification of all of the 'extremes', the more 'normals' we incorrectly identify as 'extremes' – with the 'real normals' increasing at a much greater rate than the 'real extremes' (Type I errors). So that, when we correctly identify all of the 10 'real extremes' in the area of overlap, we may have incorrectly identified as many as 95 'normals' also. If, instead, we shift our cutting-score outwards on the scale until we have correctly identified all the 'real normals', we have then incorrectly identified (missed) nearly all of the 'real extremes' (Type II errors).

In clinical work, both Type I and Type II errors are risky. If I make a Type I error, I will have increased the cost of treatment greatly, by treating more people who don't need treatment than those who do. On the other hand, if I take the risk of making a Type II error, I miss treating many of those who need it – a problem which is made greater if the problem results in pain or loss not only to the person but also to others – as where the problem is a criminal one which risks victimization of others.

The best way to reduce the risks of making either Type I or Type II errors is to employ more than one 'screen' or more than one type of measure of the dimension in question through which people are processed prior to making an identification decision about an individual's differences.

Many psychologists seek to accomplish these multiple 'screens' by using more than one test providing information about each dimension in a battery of tests. This is probably the most practical solution, but it still runs the risk that errors of measurement are, for example, at least partially related to the day or time when the assessment is undertaken – so that the errors affect all the measures taken at that time. Because of this, also relatively rare, risk, it is slightly better to use 'successive screens' – that is, observations or measures taken at different times, and preferably based on different types of data so that errors of measurement can at least be recognized.

But, you see, that can create problems too. You might think that the more information you have on a person, the more information you have. Actually, that's not true. When you add together bits of information to draw a composite conclusion, a funny thing happens. The more information you try to include, beyond a rather limited amount, the poorer your ability to predict and the poorer your ability to create therapeutic effects. Now, everybody knows that what has just been said is both flat wrong and utterly mad. However, strange to say, a good principle to consider in most things you do is 'less is more'. Felicity kept forgetting this principle.

The principle involved starts with the observation that each bit of information concerning anything contains *both* information and error – for example, in making a prediction. The information part is narrowly concerned with the issue being predicted. The error part may be related to all sorts of other issues it might predict – so that different bits will contain different 'kinds' of errors. The first bit of relevant data or information used contributes all of its information and all of its error – so that, by itself, it predicts imperfectly, but as well as it predicts. The second bit of relevant data, also containing information and error, contributes that *part* of its information which is not yet accounted for by the first bit of data (i.e., less than all its information), *and* that bit of its error not yet included – which may be a quite different 'kind' of error from that in the first variable, and so may add *all* of its error. By the time we add in the third, fourth and fifth bits of relevant data, more and more of the informational elements have already been included. But, since the error parts can relate to all sorts of other predictions, the contribution of error from each additional variable continues to increase the amount of prediction error.

The point of diminishing returns from adding information is reached very quickly in dealing with 'uncorrelated' variables – that is where the variables may predict what you're after, but also predict all sorts of other different things. With 'uncorrelated' variables, the optimum level of prediction is usually achieved using no more than five to seven separate variables. The point of diminishing returns is reached a little later when the variables being used are 'correlated' – that is, they all commonly predict the same kind of thing. With 'correlated' variables, the optimum level of prediction is usually achieved using about sixteen (12 to 20) variables. Above or below these numbers of variables any predictive efficiency tends to decline. Now that sounds like numerological nonsense to anybody with any brains. But it isn't.

Like all scientists, including psychologists, Felicity learned this sort of nonsense at school. Like you, he knew it had to be tommyrot. So he had to keep 'reinventing this wheel' all through his career. He thought psychiatric conferences, which tried to bring together everything that could be known about a patient, must be the way to reach good and reliable evaluations of patients. It took quite a long time, and a lot of reliance in his research work on this unreliable source of information, before he had disabused himself of that idea.

He was working on some research with the Rorschach inkblot test. He found about 120 heterogeneous ('uncorrelated') variables all of which, individually, significantly but imperfectly predicted something he wanted to measure. He combined all of them into a single scale, and it lost all predictive significance. After much fiddling around, it ended up that combining *any* five to seven of these variables in a scale produced the best level of prediction, better than combining any fewer or any more variables.

In the same research, he found 32 homogeneous ('correlated') variables all of which, individually, significantly but imperfectly predicted something else he wanted to measure. When he combined all 32 in a scale, he lost all significance in his prediction – it did not predict at all. After much fiddling, it ended up that *any* 16 of these variables combined in a scale produced the best level of prediction, better than combining any fewer or any more.

Later in his career, having forgotten this experience, he tried combining a group of 50 and a group of 100 questionnaire items all of which significantly predicted what he was trying to measure. He got no predictive efficiency at all. The 50 items were uncorrelated (heterogeneous), and it turned out the best predictive efficiency was obtained using any 7 of the items. The 100 items were inter-correlated (homogeneous), and it turned out the best predictive efficiency was achieved using any 16 of them.

When he started working in psychotherapy, he surveyed the available relevant research literature. He concluded that, in general, those methods that sought to address the greatest number of variables (the most complex) had the worst outcome rates, whereas those that were the most simple, addressing the fewest variables, had the best outcome rates. Of course, he didn't believe what he thought he had found from the literature. So he had to invent the wheel all over again. He started off working with the more complex methods – the ones that 'really' address the complexity of a human being, and which sought to get at the 'depth' and the 'range' of human experience. And his results were such that he felt he could not, in all conscience, keep working as a psychotherapist if that was all that was achieved (basically no better results than 'no treatment'). As he tried other procedures his results improved, keeping at first with the ones which looked as though they 'did justice' to at least some of the complexity of human living and problems. But he was using more and more simple methods. In fact, with each step toward simplification and reduction in the number of variables addressed, the higher the success rates, the shorter the treatment time, and the broader the range of human problems that could be addressed with them.

Just about everything that happens in his life shocks Felicity almost to the point of stupor. It would seem that the best ways to predict anything in the clinical area involve using a series of very brief and simple assessment 'screens', trying not to get too complex, tricky, or sophisticated with them, and preferring to take the risk of Type I errors rather than Type II errors. At least, that's the 'intelligence' that Felicity seems to have come to.

You may wonder what importance the foregoing may have to fantasies about psychotherapy. You probably know that everything written these days is done according to a 'formula'. In writing science fiction for a contemporary audience, the 'formula' requires that some pseudo-scientific mumbo-jumbo, irrelevant to the plot, be included to make everything sound precise as well as mysterious and futuristic. Can you imagine an episode of Star Trek in which some of the crew do not sit at computers, wiggle sticks, and push buttons while talking about warp speeds, black holes, and navigational coordinates? It's all part of the necessary illusion. Well, here we have tried to emulate that wisdom in writing this nonsense.

Ethical Errors – Errors of Propriety – Consequential Consequences

As we approach the end of this volume about people who have allowed Felicity to peek into their lives, it seems only right to tell a story about a mistake he made and the terrible effects of the mistake. It's true that 'anybody could have made the mistake' he did. But he made it. And he has never been able to forgive himself for his mistake.

The mistake he made was that he failed to consider a simple, and almost too obvious, requirement of the Ethical Code, and what he did had awful consequences which nobody could have anticipated. Felicity feels he must constantly remind himself that each, however apparently irrelevant, requirement of the Ethical Code is there for a reason. The reason may not be clear in every case, but the rules are broken at *the patient's* peril.

<u>A Remorseless Remorse</u>

One day, Felicity was sitting in his office at the old mental hospital when he received a call from his neurologist friend. Without even a 'how do you do', the neurologist responded to Felicity's 'hello' with, "Felicity, drop everything, bring your movie camera and lights and get down here now. We must film something going on here." Felicity acknowledged the curt message, hung up and took his photographic equipment down to the EEG lab to film whatever it was that was so urgent.

A very attractive young lady in her late twenties was lying on the EEG couch with EEG electrodes attached all over her scalp. She was undergoing a diagnostic EEG. She was also in the process of having what was manifestly a grand mal epileptic seizure. The neurologist excitedly drew Felicity's attention to the polygraph tracings on the EEG machine. Felicity bent over the paper moving under the eight moving pens and examined the tracings. He looked up in confusion at the neurologist, glanced quickly at the patient, and then back with a questioning expression at the neurologist. He whispered, "Alpha?" The neurologist radiated delight as he nodded his agreement. The patient, in manifest grand mal seizure, was pumping out pure, 'normal' alpha activity on the EEG. This was indeed a phenomenon that seemed to need to be recorded somehow.

While he prepared to photograph this apparently inexplicable event, he took note of the lady on the couch. In spite of the muscular contortions of the seizure, it was evident that this was a very attractive young lady. Her skin texture was smooth with no lines or other signs of age. Her hair had a soft middle to light brown tone. Her figure was slim but well-rounded. She was the very image of a nubile young woman.

The old building's ceilings were high, and Felicity thought he could photograph the lady best from above. He pulled up a table, put a chair on it, clambered up on the chair, turned on his photographic light bar and proceeded to run off some movie film showing both the lady and the EEG equipment to which she was attached. The filming done, he replaced the furniture, collected his equipment and returned to his office. He also obtained the patient's name for the record. The patient's name was Veronica.

About two weeks later, Felicity was asked if he would accept a new patient to his Behaviour Therapy Unit. There was a vacant bed and the chief psychiatrist seemed to think the patient would be an appropriate case for the Unit. Without further thought or question, Felicity agreed. However, he was rather busy at that time and so he was unable to get up to the Unit to meet the patient for a couple of days. This gave the new patient time to settle in and to hear from the other women on the Unit about the weird magician under whose care she had been placed.

After she had been there for about two days, Felicity made arrangements through the nurse for the patient to remain in the Unit at a certain time so that she and Felicity could meet. Felicity arrived at the appointed time and walked into the large dormitory. The new patient, and she was Veronica, was coming toward the door from the far end of the dormitory as Felicity entered. She saw Felicity and stopped in her tracks. Felicity saw that something was wrong, and he stopped in his tracks too. There followed the most terrifying three minutes Felicity has ever experienced. Of course, he is unable to state whether the time involved was one minute or one hour. He was transfixed.

As soon as Veronica saw Felicity she froze in obvious panic. Felicity waited and watched to see if he could discern the nature of the problem. What he saw was a young lady rapidly aging in front of his eyes. Her eyes became glazed and dry, like those of an old person. Her skin started to dry out and to shrivel up as deep, grey furrows etched themselves on her face. Her breasts visibly drooped under her loose hospital frock. Her legs and arms lost the fleshy look of youth and became skinny and tendonous like that of a very old person. Her soft brown hair streaked with grey. And her whole body seemed to draw itself inward as if losing much of its flesh and fluids.

By the time Felicity had come to his senses, Veronica's whole appearance was that of at least a sixty-five year old lady. In perhaps three minutes, her appearance had aged by easily forty years. Felicity grasped that there was nothing he could do to help Veronica, and that his presence obviously had something to do with her unbelievable transformation in terror. He turned and fled the Unit, found the nurse, rushed her into the dormitory, and alerted the medical staff.

Veronica stopped aging when Felicity ran out of the dormitory. But she remained the sixty-five year old woman she had become. She moved herself around the ward with stiff, halting steps. She ate her meals, made her bed and helped clean up the living quarters. But she remained mute and she would not involve herself in any of the treatment programs on the unit or with Felicity, nor even with his female staff.

Two months passed. During this time Felicity racked his brains and consulted with everyone he could think of to try to understand what might have gone wrong or to find a means by which to treat or correct whatever the problem might be. Nobody could understand what had happened. In desperation, Felicity asked the female psychiatrist serving the ward to undertake a sodium amytal ('truth serum') interview with Veronica, if only to find out what had happened. The psychiatrist agreed. Of course, it was clear that, since Felicity was so obviously a part of the problem, he should not be present during the amytal interview. A nurse would be present to assist the psychiatrist.

As soon as the psychiatrist returned from the sodium amytal interview, Felicity anxiously asked what had transpired. The psychiatrist was obviously shaken by the experience, but she wanted to share what had happened.

Sodium amytal is injected slowly, and its effects emerge at a steady but slow pace. The psychiatrist reported that as the amytal effects started to be manifest, Veronica started to rejuvenate. The deep lines in her face smoothed out. Her arms and legs lost their thin, tendonous appearance and became round and fleshy. Her breasts regained their tone and heaved up under her frock. Her eyes became moist and reactive once more. And the heavy grey streaking of her hair turned back to its soft brown colour. She began to talk, and told a strange story.

Before she came to the hospital, she had been living in what must have been a kind of commune. The dominant resident in the house had encouraged those living there to participate in group discussions which sounded like group therapy sessions. He tape recorded these sessions. According to the patient, "I poured my soul into those tapes."

By and by, she found herself in a different place – presumably the admission ward of the hospital. There, one day, she had a remarkable experience (presumably, the 'seizure' in the EEG lab), during which she saw God in the sky, surrounded by light (presumably Felicity behind his photographic light bar).

Then, again, she found herself in another place (presumably the Unit). This new place was apparently heaven, because there was God in charge of healing her. She was terrified because, she found herself in heaven, standing before God, but without her soul.

The mystery seemed solved and Felicity was about to breathe a heavy sigh of relief when the psychiatrist indicated that her report was not yet completed. The psychiatrist looked shaken again, and Felicity could feel the hair rise on the back of his neck as he waited for what was to come. As if to verify his worst fears, the psychiatrist told him that, as the effects of the sodium amytal started to wear off, Veronica started once more to age, returning back to her sixty-five year old state.

Another month elapsed while Felicity and the psychiatrist went over the case again and again to see if there was anything that could be done. The only hope was that another sodium amytal interview, with its abreaction, might stabilize her back at her real age. It had to be tried.

Following the interview, the psychiatrist and Felicity closeted themselves to review what had occurred. The psychiatrist said that exactly the same sequence of events had occurred. As the amytal effects took hold, Veronica started to be rejuvenated. Her appearance returned to its original state. She told the same story about what had happened. And, as the amytal effects wore off, she aged once more back to her condition as a sixty-five year old woman.

There was nothing more that could be done under the present circumstances. It was decided that Veronica had to be removed from the Unit to a ward where she would never again encounter Felicity. Perhaps, in time, with care and further sodium amytal interviews, her bodily habitus might be stabilized once more as a young woman in her late twenties.

Felicity's co-workers and friends tried to help him to recover from his crippling remorse about Veronica. They pointed out repeatedly that he could not have known that taking her picture would become integrated in her complex delusions. They said that no one could anticipate the manner in which her schizophrenic logic would incorporate a simple filming into her ego in such a devastating manner. And they remarked that lots of patients were filmed for all sorts of reasons without their prior consent. But there was the problem. Felicity had filmed Veronica without her prior consent, and in a mental condition in which it would be impossible to ensure that she would not misconstrue the event.

It is true that, in those days, paraseizures were not really recognized, nor were they understood. They were usually called 'hysterical' seizures, and 'hysterics' were thought to be resistant to schizophrenia. Also, the conventional wisdom was that patients in grand mal epileptic seizures would be unconscious. Even if they were not, the post-ictal (i.e., post-seizure) confusion would be expected to erase any memory of seizure events. But, then, this was not an epileptic seizure, in that the concurrent EEG was behaving normally. Of course, all this rumination merely expresses 20/20 hindsight.

The truth reduces simply to this: ethical considerations demanded that Felicity not use any means by which to invade the patient's privacy without her prior informed consent. Felicity hopes he has learned the lesson that the requirements of the Ethical Code are all there for good and sufficient reasons.

Chapter 12

ACCESSORY THERAPEUTIC AGENTS – WEIGHTY WAITING

You may think that the main therapeutic agents are surgery and medications, perhaps throwing in physicians and some other people – such as nurses, of course. Well, the world is not restricted to realities as we might conceive of them. In addition to those already mentioned, all sorts of other things interfere with or get in the way of effective therapy. You may be interested in hearing about a few other counter-therapeutic agents.

A Devil's Deviltry

Some people actually like talking on the telephone. Felicity hates it. It seems to him that it was designed to be misused. In every place where Felicity finds himself, there is one lurking around waiting for the most inopportune moment to invade his privacy. It comes supplied with a loud buzzing noise calculated to create instant arousal approaching panic. And if it is not answered immediately, putting all else aside, it disturbs the quiet of life by repeated and insistent alarms, demanding that it receive attention before anything else that happens to be in progress. And we sheep, enslaved by the mechanical world we have created for ourselves to make life easier and more pleasant by giving us control over our worlds and the things in them, obediently answer the damned thing instantly when it commands. And the reason why it is ringing is nearly always inappropriate.

During the working day, its summons are sometimes appropriate. It sometimes brings contact from someone who wants to share his or her wealth with Felicity. But that's only during the working day.

After working hours, it becomes a nuisance. Felicity had the misfortune to be in his office after working hours one day. The switchboard therefore funnelled a call to him. The caller identified himself as an oculist who had a patient who was suffering acute panic because he had the idea the world was about to come to an end. The caller wanted to know what to do with his patient. Instead of expressing the view that he hoped the patient was right, Felicity wondered what an oculist was. He asked the caller to spell the name of his occupation. The spelling was 'occultist.' Felicity suggested it might be a superior idea if the occultist took the patient to the nearest hospital Emergency Department.

During evening hours the telephone, as a therapeutic agent, becomes a genuine hazard to treatment. The patient who calls is most probably lonely and, in order to justify calling, has to induce in him- or herself some set of urgent symptoms – most often depression. The purpose of the symptom, of course, is to demand the attention of the callee, and the counter-therapeutic gain is the reliance on another to dispel the felt loneliness. These calls, if rejected, may prove dangerous for the patient; if accepted, they foster dependency and prolong the regular treatment.

At night, almost all calls received are deemed by caller and callee to be concerned with crisis, again, most often depression. The trouble is that if the call is to be made after bedtime, the caller usually considers it necessary to feel and present him or her self as suicidal. This adds to the anti-therapeutic value of the call by increasing crisis in the person's life, distracting the callee from the ongoing therapy by having to deal with the threat of suicide, gets the patient thinking about catastrophic events, and robs both ends of the line of healthful sleep.

First thing in the morning calls, unless prearranged to serve as alarm clocks, are properly responded to only by tearing the caller's phone out of the wall (if only it could be reached) and consigning it forever to the perdition from whence it came.

The telephone, as a contemporary therapeutic agent, is almost always a counter-therapeutic agent. Those who construe it to be the instrument of the devil that it is will someday emerge the victors. Felicity looks forward to the time when the infernal telephone will come equipped with a video screen so the caller and callee can both hear and see one another. When that blessed day arrives, the early morning caller will be privileged to be greeted by the same visage as that which welcomes Felicity each morning – baggy eyed, unshaved, and scowling fiercely.

Valuelessness Re-Vivified

In terms of sheer valuelessness, the ultimate form adopted by the devil in constructing counter-therapeutic agents is to be found in the person of the lawyer. These immaculately groomed accomplices in every kind of crime are constructed (as automatons they are not created) with care to practice the absolute refinement of conflict instigation and maintenance – of course, earning them economic advantages both coming and going. Lawyers are the robots most carefully programmed to instigate and benefit from adversarial wrath. Governments blindly hire them to write, and then later to adjudicate, laws that can only result in human conflict. As a result of this pre-arranged collusion, court lawyers can hoodwink the rest of us into believing that their advocacy is needed in order to protect us from the exercise of those laws. They create our problems and then offer to help us solve the created crises. But they don't help. They enmesh us deeper and deeper in the hopeless morass of our artificially created pains. Counter-therapeutic is the weakest charge that can be laid at their door – counter-productive and criminal deviltry is more apt.

Treacherous Teaching

But then educators or teachers must surely lie at the other end of that spectrum. Not by much. Education expands our horizons and allows us to see the world through eyes other than our own, right? Some education may do that. Most, however, has the effect of radically restricting our purview on things. A couple of extreme examples are used here to illustrate the point because a few paragraphs would hardly serve to bring education to task.

In principle, a main aim and purpose of learning, for example in psychotherapy, ought to be to increase the freedom of the individual – extending the range of options of response available to him/her. But surely that's what education also tries to do. Oh, is that so? Think about this.

At the point of birth, an infant's vocal options are virtually infinite, potentially encompassing all the sounds of all the languages on earth. The function of linguistic education by parents, which is extended and refined torturously by the schools, is to restrict the range of sounds the child, and later the adult, can make in vocalizing. Linguistic education simply robs the child of potential vocal sounds as he or she is encouraged, say rather enforced, to make increasingly accurate his or her reproduction of the literate use of the language(s) he or she is taught.

Moreover, children don't work with stereotypes. They are in awe of the world around them, and they hold no lasting enmity about any part of their world. Prejudices and hatreds, political pre-dispositions and pre-suppositions, and just plain ordinary malevolence have to be taught to them. In doing so, we rob them of flexibility, freedom, and the capacity to relate peacefully and healthfully to the world and those around them.

As education is practised in most societies, it is in many ways a strong counter-therapeutic agent. Of course, Felicity would argue that the same is not true of Psychology and psychologists. However, as usual, he may very well be wrong. But let's turn to psychologists next to see how they have gone about the task of trying to avoid being anti-therapeutic agents and, like the rest of the world of (ill-)health practitioners, may have failed.

CHAPTER 13

PSYCHOLOGY AS A PROFESSION

Some of the Pain of Psychologists – Variations on Felicity – Why Few 'Get' Psychology

Psychology is the most popular university course worldwide. That doesn't mean that the largest number of people are graduated from universities into the profession of Psychology. No, a rather modest number of people graduate as psychologists. It is people's curiosity that leads them to take a Psychology course or two at university. And, of course, those courses are mostly introductory courses, and they don't really teach students very much, although the students think that they do.

What such courses sometimes provide for those who are paying attention is a way of understanding how a science and a profession of Psychology are possible. Everybody has some exposure to the 'hard' sciences like Physics and Chemistry at secondary school – the disciplines that deal with the 'spatially-distributed' things of the physical universe. Everybody has some exposure to the humanities like Languages and History at secondary school, and to computational disciplines like Algebra and Geometry. There may even be an attempt to give secondary school students some exposure to the 'social sciences' in courses concerned with family life or man in society. But these courses are token courses and don't really provide any information about or from the science. They are typically taught by teachers who have received no training in science and have no idea how a science concerned with ephemeral things or 'temporally-distributed' behavioural events is possible.

Given that, introductory university courses in Psychology are about at the level of secondary school courses in other fields or disciplines. That is unfortunate. You see, the sciences of the spatially-distributed physical universe, computational disciplines, and the humanities all deal with dead things or things of the past. Even medicine and health are largely concerned with dead things. The anatomy and chemistry of the body are virtually the same whether the person is alive or dead. It is not until we reach functioning and motion that we move to the sciences concerned with life and living. And what each of us has that is most precious, and most makes us who and what we are, is life or living. The basic science of life and living is Psychology.

One of the reasons why such a modest number of psychologists is graduated from universities is that, given the introductory nature of most general level Psychology courses at university, most people 'don't get it' – they don't understand how a science of Psychology works or is possible. And they tend, therefore, to imagine that Psychology involves the exercise of personal reason or logic and the application of personal experience and philosophy.

Retiring Retirees

Another reason why few psychologists are graduated is that Psychology is the most expensive profession in which to educate people, with the least financial return. Does that surprise you? In order to become a psychologist you usually have first to obtain the highest academic degree – the **Ph.D.**, or Doctorate of Philosophy – the degree university professors usually have to have. That takes an average of nine years at university, with a range from seven to fourteen years. (By way of comparison, medicine and law require only five to six years at university.) After that you have to serve at least a year of internship under supervision, followed by written and oral exams that you must pass before you can be licensed to practice Psychology. Then, if you want to become a specialist, in the usual instance, it is expected that you will work under supervision in the type of specialty work you plan to do for about five more years, often followed by further exams.

By the time you have completed all this, you are almost ready to retire. But you can't afford it yet. You see, you first have to pay off the debts you have accumulated during the years of university. Meanwhile you have to build up a suitable retirement fund. But these two tasks are not as easy as you might think. You see, psychologists are one of the lowest paid of the professions, even although they function as one of the half-dozen professions practising absolutely independently – that means there is no other type of profession in the area which is better-trained to assume the responsibilities of independent practice.

However, you may well say, after all that preparation, psychologists get to do some of the most interesting things with some of the world's most fascinating and wonderful people. Now, that's true. But the costs are not yet fully laid out for you. You see, when they finally start practising independently, they have a choice to make – perhaps depending more on temperament than on free choice. They can be sort of flamboyant, get to be well-known and perhaps get enough business to make the whole endeavour economically worthwhile. Or they can be sort of retiring, not noticed by anyone, and scrape through life on the edge of poverty.

For most of those who choose the latter course, about the only way to survive financially is to become employed as a guest in someone else's 'house' – in physicians' houses called hospitals, or in social workers' houses called agencies, or in teachers' houses called schools, or in correctional officers' houses called jails or correctional centres. They have to work in 'someone else's house' because Psychology, as a science and a profession, is unlikely ever to have its own institutional base so as to allow psychologists to command good incomes. Institutions are set up to establish and perpetuate fixed procedures and products. That's why institutions do not accommodate well to change. Psychology is not likely to create institutions of its own because, as a science, the knowledge on which it bases its work is always changing. [All of which tends to make psychologists rather curmudgeonly, like Felicity and, parenthetically, myself. RR]

Felicity is a sort of retiring (soon, but not yet) person. Nobody notices him or cares whether he goes to work or not. You may well ask why anybody would be like that if to be flamboyant results in more money pouring in. Well, everything that has its upside also has its downside. Some of Felicity's friends who are also psychologists have chosen the more flamboyant route. Perhaps you would like to hear about the exciting life one of them leads.

So You Thought You'd Like To Be A Psychologist, Eh? – Bad Job's Bad Job

Of course, the practice of psychology is one of the best jobs one could have. The infinite variety of people precludes boredom. The opportunity to get to know people rather well, as well as the fact that the task by its nature demands that no personal judgements be made, ensures that the psychologist, at least eventually, always likes everybody he deals with. There is no responsibility in the job, since the psychologist always has to deflect responsibility back to the other person – except for what he, himself, does, and that is pretty clearly prescribed for most procedures. He doesn't even have to take much responsibility for what he says, since nobody believes anything a psychologist says. And he can be as kooky as he wants because everyone expects it of him anyway. So what could possibly make the job less than ideal?

Malice As Misfortune

Just thinking about Fortunato makes me grateful that Felicity is the comfortable, over-fed, docile, and lazy slob he is. You see, Fortunato was misnamed, at least as an Anglophone. Fortunato seems to have the kind of fortune that never misses – you know, misfortune.

Un-Fortunato started his working life educated as a clergyman. He soon discovered that he was suited best to pursue a career as an educator and a concerned reformer of wrongs against people – which means that he became deeply concerned about people's human rights. Then he realized that in order to perfect his knowledge background to be most effective as an educator, he needed to learn psychology. So he went on to get his degrees and to become a psychologist.

But he was unwilling to delay addressing some of the wrongs he saw around him inflicted on the helpless and the disadvantaged. So he did not simply spend the time of his life going to school to acquire the knowledge and skills he needed to do the kinds of work he felt needed to be done. He began, right after he had completed his required two-year stint in the army, to dig into life and to contribute his energies to help others achieve at least a bare share of the advantages the rest of us enjoy.

He started by developing a school in one of the southern states to provide some education for migrant farm workers from Mexico. That didn't sit too well with the radical right which tries to hide its red necks under white sheets. So he was burned out by the K.K.K. one night, barely escaping alive with his family.

Being a fairly quick learner, he concluded that times were not yet ripe for the South. So he went north. He set up a storefront school for street gang kids in a major northern city. Now these kids were not popular with the school system from which they had escaped. It didn't seem right that they should obtain an education without going through exposure to their share of the boring, the irrelevant, and the immaterial to which everybody else had to be subjected during their sentences to school. So the state Department of Education moved to close the storefront learning centre on the grounds that Fortunato did not have a teacher's license valid in that state.

Fortunato moved to the mountains in the north of the state. He bought a farm, hired qualified teachers and started a school for disadvantaged and impaired kids who could not be handled in the regular school system. The Department of Education could not fault him now for not having licensed teachers. So, instead, it imposed interminable inspections of the premises, demanding every kind of device and facility that could be found to be required buried in its ancient statutes and, failing that, flooding the campus with inspectors and assorted other misfits and microcephalic aments.

In sheer frustration, Fortunato moved his main campus to some property he acquired in another state. He developed a program for delinquent and mentally ill young people from all over the country, most of whom had been psychologically and physically destroyed by mistreatment and substance abuse before they arrived at the campus. The program, which was formed in consultation with literally hundreds of top-level educators, psychologists, and other specialists, began to produce truly miraculous results in nearly all those who stayed with it for any significant period of time.

However, on the strength of absolutely baseless allegations of drugs on the campus and politically-motivated media innuendos about sexual irregularities, the local sheriff's department planned a raid on the school. At one a.m. one morning, a hundred unmarked cars containing deputies, each carrying a mimeographed sheet of paper deputizing him, along with a host of T.V. cameramen and assorted other press, descended on the campus. They rousted the hundred or so panic-stricken, emotionally-disturbed children, the staff and their spouses, searched the premises and the scantily clad victims, and filmed much of the invasive proceedings. The entire cache turned up in this destructive search was two sticks of marijuana (about a thousandth of what could be turned up in any ordinary day school) found in the possession of two probationary staff who had been fired the day before for having drugs on campus but who had not yet left the premises.

Presumably to justify this inconceivably barbaric and inexcusable assault, Fortunato and his principal were arrested and carried off, leaving the campus in a terrified uproar. Of course Fortunato and his principal were released the following day for want of any charges on which to hold them. But a local red-neck politician obtained for himself a good deal of press coverage by bad-mouthing Fortunato and his efforts to save children destroyed by the society that produced them.

In spite of this and a host of lesser, but also damaging, related experiences, Fortunato hung on to his miracle school. But the bad press he had received made it seem as though he was unusually vulnerable as a provider of publicity for unscrupulous politicians. Consequently, when a senate sub-committee was examining expenditures of federal funds, one of the smallest users of such funds, Fortunato's school, was chosen for a so-called investigation – really a witch-hunt. The public week long hearings called witness after witness. All of these people had been either former staff fired for incompetence or unscrupulous practices or investigators who had been given the freedom, by decree, to harass the school and its staff under the guise of a formal investigation – hardly an objective crowd, and all with axes to grind. His staff and students and a host of senior health and educational professionals took the time to attend the hearings waiting to be allowed to provide testimony in support of Fortunato and his school. None was allowed to speak. Fortunato and his principal were each permitted one hour toward the middle of the week (before they knew what allegations might be made) in order to provide 'rebuttal'. During this time they were scorned and harassed by a lawyer, given free-rein to slander as he wished.

This tiny morsel of justice and democracy provided the last straw. Fortunato closed the school in sheer frustration and with a sense of helplessness in trying to protect those for whom he had accepted treatment responsibility. He took a couple of years to heal the bruises and wounds inflicted so lavishly upon him. Then he went into private practice as a psychologist. He still provided immense amounts of loving care to those who had been at his schools and to others who sought his help from all over the country, and from as far away as Europe. And his open-heartedness resulted in a steady decline in his personal wealth. At least he felt safe from the attacks of politicians and red-necks in the relative obscurity of a private health practice.

But no, he was not to be granted peace there either. Health practice in the United States is a fairly competitive business. Apparently Fortunato was competing too successfully to suit some anonymous other health practitioner. A complaint was lodged against him for 'practising medicine without a license' – about as empty of substance as any with which anyone was ever charged. As he sat in his office one day involved in psychotherapy with a depressed and fearful patient, there was a knock on his door. He opened it. The intruder identified himself as a police officer. Fortunato was arrested, his arms were handcuffed behind his back in front of his patients and staff, and he was pushed unceremoniously into a police car and taken to jail. It remains a mystery why it was necessary to subject his patients, his staff, and him to these appalling procedures conducted in this manner. Even if the charge had any substance, the nature of the charge would have required no more than a mailed or delivered subpoena. Why would police be accomplices in economically-motivated malice?

A tall, good-looking, ebullient, involved and politically-active man, like Fortunato, who is caring, who is willing to take his time to help others and who is effective in what he does, is at risk of evoking the enmity of others. Felicity is pleased to be a short, ugly, unprepossessing man that nobody notices. He says he's glad he hasn't got a complex – that he *is* inferior.

Post Script

If, by mistake or mischance, you happen to have read your way through this volume, you must by now be wondering what sort of a creature Felicity might be. Contrary to conventional wisdom, the nuts and dolts of psychotherapy are not the clientele – they are the practitioners. However, notwithstanding appearances to the contrary, Felicity believes himself to be really quite a nice man. He loves spinning stories for me, and I love listening to them. He knows that I like a story to sound at least a touch psycho-logically plausible, so I can 'enter into it' to some extent.

However, any clear thinking and reasonable person, who has any critical faculties at all, will know that the stories you have read here are pure and manifest fiction. Right?

Appendix A

HOW TO DO PSYCHOTHERAPY

Starters' Starters – According to Felicity

An appendix is a part of the body thoughtfully afforded by Providence to be deleted, to his pecuniary advantage, by a surgeon or other person who edits parts. It is an unnecessary appendage attached loosely (for easy removal) to the non-functioning end of the colon – which is a device to mark antithesis, illustration, or quotation. This appendix is no different from any other.

It is manifestly superfluous, even stupid, to tell anyone 'how to do psychotherapy'. Everyone knows how to do psychotherapy. It just involves pretending to listen to the other person until he or she can be cut off politely. Then, returning the attention to its proper focus (oneself) and, using the vast array of one's own personal experience, the assumptions of one's favourite notions about personality and how people change, and one's own good common sense, it involves telling the other person what to think, believe, feel, and do – knowing full-well that he or she has never before considered that particular and insightful way of viewing things. [Shades of Jonathan Swift's *A Modest Proposal*. RR]

Felicity does not doubt that the last paragraph describes the facts – about how the majority of what passes as psychotherapy is practised. Psychotherapists, trained or otherwise, are to be found lurking everywhere. They are almost as populous and demoniacal as the telephone, and even more extravagant, infesting the entire habitable world as well as the United States. Probably many (not all) of them have mastered the first of the four basics that are required *before* one *starts* to learn how to do psychotherapy. What most of them lack is basic training in how human beings function (i.e., the science of psychology), how things go wrong in human functioning (i.e., clinical psychology), and how human functioning is induced to change or correct itself (i.e., learning). After mastering those basics, it becomes meaningful to proceed to learn how to do the many procedures necessary for effective psychotherapy, then to acquire experience in doing and evaluating psychotherapy, and maybe then to become a proficient psychotherapist. Many psychotherapists seem satisfied to practice after achieving some skill in one, two, three, or none of the necessary steps. The steps are: (1) personal socialization, then (2) qualifying in psychology, (3) qualifying in clinical psychology, (4) qualifying in learning, (5) qualifying in some psychotherapy methods, (6) acquiring experience with a wide range of psychotherapy methods, and finally (7) experience in evaluation of psychotherapy outcomes. No wonder psychotherapy is gaining so rapidly in disrepute.

Will this appendix, or perhaps this volume, provide a means by which to progress through the seven steps to good psychotherapy practice? It will not. It does offer a few hints about (3) the general field of clinical psychology, (4) the relevance of learning, (5) a sample of some psychotherapy methods, and (7) a glance at a few single case methods for evaluating psychotherapy outcomes. This appendix will also offer a couple of hints about the role and use of (1) personal socialization and (3) another part of clinical psychology, namely, that concerned with the selection of treatment methods appropriate to the presenting problem.

If it can accomplish that much it has met its goals. But if any reader misconstrues this introduction as a means by which to grasp psychotherapy as a whole, it has failed dismally in its task.

(1) The First Basic – personal socialization

Everybody goes through an extended period of growing up and achieving basic personal socialization. Socialization is the process by which each of us learns how to communicate and act with other people and how to influence them.

But perhaps you think that to try to 'influence' others sounds too 'manipulative', or that it shouldn't be talked about so openly. If you feel that way, consider what follows. Almost every human action or interaction, particularly communication, involves the attempt to influence another. Make-up, the clothes we wear, the way we say things, what we say and do, and even standing passively by and doing nothing, all are selected to have an impact on and to influence others. We are all trying constantly to influence one another. Psychotherapy and sales activities are nothing more than enterprises that set out formally to achieve success in this universal human pursuit. What sets psychotherapy apart from the rest of this vast human enterprise (and particularly sales) is that it is devoted almost exclusively to the attempt to influence others to achieve *their own* needs and to correct their own problems, with no concern for the psychotherapist's wishes, attitudes, beliefs, values, or interests. And what makes it so important that the psychotherapist possess all the knowledge and skills he or she can acquire to achieve this purpose effectively and efficiently is the fact that what is at stake is absolutely the most precious and priceless thing there is. What is at stake is no less than the survival, happiness, comfort, self-fulfilment, and human condition of each individual human being. Any delay in this task robs the person of time in joyful living.

But let's get back to the first skill required for effective psychotherapy. Many of us have failed to achieve a basic standard in the socialization process. Some of us became satisfied with ourselves prematurely. Some of us have given up, having felt we failed (or some think others failed them) too often in the process. The outcome of the socialization process leads to at least two main classes of people who may want to become psychotherapists. One group is motivated by its own (felt) failure to achieve comfortable socialization, and its interest in psychology or in psychotherapy is commonly predicated either on an inquisitive interest in how others adjust or on a desire to achieve belated socialization or 'self-improvement'. The other group is motivated by the reward value of its successes achieved in social interactions with others and in its efforts to influence others – solely for the benefit of 'the other' (this last stipulation distinguishes psychotherapy from other influence initiatives, especially sales and advocacy). On the whole, the latter group should achieve better results than the former in the practice of psychotherapy.

There are those who appear to practice psychotherapy as though basic human socialization provided all the necessary skills for the task. The first step in becoming a useful psychotherapist is only partially achieved by becoming skilled in attending and listening to the needs and feelings of others (empathy), in confirming with them the meanings of their communications (reflection), in expressing appreciation and 'support' for them (positive regard), in acting in ways to parallel their behaviour (pacing), in offering occasional guidance (leading), and the like. These skills have variously been designated as 'therapeutic', 'assertive' or 'social' skills. They are merely the results of good human socialization. Of course, they are essential to good psychotherapy, but they form only part of the basic first step in mastering psychotherapy. They are necessary, but by no means sufficient. They seem to provide the fertile soil in which personal and personality change can occur, and without which such change cannot occur (except with great difficulty). Psychotherapy using these skills alone is, at best, only one step beyond what most people can obtain without cost from their relatives and friends and the local bartender. And, by itself, the exercise of such skills can hardly be claimed to be competent psychotherapy.

Some psychotherapy trainers, and even some schools of psychotherapeutic thought, have focused almost exclusively on the development of these basic social skills in psychotherapists-in-training. One outcome of their efforts seems to have been the discovery that the best way to help another person to grow in these skills of socialization is to expose him or her to the exercise of such skills. Whether by precept, example, or the natural process of growth, at least socialization seems to grow in the fertile soil of the exercise of its skills.

But the exercise of well-habituated and perhaps automatically employed social skills is not enough even for this step in the development of psychotherapy skills. The purposes of the exercise of social skills in psychotherapy are (1) to foster the development of a working relationship, (2) to foster growth in socialization of the other, and (3) to provide the fertile ground in which change can occur. These purposes might be served by the automatic application of learned social skills. But its purposes also include (4) to aid in the understanding of communications and (5) to assist in the grasp of 'where the other is' at any given moment. At least the last two of these purposes probably require conscious awareness of many of the elements of socialization both in oneself and in the other. This last statement can be illustrated by an example.

As a result of the process of socialization which everybody goes through, every social interaction is comprised of a standard series of steps. Few people are conscious of these steps even although we all employ them in every interaction, and derive and communicate information with them – whether the interaction is a formal clinical interview, a social encounter, or two acquaintances passing on the street (even without exchanging any words). A brief description of the steps involved in social interactions, and an explanation of their therapeutic uses, may serve to illustrate why psychotherapists need to be conscious of this and other phenomena.

The stages of every social encounter or interaction alternate between cognitive (thinking, intellectual) phases and affective (feeling, motivational) phases. The steps are as follows:

1. Familiarity: A familiar something draws the attention. It may be a familiar face at the door or approaching on the sidewalk. This is the first 'cognitive' step. The sense of familiarity activates a reflexive orientation toward it.

2. Orienting: The orienting reflex involves an autonomic arousal whose function is to motivate the action of 'turning toward' or 'fixating the eyes on' the familiar thing or person. This is the first 'affective' step.

3. Recognition: The act of recognition starts with awareness of the identity of the other and the appropriateness of some kind of response to the other. If the response is negative, the glance is averted. If the response is friendly ...

4. Welcoming: The eye contact is maintained briefly. The positive feeling may lead to a smile or full-face orientation toward the other. The plan of interaction is then identified.

5. Greeting: If no interaction is to occur, the gaze drops to represent this plan; if interaction is to occur, the greeting is given. The way in which it is given defines the level of formality of the intended interaction (for example, 'Hi' may denote an informal interaction, 'Hello' implies a formal but friendly interaction, 'How do you do' may indicate a stiffly formal interaction is intended). Warmth is implied by ...

6. Activation: The activation may involve a broadened smile (to denote warmth), or increased speed or variety of movement (handshake, to imply intensity), or intensified eye-contact, or by a slight frown (implying no interaction will take place).

7. Identification: If the other's name is used, it implies a degree of personal involvement; if no name is used, it may imply a degree of 'distance' from the other.

8. Pace: The pace of the interaction is set by the degree of restlessness (will move along soon) or quiescence (sit down to talk) of the parties. This starts before the definition.

9. Definition: The definition sets the stage for the coming interaction. 'How are you' asks about health, 'How do you feel' asks about psychological state, etc. A brief smile and gaze away from the other indicates no time for interaction. This phase defines the initial focus of the interaction.

10. Abreaction: The abreaction ('spilling the guts') is a relatively emotional out-pouring evoked by the definitional questions.

If the abreaction is encouraged or extended, the interaction is either between intimates such as family members or is exploratory or expressive or evocative psychotherapy.

11. Problem Solving: The problem-solving phase seeks to 'cap' or to find solutions to the abreactive phase. It addresses possible ways of looking at or dealing with the circumstances or feelings shared. Extending this phase implies that the interaction is between colleagues or equals, or is directive or behavioural psychotherapy.

12. Ending Anticipation: The end of contact is anticipated with a slight jolt, glance at watch, look away and frown, etc., or (in non-interactive passing) by a furtive glance and frown. This phase prepares the motivation to break contact.

13. Homework: Some plan or intent is formulated to maintain implicit contact during separation or to anticipate a future contact (i.e., to continue friendship), or a final furtive smile is shared while in the act of passing on the street.

14. Mourning: Pace of action slows, a slightly sad frown is given and the actions preparatory to separation (for example, shaking hands) occur to represent mourning about parting.

15. Parting: The interaction ends with its participants withdrawing in different directions.

All these steps of interaction are obvious to any sensitive person, especially once they are drawn to his or her attention. But why must the therapist be conscious of them? Only a couple of the answers are addressed here. First, of course, in order to exercise maximum influence over the client, the psychotherapist needs to know what he or she and the client are doing, if only to ensure that the interaction progresses at the speed and in the directions set by the therapist – the presumed 'expert'. If a purpose of psychotherapy is to influence another to change in any way, then part of that influence will be exerted through regulation of the nature of the interaction.

Second, the state of the other will be revealed in the nature of his or her contribution to the interaction. The process of social interaction is a well-learned tool that the client will also use as a communication tool, i.e., sharing of information in such a way as to influence the therapist. If the client does not follow all the steps in the normal interaction sequence, he or she is communicating that something is wrong that demands the therapist's attention. For example, if the client's opening utterance is most relevant to the 'abreaction' phase, the client is indicating acute distress – such that he or she cannot wait to 'unload' something important. Any such utterance ought to be recorded verbatim as it will certainly be revealing – and probably rather cleverly revealing. Alton's first contact with Felicity illustrates this phenomenon. If the client's opening interaction is most properly relevant to the 'termination' or 'parting' phase, the client is indicating acute depression, and probably suicidal feelings or ideas. Alvin's third meeting with Felicity illustrates this phenomenon.

(2) Psychology

At the risk of repetition, extensive basic training in the science of psychology is also a necessary, but not sufficient, basis on which good psychotherapy is built. The psychotherapist-to-be needs to know what is known (not what he or she believes or 'knows' is known) about human psychophysiology, neuropsychology, development, socialization, social interaction, perception, motivation, memory, learning, cognition, response and behavioural characteristics, and a host of other lawful characteristics of the human condition. He or she needs to know what is known about recording and measuring human characteristics, about how to process the information acquired and how to avoid misunderstanding or drawing faulty inferences from observations and measures. And he or she needs training in the skill of evaluating his or her own beliefs and observations in the light of scientific research, the history of human thought, and the evidences of contemporary societal issues and concepts that certainly affect how the client sees the world.

Most psychotherapists are acutely unaware of the limitations of their background training. Relatively few have anything near the basic training and experience required to enable them genuinely to appreciate the other person and the conditions of life with which he or she has been struggling. Without wishing to malign anyone or to deny to anyone the right to practice in a field in which he or she has been trained and has proper expertise, it has to be stated that most physicians, including most of those in the medical specialty of psychiatry, have not received anywhere near adequate training needed for psychotherapy practice and so they should not be, and really are not, performing formal psychotherapy.

(3) Clinical Psychology

Clinical psychology is the branch of psychology that seeks to find out how things can go wrong in human functioning and living. Actually, the things that can go wrong are not nearly as varied or numerous as most people might suspect. The possible range of human ills and the variety of factors either limiting or contributing to joy and fulfilment in life do not extend even to a small proportion of the enormous range and variety of human experiences. For the most part, human ills and the impediments to joyful living derive from a relatively narrow range of aspects of human functioning which, although supporting survival in adversity, serve to interfere with adaptation or adjustment under certain fairly simple, knowable, and modifiable habitual response errors and conditions of daily living. However, any adequate treatment of this subject is beyond the scope of this volume, let alone this appendix.

While clinical psychology, as a science, is concerned with adducing knowledge about the factors contributing to human ills, as an applied discipline its purpose is to correct or 'cure' human ills and to contribute to each individual's full and joyful living. That is, the aim of the applied discipline is to find and employ effective and efficient (so the good life is not delayed) methods of treatment. To do this, it is necessary to grasp (1) what is wrong that impairs the client's joy in living, (2) how that developed and (3) the options available to achieve recovery. Ideally a flow chart or a 'fault tree' could be constructed to represent the logical steps involved in the examination, assessment, or investigation of any human problem. And this chart or 'tree' should lead the clinician through the process of his or her inquiry inescapably to the identification of the areas or types of anomaly involved, to a clear specification of the elements of which it is comprised and of the causes which initiated and shaped it, and then to a definite series of options for its correction or normalization. Although most practitioners may not be aware that they are processing information in this manner, nearly all good ones do follow a process of reasoning that could be represented as a flow chart. And it seems likely that, to enforce consistent use of information processing by logic of this kind, eventually the human reasoner will replace his own fallible logic with a programmed computer.

A decision chart at least reminds one to make his or her assumptions conscious. It affords the care of a step-by-step analysis of the issues to be examined. As implied above, many logic charts are needed. Intervention charts list the available treatment options for each type of cause and learning of each possible condition. They include options about how each method can be carried out (on the person's own, in large or small groups, or in individual therapy), the amount of work involved in each and its duration, the probabilities of various types of outcomes and their durabilities, and any inconveniences, discomforts, complications, or side-effects associated with each. The needed information about interventions is obtained from the research literature and from the evaluation research concerned with the therapist's own practice (necessary in learning psychotherapy as well as a continuing part of responsible psychotherapy practice – affording self-improvement and quality control). If the literature's (other people's practice) and his or her personal outcomes differ by much, this too is part of the information relevant to interventions. If personal results fall much below the literature's, it is correct practice to transfer the case to someone demonstrating greater skill.

But why talk in this esoteric way? Talking about logic charts affords a simple way to remark that a psychotherapy practitioner is not competent to practice in any area associated with

- a blank (weak understanding) in any part of any flow chart, or
- failure to check on issues at any step in a relevant chart, or
- no concrete means to assess relevant states of the client, or
- no communicable understanding of the causative processes, or
- weak means to test the appropriateness of the diagnosis, or
- no intervention options among which the client may choose, or
- no knowledge of complications or side-effects of treatments, or
- no way to know or control the duration of interventions, or
- no concrete means to evaluate intervention outcomes, or
- no adequate durability of outcomes achieved, or
- no knowledge about personal outcome rates, or
- personal outcome rates poorer than literature rates, or
- personal rates poorer than with other methods others use, or
- no knowledge of or means to limit client suicide rates, etc.

These criteria are some of the ways by which a psychotherapist can determine whether he/she knows what he/she is doing.[9] Offering to provide psychotherapy without being able to demonstrate adequate knowledge about what one is doing is at best fraudulent behaviour. To do so, at least implicitly, takes responsibility for another person's most precious possession and most prized hopes without a justifiable basis for assurance that any benefit at all will be achieved, that no harm will be done, and that what is done or left undone will not contribute to increased suffering or even to the risk of death. It seems fair similarly to damn with faint praise one who, knowingly or not, unnecessarily extends the duration of psychotherapy by using ineffective or inefficient methods.

---

[9]   And reading them reminds me of just how often I have fallen short of any reasonable expectation of competence. RR

(4) Learning

The reason for doing psychotherapy is the presenting problem; the purpose of the payment for psychotherapy is the client's desire to be rid of the problem effectively and efficiently; and the level of intervention in psychotherapy is that of learning. Each treatment discipline uses its own level of intervention. Surgeons mend or cut out anatomical tissues. Other physicians alter the body's chemistry to achieve their effects on the body. Masseurs and chiropractors manipulate the body's muscles to effect often-temporary relief. Psychotherapists use the learning function of the brain to modify, temporarily or permanently, the habits and directives by which the brain regulates and controls itself and the rest of the body. The brain is indeed a marvellous apparatus that constantly strains to appreciate the conditions of life which surround it and which exist from time to time within it, and to use a host of different methods by which to learn how to adapt the world to it or itself to the world. It is an exquisitely delicate and immensely powerful learning machine.

But what can it learn? In that it regulates everything within the body, it can learn to do (almost) anything required of it. It controls the production of growth hormone, which is the means by which body parts grow and repair themselves (or become cancerous). It controls the body's immune response by which the body fights off infections and resists communicable diseases (or by which the body afflicts itself, as in arthritis and allergies). It controls the production and allocation of chemicals in the body to maintain health and energy production (or to create deficiencies). It controls its own reactions by creating pain (or by taking away pain, as in hypnosis) or fear (or by generating strength and courage) to ensure that it looks after its own integrity and survival. It determines how we relate (or fail effectively to relate) to others. It controls and creates what and who we are. And, comprised as it is of billions of nerves, it not only can communicate (receiving information through the internal and external senses, and sending directives to all the body's parts) and provide executive functions, it can also learn to do differently whatever it is that it does.

How it learns is beyond the scope of this work. However, it is easy to understand why it sometimes fails to learn what it might be expected to learn in order to minimize suffering. It sometimes chooses the wrong habits or strategies. But it can be taught.

(5) Psychotherapy Methods

At last we come to the advertised topic of this appendix, only to be disappointed once more. The techniques of psychotherapy are more numerous than the ways in which people have tried over the centuries to influence one another – many possible ways have not yet been tried. Some work, and some don't. Practice is not even a major determinant of success in psychotherapy. The effectiveness of the method(s) chosen is the first determinant of success. Strategies work well, work poorly, don't work at all, or do more harm than good. The real determinant of good psychotherapy is the process by which the method(s) are selected and are shown to work effectively, reliably, and efficiently to achieve the purpose of modifying the problems people present.

Years of exploring the literature in all the fields addressed above, of carefully evaluating the effects of what he has tried and of trying to be as honest as he can with himself, have led Felicity to his own personal understanding of what is good psychotherapy. However, he is not prepared to affirm that his grasp of the issues is better than that of another. All he feels justified to do in this connection is to tell some stories about treatments of some people's problems and how he conceptualized what was happening. You have already read some of those stories.

(6) Evaluation Research

This section will be just as unsatisfying as the last. Some of the evaluation methods Felicity has used have been illustrated or described in the main text. Even his views about how to think about information and its verification have been treated already. The main point here is that psychotherapy is comprised of those procedures that have been demonstrated objectively (evaluation research), reliably, and preferably efficiently to rid people of their presenting problems and thus to enhance for them the value of living. To accept a suffering person's trust by offering to help, and then to exercise personal attitudes and beliefs, even if they seem to be verified in one's own life experiences, is tantamount to wilfully intending to inflict suffering (or worse) on the other.

(7) Practice

Given that the psychotherapist has mastered and executed the foregoing six preliminary steps to psychotherapy, the seventh step is to keep practising toward the goal of achieving some degree of perfection in the art of psychotherapy. The practice of this art is unutterably rewarding and worthwhile. It may be said to represent the ultimate pursuit of humanity, as it involves spending ones energies in the loving pursuit of the joy and fulfilment of one's fellow humans. The enterprise is not only valuable and engrossing, it's also heaps of fun.

APPENDIX B

INTRODUCTION TO F.A.C.T.
– FUNNY THINGS THAT
FUNNY PEOPLE DO

To our alleged patients

Whenever I meet someone, it seems only proper to introduce myself before I expect the other person to divulge much about him or her self. As you read and react in your own special way to each of the stories about which I plan to gossip, it seems likely that you will reveal a good deal about yourself – to yourself. So it seems only right that I should begin by telling you something about myself and about the rather improbable protagonist in this set of mystery stories. Bear with me while I do that.

Like most people I know, I was born some years before I grew up. If you wonder how many years it has been since I was born, the answer depends on who you are. Everything is relative. If you happen to be a client, you will want me to be and to look older than I am – which, of course, I am and do. If you are not a client and you are male, I would state with conviction that I am older than I look. If you are not a client and you are female, I would state with certainty that I seem older than I am. And if you are none of the above, with as much assurance as I have about your identity, I would affirm with a definite maybe that I am every bit as old as I should be. One thing is sure. By western standards, I was born on a truly auspicious date, namely, 7/11. Of course, if you're American, this means I was born in July; whereas, if you're British, it means I was born in November. It seems only right that you should be yourself, even if you are none of the above.

When I was born, I was named. Although we could dispense with it, in case you were wondering how I got my name, let's get that unpleasantness out of the way. My mother had a number of character traits that endeared her to nobody. In particular, three of her traits left me just plain cold. These were her impatience, her assurance that if she had even a passing thought it was bound to be absolutely true (probably justified to her by her acquired surname), and her insistence that nothing interfere with the serenity of her life. That's how I got my name.

During the entire time of her 'confinement', my mother was absolutely convinced that I was a girl. Not even my wizened, prune-like appearance when I emerged with my extra little gizmo could shake her unfailing belief. Of course, having decided on my gender in advance, her impatience demanded that I be named long before birth. That's how I got girl's names. I suppose it was to ensure that I got the message to behave myself, and not to upset her in any way, that she dubbed me Felicity. She added the other names out of spite, to get back at me for having failed to be a girl. Alice and Connie were my two, much despised, spinster aunts. Their dislike for my aunts Alice and Connie was the only subject on which my parents and me were ever known to agree.

Of course, my initials did help to shape my destiny. It was inevitable that I'd become a physicist or an engineer. So, naturally, I became a psychologist. And, naturally again, being destined for a career in the 'hard' sciences, I became a psychotherapist.

How that came about is easy to understand. I don't know about you, but I hated school. But I hated the thought of having to work even more. So, upon completing high school, I found an expedient way to postpone the need for the employment market. I registered in university. Then I was faced with another problem. I was chronically confused about who or what I was. So I had no idea which of the available courses of study to pursue. Providentially, to support the indecision of the indecisive, the university had an entry program in Arts that served as the first year for a host of disciplines. I enrolled in this entry program and chose courses with the help of a dartboard and a set of dice – I never did figure out how to get a die to stick to a dart board. One of the courses I carefully selected by these means was Psychology. It was in this course that I found the discipline most suited to my nature.

As you might imagine it, I had learned everything I cared to know about health in high school, where I was taught an assortment of useful things such as 'Flies spread disease; keep yours closed'. Now, only in my first year at university, I was taught the rest of what it was felt I needed to know – that 'Psychology is the study of the id by the odd'. Although I had attended the world's most advertised school (you know, everywhere you go you see its sign 'Slow School'), I was quick enough to see at once the discipline I was destined to follow. It occurred to me in the twinkling of an eye (or the twitch of an nose) that I would someday be doing, in my own odd way, the funny things with the id that those funny psychologist people do.

In the course of a long career, replete with improbable experiences, I encountered many strange events and a great many wonderful people. Most of these people managed to effect almost miraculous changes in themselves during the time in which they allowed me the privilege of peeping into their lives. Of course, I never had the slightest idea about how they performed their feats. But, because they impressed me so much, it always distressed me that their accomplishments could not be shared with others. Unfortunately, nobody would believe most of the stories I could tell about these people, even if they were recounted face to face, and even if the listeners were the closest of friends. So I had resigned myself to the fact that these improbable events were never to be recorded.

However, a friend and colleague, who was enamoured of the tales and who was concerned lest my final breath be drawn without some of these fanciful stories seeing the light of day, concocted with conviction the original form of the Principle of Perversity (Felicitations, 1980, 1, 1, 1-2). He pointed out that, human nature being what it is, it is much easier to believe that which is presented as patently fictitious than it is to believe that which is presented as fact. Why not, he suggested, write up the cases as the pure fiction they clearly are, uncluttered with any attempt to make them sound plausible? Then everybody could believe them if they chose to do so. He added that if I felt it necessary to expound profound truisms and assorted meaningless justifications about what was purported to have taken place, or about how the effects noted might be explained, I might choose to expand at length on the tales in a companion work. In this way, it would be possible to make reading about psychotherapy tolerable, even fun, while at the same time introducing students to the demanding discipline of psychotherapy with the least possible pain.

Accordingly, this is an improbable work of fiction. It contains yarns about people who never existed, identified by their real fictitious names. Of course, it must follow that any resemblance between these people and anybody living or dead, or even eventually to be alive or dead, is purely and completely accidental and unintentional. The companion work, aptly entitled *A Companion's Work*, containing all the associated clutter of irrelevant thoughts, unlikely schemes and fantastic fictional and pseudo-scientific explanations, all expressed in the pedantic and mind-destroying forms of non-communication commonly used by psychologists, you will be happy to hear, is not going to be written. You may be less happy to hear that its contents are contained instead – I hesitate to say this – under the covers of this volume, although frequently in chapter introductions, which can easily be skipped if you like.

By now, the fact that one aim of this work is to formulate psychotherapy fiction under the guise of science must have been only modestly obscured. Of course, everybody knows that science is a process by which statements (called hypotheses or theories) are tested for their truth or validity. Although normally based upon fairly firm grounds (usually stated in a scientific report), an 'hypothesis' is a guess, the truth or validity of which is to be tested in an experiment. This *hypo*-thesis is a little thesis or a incomplete (less than complete) theory. As the statement or little theory to be tested in any experiment, the hypothesis is the central and organizing idea that selects what is to be explored. What marks these stories as being beyond the fringe (or off the wall) is not only their manifestly fictional character, but also the fact that the hypotheses tested are often perhaps a trifle unusual, and sometimes even quite strange.

Also, in experimental tests of hypotheses, a plurality of individuals or observations is usually included in order to avoid the pitfall of drawing a mistaken conclusion due to the chance peculiarities of one particular individual or observation – a problem most readily seen in the work of Fraud … err … Freud. In clinical work, it may be impractical to employ more than one case in a given experiment. So it is accepted practice to do 'single case' studies. However, when single case methods are used, it is considered inappropriate to draw widely generalized conclusions from them. For this reason, where convenient, two or more case stories are fabricated here to illustrate the possibility that the conclusions dreamed up may be suitable for generalization to whole populations of events or people. How's that for a way to get around a methodological problem?!

Finally, may I add a note of welcome to these pages. I would invite those, such as yourself, possessed of virtue, integrity, honesty, calculated scientific reserve, and tutored critical faculty to explore these pages. A little harmless fiction never hurt anyone. It might even poke a few holes in the blinkers with which we all restrict and fashion the world to fit our own pre-conceptions. What you will find here is a set of mystery stories in which hypothetical solutions are generated (and examined through treatment outcomes) to provide means by which one rather peculiar psychologist might create imaginary structure for himself to help himself cope – you may think in a crazy way – in the confusing enterprise of trying to help people to fix their deformed or broken worlds through psychotherapy.

ABOUT THE AUTHOR

Douglas Arthur Quirk (1931-1997)

Douglas A. Quirk was born in India, the son of missionary parents and, if I remember correctly, spent some time in boarding schools, in England. In any event, he was educated in the classics as well as in the classical English music hall ballads.

He received his B.A. and M.A. from the University of Toronto, and completed all of the requirements for his Ph.D. except for his dissertation – and he subsequently taught Psychology to Psychiatrists and Nurses in the U. of T. Department of Psychiatry for many years. He was a Clinical Fellow of the Ontario Society for Clinical Hypnosis, the Behavior Therapy and Research Society, and the American and Ontario Associations of Marriage and Family Counsellors, and he was a Fellow of the Royal Society of Health.

Doug was a prolific writer. Here is a small sample of his many publications:

> (1966) The Application of Learning Theories to Psychotherapy: Component Therapies and the Psychoses. Paper read at the Canadian Psychological Association Annual Convention
>
> (1968) Former Alcoholics and Social Drinking: An Additional Observation. The Canadian Psychologist, 9, 498-499
>
> (1976) O.P.A.'s Brief to the Royal Commission on Violence in the Communications Industry. The Ontario Psychologist, 8, Supplement

(1980) Nutrition and Crime: a review. Prepared for
    The Solicitor General of Canada
(1982) Biofeedback in Dangerous Offenders:
    Learning Normal Functioning of the Nervous
    System. Poster Session, Ontario Psychological
    Association, Annual Convention
(1986) Nutrition and Violence. Invited Address, John
    Howard Society of Canada Conference
(1991) A Practical Measure of Offence Seriousness:
    Sentence Severity. Ontario Correctional
    Institute Research Report (RR91-1)
(1994) The nature and modification of criminality.
    Paper presented (with Reg Reynolds) at the
    Annual Convention of the Ontario Psychological
    Association.

At various times during his career, he served as consultant to
the World Health Organization, (S.E. Asia Region), the Scarboro
Foreign Missions Society (Toronto), the Canadian Institute of Stress
(Toronto), Toronto Catholic Children's Aid Society, York-Lea Mental
Health Project (Toronto), the American Society for Humanistic
Education, the Institute for Applied Psychology, Humanitas Systems
(New York), Biomedical Engineering Associates (Toronto), North
York General Hospital (Toronto), and the Green Valley School &
Hospital (Florida).

From 1959 to 1967, he was Senior Psychologist at the Ontario
Hospital, Toronto and, from 1961 to 1967, Director of the Behaviour
Therapy Unit there. From 1967 to 1971, he was Director of Clinical
and Research Labs at the Clarke Institute of Psychiatry. Briefly, he
was in full-time private practice; and then from 1975 to 1995, he was
Senior Psychologist at the Ontario Correctional Institute.